100 MINDS THAT MADE THE MARKET

The Fisher Investment Series

The Only Three Questions That Count

~

100 Minds That Made the Market

~

The Wall Street Waltz

100 MINDS THAT MADE THE MARKET

KENNETH L. FISHER

BICENTENNIAL
1807
WILEY
2007
BICENTENNIAL

John Wiley & Sons, Inc.

Published by John Wiley & Sons, Inc., Hoboken, New Jersey.
Published simultaneously in Canada.

Wiley Bicentennial Logo: Richard J. Pacifico

For general information on our other products and services or for technical support, please contact our Customer Care Department within the United States at (800)762-2974, outside the United States at (317)572-3993, or fax (317)572-4002.

Wiley also publishes its books in a variety of electronic formats. Some content that appears in print may not be available in electronic formats. For more information about Wiley products, visit our Web site at www.wiley.com.

Library of Congress Cataloging-in-Publication Data:

ISBN-13: 978-0-470-13951-6

10 9 8 7 6 5 4 3 2

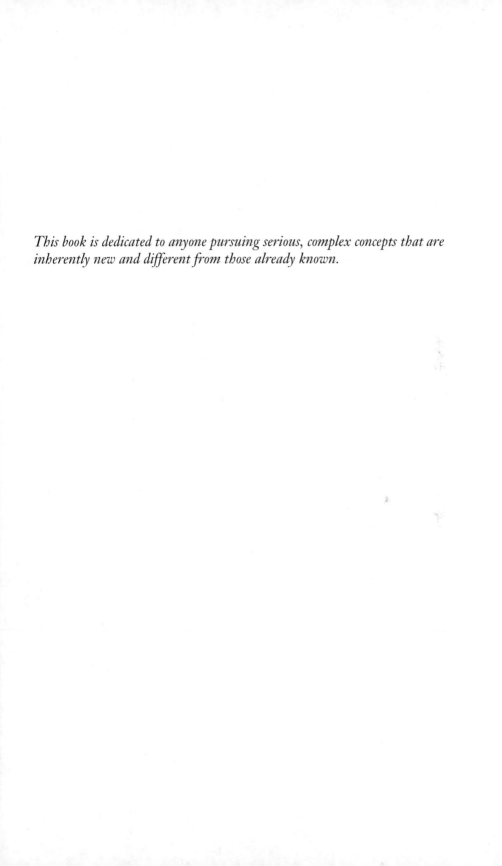

This book is dedicated to anyone pursuing serious, complex concepts that are inherently new and different from those already known.

CONTENTS

CHAPTER TWO

CHAPTER THREE

CHAPTER FOUR

CHAPTER FIVE

CHAPTER SIX

CHAPTER NINE

CHAPTER TEN

PREFACE

This book was first completed in 1993. The standard I used was to include only people who had somehow, in some way, had some material impact on finance—and who were dead—under the assumptions I could be completely critical and that dead folk don't sue. Partly, as I said in the original introduction, that also helped me avoid writing about my own father, who I felt uncomfortable about discussing in his lifetime.

In the original introduction I cited interesting people who were living, including Warren Buffett, John Templeton, Ivan Boesky, and Michael Milken. They are still alive today. But, as I mentioned then, these more modern names have a great deal of media about them readily available, so I don't feel their exclusion from this book, alive or deceased, is a major disadvantage to readers.

As for my father, who passed away in 2004, I covered him then at some length and detail in the Wiley Investment Classics edition of *Common Stocks and Uncommon Profits and Other Writings*. And you can certainly find all you need about him there. By comparison, most of the folks covered in this book are vastly harder to learn about without a great deal of effort. These cameo biographies allow you to learn a great deal of overview in a few minutes, and the appendix materials allow you to dig further if you want to really delve into these fascinating minds.

So, the list of 100 names is essentially as valid today as it was in 1993. While reviewing the book, I discovered that I would change little, if anything at all.

I have changed my mind materially about Gerald Loeb. I regret I was much too critical of him when I wrote his section. As I've aged I've come to appreciate him more and more. In my mind at the time I had been comparing him to influential shapers of market thought like Ben Graham, Harry Markowitz, or my father—and he came up short. What I didn't appreciate about him at the time was how powerfully he motivated young and new investors to get involved with the markets for the first time. He brought, arguably, hundreds of thousands to the world of stock investing at a time when there were few others to encourage them—and over decades when they succeeded. I tried to make it up to him by recently writing a new, more laudatory introduction for his updated Wiley Investment Classic, *The Battle for Investment Survival*. In some ways, as I said there, he reminds me a little of the Jim Cramer of his day: Flamboyant, seen everywhere, endlessly energetic, for the little guy, quick with a word, and encouraging everyone that they could do it themselves. He had a tremendous amount to do with moving people toward stocks from 1935, when his book came out in a bleak world into and through the 1960s when common stock investing for the little guy had become much more common. I encourage you to read his book almost as a 35 year history of the evolution of American stock markets.

After writing this book, I met Ben "Sell 'em" Smith's son who impressed upon me that how despite his father's tough and boisterous attitude in business, he was consistently a soft and gentle father. That made me realize how little I may actually have captured about any of these people's real private lives. As a student of their lives, I wrote mostly about their reputations and legends, as had been captured in books and articles. It is impossible to know the secrets people chose to keep private—these matters are often never known. But Smith's son made me realize that all these people, as exceptional as they were, were also probably more complex than I gave them credit for.

There is one point I didn't cover in the book that is clear to me now as the years have rolled by: With very few exceptions like John Law and the Rothschilds, these *100 Minds* were Americans. Finance and capitalism have been infinitely more impacted than the rest of the world. It may be a deficiency that I didn't include that great Scotsman, Adam Smith, whose book from the year of our nation's birth is still a beacon of influence, hope, and direction, and almost divinely inspired as if by his own infamous "invisible hand." But like many of the living modern names, a quick internet search for this famous man will render a large collection of material. If you haven't studied Smith, I encourage you to do so, as he is one of the most influential forces on the creation and evolution of capitalism.

Most of the people in this book are harder to learn about. And an overwhelming number are Americans. It is irrefutable that most of the big forces on capitalism and capital markets have been American. The more I think, the more I see that there just aren't many from abroad. The people who had the impact and changed the way we thought came from America. That is still true today when we look at the living. The legends and the influencers come from America, few from elsewhere.

Why is this? Increasingly I've come to see it as a function of America being the "un-culture." In most countries it has always been true they have a monolithic or dualistic culture. One dominant culture and maybe one or a few lesser ones! France, for example, was always based primarily on a single nationality and Catholicism. While in various countries the Catholics and the Protestants squabbled, the culture was narrow at best. But in America more than anywhere and from its more recent beginning, everyone came from different backgrounds, without a common culture, creating the un-culture that is America. And I submit that an un-culture is more fertile soil for capitalism and capital markets than any culture.

In America a product that may start out catering to a tiny minority can break out to the vast majority. The same goes for the bad as for the good. The Klu Klux Klan came from the Deep South and became long and strong regionally but didn't sweep the nation. But Coca-Cola and the blues also came from there and swept over the world. Just so, today someone might start a product, financial or not, aimed at some small subset of America that comprises a large number of consumers, for example, Chinese Americans—and have the product take off and cross over to the rest of America. Sound far-fetched? It happens all the time. The burrito, for example, is not really Mexican food. It was created in California for Mexican-Americans and is now eaten everywhere. Examples are endless. But this book is about finance and in finance the new ideas come from America. Whether modern finance from the mind of Harry Markowitz à la mean variance optimization, or original commingled mutual funds, or, more recently, exchange traded funds, the discount broker, collateral derivative obligations—the list is endless. The new ideas come from America.

In a strong monolithic or dualistic culture it is very difficult to establish new ideas, challenge old ones, and change the status quo because the dominant culture can suppress socially with impunity. It is, for example, how and why it was so easy to excommunicate Galileo. But capitalism draws its success from change, creative destruction, renewal, the young upstart wiping out the old guard, then becoming the new old guard about to be wiped out. This occurs best where cultural impediments are fewest, in an un-culture. People from every country, national origin, religion, and race have succeeded here.

Look at the success of those of Jewish descent in American capital markets. Whereas Jews were discriminated against in most European nations, in the un-culture the Jews could have their most maximal impact and success in capital markets. As you go through the book notice how many Jewish Americans you see. To be clear and fully disclosed, I'm of Jewish descent so maybe my views are biased here. But my paternal family left the town of its origin, Buttenheim, Germany in the 1830s. By the 1880s all Jews had fled Buttenheim—all! And where did they flee to? America, of course! Why, because they faired better in the un-culture. But innovation by immigrants in America has been ubiquitous, and more so than in their native countries.

If I were writing this book over from scratch I'd put more emphasis on each participant's pre-American origins because they come from all over. I've become firmly convinced in the last 15 years that only in America could the nature of capital markets innovation flourish as it has—that it isn't just chance that the overwhelming bulk of those impacting thought, product, innovation, marketing, and the technology of capital markets came from America.

KEN FISHER
Woodside, CA
May 2007

ACKNOWLEDGMENTS

The acknowledgments sections in my first two books were quite lengthy because those were serious books including a lot of work by a lot of people. This one isn't and wasn't. This was a fun book—fun to create and I hope fun to read—so I kept more of it to myself than before. But certain key thank-you's are in order nonetheless.

First and foremost, this book never would have happened without Barbara DeLollis. I came up with the idea, the title, a list of names and a lot of my ever-eccentric views. Barbara then, under my guidance, set out to research each of these 100 fabulous financial figures, plus a good many we ended up deciding not to include in our final list of 100. She spent hours and hours on each one, and then, with my input, handed to me a first draft of each life story which I could massage into that which you now read. I'm too busy running a financial firm to do all that. I'd never be able to take the time. Was she a ghost writer? No. I've been writing for years—my books, my *Forbes* columns, and an occasional piece here and there—I love to write. So the writing is mine. The ideas are mine.

Barbara's contributions were considerable, but any shortcomings in the book are obviously my responsibility. The conclusions and views on each of the *100 Minds* and their roles in history were always mine. Where I felt uncomfortable from time to time with Barbara's research, I checked up on it and always found her digging to be more than adequate. She was dealing and redealing in detail, and I used her as a resource. She also indexed the book, got the photographs, and just kept moving forward toward the book's completion until it was basically a finished draft. Thank you and good luck with your future in New York.

As each story was finished, Sally Allen, Marguerite Barragan, and Martha Post (all regulars in varying capacities at Fisher Investments) put in considerable time editing. Their contributions ranged from simple grammatical niceties to curbing me in when I would wander too far on tangents, as I sometimes am prone to do. My father, Phil Fisher, racked his brain for me remembering some of the people from his youth who otherwise might not have been included, and so you have names I might not have otherwise seen.

David Mueller, formerly of my firm, prettied up the book's appearance and format through computer graphics and guided its indexing. But it was really, and always is, my wife Sherri who took the bull by the horns, pulled in our first editor Barbara Noble, and drove the manuscript into book form so you now can read it. Without her push and guidance it would have died in a desk somewhere. To all of you I owe my thanks.

KEN FISHER

FOREWORD

The adventure of investing engages us intellectually and spiritually—often even more deeply than our obvious financial engagement—and through this engagement we almost inevitably become members of a community of similarly engaged colleagues.

At first, we may only recognize those we see and speak with daily as the other "players of the game," but as we travel and meet more and more people in more and more organizations, over more and more years, we realize, with expanding interest and pleasure, that the investing "crowd" is very large.

We also learn how richly dynamic, creative, and powerful this, our crowd, truly is. It is a communications village and we are the better for being members of this very special community.

One dimension that enriches our own experiences is the challenge and the fulfillment of learning—partly by trial and error. (We err and err and err again. But less.)

Fortunately, we have many, many "instructors" with whom to learn. Our great teachers are often truly fascinating people whose lives and adventures enrich our own enjoyment and fascination with the adventure of investing. "The play's the thing," as Shakespeare put it. Or as 'Adam Smith' so aptly said, "It's the money game!"

This easy reading introduction will enlighten and intrigue you—and introduce a splendid group of gamesmen who have played before us. Ken Fisher adds an important dimension by sharing his wise interpretations and perspectives on their experiences. As a result, he enables us to learn much from the experiences of others—so much easier, faster, and painless than learning only from our own experiences.

In his engaging book, Ken Fisher tells the stories—in a breezy, irreverent, friendly way—of 100 remarkable people. Some you already know, some you will feel you almost know, and some you have not yet come upon. They have "made the market" what it is today. Some have played their role as heroes; others have been villains. We can learn life's lessons from them—particularly with the thoughtful and thought-provoking insights and commentary Ken Fisher provides us on this guided tour.

Charles D. Ellis
Partner, Greenwich Associates

INTRODUCTION

Why should you read this book? To have fun. As its author, my highest hope is for it to be fun for you. The 100 subjects I've chosen are fascinating, wacky, wild, and often just weird—yet they are powerful and at times very funny. Their lives are as fun to read about as they were to write about. Depending on who you are and what you do, want, and like, you might also benefit from the professional and personal lessons of their lives and learning more about the American financial markets' evolution. If you are a market practitioner in any form, these lives are role models of what works and what doesn't, how far you can bend things and when they break down, and what human traits go with market success and failure. But, as I said, the main reason to read this book is to have fun.

DON'T TAKE IT FOR GRANTED

Wall Street is an institution that some, especially today, seem to take for granted. It didn't appear one day from some biblical fairy tale. Instead, Wall Street exists as it does because of nearly two centuries of pioneering, innovation, perspiration, mistakes, and scandals. Throughout Wall Street's evolution, survival of the fittest dictated which innovations would be incorporated and which mistakes would be corrected—and it was these improvements that made the market the wonderful institution so many now take for granted.

But it was the individuals behind the improvements who drove the making of the market. This book presents 100 such people, each of whom contributed something—a lesson, an innovation, or a scam. Their minds made the innovations and their impact made the market what it is, so ultimately and simply, it was their minds that made the market—hence the book's title.

Looking back on their lives is invaluable for anyone who never stopped to think how the market came about and essential for everyone connected with today's market and tomorrow's future. As the saying goes, "Those who do not learn the lessons of the past are doomed to repeat them." Here you have 100 of the best teachers available to save you from learning the hard way the lessons their lives so vividly portray. In reading *100 Minds That Made The Market*, you will find the story behind Wall Street's gradual formation as fascinating and engrossing as the market itself.

HOW TO READ THIS BOOK

100 Minds is presented in a form that chronicles Wall Street's evolution. Eleven categories (chapters) describe people who laid the basis for the institution; those who chronicled its growth and the deal-makers who financed it; those who innovated it; and those who assimilated it into the American economy. Then came those who reformed it, systematized it, scandalized it, and those who made and lost money in it; plus a few miscellaneous others. Within each category, the stories are presented in chronological order so you can follow the flow of time.

It's important to remember that the categories aren't as important as the people themselves. In writing the book, the people were chosen first and categorized later. The descriptions of each of them needed to stand on their own as cameo biographies before being fitted into any particular framework. Only after the 100 were written were they placed into groups that logically flowed from the stories themselves; then chapter summaries were written to bring the 100 together with overarching themes and lessons.

As important, I wanted you to be able to choose between reading the book cover-to-cover and just picking it up from time to time for a quickie on a single person whenever someone becomes of interest to you. As a writer of two previous books, a columnist in *Forbes* for eight years, and an author of a lot of other material, I hope *100 Minds* is entertaining and educating enough to be worthwhile to many of you in a cover-to-cover format. But I am also mindful of how many more things I would like to do than I ever have time for and presume the same is true for you. By putting it in a format where you need not read it cover-to-cover, I am freeing you to use whatever bits of the book benefit you most. If one day someone mentions Lucky Baldwin and you haven't the foggiest as to who he was, you can save yourself the embarrassment of asking or doing a lot of library legwork by simply flipping to the index and reading a four-minute cameo story. If you want to read further about Baldwin, just flip to the appendix where there's a bibliography for each story that shows you where to go next. And if you want to find more subjects like Baldwin, just browse around his chapter.

Many of these fascinating folks can actually be placed into several different categories. How can you put J.P. Morgan into one box? And Ben Graham was an author, but he was much more, as were so many of these great pioneers. Yet I had to categorize them somewhere and did so where they made most sense to me. If you see it differently, I beg for your patience. Also note that many of these lives are interrelated, so when one subject is mentioned in another's story, he or she is cross-referenced by boldfacing their name upon first reference, so you can quickly flip to that story for more.

WHY 100 INSTEAD OF 103?

I had to stop somewhere! And *100 Minds* sounded good to me. Admittedly, this isn't the perfect list of *100 Minds That Made The Market*; that would be impossible to compile—no one could ever track every single contributor. It is almost certain that many material but quiet contributors were simply lost to history because, while their contributions may have been significant, they as people weren't noted by society.

These 100 are my 100—based on what I've learned from 20 years as an investment professional and prior schooling in finance and history. They were chosen as my interpretation of the big contributors as opposed to finding people somewhere to fill certain slots ("Oh, I'd better find five more chartists and two more bankers!"). Yes, this is my list of *100 Minds*. If you shuffled history you might come out with a few different names, but I'd bet most would be the same. We might disagree on a few, but it would be fun debating why some folks deserved to be included while others didn't. So hopefully you will enjoy reading about my choices even if you disagree.

MADE IN AMERICA—AND OTHER EXCLUSIONS

Most of these *100 Minds* are Americans. There were only a few foreigners I could envision whose contributions to the evolution of American financial markets were so great that they couldn't be excluded. This isn't an attempt to chronicle those who made hay in the evolution of European markets or markets as a whole. This simply details who made our market "the" market, for despite all the current fascination with global investing and overseas diversification, the American stock market is still the bellwether market of the world; the one on which everyone around the world focuses.

Some notable American financiers didn't make it on the list for reasons such as being too industry-oriented or being too obscure in the history books. Automobile empire builder E.L. Cord, railroaders Collis P. Huntington and Leland Stanford, and investment banker August Belmont, Jr., were among those too industry-oriented to have made any significant contribution to our market system. This doesn't discount their own unique contributions in their respective industries, but it puts them behind others who significantly affected our markets in a direct way.

Those who were too obscure in history were sadly left out because adequate biographical material was not available. Kuhn, Loeb partner Otto Kahn, technical analyst (and John Magee's inspiration) Richard Schabacker, and even E.F. Hutton were all quite famous on Wall Street, yet surprisingly little was written about them, so I couldn't really penetrate their lives or their minds. In Kahn's case, there was plenty written about his wardrobe and love of opera, but the heart of the matter—his deal-making—was too inadequately described to get a good enough handle on him. I really wanted to cover him because I've always sensed his importance, but he seems beyond my grasp.

Richard Wyckoff, who pioneered ticker tape reading with his book *Studies in Tape Reading*, also falls into the too-obscure category, as does Addison Cammack and the Claflin sisters. Cammack was credited with coining the warning, "Don't sell stocks when the sap is running up the trees!" He was described as the consummate trader in Edwin Lefevre's *Reminiscences of a Stock Operator*, but I've never found anything in-depth on him . . . If you ever do, I'd love to hear from you.

The Claflin sisters—possibly the first female stockbrokers—rate mention in this introduction, if only because their story is so sensational. Outlined in Dana L. Thomas' *The Plungers and the Peacocks*, the flighty, calculating pair—Victoria and Tennessee—went to New York in 1869 to court one of my *100 Minds*, Cornie Vanderbilt, a genuine dirty old man. In 1870, he set them up in their own brokerage firm, feeding them lucrative tips and loving the commotion they stirred! While Tennessee presumably minded the mysterious business, Vicky advocated free love, women's freedom, and a host of other then-radical ideas, and became the first woman to be nominated for the U.S. Presidency! After Vanderbilt died, his son and main heir, William H. Vanderbilt (who you can also read about here), bought the Claflins' silence regarding their escapades with the old man. Both sisters eventually left New York and married British aristocrats. While interesting, the Claflins didn't really make the market; a true contribution is hard to define. But they are a nice complement to Vanderbilt, who actually was a major contributor, which leads to another point.

This book is primarily about men, and in this day and age women may take offense at that. I beg your pardon, but Wall Street's early years were almost exclusively a man's world. The role of women in this book is almost totally confined to aspects that today would be thought of as stereotypically sexist: housewives, bimbo-mistresses and supportive seconds to the men who are featured. In terms of women who independently affected the market, I am sadly able to feature only three: Evangeline Adams, Natalie Laimbeer, and Hetty Green. But even among them there is some taint of oddballism that modern woman may find offensive. Adams was too astrology-oriented to be taken seriously, and Green was fabulously chintzy. If women are poorly represented in this book, I apologize and defer to the simple fact that the book is an accurate portrayal of the historical information available. Despite modern day desires for coverage of women in history, you can't do that in this case and be historically accurate.

TRYING TO BRING THE DEAD TO LIFE

Note that everybody in the book is dead: This is not a scorecard of today's players. (Four of the *100 Minds* I can't actually say are dead, but they have dropped from public view long enough to be presumed dead. When out of public view, it is virtually impossible to find obituaries.) Why dead heads instead of current market moguls? Clearly some of the living have made huge contributions—measurably bigger contributions, for good or for bad, than some of my *100 Minds.* But, with no disrespect to folks like Warren Buffett, John Templeton, Ivan Boesky, and Michael Milken who have had great impact, they and others like them have already been heavily covered by the press; so today, anyone who has the slightest interest in financial types already holds his own views about them. No value added by covering that turf, so I don't.

Furthermore, I can be openly critical of my subjects when appropriate, simply because dead people don't sue. Among these stories you will see men I praise and others I damn. But with the dead I can't be accused of ruining a career no longer in existence. Then, too, there was my father, Phil Fisher. In some ways he made me realize the beauty of limiting my book to the dead. When I first contemplated the book I envisioned including about a dozen living legends—and that would be impossible without covering my father, due to his vast formative and seminal contributions to the school of growth stock investing.

But I felt too emotionally uncomfortable writing about him: it was too easy to lose the forest for the trees...too easy to be too laudatory, or to compensate for that by putting up artificial walls to distance myself from him. In many ways I would rather have someone who is more naturally distanced than I write about my father. Of course, John Train did that when he wrote his classic book, *The Money Masters*, which chronicled nine great modern-era investors. Warren Buffett also wrote of him, and he has been covered at some length in the press over the years: In time, others will write more. Then it dawned on me: The living get covered and it is the dead who fall from sight and whom I can bring to life for you.

Most of the names in this book are fairly obscure—perhaps only a quarter of them are easy to learn about in the library. But the rest provided slim pickin's and required digging; in many instances, this is the most complete and condensed account of their lives. If you decide you want more on a subject, just look up his or her bibliography. But what you won't find in any biography is meaningful analysis of these lives regarding their impact on the market—and that is what I think my other contribution in this book is. As in my second book. *The Wall Street Waltz*, which operated in a short-story format, and as with my *Forbes* columns which operate in a single-page format, I'm used to condensing an entire saga into a few paragraphs. Because I've done a lot of that, I hope my experience makes me better able to do so for you with these 100 wonderfully interesting people. In each case, I have tried to put their contributions into perspective, give you overview, and show you a key lesson or two.

AT THE CORE OF FREEDOM

None of these characters are ordinary. You see extremes, from the most flamboyant to the most introverted, to the most brilliant, to the most crooked: None are run-of-the-mill. Before there was ever a thought of *People Magazine* or *The National Enquirer*, many of these market leaders were folks about whom gossip flowed. Many of their lives read like novels, but in many instances, fact is stranger than fiction! Above all else, these were people who did not feel constrained by those around them. They allowed themselves the freedom to do what others hadn't or couldn't do; and they wouldn't be ruled by convention, history, society or, in many instances, the law. They gave themselves permission to bend, push, stretch, and at times simply break the rules that others all around them obeyed.

Allowing for innovation is the fundamental determinant of success or failure of economic systems. As Milton Friedman wrote so well, capitalism and freedom are truly impossible to separate. Democracy without capitalism is far from freedom because all the decisions are cast in a mode where some 50 percent win and 50 percent lose—which is a hell of a way to run a railroad. Too many lose. Only in the marketplace is everyone acting on decisions when it is in his best interest. And obviously, as recent history shows, non–self-interested central control, as in communism, fails because, basically, if people can't do what they want, they won't do very much of anything. Likewise, self-interested business in a totalitarian state is destined to failure. Without the regulator of competition—what Adam Smith referred to so well in *The Wealth Of Nations* as the almost divine "invisible hand"—capitalism is destined to go astray. Consider what occurs in all fascist countries eventually.

And everywhere capitalism and freedom reside in a modern economy, there must also be capital formation, and thereby the financial markets. And it is in the financial markets where capitalism has its most potent effect for good or bad. It is here where innovation is the most fluid—the very nerve center of capitalism. Here where fear and greed are so easily stampeded into action. Here where the wealth of nations burns like gas on a fire, at times exploding in our faces. Here where unique individuals expose themselves at their best and worst and most bizarre. It is because Wall Street is so potent and important to the functioning of capitalism that the *100 Minds That Made The Market* are so important to our past and future.

All these *100 Minds* were innovators. And because innovation is what makes Wall Street and capitalism great, fluid, and ever current, the 100 are in many ways the very personification of what made and makes America great. If you love the market, remember that it is made up of people, and you will love these 100 fascinating people. Their lives are telling—telling the story of Wall Street.

CHAPTER ONE

THE DINOSAURS

BIG AND RUTHLESS WHEN THAT WAS ALL THAT COUNTED

Before civilization, dinosaurs roamed the earth, doing as they pleased. They could do whatever they wanted back then; there were no rules to follow, no structure to live or work within and nothing bigger than they were. The only thing governing them was their environment, and because of their intimidating size, they were able to dominate that with unquestioned power.

The Rothschilds, Stephen Girard, John Jacob Astor, Cornelius Vanderbilt, George Peabody, Junius Morgan, Daniel Drew, and Jay Cooke are our financial Dinosaurs. They operated prior to order and organized structure within the capital markets. They too dominated their society through their magnitude and ability to simply surpass the rest of the population.

In creating the basis for our capital market system, they were viewed as ruthless, lawless and merciless. With a single, foreboding footstep, they were able to crush lesser creatures sometimes without really intending to. Like dinosaurs, they were big and awkward and not really civilized—at times completely unaware of their strength and the effects it had on others—whether for better or worse.

Astor, Vanderbilt, and Drew were perhaps the most notorious Dinosaurs, infamous for their foul treatment and manipulation of others. Regardless, during his lifetime, Astor became the "landlord of New York" and amassed a fortune. Vanderbilt pioneered transportation, building up the shipping industry and a railroad empire to accommodate the country's growth. Drew was the father and most rigorous practitioner of stock "watering."

You might view these three men as carnivorous dinosaurs. Each relied on another bite of flesh to build his immense fortune (and then lose it, in Drew's case). But another group of Dinosaurs created and built an economic society without directly harming anyone in particular. The Rothschilds, Girard,

Peabody, Morgan, and Cooke might be considered the vegetarians. They were much more gentle and docile in their way of promoting progress—but certainly no less effective.

The Rothschilds, father Mayer and son Nathan, were workhounds who emerged from the German Jewish ghetto to become the first power in world banking. They financed kings, princes, foreign countries, European industry and, when the time was right, America's gradual transformation from an agricultural society to an industrialized nation.

Girard, who really was a vegetarian, financed America's earliest trade endeavors, becoming America's first richest man. He was a mercantile trader who financed import-export voyages and was among the first to support central banking in America (long before its time). Cooke financed the Civil War, becoming the first American to make large underwritings—and their sale—possible.

Peabody and Morgan, both based in London, took up what the Rothschilds started, becoming links between an economically advanced Europe and a cash-needy, emerging America. Peabody was the first to funnel European capital to things like state governments and early forms of industry; Morgan financed our railroad boom starting in the 1860s.

Morgan was perhaps our most important link to modern capital markets in America. His railroad financing sparked a flurry of economic progress, and he funneled much of that progress to his son and American business contact, J.P. Morgan. Young Morgan, whom you can read about in Chapter Three in his role as an investment banker, emerged as a Dinosaur-like power in his own right. Back when Wall Street was little more than a dirt path, young Morgan ruled the road with an iron fist. He was bigger than society and larger than the law, creating structure with each new idea he initiated. Instead of being described in the investment banking section, J.P. Morgan could as easily have been included in this section, as the last of the Dinosaurs, and perhaps the greatest and most powerful of them all.

Despite their larger-than-life personifications, the Dinosaurs didn't live forever. They couldn't. The very structure they created dated them, made them obsolete; the social response to their very existence outlawed them and eventually destroyed them. The progressive era, for example, coming at the height of Morgan's power, was a direct reaction against decades of Dinosaurs and aspiring Dinosaurs who thought they could do as they saw fit in society. The Dinosaurs could. With the rise of the Progressive movement, Roosevelt, Wilson and the income tax. and all the rest of the evolution that ran through the eventual creation of the SEC, no one would ever again have so much total financial autonomy.

It's hard to truly get a feel for the Dinosaurs today, while viewing them from our world—one that evolved through decades of innovation and Dinosaur-bashing and still more innovation and decades where Dinosaurs have since become nothing but memories. Yet, through their existence they provided us with the very beginnings of financial order—when there had been none. With their mass they tromped down the vegetation to make the first crude paths through the financial wilderness. They fought financial battles of a magnitude that could only be viewed as we now would view prehistoric dinosaurs in battle. And from the backlash of those battles came trends to follow and to buck just as early mammals learned to get out of the way of prehistoric dinosaurs and to scavenge their left-behinds. Finally, Dinosaurs gave us the beginnings of a loose set of ethics (both by positive and negative role models). For decades, good and bad would be defined in terms of the Dinosaurs' actions. Men would aspire to emulate their successful market actions, and the outraged would create social foment aimed at early governmental control.

The Dinosaurs will never return. Occasionally a mutation occurs that attempts to be a Dinosaur. But that wanna-be can't survive for the same reason prehistoric dinosaurs can't survive now—regardless of climatic conditions. Simply put, human society wouldn't allow it. Today we have a well defined civilization oriented toward protecting our social order, including the weak and unfortunate. And our social order won't allow Dinosaur-like action. To wit, we have Michael Milken, who came as close to a Dinosaur as anything we've seen in decades. Note how easily the government put Milken in jail on violations which were miniscule relative to the overwhelming mass of his overall junk bond financing activity.

If somehow the Loch Ness monster were to come out of the lake and start strolling in toward town, our authorities would find immediate justification to take action and control it long before it ever got close to population centers. A big wild thing just can't be totally free now, and what is a Dinosaur but a big wild thing? It's actually been a fairly long time since you could be a little, wild thing. Think back to 1911, when Ishi, the last of the wild native American Indians, came in from the woods to give himself up. We took him captive and put him on display in a museum, and in a few years he died of diseases he had never been exposed to in the wild. Our modern societal need to control freedom—lest something damaging occur—will never again allow the evolution of men like the Dinosaurs depicted in this section.

So enjoy these big and wild Dinosaurs. They were among the very first minds that set the market on the path to what it has become.

MAYER AMSCHEL ROTHSCHILD

OUT OF THE GHETTO AND INTO THE LIMELIGHT

Deep in the dank, damp and cramped Jewish ghetto of Frankfurt on the Main in the late 18th century, a nondescript, dark-eyed pawnbroker named Mayer Rothschild created a financial dynasty that grew to finance the development of western civilization. Because of Rothschild and the banking house he built with his five sons, money flowed throughout Europe with ease, enabling the industrial revolution to take place and lift Europe from the dark ages. As a direct result, America—then practically a Third World country compared to prospering Europe—received the financing it needed to transform itself from a provincial, largely agricultural country into a great industrial nation.

Mayer had begun his career by age 10, discovering the ins and outs of money at his father's pawnshop and money bureau. Currency during the 1740s was quite complex, as each of the hundreds of states comprising Germany (still the Holy Roman Empire) minted its own coins. Being astute, he caught on quickly and soon could translate gold and silver into coin and calculate exchange rates with lightning speed.

Orphaned at age 11 in 1755, Mayer followed the sound of clinking coins rather than his parents' idea that he become a rabbi. Over the next decade, he ran a small trade business and pawnshop, selling tobacco, wine, and cloth in exchange for coins. And knowing what a royal connection could do for his career, Mayer courted the business of a numismatic prince—not just any prince, but one of Europe's mightiest and richest, the billionaire Prince William. Mayer sold him his antique coins at ridiculously low prices for years—foregoing immediate profits for long-term favor. He had no intention of staying a small time pawnbroker the rest of his life!

Back then, being a pawnbroker-merchant was one of the only career options available to Jews. Thanks to a papal decree centuries earlier, usury laws forbade Christians from lending for profit. So Jews took over the money-lending trades, becoming pawnbrokers, small trade merchants, and wizards of finance. By the 18th century, it was tradition to trek over to the Jewish ghetto when you needed to pawn a possession for cash or to buy trinkets or second-hand goods. Had Mayer been content with his common role, it's unlikely the Rothschild name would mean what it does today in the financial world.

Tall, black-bearded, with an odd, quizzical smile and a ghetto dialect of Yiddish-Deutsch—Mayer produced 20 children with his wife, Gutle, between 1770 and 1790, with only five girls and five boys surviving. Despite Gutle's harsh life, she was tough, and lived to age 96—which was exceptionally old back then. Seeing the future in his boys, Mayer taught them to buy cheaply and sell dearly before they could walk, and when they reached age 12, he put them to work in the family business. Ultimately, it was through his sons that Mayer realized his ambitions.

Operating from his house, Mayer and sons Amschel, Salomon, **Nathan**, Carl, and James built the business into a strong importing house. This was at the turn of the century, when dry goods were hard to get in Germany unless someone imported them—and that someone was Mayer. Foreseeing the demand for cotton—and perhaps the expanse of his later empire, Mayer sent Nathan to London to make sure cotton shipments reached Frankfurt.

As a big wartime supplier, the Rothschilds piled up the profits. Mayer, still not content with the excess, next began operating a money exchange bureau in their yard. What's considered the very first Rothschild bank appeared to be a nine-square-foot hut—but things weren't quite what they appeared to be. Mayer installed a large iron chest that, when opened from the back, revealed a stairway leading to a secret storage cellar.

Mayer's scheming finally paid off when Prince William of Germany, the man to whom he'd been selling coins, gave him the business he'd been hoping for all along. It started with Mayer acting as the prince's independent agent in an anonymous loan to Denmark. He was the prince's chief banker in 1806 when the prince was forced to flee in exile, leaving his fortune in the Rothschilds' hands.

In the following years Mayer had his sons fan out across the European continent: James went to Paris, Salomon to Vienna, Carl to Naples, Amschel remained in Frankfurt, and of course, Mayer's successor Nathan stayed in London. Each son followed in Mayer's footsteps, courting profitable royal connections, and later each made his own mark by financing kings, wars, and Europe's first railroads. Ultimately, the Rothschilds united to form a sturdy, efficient moneychain across Europe that financed its industrial revolution, creating a common money market for the first time.

By Mayer's death in 1812, his ghetto hopes and ambitions had been realized through his sons, who were well on their way to becoming the world's largest private bank. Without his sons, Mayer might have wound up wealthy, but never world renowned. Why is it that in a book of American financial biographies and American markets there is mention of this European? Simply put, at a time before America had developed its financial markets, the financing of American commodities and government bonds would have been impossible without the flow of funds from Europe. The House of Rothschild, derived through Mayer, was the center of Europe's money markets. Without Mayer and his generational empire, it is unclear that America would ever have developed its own industrial revolution or financial markets. His genes were the seeds through which America's industry got its original lifeblood. In that respect, the seminal tinkling of this German pawnbroker's coins and the thinking that went on behind it are every bit as important to the evolution of American financial history as the life of any American.

The Rothschilds: A Family Portrait, 1962

NATHAN ROTHSCHILD

WHEN CASH BECAME KING—AND
CREDIT BECAME PRIME MINISTER

Money became king when Nathan Rothschild rose to power over Europe in the 19th century, forcing people to recognize finance over divine right. More powerful than monarchs, Nathan masterminded the Rothschild money-factory by sparking Europe's industrial awakening. He financed governments, wars, railroads—anything that stood for progress. At his death in 1836, he left an undisclosed fortune (secrecy was a Rothschild trademark), a legacy of Rothschild bankers, and most importantly, the earliest and most abundant source of credit for a burgeoning America via his American agent **August Belmont.**

Although banking was then still in its rudimentary state, Nathan fully understood the interplay between finance and economics, the effects of political news on the stock exchange, the quickest way to bull or bear a market, and how gold reserves affected the exchange rate. Born in Frankfurt, he founded London's N.M. Rothschild and Sons. He spent half his day at the bank and the other half at the Royal Exchange leaning against the same pillar, knowing he was the center of attention. While brokers watched his short, stout figure, hopeful for a sign or a gesture that might foretell his next move, Nathan kept an utterly blank expression—his hands thrust inside his pockets and his hat pulled over his eyes.

Round-faced, red-headed with pouty lips, a sour personality, and arrogant manner, at age 33 Nathan built the family fortune in a single move at the Royal Exchange—with a prince's royal booty! His father, **Mayer Rothschild**, had advised a German prince to buy British consols (English government bonds) and to use Nathan to do so, since Nathan was in London and would only charge a tiny brokerage fee of one-eighth of 1 percent. The prince agreed and sent Nathan the equivalent of $5 million—which was a lot of money back then—all earmarked for oodles of consols, priced at 72.

Quick-thinking Nathan eventually bought the prince his consols, but he first used the money to successfully speculate in gold bullion, making a killing and a reputation for himself in the London exchange. That would be considered highly unethical today because using a client's money for your own benefit is dishonest and generally slimy. But in those days, notions of highly unethical behavior didn't exist. Had Nathan's gold speculation failed, we wouldn't be reading about him now.

When the prince grew impatient for his securities, Nathan simply bought the consols at 62, making another killing by charging the prince the expected 72 and pocketing the difference! Amazingly, it was three years from the time the prince first advanced the money that Nathan actually got the consols for him—1809 to 1812. For three years Nathan used the money, interest free, and from it made two fortunes. If a broker did that today, he would be banned from the industry for life. Nathan just might have been the first of the big-time brokerage scoundrels. Yet five years, later, at 38, he was banker-in-chief to the British Government.

By the 1820s, Nathan and his four brothers were operating from five capitals, creating a financial network that sprawled throughout Europe like never before. Cultivating Europe's wealthiest as clients, Nathan masterminded the family's coups while his brothers successfully carried them out. For instance, Nathan concocted a loan—carried out by brother James in Paris—to finance the return of Bourbon Prince Louis XVIII to the French throne. When Naples was overcome by a revolution, Nathan dreamed up the loan that financed a military occupation by the Austrian army—and brother Carl saw it through.

With communication systems practically nonexistent except for word of mouth, the Rothschild brothers stayed in touch via their famously efficient private courier system that consisted of a network of men, ships that sailed regardless of weather, and, most importantly, carrier pigeons. Even folks unfamiliar with Nathan Rothschild knew about the famous carrier pigeons. Their fame is based to a large extent on how the pigeons enabled Nathan to know before anyone else outside the battle zone of Napoleon's defeat at Waterloo. While others feared England might lose, Rothschild knew otherwise, and by knowing before others on the floor of the London Stock Exchange, Rothschild bought and made another fortune. Rothschild truly brought a different meaning to the phrase, "a bird in the hand is worth two in the bush."

While today money can be transferred almost anywhere with the blink of an eye and a phone call, Nathan lived when the actual, physical currency—often, heavy gold bullion—was physically moved to show proof of deposit. Knowing how inconvenient this was, Nathan replaced this old credit structure with a worldwide system of paper credit. In this way, Nathan enabled the British Government, in its fight against Napoleon, to pay out some 15 million pounds to the continent between 1812 and 1814. He handled the transaction so deftly that the exchange rate was left intact. Until then, a government advancing money was faced with the prospect of losing much of it. In this respect Nathan pioneered international credit.

The Rothschild brothers—Nathan, James, Amschel, Carl, and Salomon—comprised the world's largest private bank. No one else even came close. The House of Rothschild was sort of an international central bank at a time when America barely had a grip on central banking, and couldn't hold on to its grip for long. The Rothschilds were not only capable of financing industries, governments and wars, but they were also able to stabilize panics, pioneer the western world, and outlive the many unstable governments with which they did business.

The Rothschilds were capable of affecting history to their liking. For example, when there was cause to worry about war between two German states, the Rothschilds' mother, Gutle, laughed and said, "Nonsense! My boys won't give them any money!" But perhaps the best example of their power was when Nathan, in all his glory, managed to save one of England's greatest institutions, at a time when England was by far the most powerful economic and military force in the world.

He rescued England's central bank, the Bank of England, from bankruptcy in 1826. The year before, hordes of English firms had invested in newly-independent Latin American countries on a long shot. (Nathan, luckily, had been too busy with affairs back home to bother.) Within a year, the countries had defaulted on their loans, leaving the British investors holding the bag, and as a result, some 3,000 firms went under. The Bank of England, meanwhile, was the ultimate loser, for it had loaned those 3,000 firms the money to invest in Latin America. So, just as the bank was about to close its doors, Nathan stepped in and arranged for an emergency transfer of gold bullion from France via his brother to save the bank. It was about the same as if our central bank could rely on the Bank of Japan to bail it out or vice versa.

When not working—which wasn't often—Nathan stayed at home with his wife and seven children. She was his best friend, and they rarely sought the company of people outside the family, unlike some of his more society-minded brothers. Like his father, Nathan kept a close-knit family and wanted his four sons to continue the family business. "I wish them to give mind, soul, heart, and body—everything to business." Fond of making money, but not spending it, he added, "It requires a great deal of boldness and a great deal of caution to make a large fortune, and when you have it, you require ten times as much wit to keep it."

Nathan died in 1836 at 59, leaving a depressed London stock market and his youngest brother in charge of the family fortune. At the time of his death, the famous Rothschild carrier pigeons were released from a London rooftop at midnight, notifying all Rothschild brothers and agents that Nathan was dead. The pigeons carried the simple message, "il est mort," or "he is dead."

The importance of Nathan Rothschild is his essential creation of a European money market. Before him, every country was a financial island. The Rothschild family under his direction made a worldwide force that provided not only the first material international financial interplay throughout Europe, but also spread its web to America via August Belmont. Without the Rothschilds, led by Nathan, there probably wouldn't have been enough of a European money market to fund the conclusion of their industrial revolution, much less the beginning of ours.

STEPHEN GIRARD

THE FIRST RICHEST MAN IN AMERICA FINANCED PRIVATEERS

S tephen Girard had a lousy home life, but in exchange, he had the drive to build a million-dollar shipping empire in the early 1800s—and with his millions, open his own private bank. As eccentric as he was rich, the one-eyed, embittered Frenchman never rested, believing "labor is the price of life, its happiness, its everything."

Starting each day with a spoonful of Holland gin and the strongest black coffee, Girard had labored for over 65 years when he died in 1831. Born near Bordeaux, France in 1750, he went to sea at 14, following in his father's navy-captain footsteps, and became France's youngest captain at 23. In 1774, after his first lone voyage left him in debt, he set sail for New York, never to return home. Girard, who spoke with a thick French accent, worked for a N.Y. shipping firm and half-owned a vessel—but grounded her in Philadelphia when the Revolutionary War broke out, barely escaping British warships. Ambitious and never content, Girard set up shop there in a dingy waterfront office, returning to foreign trade.

While making a name for himself and his maritime firm, Girard married a servant girl in 1777, but the marriage was doomed. After their only child died at birth, his wife went crazy, living the rest of her life in an insane asylum. Girard never remarried, and he never had much fun. To take his mind off things he worked harder, financing privateers and building profitable trades in the West Indies, Europe and Asia. As an American citizen, he built his fortune via hard bargains, persistence and planning. Controlling an 18-vessel fleet named after French philosophers, he transported wheat, fish, flour, lumber, sugar, and coffee, despite frequent embargoes, blockades, pirates, and seizures. Of course it probably didn't hurt him any that he had financing relations with many of the seamiest souls on the docks. A shrewd dealer without patience for stupidity, he declared work "the only pleasure I have on this globe." (Actually he got a big kick out of the singing yellow canaries he kept on his desk.)

As his "only pleasure"—and international reputation—flourished, Girard kept a million-dollar booty with the Baring Brothers in London while investing in Philly real estate, insurance and the First Bank of the U.S. So, when political turmoil brewed and the First Bank's charter was discontinued by Congress in 1811, Girard reeled in his overseas capital to create his much-celebrated Bank of Stephen Girard with $1.2 million in the U.S. Bank's old quarters. While Girard's investment choices were unlimited by his vast capital, he chose a private bank to supplement his maritime firm's credit. "My commercial capital enables me to sell my goods on credit and to carry on my maritime business through cash on hand without the aid of discounts," he once told a Baring brother. Yet, unlike other private banks which were usually connected to large merchandising outfits, Girard—known for his honesty—kept his bank and business scrupulously separate.

Operating at a time when private bankers fell out of favor to chartered, commercial banks because of their increased functions, Girard faced stiff competition from other Philly banks. But immediately securing sound connections—the Treasury and national Second Bank of the U.S.—he successfully led his bank through all economic weather, including suspended specie payments. Floating loans to finance the War of 1812, his bank became heavily involved in Treasury financing, and in 1813, participated in one of the nation's very first syndicates, floating a $16 million loan—then the largest in America's history. En route he was foreshadowing the path that many others would follow later in a myriad of syndicates to finance virtually everything that has ever been financed in America since.

With a sound reputation, Girard's bank acted as a central reserve for rural banks and as a local bank for Philly residents. And since the bank didn't have to answer to a government charter, Girard used his privacy and flexibility to his advantage, quickly adjusting to changing market conditions, perhaps increasing the proportions of loans, or enacting new services, like investment banking. In essence, he was the first free-wheeling wheeler-dealer in the history of banking and finance in America.

Following the war, Girard, a proponent of central banking, was appointed one of five government directors of the new Second Bank of the U.S. When no buyers were found for the $3 million of new stock needed to capitalize the bank, Girard subscribed for it all in 1816. But when possible corruption clouded the bank's policies, Girard refused another appointment to the board and returned to running his bank's day-to-day activities as president. Girard brought his bank prosperity, making him worth nearly $5 million by 1815.

Aside from his independent, yet conservative banking practices, Girard is recognized as a unique symbol of his times. He combatted wine-swigging, cargo-stealing pirates to get rich in a mercantile economy—then took on the up-and-coming commercial bankers in an increasingly corporate and civilized world. He was uniquely versatile, commanding fear as easily as respect from those with whom he dealt. And as the new era of commercial banking was ushered in, the aging Girard, continually resisting its corporate nature, foreshadowed what was to come—the all-powerful and private investment banker. Had he lived another 75 years, the wealthy, influential Girard might have rivaled the powerful **J.P. Morgan!** Unlike Morgan, however, Girard's empire died when he did in 1831. His bank's books were closed four years later, giving rise to the chartered Girard's Bank.

At the time of his death, from influenza, Girard was worth some $6 million. Of course, that is not actually as much as it might seem. Somewhere along the way he must have lost a bundle that isn't recorded anywhere. Consumer prices were very high following the war of 1812, and soon thereafter they peaked and then fell steadily, so that by his death they had fallen by half. $6 million in 1831, adjusted for changes in consumer prices, would miraculously be worth only about $80 million today. So while our first richest man was certainly prosperous, he wasn't as prosperous as any of the *Forbes* 400 today. In a sense his riches are a reflection of how financially poor life truly was in early America.

Not always the miserable man he was reputed to be, Girard liked children and willed the majority of his estate to establish a college for orphans. Converted to vegetarianism in his older years, and a nature enthusiast who spent most of his later days on his Delaware River farm, Girard was convinced "to rest is to rust." He stated a month before his death, "When death comes for me he will find me busy, unless I am asleep. If I thought I was going to die tomorrow, I should nevertheless plant a tree today." It's likely he did.

Girard had no road map of prior travelers in banking and finance to follow. He was a pioneer. He was also the essence of the early American rugged individualist who could deal equally with pirates or politicians (much the same), but also with bankers and merchants. The future is always rugged, and there are always modern era pirates, politicians and bankers to get in your way. But the good news from Girard's life is that in many ways the future is always an unmapped path, and any of us have just as good a chance to lead the way now as he had then.

JOHN JACOB ASTOR

A ONE-MAN CONGLOMERATION

A stout, thick-headed German, John Jacob Astor had his finger in practically every profitable pie of the early 1800s. Fur, shipping, money-lending, real estate, railroads—if it was profitable and safe, Astor bought it. At his death in 1848, he left some $30 million, though his lawyers claimed it was as little as $8 million—and the public estimate was as high as $150 million! Astor was among his era's most controversial figures because of his millions—and the methods by which he earned them. Upon his death, in fact, a *New York Herald* editor proclaimed that half of Astor's estate should go to the people of New York City for having augmented his properties' values. Astor probably chuckled in his grave!

Born in Waldorf, Germany to a butcher in 1763, Astor never took public uproar too seriously. He was stubborn and gruff in manner, which is why he had the gall to go through with this very telling real estate deal: One day, a lawyer told Astor that over 50,000 acres in New York's Putnam County did not legally belong to the 700 families that had purchased their farms from the state 50 years earlier. The land had been illegally confiscated from Roger Morris. Astor immediately bought off the Morris heirs for about $100,000, then notified the 700 farmers that they were trespassing on his property! The dumbfounded farmers ran to the state, which at first refused to recognize Astor's claim, but after lengthy legal battles, Astor won $500,000 from the state in 1827!

In keeping with his ruthless reputation, "the landlord of New York" foreclosed mortgages at the drop of a hat and bought properties for fractions of their value whenever hard times hit. Even on his deathbed, he was concerned with collecting the rent. In one case, when Astor inquired about a particular tenant's rent, his agent replied that the rent could not be paid due to a misfortune. "No, no, I tell you she can pay it; and she will pay it!" Astor screamed. When the agent told the story to Astor's son, the son forked over the "rent" for the agent to give to his father. Waving the money around with a smug grin on his face, Astor said in his thick German accent, "There! I told you she would pay it!

Standing 5'9" with a high, square forehead and long silver hair, Astor came to America at age 20 with seven flutes to sell and speaking broken English. After unloading his flutes, he married and went on to build a small fortune in the fur trade. He bought off government employees and politicians to receive exclusive rights and a virtual monopoly in America's fur industry. Having put together the monopoly in a string of seemingly unrelated deals, he then incorporated the American Fur Company in 1808 as a holding company. He then taught Wall Street one of its early lessons in stock watering and cheating employees. He formed a relatively unimportant subsidiary and distributed some of its stock to a few partners and employees to heighten their interest in the firm—and maximize their use. It was eventually dissolved. Throughout his life he had a knack for using people for all they were worth.

In the fur industry, Astor made trading an art form. It was easy. In order to buy skins cheaply, he had his traders get Native Americans (his main suppliers) drunk before trading. To keep a handle on his traders, he paid them cheaply—not in money, but in overpriced goods sold at Astor's stores. To check politicians and legal watchdogs, he kept a stream of top-notch lawyers on hand. And while there was nothing wrong with it, he shrewdly boosted his profits further by shipping his furs overseas, where they sold for five times the profit. And, naturally, rather than watch an empty ship cross the Atlantic, Astor started up his shipping business and trade with China.

Some of his more sedate dealings were in stocks and banking. Ever-faithful to the American economy, Astor bought state and federal government securities for years. During the War of 1812, he and **Stephen Girard** joined to loan the government millions. They bought blocks of bonds priced from 80 to 82 cents on the dollar, paying for them in bank notes worth half their face value! Four years later, he helped arrange the Ohio canal loan and invested heavily in New York, Pennsylvania and Massachusetts bonds. Astor also invested in both the first and second Bank of the United States, becoming New York branch president of the second Bank in 1816. Later, he speculated in banks, but refrained from an active role.

In Astor's old age he was sickly, often bedridden, and suffered from palsy and severe insomnia. When he died at age 85, his son and partner since 1831, William B. Astor, took over his estate and continued the legacy. Ironically enough, Astor's namesake, John Jacob, Jr., who was supposed to be groomed for business, was born mentally deficient.

In all fairness Astor was doing rough things in a primitive world. He didn't break the law or defy convention. What he did in the early 1800s was help establish the conventions that would rule Wall Street into the later 19th century. The stories condemning Astor most likely abound because he died at the onset of muckraking in 1848, and because in a very rough world and one with few rules, he was the richest and most successful man of his time.

AMS Press, Inc.

CORNELIUS VANDERBILT

A MAN ABOVE THE LAW

Cornelius Vanderbilt did what he damn well pleased. When his wife refused to move his family to Manhattan from Staten Island, she was promptly committed to an insane asylum until she changed her mind. Several months later, she obediently scurried to her relocated family. In his later years, he played cards all night long and meditated with mediums. Some attributed his eccentricities to his old age—he was 83 when he died in 1877—but his wife knew he did just what he wanted.

The hulking, fiery-eyed, and pink-cheeked Vanderbilt was no old coot—in fact, quite the opposite. A bright, ambitious, never-take-no-for-an-answer go-getter, "the Commodore" built his fortune by sheer persistence, first in shipping, then—at 70, on the wave of the future—railroads. Always ready for a fight and letting no one get in his way, Vanderbilt woke each dawn, fueled himself with three egg yolks, a lamb chop, and tea with 12 lumps of sugar, and planned his schemes for the day. Stock watering, bribery, and stock corners were all methods to his madness, but for good reason. "My God, you don't suppose you can run a railroad in accordance with the statutes of New York, do you?"

The Commodore taught the financial world how to corner stocks, something illegal these days. But back then it was quite a feat. In 1863, when the Commodore first started buying railroad stock, he was practically laughed off Wall Street. They saw an old shipping magnate who knew absolutely nothing about the rails and, to top it off, he was buying up the depressed Harlem and Hudson River lines! Let them laugh, Vanderbilt roared—he never gave a hoot for public opinion. He gained control of the two lines in hopes of merging them. Then he set about getting what he wanted, obtaining a charter from Manhattan politicos through bribery to connect the Harlem line with city streetcars.

As a result, the stock zoomed, attracting **Daniel Drew** and the same city politicos. Licking their chops, Drew and his corrupt cronies sold Hudson short, then prepared to reneg on the charter, while the old Commodore bought all he could. When the streetcar charter was canceled, the stock dropped and Drew's group further sold short at 75—but when they tried to buy back their stock, they found Vanderbilt had cornered it! Harlem jumped to 179 and Vanderbilt settled at top price, letting the group off the hook for a million and Drew, $4 million.

Wall Street still giggled at him—but not after 1864! As state legislators considered a bill allowing his Harlem-Hudson merger, they pocketed his bribes. Then, sniffing quick profits, they called in Drew to lead them in again selling the Harlem short at 150. The bill was naturally defeated, causing the Harlem to plummet. Drew's group waited until it reached 50 before covering its shorts. Meanwhile, as it fell, Vanderbilt bought and bought until he had accepted 27,000 more shares than actually existed. He had cornered Harlem again!

The old Commodore whistled to the defeated Drew, "Don't you never buy anything you don't want, nor sell anything you hain't got!" This time the stock jumped to 285, knocking the bears to their knees, but the Commodore wasn't satisfied. Heartlessly he cried, "Put it up to 1,000. This panel game is being tried too often," but in light of an overall panicky stock market, and one particularly spooked by the Commodore's corner, the old coot settled at 285.

Vanderbilt bought bankrupt railroads and made them pay. He replaced old iron tracks with steel and built New York's Grand Central Station—because they were good for business and built earnings. While he claimed, "I am a friend of the iron road," he was equally a friend of stock-watering schemes. For example, The New York Central, which remained in the Vanderbilt family for years, was watered twice by $23 million. The first time he cranked out bogus new shares at midnight in a secluded basement. "I never tell what I am going to do 'til I have done it." So, when his roads finally paid, you were certain the public was also paying. When he raised dividends called for by the newly-created "water" shares, freight rates were jacked up sky-high, repairs postponed, and employee wages cut.

The Commodore practiced his ruthless ways for over 50 years. Once, early on, while still engaged in shipping and sidetracked by a rare vacation in his lavish, specially built yacht, he came back to find that his partners had ousted him from his firm. The classic Vanderbilt response? "I won't sue you for the law is too slow. I will ruin you!" His demeanor rubbed off on at least one of his 12 children. **William Henry Vanderbilt**, his son and heir to three-quarters of his fortune, was known to revile the public as much as his father did, once screaming, "Let the public be damned!" And pretty regularly it was.

The Commodore's harsh, sometimes lawless tactics paid off. It certainly didn't bother him. He was a vain man who thought he superseded law. "Law! What do I care about law? Hain't I got the power?" Vanderbilt got just what he wanted—over $100 million—but, aside from that, he lived in hell. In his old age his only pleasures were chasing young female servants around his room as best he could and yelling at his doctors while throwing hot water bottles at them. Despite his riches, he was a classic crotchety and dirty old man. His energetic youth gave way to a handful of illnesses—his kidney, intestines, liver, and stomach were all used up. He once told a doctor, who I'll bet couldn't sympathize, "If all the devils in hell were contracted in me I could not have suffered any more."

There is a hidden message in Vanderbilt's life. Just as he said, the markets are more powerful than the law. While it is less true now than in Vanderbilt's day, it is still true today. Those who have economic power and skirt the law for their own benefit are rarely brought legally leveled to their original condition or worse, unlike what happens to other kinds of criminals. For example, the amazing thing about all the 1980s insider trading trials is how light the sentencing was and how few of those convicted ended up less than very rich. Most American poor folk may well think these modern-era Commodores did pretty well for themselves over the course of their lives. But smiling from his grave. Commodore probably just muttered, "Hain't done what I coulda done—hain't even done what I did."

GEORGE PEABODY

A FINDER OF FINANCING
AND FINANCIERS

Before there was Morgan, there was Peabody. George Peabody. He started out as a Baltimore dry goods merchant, then left his native America in 1835 to become one of the most powerful merchant investment bankers in England. Hard work, dedication, and a willingness to take a chance gained him a topnotch reputation in both Europe and America. He accumulated over $10 million before dying in 1869, leaving an empire that eventually led to the rise of the all-powerful House of Morgan.

Peabody's transformation from merchant to merchant banker was ambitious, but not atypical at the time. Many bankers' businesses grew as an outgrowth of their mercantile businesses—for example, financing ships' voyages abroad and selling their cargoes. Peabody had good credit, capital, and a knowledge of world commerce and banking houses—he had been dealing with them for years in the dry goods firm. He did lots of banking-type favors for friends, including selling stock in London that an American friend had left with him, watching over others' investments, and writing letters of credit for travelers. He was trusted—so trusted, that his name was a source of credit for friends in either country.

Serious, sedate, and sincere, Peabody began building his house piece-by-piece with American securities, selling them in the London market, where he came to be known as the expert in American securities. An American himself, he symbolized security, integrity, and stability, and that reflected well on his wares. During periods of declining confidence in America, Peabody "bought American" himself, investing in the Bank of the United States, busy canal companies, insurance firms, and railroads. He bought cheaply, on a large scale, between 1837 and 1843, after the famous Panic of 1837. During the tremendously long and deep economic depression that followed, he made a fortune when the stocks jumped in value.

Peabody believed that in the long run, American investments meant sound investments. So, naturally, when it came to underwriting bond issues and selling them in the London market, he was quite a convincing salesman—he truly believed in his products. To push things along, Peabody promoted American securities through excellent English-American business relations. He threw elegant parties in the poshest places whenever Americans visited and though he usually drank little and ate plain food, he made merry for the sake of advertising America, its people, and its products.

Peabody had tremendous success during his career, not only because of his salesmanship, but also because of his optimism. But optimism wasn't nearly enough in the case of an $8 million bond issue meant to finance construction of Maryland's Baltimore and Ohio Railroad in 1838. Appointed one of three financiers to float the issue, Peabody had a bad time of it due to America's poor financial condition following the Panic of 1837. Mention Uncle Sam to an Englishman, and he went running! America was on its knees for years after the panic, which meant a greater chance to default on loans and interest payments.

Like a broken record, persistent Peabody repeated his America-is-a-good-investment spiel, and finally he unloaded the bonds on the Baring Brothers at a ridiculously low price—which should have made him feel good. But it didn't. The fact that Maryland had urged him to sell at any price left him uneasy. In 1841, his uneasiness was confirmed when Maryland defaulted on the bonds.

Tall, stout, and good-looking with clear blue eyes and black hair which he dyed, Peabody's personal life was equally uneasy. Though he was seemingly London's most eligible bachelor, he remained single all his life. He tried to marry a 19-year-old American at 43, but she never went through with the wedding—she loved another. Forlorn Peabody never married, but instead kept a rigorous work schedule—10 hours per day, and often evenings and Sundays. He never took a day off until 1853! He also kept a long-time mistress, with whom he had a daughter, tucked away in Brighton, England. By some folks' standards that would be better than getting married.

In America, as well as England, Peabody had a reputation bigger than life. During the Civil War, the Confederate government called on him to negotiate a loan for them in England, which was chock full of Confederate sympathizers—but because of political feelings, he declined. At that stage in his life, he could well afford to pick and choose his business. So the Confederates sought the loan themselves, calling on London capitalists for $75 million in exchange for their bonds at 50 cents on the dollar. Queasy about granting the loan without the American securities expert's blessing, two of the Londoners relayed the proposition to Peabody who said he believed the bonds could be bought for 25 cents on the dollar within a year.

"To prove that I am sincere, I will stipulate to sell you a million dollars worth in one year from today at 25 cents on the dollar." So the men declined the Confederates' deal and took Peabody up on his. Sure enough, "the year came round and Confederate bonds were worth less than even I anticipated," Peabody wrote. He held the men to their deal and collected $60,000!

Hurting from gout and rheumatism, Peabody allowed himself to take a breather from work. During the last years of his life, he went to spas, visited friends, and went salmon fishing, besides giving most of his money away. He was known for his generosity to the people of both his countries; endowing schools, libraries, museums, and people. Peabody, Massachusetts, which was once called South Danvers, was named after him in honor of his birthplace and donations.

In addition to his large donations, Peabody is most well known—on Wall Street—for giving **Junius Spencer Morgan** (**J.P. Morgan**'s father) his start in investment banking. A great judge of character and a bit of a visionary, Peabody selected Morgan as his partner in 1854, allowing Peabody to take a breather from the firm. What he looked for in his partner were qualities he himself parlayed: integrity, daring on occasion, caution, and a shrewd mind. But Peabody represented much more than giving a boost to the long line of Morgan leaders. He brought us much-needed European money, in large chunks, without which we wouldn't have developed the infrastructure which subsequently let us develop industrially in the 19th century. Industry follows finance, and everybody followed Peabody.

JUNIUS SPENCER MORGAN

THE LAST OF THE MODERN MANIPULATORS

Junius Morgan was the first to make the Morgan name what it came to stand for under his only son, **J.P. Morgan**—integrity, trust, competence and power. Standing over six feet tall, with a strong frame, sharply defined features and a straightforward, trustworthy manner. Morgan challenged London's established banking firms and eventually surpassed them, becoming the most important American banker in London in the 1860s. When he died, he left his son an international legacy and his old-fashioned business ethics—a firm basis on which to build the infamous House of Morgan.

Born in 1813 the only son of a wealthy landowner-investor, Morgan grew up in West Springfield, Connecticut, well educated and surrounded by his father's sound investments. He was no stranger to success. Still, he worked hard to climb up the ladder, first interning at a Wall Street banking house for five years. At age 20 he became a partner in Ketchum, Morgan & Company. But when he learned his partner was an unscrupulous speculator engaged in shady deals, Morgan immediately escaped the partnership and began again on the right track, settling in New England, marrying and starting a family of one son and two daughters. (The son, of course, was J.P. Morgan.)

Morgan climbed his way to the top via the country's premier wholesale dry goods and importing house, James M. Beebe & Company, which became J.M. Beebe, Morgan & Company in 1851. In those days, importing and finance were very close to each other since it was impossible to import without financing. He became known for his integrity, firmness, and fairness and was well on his way to prominence in American finance, financing Boston's bustling clipper ship trade with Europe and Asia. But while in London discussing his firm's credit account with **George Peabody** of the highly respected London merchant banking firm Peabody & Company, Morgan traded in his American dream for a chance at the big time after Peabody made him an offer he couldn't refuse.

A former dry goods importer like Morgan, Peabody specialized in underwriting and selling American securities overseas, but was looking to retire and needed a replacement he could trust. Though Peabody was picky, he saw in Morgan the drive, ambition and dedication needed to follow in his own ambitious footsteps. Morgan, in turn, saw a chance to increase his already large fortune and, better still, link English capital to New England needs. So he made the plunge, packing up his family at age 38 and heading overseas to a new world.

Morgan quickly mastered the typical merchant bankers' trade—providing credit for the world's expanding trade business, trading commodities, shipping bullion, exchanging currencies, and financing importers and exporters. By the time the 1857 Panic hit in America, Morgan was ready to take action. Since Peabody & Company was closely linked with American securities, the panic had drained the firm's bank account; American creditors could not pay money they owed Peabody & Company—money the firm used to pay its own debts. Morgan solved the problem by negotiating a loan for the firm from the Bank of England—a loan so prestigious it might as well have been the Queen's blessing!

Feeling he was in good hands, Peabody gradually withdrew from the firm and Morgan's flair began to flavor the firm (renamed J.S. Morgan & Company once Peabody fully retired). Though he continued trading in the usual—spices, tea, coffee, wheat, flour, sugar, and the like—he saw to it that the firm's most important commodity was American railroads. Railroad construction was so expensive that America was forced to rely on European capital—and that suited Morgan just fine.

Peabody had been dabbling in railroads and railroad materials such as iron for some time, but Morgan knew America was beginning to depend on a sprawling railroad network. He dove headfirst into railroad financing, taking carefully calculated risks (his trademark). For example, he negotiated the sale of a $4 million bond issue for the Erie Railroad when Erie credit was at an all-time low, making it one of the first large American rail offerings in the London market and the most profitable. By the 1850s, his clients included most major lines: the New York Central, Illinois Central and Baltimore & Ohio.

Meanwhile, Junius' only son, J.P., was coming of age and searching for his own place in Wall Street. But his father, even though in Europe, still had tremendous influence in his son's life via the mail. Between 1857 and 1890, the two passed back and forth lengthy letters (often a dozen pages long) containing their most intimate and confidential thoughts. Junius catalogued his son's letters in yearly, leather-bound volumes that were locked and shelved in his library.

In a typical letter, Junius wrote to his young son, "I want you to bring your mind quietly down to the regular details of business. I do not like it (to) be excited by anything outside, and I would recommend your forming a resolution never to buy any stock on speculation." But such fatherly advice surely didn't warrant the letters' destruction—you could only imagine what the young son must have written to his father! J.P., who at one point was Peabody's confidential agent, renewing magazine subscriptions as well as negotiating loans for the Illinois Central, crammed into his letters political and economic developments, and perhaps a few entrepreneurial ideas of his own. You can't help but hear J.P. telling his father of his hopes for Wall Street—and Junius' empowering replies! Sadly, particularly for historians, J.P. got his hands on the volumes when his father died and tossed them all into his blazing fireplace one by one.

Junius became a true power in international finance in 1870 with his famous French loan following the Franco-Prussian War. He organized a syndicate—when syndicates were still recent innovations—to float $50 million when no one else would. "This was no gamble," he later told the *New York Tribune*. "I thought it was a safe operation." He floated the loan at a low interest rate but high commission rate, and within a week European investors clamored to invest.

The next year, however, Morgan was forced to buy back large amounts of the issue at heavy discount when Prussia threatened to make the loan's repudiation a condition of peace. So in 1873, when a defeated France redeemed the entire issue at par, Morgan made a killing. Altogether his firm netted 15 percent of the issue's par value through commissions and the resale of bonds bought at discount. Aside from profits though, the loan boosted Morgan into the upper echelon of private international bankers.

While Morgan—who died in 1890 after falling off his horse-drawn carriage near the Italian border—must be remembered for laying the foundation for the House of Morgan, he also had great significance in linking the flow of European money to America at a time when America needed it most. At the onset of the great railroad development, Morgan financed huge deals that would have been too big for financiers in America had they had no European help. Railroad development would have been slowed greatly, which in turn would have slowed America's industrial progress. And slow industrial progress would, in turn, have left J.P. Morgan twiddling his thumbs at his giant Wall Street desk!

DANIEL DREW

MUCH "TO DREW" ABOUT NOTHING

Friendship is okay for weekends, but when Monday rolls around, forget about it. Daniel Drew did. He had no friends to speak of—when he did, he double crossed them. This shifty-eyed scoundrel was a Wall Street tiger, both powerful and biting. But, as they say, what goes around, comes around, and that's exactly what happened to Uncle Dan'l.

Drew was the market's first major speculator to venture inside business. Instead of just buying and selling stock as a speculator, he was the first of what we today would see as takeover artists, using the stock market as a way to acquire controlling interests in businesses, then get inside them and alter their destiny.

Illiterate and a religious zealot, Drew speculated in railroads, most notably the Erie, operating by trickery and gut instinct. "I got to be a millionaire afore I know'd it hardly." Drew typically printed and sold company stock when needed, raided the market when he caught the scent of cash and used deceit when desperate. A truly ruthless man, Drew coveted his enviable insider position. The irony is that a man so religious could be so dishonest. He even went so far as to plant phony buy orders, "dropping" them and leaving the tickets behind during lunch at an eatery frequented by speculators; once the crowd started buying on his coattails—as he knew they would—he sold all they could handle!

Whenever Drew was hounded for "insider" tips, which was all the time, he would finally relent, give a false tip, and extract a vow of secrecy from the recipient. The tip would always be exactly the reverse of what Drew himself planned to do. Of course, once the coattailer bought or sold according to Drew's instruction, he could never keep his mouth shut, and all manner of too-greedy and seedy operators would jump on the bandwagon. Drew, in waiting, would double cross the entire lot of them with huge disguised orders that ripped through the price like a razor to paper, giving himself a tidy little profit and them, perhaps, a useful education. It may have been Drew who inspired the following saying:

> The stock market is a place where a man with experience gains money and a man with money gains some experience.

A War of 1812 veteran, Drew discovered Wall Street tactics as a cattledriver in 1813. He was 16 and acquired cattle by smooth-talking local Carmel, New York farmers. Having little money to actually buy cattle, he bought the cattle on credit, but never actually paid for them. As he drove his stock to Manhattan for slaughter, he stumbled upon the benefits of "watering stock"—feeding his cattle salt, then watering the thirsty critters prior to their weigh-in at purchase time.

When butchers like Henry Astor suspected his scam, Drew switched to steamboats, buying a dilapidated tub in 1834, and calling himself a steamboat line. Steamboat magnate Cornelius Vanderbilt called Drew a nuisance when he announced cutthroat fares on the Hudson, forcing Vanderbilt to buy his line for a tidy sum. In 1845, he formed Drew, Robinson & Co. and joined in bull and bear stock market raids preceding the 1857 Panic.

In 1857, at age 60, his firm was a dozen years old. Drew was no spring chicken, but his trickery and avarice were ripe for market mischief. So, the Bible-spewing Drew dissolved the firm and began operating alone. He single-handedly seized control of financially-ruined Erie—he said "Airy"—in 1857. Controlling Erie's board, Drew easily manipulated company stock, printing up fresh batches whenever he sold short. He had an entire treasury to do with as he pleased! Nine years later, Drew met budding market manipulators young **Jim Fisk** and **Jay Gould**, his ultimate rivals. Liking them, Drew as a mentor unknowingly let them in on his plans and taught them his treacherous ways.

The Erie War was waged between 1866 and 1868 with Drew and his two-man army charging full force against their foe, Vanderbilt, who stupidly initiated the battle. At first, Vanderbilt bought Erie heavily in hopes of monopolizing Manhattan railways—and just as he thought he had controlling interest, Drew pounced, initiating a bear raid. Drew loaned Erie $3.5 million, received 28,000 unissued shares and $3 million in convertibles, then flooded the market. Vanderbilt, a typical bull, bought heavily, but what he didn't know was that he was buying stock watered by Drew, just like the old cattle trick.

Merrily Drew chanted, "He who sells what isn't his'n must buy it back or go to pris'n!" Silently printing stock was far easier than selling short. Sensing a scam, Vanderbilt's well-bought "pocket" judge issued an injunction prohibiting Erie directors from issuing more stock. Ultimately, it was Gould who took care of the injunction by greasing a few palms. Gould then took to the printing press, dumping an additional 100,000 shares on the market.

Vanderbilt roared, and soon Drew, Gould and Fisk were wanted for arrest, again courtesy of Vanderbilt's judge. To escape arrest they "crossed the border" to Jersey City. But after a month, the now 71-year-old Drew felt homesick. He was intrigued when he received a private Vanderbilt note that read, "Drew: I'm sick of the whole damned business. Come and see me." So, while Fisk frolicked at the hotel with his mistress and Gould attempted to undo warrants for their arrest via bribery, Drew—on the sly—ferried back to Vanderbilt's quarters to fix the situation. Vanderbilt and Drew settled on a deal to pay back the loser's losses out of the Erie Treasury—Vanderbilt didn't really care where the money came from. But Gould and Fisk discovered the deal and fumed, deciding to honor the Vanderbilt-Drew deal—but oust Drew from the Erie. They successfully extracted their pounds of flesh from Drew in a treacherous stockwatering bear raid that drove Erie stock below Drew's margin call price, forcing Drew to take losses. They gave to Drew an ironic taste of his own medicine.

But Drew was not broke. He still had about $13 million. And he was still an operator. Stripped of his golden goose and, with his vicious character exposed, he aroused suspicion in his fellow Wall Street insiders. On one occasion, Drew used this suspicion to his advantage, setting a past associate up for a big fall. He tipped the sucker to an impending Erie bear raid while he himself sold heavily. When the sucker suspected Drew's plan—despite Drew's denials—he locked Drew and himself in Drew's office to see if the market was still supplied with Erie when Drew was out of circulation. Ever street-wise, Drew out thought his suspicious sucker. Pretending to be hurt by this loss of faith, Drew started a heated argument with the man and, enraged, banged on the table. Little did the man know that each bang told his brokers to sell 1,000 shares of Erie!

Shunned by Wall Street, Drew came to a rapid decline. Gould and Fisk falsely refriended him and again included him in an Erie bear movement, tempting Drew to sell heavily short. But at the last minute they bulled, leaving him 70,000 shares in the hole. Drew lost $1.5 million. When he begged for mercy, they laughed! Slower and less adept, the 76-year-old former cattle swindler lost everything in railroad speculation in the 1873 Panic. While this panic was among the largest and longest running declines of U.S. economic history, in his prime, Drew would have almost certainly sidestepped it with fast footwork and deceit. At 76, he was too slow. In filing bankruptcy he tallied debts exceeding $1 million and assets less than $500. He spent the remainder of his 82-year life as a Wall Street outsider and as squirrel bait in his hometown. Back in Putnam County, where Drew had deceived many a cattleman 60 years ago, decrepit farmers, one of them over a hundred years old, nipped at his skin, demanding their age-old payments. Drew was haunted by his sins and died a forgotten man. Not even the newspapers mentioned his death.

Drew was a sad case in many ways. His wife and son seemed relatively unimportant to him. He never built friendships. He had no major social interests, and in a rare instance of charity, while creating Drew Seminary (now Drew University), he welched on his financial commitments to the institution. If he were the type of philanderer that Jim Fisk embodied, or if he had died rich, he would be easy to despise. But pity is better placed.

The lessons of his life? There are lots—the simple ones your mother taught you as a child—the lessons of his mistakes. Start out with a good education and play by the rules—he didn't. Quit while you're ahead, before you've stayed at the game too long—he didn't. He who doesn't build enduring associations doesn't build much. What your mother may not have told you, because she probably never thought about it, is that swindlers get swindled eventually. Old swindlers get swindled sooner.

AMS Press, Inc., 1969

JAY COOKE

STICK TO YOUR KNITTING

From a dank and dingy office on Philly's waterfront, where wharf rats scurried on sweltering days, flowed the millions of dollars used to finance America's Civil War. This was the office of government fiscal agent Jay Cooke & Co., wartime America's most respected banking house whose founder helped mold today's banking system. A fierce patriot and believer in the American economy, Jay Cooke floated the war debt creatively, advertising bond issues and selling bonds door-to-door to small investors. Known as "the tycoon," Cooke was a charismatic, imaginative banker who used innovative ways to boost our economy.

In a seemingly dubious era—just as Lincoln was elected President and North–South tensions ripened—Cooke, 39, began his firm in 1861. He climbed to primary floater of the war debt by being resourceful, focused, confident, a little daring—and it didn't hurt to have a partner and brother who knew Treasury Secretary Salmon P. Chase! Always keeping an eye on the Treasury prize, Cooke declined profitable propositions to speculate in government supplies. Instead, he stuck to his knitting and flaunted his revolutionary distribution methods, obtaining a $3 million loan for Pennsylvania, hurdling the state's notorious credit by distributing bonds in nearly every state of the Union. So, in 1863, when the Civil War broke out, Jay Cooke & Co. was solely awarded Chase's Treasury business—his just reward for such fierce focus.

Cooke worked miracles for Uncle Sam, selling millions of war bonds to a seemingly unlimited market of ordinary people who had never before heard of stocks or bonds. He literally and skillfully brought Wall Street to middle-class America's doorsteps for the first time, appealing to citizens' patriotism and using rather unorthodox methods. His most grandiose scheme, surrounding a $500 million issue (underwritten by a syndicate of Wall Street's major houses), consisted of 2,500 canvassers touring the country door-to-door, personally soliciting investors. In another instance, Cooke, also an engaging speaker, advertised in over 1,800 newspapers to promote bonds. He was amazingly resourceful and always optimistic. By 1864, over 600,000 people owned shares in the war debt, all of which had passed through his firm's hands! A year later, at war's end, Cooke sold another $600 million in bonds—no other banker even came close. He was hailed by the press as "savior of the nation."

Born in 1821 the son of an Ohio lawyer and congressman, Cooke was known as a fiercely patriotic man and sincere in his dealings. An Episcopalian and Republican, he nurtured a clean, dignified public image, conducting business openly, firmly, and fairly (uncommon back then). Marrying in 1844, he built a family of four kids, including a minister and a banker, Jay, Jr. (Cooke's grandson, Jay, III, was also a well-known investment banker in his own right.) Lesser known is that Cooke, who went to work at 14, was an avid advocate of national banking to provide uniform currency. A former "counterfeit clerk" in the days of wildcat banking, Cooke remembered days of common counterfeiting and frequent bank failures. So, naturally, he supported Chase's National Banking Act of 1863, helping organize many of the first national banks.

But after phenomenal success during wartime, Cooke lost focus and conformed to the times—his biggest mistake. Easing his reins on the government, where his skills truly lay, he delved into railroads, particularly the yet-to-be-built transcontinental Northern Pacific in 1869. Through his N.Y. and London offices, he floated $100 million for the line overseas in his ballyhooed fashion, buying newspapers and a reporter to promote his project. The more he became involved with his railroad, the less he focused on his forte—government financing. So, when the line never got off the ground, Cooke woke up to find that most of his government refunding operations had been wrestled away by the Morgan-Drexel group and that most of his money tied up in the Northern Pacific was gone!

Cooke's funds dwindled quickly, leading to Jay Cooke & Co.'s failure at the onset of the Panic of 1873. The firm's failure hit Wall Street like a thunderbolt, leaving Morgan to take the reins of leadership for the next few decades. The once-regaled nation's savior disintegrated, destined to deal in only small-time ventures until his death in 1905. What happened? How did Cooke manage to go belly-up after years of proven success? We learn from Cooke three simple little lessons—Don't falter in your focus after consistent success; don't go with the flow; and never put all your eggs in one basket. Not terribly difficult lessons, but important ones.

Cooke, the first to make large underwritings possible, ventured into new ground when he took on operating a railroad, leaving his specialty—government financing—fair game for the likes of Morgan. He was a financier and promoter, never a manager—so why try to be one at 48? Then, he disregarded diversification! If it wasn't stupid enough gambling his meal ticket on a new trick, Cooke went a step further, betting it all on one trick! By dumping his firm's funds solely in the Northern Pacific, he took the big fall when the line went under.

Worst of all, Cooke lost his head in the excitement and rigamarole that surrounded the transcontinental race. His imagination getting the best of him, Cooke got caught up in his own promotions, compromising himself and the firm he had nurtured for years! He lost his focus, walked the wire, took the gamble—and lost. Maybe if he hadn't ignored his original golden goose, his would have remained the preeminent name on Wall Street, instead of Morgan's. Now, Cooke is just a long-lost lesson to be learned.

CHAPTER TWO

JOURNALISTS AND AUTHORS

WALL STREET'S INFO FLOW: NEWSPAPERS, MAGAZINES AND BOOKS

Imagine not being able to pick up the *Wall Street Journal* (*WSJ*) to check instantaneously on your stock's price or even refer to *Forbes* and *Barron's* for business news! It's hard to fathom, but in Wall Street's early days, this was very much the case. Whether you were inside the market or just a curious outsider, information was scarce and hard to come by, and even when you got some, it was likely to be very inaccurate. It wasn't until the late 1890s that the creation of the granddaddy of financial information, the *WSJ*, sparked a slew of periodicals and books that would interpret, analyze, describe and promote stock markets in future years. Wall Street became more practical. Without good information flow, you can't have broad financial markets that incorporate different types of investments and investors.

Financial news and information was made available first by a handful of firms that hired reporters to snoop around Wall Street for scoops, writers to create the stories, and messenger boys literally to run the stories to local subscribers waiting to act on the news. Obviously this wouldn't help if you were located outside of the immediate Wall Street geography as so many professional investors are now. The dispersion of professional investor activity across America and around the world was made possible only by the increased information flow created by journalists and authors. Many of the fathers of financial journalism made their mark on this industry. Charles Dow and Eddie Jones ran a similar service on Wall Street prior to publishing the *WSJ*.

With the advent of the *WSJ*, interpretation and analysis soon followed. At first, it consisted of sensational, easy-to-digest muckraking, believed and widely read by the public mainly because there was no other credible, objective writing to counter it. A classic example was speculator-turned-author Thomas Lawson, who wrote prolific accounts of corporate abuses after losing big in the stock market! His accounts of Wall Street were biased from a loser's viewpoint, but at least they provided juicy reading and got people thinking.

Comparable to today's tabloid stories, Lawson's brand of journalism quickly grew dated when more credible insiders' views of the financial world were aired in *Forbes*. B.C Forbes started my favorite magazine in 1917, becoming one of the first to legitimize and personalize financial writing. Edwin Lefevre followed, in the 1920s, in the *Saturday Evening Post*. But instead of being a publisher/author as Forbes was, he stuck to churning out articles for others, and almost every popular organ carried at least one Lefevre story. Why? Because he humanized Wall Street, giving it detail, emotion and personality. He made it intriguing enough for the masses to enjoy.

Interpretation progressed with Clarence W. Barron's news and analysis in *Barron's*. Then Arnold Bernhard gave us the *Value Line Investment Survey* featuring quick overview and analysis of single stocks. Now you could read about the world in the *WSJ*, get the trader's view in *Barron's*, have it all interpreted and personalized by *Forbes* and Lefevre, and even keep updated on single stocks via Bernhard—and all that evolution in 50 years.

In the 1930s Ben Graham pioneered investment analysis with his book *Security Analysis*. The world has never been the same. Suddenly investment analysis became a generally accepted body of knowledge. Graham brought to investment analysis what the germ theory of disease brought to medicine—cohesion and a central core against which no one fundamentally rebelled. It is hard to find a professional investor who will admit to not having read Graham. Yes, Graham was also a teacher at Columbia, and no doubt had a material impact there, but it was his writing that changed the world forever

And, as part of Merrill Lynch's plan to court Main Street onto Wall Street, Louis Engel penned *How to Buy Stocks*, of which there have been more copies read than any other stock market guide ever—perhaps as many as all other stock market guides put together. Engel showed the little guy how to get started.

As I write this book, my third, and after having penned more than 100 *Forbes* columns since 1984, I am ever reminded when I hear from a reader on the other side of the country—and sometimes ones that are in amazingly powerful positions—what an amazing force the pen is. I'm not a pimple off any one of the guys in this section, but my writing has affected the financial world. It has been included in the Chartered Financial Analyst (CFA) curriculum—my writing also first introduced the world to Price Sales Ratios, and little bits and phrases of my writing have been reprinted and quoted by sources I never thought would ever bother to read my thoughts. Yet my writings have been little refinements in a world financial structure that was already pretty defined before I came along. If I have had some small impact on an existing structure, imagine the power these financial pioneers of the pen wielded at they broke virgin turf. They provided the informational and educational guidance which in some cases paralleled the flow of Wall Street's evolution, and in others made it what it was and now is.

CHARLES DOW

HIS LAST NAME SAYS IT ALL

C harles Dow is one of Wall Street's most significant legends for two very significant reasons—he created our financial bible, the *Wall Street Journal (WSJ)*, as well as our first market barometer, the Dow Jones Averages. He is also the father of technical analysis. Ironically, Dow went relatively unnoticed for his achievements and died quietly at age 51 in his modest Brooklyn apartment in 1902—years before he was credited with revolutionizing the way we now talk about the stock market.

You could explain "his" theory and its technical applications, but during his lifetime, he never laid out a "Dow Theory," per se. When he first began compiling stock market averages in 1884—before the *WSJ* even existed—he hadn't established much besides an index with an all-inclusive "index number" by which to measure the stock market. Later he added his intuitive opinions. In fact, the Dow Theory as we know it today was only named and extracted from his *WSJ* editorials twenty years after his death by other market technicians, like **William P. Hamilton.**

Standing over six feet tall, yet slightly stooped and weighing over 200 pounds with dark eyes and brows, a jet-black beard, and walrus mustache, ultra-conservative Dow had a grave air about him, spoke with measured speech and was reminiscent of an overly serious college professor. He never raised his voice and often said it took him a full 24 hours to get angry, and once angry, he stayed angry. The professorial analogy is strengthened by the fact that, working during the end of the robber baron era, he never chose to play that game, never tried to make a market fortune for himself; he instead chose, to be a sidelines observer and commentator.

He was born on a Connecticut farm in 1851 and worked odd jobs as a kid. His father died when he was six. When he was old enough to choose his career, he chose to abandon farm life for the pen. Following a scant education, he apprenticed for six years with the influential Massachusetts newspaper, the *Springfield Republican*. Then he moved to a Providence, Rhode Island paper, where he found his niche in financial writing while covering the mining industry beat.

Having made a modest name for himself, Dow, at 31, next ventured to New York and in 1882, founded Dow, Jones & Company with fellow reporter **Eddie Jones**. They used second-hand office equipment and worked out of a tiny, one-room office in a ramshackle building at 15 Wall Street, building a profitable news agency. They provided daily financial news updates to subscribers, who were mostly typical Wall Street wags. Printed news was scarce on the Street, and there was a value to being plugged into news sources even if they were little more reliable than the gossip proliferating through the crowd. So, their service was cherished, and the firm grew rapidly within the year. Soon, they started publishing a two-page newspaper called the *Customer's Afternoon Letter*—the *WSJ*'s predecessor.

It was in the *Letter* that Dow first published his average, which he left unnamed. For example, on February 20, 1885, his average was compiled from 14 companies—12 railroads and two industrials—whose closing prices totaled 892.92. Dividing this figure by 14, he came up with 63.78. Since the previous day's close was 64.73, the market was said to be down nearly a point for the day. A more precise observer might have been able to note that it was down 1.47 percent. The index was the first enduring attempt at precise market measurement. The index also gave birth to what would later evolve into the entire realm of "technical" analysis, wherein people forecast future price activity based on pricing history.

The *Letter* grew into the *WSJ*, in 1889. Costing $5 for a yearly subscription, 2 cents per copy and 20 cents per line for ads, the *WSJ* contained four pages of financial news and statistics, including bond and commodity quotes, active stocks, railroad earnings and bank and U.S. Treasury reports. At a time when there were about 35 major stocks and several hundred less widely followed names, an authoritative news source began to create, in effect, a standard by which reality was to be measured. We use the same standard today, published by the same firm. That function alone insures Dow a seat in the financial hall of fame.

Dow was a perfectionist. He worked quietly and intently, using his market averages to pursue his theory of market behavior in a series of editorials between 1899 and his death in 1902. Although he predicted the bull markets of the early 1900s, Dow disciples believe the furthest thing from his mind was creating a system of buy and sell recommendations; they say he used his own theory to review market history, not predict future activity. Regardless, his efforts linking past and future pricing activity were the seeds of technical analysis, a field which today involves thousands of investment professionals and a major investment of time and money.

The theories Dow put forth in his succinct editorials are technically described in this book's biographies of **William P. Hamilton**, Dow's successor at the *WSJ* and major contributor to the Dow Theory; and **Robert Rhea**, who transformed Dow's and Hamilton's principles into a system.

It is impossible to think of how the Wall Street landscape would look today without Dow's influence. Whether because of his newspaper or technical analysis via his indexes, the name Dow cannot be separated from the market. Dow lived before the beginnings of "the information age." While no one would create an index today that operates in such a bizarre and inferior manner (coupling just a few stocks and price-weighting), nonetheless, it was a breakthrough for its time.

In a world of computers the Dow seems to be our worst major index, poorly conceived and non-reflective of the typical stock in America. But that is looking at it from our perspective today, on the back-end of an information and electronics explosion. Back then it was an easy-to-calculate index, and price-weighting made more sense because the data required to build market-cap and unweighted indexes was not readily available and updatable. And the Dow Series was more complete then, because the few stocks they covered were a higher percentage of the relatively few big stocks traded.

Dow was an innovator, foreseeing what wasn't yet there. Several lessons can be extrapolated from Dow's life. First, is the importance of news and information. Second, the importance of perspective—something this author feels is increasingly lost in a world that now sometimes seems too bombarded with news, opinions, and media. And finally—the importance of foresight and the ability to see what wasn't yet in the market, and would be important to the future. If instead of being *100 Minds That Made The Market*, this book were to focus on only a dozen names, Dow would still be one of them.

EDWARD JONES

YOU CAN'T SEPARATE RODGERS AND HAMMERSTEIN

Lively, red-headed, and dimple-chinned Eddie Jones was a journalist in every sense of the word. He was a go-getter, a hard drinker at times, a gossip monger, a networker, and nosey. But he was no ordinary reporter, for he and colleague **Charles Dow** went beyond writing financial news—they created the century-old business bible, the *Wall Street Journal (WSJ.)* And though Dow usually overshadows Jones because of his Dow Theory, there was no way the *WSJ* would be what it is today—or even exist—had it not been for Jones and his zany personality.

Tall and lanky, partially bald, with ruddy skin, smiling blue eyes, and a flowing red walrus mustache, Jones was born in Worcester, Massachusetts in 1856. While attending the prestigious Ivy League school, Brown University, he interned as an unpaid drama critic for the local city paper. When the internship blossomed into a full-time job, Jones dropped out of Brown to follow his love, journalism, which was then considered just a trade. His well-to-do, well-educated family was horrified, but Jones was indignant and independent right down to his bones, and he did as he pleased.

While working for several Providence newspapers in the 1870s, Jones met the introverted and grave Dow. Though the two were seemingly opposites, they got along, worked well with each other and complemented each other's style. Jones' Providence career, however, was not a happy one. Known to go on prolonged drinking binges, he was unhappy with his work, the area, and his prospects. He had bought into a paper with hopes of creating a financial page to follow what he saw as an emerging world. But when his senior partners disagreed, and he didn't back off his ideas, he lost his job and his investment. So, when Dow began working for a Manhattan financial news service, he convinced his boss to hire Jones. Jones, no doubt drunk out of his mind, popped up in the Big Apple mumbling something about marriage and financial worries, but he quickly adjusted to work, brought his wife to the city and settled down—for a while.

Restless and dissatisfied with working for anyone else, both Jones and Dow talked of forming their own news service and did so in 1882. Jones, 26, and Dow, 31, formed Dow, Jones & Company with a third, silent partner, determined to write about Wall Street objectively. This was in an era (that continued for decades to come) when many reporters supplemented their measly salaries by taking bribes for printing marked-up numbers given to them from overeager corporate presidents. But Dow, Jones was going to be different.

Before the *WSJ* existed, Dow, Jones & Company specialized in the delivery of accurate financial news, like management changes, interest rate changes, strikes and dividend announcements. It was a news service. You subscribed, and when stories broke, Dow, Jones & Company would write them up and run them out to you—literally, via messenger boys—so you could act on the news before others might know of it. Jones had their early system down to a science: Reporters snooped through brokerage houses, banks, and corporate offices for hot stories, ran the stories back to the shabby Wall Street office and dictated the stories to writers, who took over from there. The writers then copied the stories onto short white sheets separated by carbons, producing about two dozen copies each time. The messenger boys completed the cycle, running the copies to subscribers—every time a story broke, often eight times per day.

A mathematics whiz, Jones covered financial reports. His specialty was railroad earnings reports. He could spot hidden meanings and mistakes in them when no one else could, and like a good journalist, he exposed them. Jones also kept abreast of the fast-breaking news, making sure it got out to subscribers as soon as stories broke. He was constantly out on the Street, hustling subscriptions to Wall Street bigwigs like William Rockefeller, picking up news bits, and keeping track of the messenger boys who delivered the final product. By far, his favorite duty was making contacts in the Windsor Hotel bar, sometimes called the "All-Night Wall Street," where all the big-time operators like **Diamond Jim Brady** hung out.

Emotional, explosive, excitable and headstrong, Jones was clearly the boss in the office. He reclined in a lean-back chair with his long legs and feet resting on his desk. Sometimes, he'd get up from his chair in a rage, scream-ing four-letter words to whomever was closest to him without anyone ever knowing what set him off. Yet, when crises arose, he was always the calmest; people—even Dow—turned to him for direction. He was the lonely-at-the-top type of guy who could make the tough decisions. Dow, on the other hand, was mainly the ideas and editorial man who constantly tucked himself away in his office to work on his number-crunching, charts, editorials, and the Dow Jones Averages.

Ironically, Dow was entirely helpless when it came to business within their firm. In 1889, when they decided to create the *WSJ*, it was Jones who projected initial costs and circulation possibilities—the very foundation of the paper. And this was Jones' most important contribution to Wall Street—his handling of financial news and Dow's editorial work. He packaged, promoted, and finally sold financial news as a viable product and en route, created a newspaper that every good businessperson looks at every business day.

In 1899, a decade after the *WSJ* got underway, Jones retired from the paper and the firm. Why he left was never recorded, but there were hints of editorial clashes with other writers—more likely, it was a yearning for better pay. Jones had always run on the fringe of the fast and rich crowd—and he wanted more. People like **James Keene** had tried to lure him into the brokerage business before—it looks as if he finally succumbed that year. And it made sense. Jones loved Wall Street and had plenty of connections. He joined Keene's son-in-law's brokerage firm and later worked for Keene himself at the height of Keene's success, so Jones presumably got what he was looking for before dying of a cerebral hemorrhage in 1920.

Just as you couldn't have had Hammerstein without Rodgers, nor Lennon without McCartney (even though like Dow and Jones they were only together a relatively few years in the greater scheme of things), you can't separate Dow and Jones. They made history together. Clearly Eddie Jones was not as important as Dow, but in every duo one must be more important. Dow was dry, and Jones was lively, and while Dow was enduring, news seldom is—like Jones' whole attitude toward life. Dow was the better market mind, but Jones was a journalist through and through, and like so many, became burned out by it. Without Jones, the landscape of American financial journalism would be different by any measure.

Everybody's Magazine, 1912

THOMAS W. LAWSON

"STOCK EXCHANGE GAMBLING IS
THE HELL OF IT ALL..."

Some folks don't take losing lightly. At turn-of-the-century Wall Street, your options were limited: You could succeed, quit, jump out a fifth-story window, or—get even. In 1905, flashy, well-spoken speculator Thomas Lawson decided to get even...

B ack when muckrakers could write no wrong and big business was the all-American bully, Thomas Lawson was a notorious Boston speculator down on his luck—Wall Street had toppled his $50 million nest egg. So, desperately in need of a new trick, he hopped off his high horse and boarded Teddy Roosevelt's anti-business bandwagon! Lawson attacked Wall Street kingpins—which he nicknamed "the System." He ripped into their practices, players, and their disregard for the masses. Trumpeting that "Stock Exchange gambling is the hell of it all, (and) the hell of it all can be destroyed," he mounted a massive publicity campaign aimed at undermining the System—and, coincidentally, replenishing his fortune. The "people" literally bought his act and even funded his "crusade"—which got him riding high again.

"My one instrument is publicity. It is the most powerful weapon in the world." Lawson was a true promoter—full of hype. A prolific writer and a bold speaker, he had an animated personality and was a split-second decision maker. During his publicity campaign—while penning for *Everybody's Magazine* two sensational series in 1912 called "Frenzied Finance" and "The Remedy"—he captured the most stubborn listener with his caressing, tender tone, vividly describing the inner machinations of his old cronies, the Standard Oil clan. Gazing with his intense, large gray eyes set under bushy brows that made him look fierce, he easily convinced people of Wall Street's wicked ways—and that his life's ambition was to free the masses from the "System's" chains and to annihilate Standard Oil. What a character!

Sporting a large diamond ring on his finger and blue cornflowers in his buttonhole, Lawson stayed true to his dramatic style during 32 years as an insider. Born in 1857 to Nova Scotia emigrants, he grew up modestly near Boston, and by 14, worked as a State Street office boy after his father died. Two years later, at the mere age of 16, he was a full-fledged operator heading his own 13-member pool which had made $60,000 speculating in railroads.

Lawson then bought into a gas firm with a city contract. Next he rigged a deal where he bribed city officials to propose and then to defeat motions to cancel the contract. With each motion to cancel the contract, the gas stock would plummet, Lawson's pool would short and rake in oodles—then, once the motion was defeated and the contract renewed, they'd ride the stock back up! But when a move to cancel the contract unexpectedly was approved, the stock—and Lawson's profits—plummeted, leaving him with just $159! The young, optimistic Lawson, however, took his loss like a trooper, wined and dined his friends with the last of the profits, tipped the waiter his last five bucks and began again with a clean slate!

His slate, however, wasn't spotless—at least according to his own later standards. At 21, having married and starting toward a family of six, Lawson opened his brokerage firm, Lawson, Arnold and Co. He made his first million nine years later by acting as agent and promoter for N.Y. financiers. As a rampant bull still speculating on a grandiose scale, he became known as Boston's best-known plunger. Then, after wrestling control of Bay State Gas and Co. for a client, Lawson's style caught Standard Oil's attention. In no time at all, he became Standard Oil's chief broker in its consolidation of the copper industry into Amalgamated Copper. By 1900, snug in his $6 million Boston estate, he was reputedly worth some $50 million! Lawson enjoyed this life, smothering himself with luxuries like the "Lawson pink"—a $30,000 specially bred pink carnation he later excused as a "business investment." In 1901, he even built a yacht to compete for the America's Cup, as did all millionaires then, though his boat was banned—and he became bitter.

What really got Lawson's goat—and wallet—was similar to what happened to lots of other folks, and not too dissimilar to what happened to his first $60,000 pool. He put too much in one pot and borrowed to do it. When a bear raid caught his huge position on the wrong side of the market, Lawson found himself without his huge fortune. Now he was really bitter—and, hence, his "reform." Joining in with the spirit of turn of the century yellow journalism and the Teddy Roosevelt reform era, he relentlessly reviled stock market sins across America, and, to gain exposure, wrote *Frenzied Finance*—what he described as "the first true-to-life etching of this romantic St. Bernard-boa-constrictor hybrid of financialdom." Personally, I don't get it.

But then came the clincher: He took out costly, full-page ads in national newspapers urging the public to support him in raiding "System" firms. Lawson's "System" was synonymous with Standard Oil and its sphere of influence, which he mistakenly saw as the central power of America's entire financial system at a time when Standard Oil was truly powerful, but no more so than several other trusts, or for that matter, **J.P Morgan**. But to him it was all Standard Oil, the "System."

One time, just as various Standard Oil affiliated bigwigs were trying to put together a "copper trust" via Amalgamated Copper, Lawson began touting Amalgamated as a valuable stock, urging the public to buy. Later that year, after his faithful flock snatched it up and Amalgamated grew top-heavy, Lawson sold out—just before the stock spiraled! And this guy claimed he was on the "masses" side? When confronted by the *New York Times* in 1908, he confessed he "cleaned up a few hundred thousand dollars," then—to unload his sin—he advised his flock, via more ads, to "sell Amalgamated to your last share. It will break from $80 to $33." Consequently, the copper stocks broke violently. Amalgamated dropped to $58 in three days, and on the worst day, Lawson ordered his brokers back in—to buy all the Amalgamated they could lay their hands on!

When scoffed at for his actions, he cried out, "Oh, ye fools of earthworm intellect. Did ye not see I blundered on purpose to hoax the System?" Predictably, after each "wrong" prediction, he'd go back to the market under the guise, "I am going back to the game to recoup the millions I have donated to my work." Lawson was either a brilliant conniver—or a warped crusader. Whatever he was, he never let on, constantly proclaiming, "My work is solely for one end, the destruction of high-cost living, and in no way is it a personal-pride-play-to-the-literary-gallery-grand-stand-work." Personally, I still don't get it.

Lawson's is a story that comes along every so often. Every once in a while a self-proclaimed social sharpshooter targets Wall Street for his sermon. The difference with Lawson is that he knew enough to condemn and make Wall Street profits all at the same time. While Lawson didn't actually hate the market—"on the contrary, it should be one of the main factors in a civilized people's business machinery, and it will be after it has been closed as a gambling institution"—he actually hated the fact that the majority of Wall Street's money lay in just a few hands, and that they weren't his. But that's capitalism, right?...

Lessons? Just as Lawson thought, the media and publicity are awfully powerful, so be skeptical about what you read. Despite securities laws that today regulate many investment professionals, nothing regulates freedom of speech in America for everyone else, and what someone says may have a hidden agenda that the regulators can't do much about.

B . C .   F O R B E S

HE MADE FINANCIAL
REPORTING HUMAN

Bertie Charles Forbes, or "B.C.," as he was known, personalized financial
writing and consequently humanized big business via *Forbes* Magazine,
established in 1917. Using his trademark corny epigrams and prolific prose,
Forbes looked beyond the factories and machinery to the men behind the
corporation, forcing his readers to look at business in a different light. His
specialty was writing lively and candid biographical accounts of his era's most
influential business leaders, concentrating on the positive traits that led them
to success. Because of B.C., by the time the great bull market took off in the
early 1920s, America was well acquainted with—and indeed, admirers of—the
men leading the firms it was increasingly investing in.

For example, he held a candle to U.S. Steel top-gun Charles M. Schwab (no
relation to the modern-day discount broker), a man who has "played the business game" and won "an unusual measure of happiness and an extraordinary
number of friends." Forbes was far from secretive about what he valued most
in life. He wrote, "Schwab, from the start, had goodwill in his heart toward his
workers and his associates . . . he has never lost sight of the fundamental fact

that, in the end, a wealth of friends means more than a wealth of gold." In an effort to steer the ambitious away from greed, he cautioned, "The final question shall be not, How much have you? but, How much have you done?" and, "What most big men seek is greater power. A few, still bigger, seek to serve."

You could say Forbes capitalized on schmoozing with Wall Street's most notorious business leaders—like bankers **A.P. Giannini** and **George F. Baker** and steel magnate Charles Schwab, to name a few. But Forbes didn't inherit his connections—he earned them, and maybe that was half the fun of his work. Back then tycoons generally kept to themselves, rarely answering to stockholders and even more rarely answering to reporters if they could help it. (**J.P. Morgan**, for instance, was notorious for scorning the press.) So, before boosting *Forbes*, the optimistic-yet-cautious Scotsman purposefully rented an expensive room in Wall Street's then-hot spot, the Waldorf-Astoria. He thrust himself into a bevy of bustling Wall Streeters who gathered regularly at the hotel bar, immediately charming them with his Scottish burr. He blended in with the tycoons and in a sense, even became one of them; after that, he was never in need of news.

Forbes loved his work and considered interviewing his subjects a form of "interpreting human nature." He was forever preaching his interpretations in his magazine, which he edited until his death, as well as in his syndicated column and the scores of books he authored over the years, like: *Forbes Epigrams* in 1922 and *Men Who Are Making America* and *Keys to Success* in 1917. A deeply moral and religious man who read the Bible every morning, Forbes' interpretations were often moral ones: "Those who have earned the greatest wealth have not always earned the greatest happiness." He took his lessons to heart and never let success infringe on his beliefs.

Gray-haired, dark-eyed, bespectacled, standing 5 foot 7, and weighing 185 pounds, Forbes was a dedicated family man, father of five and married since 1915. In his son Malcolm's autobiography, *More Than I Dreamed*, B.C. was described as being principled, hard-working and strict, especially with his boys. He demanded obedience from his sons, yet loved taking them to the amusement park. A faithful Bible reader, he was an equally devout poker player who played every Sunday, stopping only to hear his sons sing their "hymn of the week."

Born one of 10 children to a storekeeper in a small Scottish village, Forbes took pride in his heritage, going back with his entire family for visits practically every year. Later, at Malcolm's wedding and other special occasions, he was known for donning a kilt and dancing a traditional jig. In Scotland, Forbes grew up modestly, herding cattle for neighbors as a child. He left school at 14 to become an apprentice in a printer's shop, setting type. But he continued to study in night school and later, took night courses at University College in Dundee. At 21, after a stint as a reporter for a local paper, he left his homeland for South Africa, where he helped mystery writer Edgar Wallace create the *Rand Daily Mail* newspaper.

After saving every cent possible, Forbes journeyed to Manhattan in 1904. He worked for free for the *Journal of Commerce* to get his foot in the door, and sure enough, William Randolph Hearst chose him to become a financial editor and columnist. While writing his column, syndicated and distributed to 50 papers nationwide, B.C. started *Forbes* in 1917, because he was gathering more information than he could possibly use in the column! His name helped promote the magazine, and his connections guaranteed him an abundance of stories. 1917 must have been a very busy year indeed for B.C. Forbes, between writing several books and starting a magazine. It is hard to imagine anyone doing any more.

Forbes has become firmly entrenched in Wall Street, staggering only after the 1929 Crash, during which B.C.'s column profits paid payroll and printing costs. You can imagine how unpopular a magazine like *Forbes* was after the Crash drained American confidence from business, but B.C. believed in his baby and struggled to keep it alive. In return, B.C. became something of an institution at *Forbes*, holding on to its editorship until the day he died in his office from a heart attack in 1954. He was nearly 74 years old, a firm believer in working as long as it was physically possible. "Rest? Yes. Rust? No!...The self-starter never allows his steam to run down...." In many ways exactly the same things could be said of his son, Malcolm, who was continually high energy until dying of a heart attack at a similar age. Perhaps it was in B.C.'s genes to build *Forbes*.

Even today the spirit of B.C. Forbes lives on in *Forbes*. There is no other major magazine—and certainly no financial magazine—that's as personal in its presentation as *Forbes*. Do you even know who started *Business Week* or *Fortune*? It's almost impossible to envision either of them as still run by the family that started them—yet they came after *Forbes*. B.C.'s emphasis on the personal side of business and financial reporting and his high ethical standard are still evident in *Forbes* today. First, you can see the personal side in the large number of *Forbes* stories on smaller companies that don't appear in other places. Then, too, you can see the ethical side in the magazine's continuing and unswerving tendency to expose scandals like the Robert Brennan and First Jersey Securities scam and penny stock frauds, and the scandalously high pay America's top litigators had been secretly amassing.

In some ways, just as ancient time is measured B.C.—in years Before Christ, financial writing in America can also be measured in terms of years before B.C. Forbes. I argue that without B.C. Forbes and his personal touch, America never would have developed the confidence it had in its business and financial leaders and that accordingly the financial markets would have been crippled. He encouraged confidence in America, its business and financial markets as if it were lubricant to gearworks. While the *Wall Street Journal* was reporting the numbers and news in cold, dry fashion, B.C. brought them to life. The spirit of B.C. Forbes lives on in *Forbes* Magazine as no other individual's ghost haunts the financial pages. And while the organization that bears his name does not have the size of Dow Jones & Company, his role clearly leaves him in my mind as the third most influential business and financial journalist behind the legendary **Charles Dow** and **Clarence Barron**.

EDWIN LEFEVRE

YOU COULDN'T SEPARATE HIS FACTS FROM HIS FICTION

More than any other Wall Street writer, Edwin Lefevre provided America with a peek at what really makes Wall Street tick—human nature. In his day's most popular magazines and his own entertaining novels, Lefevre illustrated how—and how often—greed, stupidity, sheer luck, habitual honesty and intense cleverness came into play in finance. Whether he reported on the lives of Wall Street's biggest players or told the rare tale of the lucky guy-next-door, Lefevre always hit close to home, playing on the rags-to-riches dreams of almost every American. Via personal, candid, straightforward prose, he painted the most realistic portrayal of Wall Street and its operators. In doing so, he humanized finance, bringing it down from its pedestal and smack into the homes of the American public.

Described as being "equipped with a genius for speculation—plus the brains not to pursue it," Lefevre chose to educate his public about the stock market over some 40 years of financial writing, some fiction and some nonfiction. One point of praise about Lefevre is that it was always hard to tell fiction from fact. With pointed, logical views about how the market runs its course, he did his best to describe its function and technological mumbo-jumbo, leaving the biggest decision—whether or not to invest—up to his readers.

Typical Lefevre-esque rationale followed along these lines: "There is always a reason for bull markets. They start because the business tide turns. They run their course because human nature does not change. Before they end they are apt to degenerate into a frenzied carnival of gambling...No professional Wall Street tipster or plausible promoter can turn a sane person into a stock gambler as easily as his next-door neighbor bragging about his winnings. If all men profited by experience, the world would be peopled exclusively by the wise...."

Born in 1870 in Panama, the son of an American businessman, Lefevre was educated in San Francisco public schools, Michigan Military Academy and Lehigh University, where he studied engineering and mining from 1887 to 1890. At 20, he began his journalism career with the tedious task of gathering the daily commodities quotes for the old *New York Sun*. He loathed commodity prices—coffee, eggs, cheese, petroleum, and pig iron. He wanted to write about the industries and the real world events that moved the prices! So after countless attempts at pushing business pieces he'd written on his own time past his editor and into the paper, Lefevre eventually got his first story printed about the banana industry. Then he faked a fan letter to his editor praising his own article and from there, began his writing career. He was a financial reporter and editor, writing articles for *Harper's*, *Everybody's*, *Munsey's*, and several other popular periodicals.

Lefevre's career sky-rocketed with the 1920s bull market, when he wrote exclusively for the *Saturday Evening Post*, a magazine found in practically every American household. He explained the ins and outs, pluses and minuses of speculation to the masses, who, at the time, were getting caught up in playing the bull market. With a strict moral code, he never outwardly promoted the stock market without objectively telling the risks involved. In a confidential manner, as if writing to readers he knew personally, Lefevre wrote articles entitled: "Speculation, Both Versions," "Pick Your Seller," "Wholesale and Retail Bond Selling," "Blame the Broker," "Bulls on America" and "New Bears, Normal and Grizzly."

After the boom ended with the 1929 Crash, Lefevre tried rationalizing it to his friends, the readers. In a 1932 *Post* article titled, "Vanished Billions," he said, "Reckless fools lose first because they deserved to lose, and careful wise men lose later because a world-wide earthquake doesn't ask for personal references." Later, he addressed the ensuing Great Depression, or as he phrased it, "the stupendous landslide of fear that has changed the face of the financial world." He wrote: "To the question that thousands of Americans are asking, 'When is it safe to invest?' there are two answers...

1. Never!
2. Always!

'Never for' the crowd...'Always' for the reasonable man; for it all depends upon what you call 'safe,' in a world peopled by fallible human beings."

Lefevre liked to tell it like it was. Two years after the SEC came into existence, for example, in a 1936 analytical piece called "New Bull Market, New Dangers," he warned investors not to think of the regulatory agency as an automatic buffer from risk. "They (SEC) do not guarantee against loss, nor can they say which securities are cheap and which are dear at current prices. The public must do its own watching for danger signals. Look within yourself and then, Mister Trader, you won't have to look out."

Lefevre's catchy quotes and a sympathetic tone made him one of the most listened to, talked about and infinitely trusted financial writers ever. Of course, he also appealed to the voyeuristic—those who were simply interested in knowing the lifestyles of the rich and famous. His articles took readers on yacht cruises with unnamed highly-paid operators, whom could be easily identified by newspapers and readers.

Lefevre was a great source for juicy Wall Street gossip, presenting a wonderful, insider's account of the wild life of wild speculator **Jesse Livermore** in his book, *Reminiscences of a Stock Market Operator.* This book is one of my all-time favorites, and I don't think anyone should invest money he deems important without first having read it. In my 13th *Forbes* column (June 3, 1985), I listed Lefevre's book as among my 10 favorite investment books. It's that good, and so readable, anyone can enjoy it.

Married with two sons, Lefevre had a brother who became Panama's president. Lefevre himself was appointed Panama's ambassador to Spain and Italy in 1910 at 40. Besides writing, he loved antiques. He passionately collected early American flasks and bottles many decades before that became a fashionable hobby. And when he wasn't writing about Wall Street, he wrote about his obsession with antiques. Lefevre died at age 73 in Dorset, Vermont in 1943, having retired from writing almost 10 years previously. He made Wall Street human for non-Wall Streeters, which in many ways set the stage for the magic conversion that folks like **Charles Merrill** would create in the 1940s as Wall Street went to Main Street.

Dow Jones & Co.

CLARENCE W. BARRON

A HEAVYWEIGHT JOURNALIST

Looking a lot like a fat, jolly little Santa Claus with a full white beard, ruddy cheeks, and sparkling blue eyes, journalist Clarence Walker Barron was a glutton for food, money, and financial news—and in his lifetime he got his fill of all three. He took over Dow, Jones and Company's *Wall Street Journal* and ran two financial newspapers of his own. Then in 1921, Barron all but monopolized the financial news field by creating *Barron's Financial Weekly*.

B.C. Forbes once called him "the foremost financial editor in the world," but Barron was first and foremost an eccentric. Intolerant of failure and stupidity, he had a benevolent heart when he chose to and a personality that inspired confidence—everyone told him his secrets. Despite a big belly—he hadn't seen his feet while standing in years—he was an avid swimmer and was often found standing waist-high in the water dictating to two male secretaries. His hobbies were mapmaking and farming. He owned several New England farms and liked referring to himself as a farmer, first, and publisher, second. A religious man, Barron adhered to the Swedenborgian religion and faithfully carried a copy of the Bible and Swedenborg sandwiched between silk handkerchiefs when traveling.

Although terribly overweight, Barron was never a weight-watcher and rarely glanced at the scales. He kept a wardrobe in six progressively larger sizes and when he could fit into only the largest size, he knew he was at his maximum—350 pounds. Then it was time for another trip to his sanatorium where a doctor restricted his diet and slimmed him to his usual 300 pounds But as soon as the weight came off, it came back on—via his decadent diet For example, a typical Barron breakfast included juice, stewed fruit, oatmeal, ham and eggs, fish, beefsteak, fried potatoes, hot rolls and butter—and finally, coffee with cream from his own prize-winning cows!

Born the oldest of 13 children in Boston, ambitious Barren chose journalism as his career when he was barely 15 years old—and once his stubborn mind was set, he went after his goal with ferocity. By age 21, after learning the ropes of the news industry, he scouted his specialty—financial writing. He boldly told *Boston Evening Transcript* editors he'd start a financial page for them by covering Boston's business hub, State Street—and sure enough, he was hired. Ironically, it was his ambition that got him fired, too, when he revealed too much about an influential railroad tycoon's shenanigans.

Never discouraged and ever optimistic, Barron next became a publisher. Borrowing Dow, Jones & Company's earliest business idea, he started Boston's first news service, the Boston News Bureau. Without extensive resources, he hired a few messenger boys, found a printer, and legged it around State Street on his chubby legs, searching for stories. He charged subscribers—mainly bankers, brokers and businessmen—$1 per day for 25 to 30 news bulletins per day, and business flourished. From this business, he produced a Boston financial paper, then established one in Philadelphia, attracting the attention of **Charles Dow** and **Eddie Jones.**

Barron was Dow, Jones' first out-of-town reporter for a few years before taking over the firm in 1902 at age 46. He bought out Charles Dow, as the saying goes, "for a note"—that is, he bought the entire firm for $2,500 down and a promissory note. Just a year before, he had married a prominent Boston widow he'd boarded with for the past 14 years, and in a rare move, put all his Dow, Jones shares in her name; so, she represented him on the board of directors for the next 10 years. This allowed Barron to be more concerned with editorial content than the running of the paper—and it worked. Circulation soared, though he preferred maintaining a quality subscription list.

Barron was a staunch defender and advocate of the old Wall Street, when **J.P. Morgan** ruled the roost and wild plungers like **Jesse Livermore** constantly tried to beat the system. Following the 1907 Panic, for example, Barron desperately called for banking reform in *WSJ* editorials, but pleaded for Morgan to lead the reform movement. He generally advocated that the Street clean up its own house—not Uncle Sam.

With the newspaper a proven success and Barron's name and reputation at an all-time high, *Barron's* was established in 1921. The weekly was originally conceived as a business proposition by Barron's son-in-law, Hugh Bancroft (Barron had adopted his wife's two daughters). Bancroft later succeeded Barron as Dow Jones president after Barron's death. *Barron's* could capitalize on his name, use up idle press time and be edited by the staff of his other newspapers—pure gravy for the company. Barron penned its motto, "The application of money to practical ends."

Barron's, now something of a bible to traders, was launched in dubious financial times. Unemployment was at its worst since the 1907 Panic, yet the magazine took off. They used the ad campaign: "*Barron's*, the new National Financial Weekly for those who read for profit" and Wall Streeters flocked to buy it. Barren boasted. "Not every reader is a millionaire, but there are few millionaires who do not read religiously one of these papers." It included now-famous editorials from *WSJ* editor and *Barron's* executive editor **William Peter Hamilton** and covered financial news from way beyond Wall Street. *Barron's* presented a broad scope of Wall Street and the factors affecting it.

There is no question that news flow is fundamental to the flow of markets. Barron was not as big a mover and shaker in the formation of the financial news world as was Charles Dow, and maybe not as important as Eddie Jones to financial history, but clearly no one could rival him for the number three spot in the hall of financial news fame (B.C. Forbes would have to be counted as number four, but even B.C. would yield the higher position to Barron). As the first head of Dow, Jones after Dow and Jones themselves, Barren turned a personal business into the beginnings of an institution that has been the voice of Wall Street for half a century. Merely by creating *Barron's* he assured his name in financial history. Without Barron and the role he played, our flow of financial news in the 20th century would have been different in ways that can never be known nor comprehended. His information made the market.

Garret-Howard

BENJAMIN GRAHAM

THE FATHER OF SECURITY ANALYSIS

In the field of security analysis, Ben Graham wrote the book—literally—and transformed a discipline based on hunches into a specific, much-depended-upon school of thought. A Wall Street legend, he pioneered value investing, basing successful stock selections on current figures derived from his careful research, instead of trying to predict future markets or a company's worth in them. His essentially conservative thinking became perhaps the most success-ful widespread investment philosophy in post-World War II Wall Street. But beneath the distinguished success and achievement was a man whose life was anything but steadfast and conservative. Ironically, he was a notorious ladies' man, who took on mistresses while gallivanting among his various homes in the south of France, California, and Wall Street until his death in 1976.

Graham arrived on Wall Street in 1914, a 20-year-old classicist fresh out of Columbia University who was more concerned with securing his financial future than translating Greek and Latin for a meager living. Working his way up from chalking stock and bond prices on a brokerage house blackboard, Graham started doing write-ups and by 1917, was a respected analyst. As Adam Smith remarked, this was in a time when a security analyst was no more than a hard-working statistician; "an ink-stained wretch wearing a green eyeshade and sitting on a three-legged stool, who gave figures to the partner in charge of running that day's pool." But Graham broke the mold and started trading on his own account with terrific results.

In 1926, a friend realized he'd found his golden goose in Graham and wooed him away from the brokerage house to start the Graham-Newmann Corporation, which later put value investing on the map. A mathematics whiz, Graham concentrated on finding bargain stocks via quantitative research, then bought control of companies selling at less than their worth to force realization of the assets. He hated technical tools like charts and graphs and equally distrusted growth investors' blind faith in a company's management, upcoming products and present reputation—those just couldn't be measured in cold, hard numbers, he figured. Instead, Graham relied on earnings and dividends, and felt that book value—the physical assets of a company—was the basis for making sound investment decisions.

Typical of Graham's deals was his coup in Northern Pipeline. While examining Interstate Commerce Commission reports for pipeline companies, he found that Northern Pipeline was holding $95 per share of quick assets—and selling for only $65, at which it yielded 9 percent. Graham plunged into Northern Pacific so that by its 1928 annual meeting, he arrived with 38 percent of its proxies—and left with a seat on its board. Later, he persuaded management to shell out $50 per share to its stockholders. The remainder was still worth over $50 per share, bringing the total value to about $ 100—a keen profit over his original $65 investment.

The deal Graham-Newmann was most famous for, however, was its 1948 coup in GEICO, Government Employees Insurance Company. Graham wagered a quarter of the firm's capital on the firm, then gleefully watched its shares rise 1,635 percent over the next eight years. By the time GEICO all but collapsed in the early 1970s, Graham had long retired and given away most of his holdings in the firm.

Besides being a security analyst and investor, Graham also acted as both corporate and individual financial consultant, lectured at Columbia University and UCLA, and authored a few books. It was from his years at Columbia that his most famous work, *Security Analysis*, evolved in 1934. Written with Columbia colleague David L. Dodd, the thick text—known now by investors around the world simply as "Graham and Dodd"—detailed Graham's investment philosophy as covered in his past university lectures. They analyzed a number of industries—exploring financial characteristics and comparing key operating and financial ratios—to show how analysts determine which companies in a group of similar ones are successful, financially sound and undervalued. It was a lot to comprehend, especially for the layperson, so in 1949, Graham penned a more or less distilled version, *The Intelligent Investor*. Both books had sold over 100,000 copies by his death, and both sell more copies each year now than when they were originally published, the true sign of a classic and a feat achieved by only a minuscule percentage of books published.

Near the end of his life, Graham about-faced on the elaborate and complex security analysis techniques he'd put forth in *Security Analysis*. In a 1976 *Financial Analysts Journal* interview, he said, "In the old days any well-trained security analyst could do a good professional job of selecting undervalued issues through detailed studies; but in the light of the enormous amount of research now being carried on, I doubt whether in most cases such extensive efforts will generate sufficiently superior selections to justify their cost." He added that he'd turned to "the 'efficient market' school of thought now generally accepted by the professors." Ironically, Graham's adoption of "the efficient market" was just before computer backtests would poke all kind of holes in that theory. Graham was simply old and unable to keep up with the times.

Later that year, Graham died at age 82. Having dissolved his firm in 1956, he was far from inactive: Just before his demise, he'd completed research going back 50 years that showed he could have outperformed the Dow Jones by a factor of over two-to-one by using just part of his long list of investment criteria.

Meanwhile, Graham was also busy bustling between his homes in La Jolla, California and Aix-en-Provence, France, where he ultimately died in the company of his long-time French mistress, whom he'd courted away from his son! Married three times, Graham used to joke that this relationship with his mistress lasted because they were never married. Graham's student, Warren Buffett, once tried explaining Graham's obsession with women (usually willowy blondes): "It was all open and everything, but Ben liked women. And women liked him. He wasn't physically attractive—he looked like Edward G. Robinson—but he had style."

Stocky, but thin with age, short and dapper, Graham—original family name, Grossbaum—changed the name to Graham during World War I. He had big, wide lips, a roundish face, light blue eyes, thick glasses, and two-thirds a head of gray hair. A fountain of quotations, he was witty, sharp, sensitive, energetic, cultured, modest—and whimsical. He once told a friend he'd like to do "something foolish, something creative and something generous" every day—and he usually did! Graham was polite and an intense listener for as long as he needed to be. Nephew and money man Richard Graham recalled, "He had a habit of looking at his watch—politely, of course—and saying, 'I think we've spent enough time on this.'"

Graham had abundant interests—and not only by Wall Street standards. He could translate Latin, Portuguese, and Greek into English; loved biology and served as a zoo trustee; read six books at a time on such varied topics as history, philosophy and the classics; skied and played tennis; and loved to dance, becoming a lifetime member of Arthur Murray after signing up for thousands of dollars in dance lessons! Someone once said the only reason he stayed in finance was for the challenge. Graham certainly proved himself the exception to the rule that you must be a narrow-minded person to make it on the Street.

Ironically, of his four kids—three daughters and a son—none went into investments, though other relatives did. But Benjamin Graham left a legacy of security analysts and investors who trace their investment ancestry back to him. And he is widely known as the Father of Security Analysis. Graham was not only the original quantitative analyst, to whom today's whole school of such thinking owes its heritage, but he was also a source of much of the fundamental analysis and lore that Wall Streeters follow today. Anyone who hasn't read his books can hardly consider himself well read in the field. As the teacher, mentor and philosophical source for Warren Buffett, Graham pioneered the way for the modern era's most successful single investor. His contribution and legacy are unmatched by any other single investor of the 20th century.

ARNOLD BERNHARD

THE ELEGANCE OF OVERVIEW ON A
SINGLE PAGE

W hat started as an obscure collection of statistics on 120 stocks is now the standard and most basic reference on 1,700 stocks: the *Value Line Investment Survey*, king of investment newsletters. Lots of folks simply swear by it, and no one swears at it. Created by Arnold Bernhard nearly 55 years ago, *Value Line* packs statistics and brief, succinct analysis into one-page detailed descriptions that offer an amazing combination of detail and overview. While the *Value Line* offers specific stock forecasts on each of its stocks, most of the masses who use it do so for its reference-like functions, almost as a bible, rather than its specific stock forecasts. There are about 100,000 subscribers, each paying $525 annually, making it the nation's most successful investment letter and a tribute to what mass merchandising can do, particularly for a small financial service.

To most subscribers, the publication is less a newsletter than a handy reference source. In a nutshell, it offers facts and numbers that quickly provide a broad overview of a single company in an easy-to-fathom, single-page format. Besides a brief summary of the business, much of the information is statistical, like the financial and price histories. Then, there are predictions of how the stock will perform over the next year and three to five years. What some consider the *Value Line*'s most important feature, and which I think not too many people care much about, is its rating and ranking system, whereby the stocks are rated from 1, being the highest score, to 5, the lowest.

Initially, Bernhard set a stock's rating by what he called "taming the earnings curve with book value." An investment counselor early on, he recalled, "I was managing all the accounts and studying all the securities in each of the portfolios. I thought again that there must be some method to determine when stocks were high or low, when they were good or bad values." Math-minded, Bernhard worked with a 10-year history of certain stocks. "I multiplied a stock's earnings, added it to a percentage of the book value and found a close correlation for the years between '29 and '39, between earnings, as I multiplied them and prices." Bernhard never stopped fiddling with figures and formulae. By 1965, he and his statistician brandished their ultimate form of "disciplined analysis" called "cross-sectional analysis." the system in place today, more or less. Instead of comparing a stock against its own performance, this system compares it against all the others' (in the *Value Line* sphere).

But Bernhard and the *Value Line* were never regarded very highly for stock-picking prowess. Sometimes criticized for his simplistic approach to the market, Bernhard—a closet technical analysis buff who kept hourly charts on the Dow Jones Industrials—was thoroughly convinced of his system. If a stock ever strayed from *Value Line* expectations, he was sure it would soon slide back to its place. He admitted his system "is not infallible, of course, but if a stock has for 10 years sold at 10 times earnings and this year it is at 20 times earnings without any radical changes in the company's business character, which is the moment of insanity? Now? Or all of the past decade?"

Small but broad-shouldered, with a receding hairline, short, well-clipped mustache and large eyes framed by sweeping, dramatic eyebrows, Bernhard dominated the *Value Line* empire until he died in 1987 at age 86. With a wry wit and formal, aristocratic manner, he was known as "Mr. Bernhard" even to his managers. He was a notorious tyrant in the office. Running the show while seated behind a massive desk, he gave his higher-ups little responsibility and even smaller salary. "I'm told there are big reunions of *Value Line* alumni, but I'm never invited. I'm not as chummy a person as I'd like to be." Even so, the publication is still considered prestigious training ground for security analysts, money managers and the like.

Bernhard was born in 1901, the son of Jewish immigrants—a Romanian mother and an Austrian cigar-and-coffee merchant. Raised in Hoboken, New Jersey and Brooklyn, young Arnold left military school to study English at Williams College. A Phi Beta Kappa grad, he landed a prestigious journalism job as theater critic for *Time*. Prestige or not, the pay was the pits. So, he doubled as critic for the *New York Post* and syndicated his own column, while courting his high-school sweetheart, and wife-to-be with free Broadway shows (that he later reviewed).

An avid reader who favored books about the Napoleonic era, Bernhard became intrigued by Wall Street after reading **Edwin Lefevre**'s 1932 classic, *Reminiscences of a Stock Operator*, a fictional account of speculator **Jesse Livermore**. Inspired, he penned a play called "Bull Market." Next thing you know, he became one of Livermore's clerks! One time, Bernhard wrote his boss a glowing report recommending copper stocks; Livermore read it and immediately sold the stocks short! Another time, Livermore had his clerk hunt down a mystery stock symbol—pronto!—while he traded a large position in it, based on its tape action alone. The speculator's off-the-cuff operations fascinated Bernhard, although he voiced patent disrespect for Livermore. Yet the experience challenged Bernhard to find some sort of "system" to figure out the market.

After a three-year stint at Moody's, first as analyst, then account executive from 1928 to 1931, Bernhard came up with the *Value Line*'s predecessor in 1936. He worked out his original formulas for 120 stocks, bought a press and cranked out 1,000 copies of his results in book form, which he planned to sell at $200 apiece. But after making countless personal presentations, he sold one copy. "It was hard for me to realize how little the world would be interested." Then, a market letter writer of the moment, in exchange for a free copy and an $800 fee, plugged Bernhard's book in his own letter. The writer mistakenly underpriced Bernhard's book at a $55 price tag, but the checks poured in daily, putting Bernhard in business. the *Value Line* took off, and the Bernhards moved to stylish Westport, Connecticut.

From then on, Bernhard swore by mass merchandising. He took out his first official ad in *Barron's*, and he never quit advertising there. The original ad offered a sampling of *Value Line*'s wisdom for a token charge, which in turn, brought in a percentage of new subscriptions—which more than paid for the ad.

Because he was so sure of his product—even cocky to some degree—and because he wanted to remain neutral in the stock market, Bernhard invested most of his vast fortune in the *Value Line* empire, including various *Value Line* mutual funds. Feeding his ego and love of theatre, he also put a few bucks into producing plays, like David Mamet's critically acclaimed *American Buffalo*. In 1984, *Forbes* placed his wealth at $400 million, landing him a position in the *Forbes* 400—all based on the value of his little publication as a publishing business. When he died in 1987, the stubborn old man left his 53-year-old daughter, Jean Bernhard Buttner, in charge.

Bernhard was notoriously cheap. He had lots of bodies at work, each writing up his or her analysis of various companies, but he paid almost nothing. In the mid 1980s "analysts" were working for the firm in New York, routinely for compensation between $25,000 and $35,000, depending on duration. So, his people were usually rank beginners who were temporarily using *Value Line* as an entry to Wall Street, Wall Street is lined with good people who started in the Bernhard empire, left, and moved up—a poor man's training ground for all kinds of talent. Accordingly the staff turnover at *Value Line* is never ending.

Once, in 1982, I had lunch with Bernhard. Another fellow and I were talking to him about potentially creating a kind of training institute for young analysts and were hoping—because he had so many workers at *Value Line* — that we could get him to participate as a paid speaker and "draw." We were also hoping to get him to send his young people for training—which would be additional revenue for the project. Our idea for a training institute never got off the ground, but it was interesting to me that Bernhard was not interested in sending his analysts for training. He did express interest in the idea as a way to find and recruit more young beginners for his ever-revolving door of *Value Line* analysts. Worth hundreds of millions, Bernhard was cheap and clever to the end.

Because the *Value Line* is actively used by every major American investment firm, and because so many folks fathom companies in terms of the information it carries on a single page of analysis, it would be hard to envision the market today without the contribution of Bernhard. He gave us the capability to see an overview of almost any company on a single page. True, the analysis isn't always very deep or accurate. And yes, the system he uses for ranking stocks isn't very widely accepted. But the statistics are good. The *Value Line* format never changes, and people know it and relate to it and accept it. It is today a standard, and for that the world owes Mr. Bernhard much.

LOUIS ENGEL

ONE MIND THAT HELPED MAKE
MILLIONS MORE

Louis Engel's book, *How to Buy Stocks*, originally written in 1953, took on a life of its own as investors realized Wall Street was no longer an exclusive club for the wealthy. How a seemingly simple "how to" guide could alter the market forever is simple: In writing his book, Engel was the first to explain the market to middle-income people—the masses—in their own language. Using vernacular and real-life examples, he translated financial jargon into English, enabling the expanding middle-class to view securities as viable and safe investments. As a result, Wall Street was able to tap into an important market by bringing Wall Street to Main Street.

"If business is to have the money it needs to go on growing, somebody has to take the rich man's place. That somebody can only be the investor of moderate means—thousands of such small investors, because it takes 1,000 of them with $1,000 each to equal the $1,000,000 in capital that one wealthy man may have supplied yesteryear." Like **Jay Cooke** before him, financing the Civil War, and **A.P. Giannini**, building Bank of America, Engel turned to the "little fellow" to give Wall Street a much-needed boost during its postwar period. But instead of doing it for him as Giannini and Cooke did, Engel was to show him how to do it himself. As an ad man and journalist, his tool was language.

While an advertising manager at Merrill Lynch, Pierce, Fenner and Smith, Inc. between 1949 and 1969, Engel decided it was no longer feasible to do business "with just a handful of the rich and financially literate." The brokers, he said, needed "to do business with John Jones and Bill Smith and that means they're going to have to forget financial lingo and talk . . . about stocks and bonds in language that they and their wives understand." The alternative was that "American industry may well find itself starved for new capital." So, as part of Merrill Lynch's "Bring Wall Street to Main Street" ad campaign, in which it sought to sell its brokerage services to a lot of little investors, Engel wrote an advertisement explaining stocks in simple terms. It wound up being so successful that soon afterwards, publishers Little, Brown and Company approached Engel to expand his ideas into a book, and he penned *How to Buy Stocks* in six weeks.

Thirty-eight years later, *How to Buy Stocks* is the most successful financial book ever and still sells. By Engel's death in 1982, the book—revised seven times—had sold some four million copies. No other investment book comes even close to that in terms of cumulative sales. In a fairly objective manner, it tells the story of the imaginary Pocket Pole Company, beginning with its inception—the invention of a new collapsible metal fishing rod. From here, Engel leads the reader down the most fundamental steps to building a company: Borrowing capital and issuing stock to shareholders, electing a board of directors, conducting annual meetings, issuing dividends, issuing preferred and convertible stocks, selling bonds, and the rest of the basics needed to run a firm, expand it, and reap profits.

Short and easy-to-read chapters include: "How New Issues are Regulated," "What You Should Know about Government and Municipal Bonds," "How the 'Over-the-Counter' Market Works," "How to Read the Financial News," "The Folklore of the Market," and "When Is the Time to Sell?" What Engel writes is neither profound nor condescending, just simple and straightforward!

Naturally, being a Merrill Lynch mouthpiece, Engel took his time detailing the broker's role in the securities industry in chapters like, "Investing—or What's a Broker For?," "How You Do Business with a Broker" and "How You Open an Account." He confided, "Lots of people still shy away from the broker for a variety of reasons. Some of them feel embarrassed about the amount of money they have to invest. Maybe they have only $500 to put into stocks, perhaps only $40 or $50 a month, and they figure a broker wouldn't be interested . . . Perhaps they think of the broker as a somewhat forbidding individual who gives his time only to Very Important People, people who are well-heeled and travel in the right social circles." But Engel reassures the reader, "That's not true. There's nothing exclusive about the brokerage business today. No spats or striped pants. The club rules are all changed, and coffee and hamburgers are more popular items on the club menu than champagne and caviar."

Born the son of an auditor in 1909, Engel grew up in Jacksonville, Illinois. He graduated from the University of Chicago in 1930 and began his career as a University of Chicago Press staff member for two years. He left for New York to become managing editor for *Advertising and Selling*, then became news editor—and later managing editor—for *Business Week* from 1934 to 1946. That year, he left to join Merrill Lynch as its advertising manager, becoming a vice president in 1954 and remaining until his retirement in 1969. Engel's home life started at 34, when he married his first wife, whom he divorced a few years later. He remarried in 1954 at 43 and had three daughters. After his retirement in 1969, Engel retreated to his upstate New York home, becoming village trustee in Ossining, and town supervisor between 1975 and 1979. The man "who brought Wall Street to Main Street" died at 73 in 1982.

There is no doubt that Engel's book was a Merrill Lynch promotional piece. For decades Merrill Lynch brokers have given copies of it away to prospective clients as an enticement to do business with them. But at the same time, his book took on a life of its own. I've never had anything to do with Merrill Lynch, yet I've given away dozens of copies over the years to folks interested in a first book on investing. I've never really seen a better first book on investing than *How To Buy Stocks*. Engel's sheer simplicity and straightforward approach, coupled with the innate writing skills he picked up in business journalism, allowed him and his thoughts to be the conduit for millions of modern era investors in their introduction to Wall Street. Not only was Engel one of the minds that made the market, he helped make millions of minds through his one little book.

CHAPTER THREE

INVESTMENT BANKERS
AND BROKERS

THEIR ALLOCATION OF CAPITAL IS WHAT
CAPITALISM IS ALL ABOUT

Financial markets via Wall Street and their counterpart cousins of capitalism on Main Street allocate resources more efficiently than a centrally planned economy ever could. Day-to-day prices are decided by financial markets, but the deals where the money actually changes hands (and is thereby allocated to specific projects) are put together by savvy deal makers like the folks in this section. Deals are at the heart of financial markets, and are one of the prime reasons for free markets to exist and freely "do their thing." Deal-makers keep it pumping.

Vision, detail, and salesmanship are what the deals are all about, and good deal-makers possess all three. First, they are visionaries, envisioning the deal as one whole fluid process, from figuring out the cast of players to setting ideal prices. Second, they must be detail-minded before, during, and after the deal goes through. That means considering everything from the details of how the deal is cut to legal issues like SEC regulations, to what is going on with competitors with wanna-be deals. Third, they are super-salesmen, because selling completes deals and brings in new ones. Without it, the deal never happens.

This essentially describes the people in this section. August Belmont, the Lehmans, J.P. Morgan, Morgan Jr., Jacob Schiff, George Perkins, Clarence Dillon, and Sidney Weinberg were the most capable in their field—they closed deals that shaped modern corporate America.

It was all made possible by America's earliest large-scale deal-maker, August Belmont. He united Wall Street with a force much bigger than itself, a force that made it possible for our capitalist markets to expand beyond their local roots—European capital via the Rothschilds.

Once the capital flowed, J.P. Morgan put it to use. Morgan pioneered investment banking and is someone we think of as the quintessential deal-maker. He epitomized trust, competence, decisiveness, fairness, and a sense of responsibility. He literally carried the world on his shoulders and with seeming grace. He saturated early American finance and wielded a power that no one in history has wielded since. The House of Morgan became synonymous with power, and in his prime no one had the gall to buck Morgan.

Morgan used his power to create giant companies that ultimately transformed America from an emerging country into a powerful, industrialized nation. He financed railroads in the 1870s, transporting progress among states. In 1901, he formed the first billion-dollar company and the stalwart of modern industry, U.S. Steel. He kept the entire American economy afloat during the 1907 Panic. He was big. He was more than big.

Nearly as big, but in a different way, were the Lehman Brothers. Initially a cotton brokerage firm in the pre–Civil War South, the Lehmans represented the other side of Wall Street—the Jewish side. The Jewish houses never really rivaled Morgan; instead they coexisted, sometimes working together when Morgan needed extra funds and sometimes financing completely different industries. For example, the Lehmans discovered their own niche financing new technologies like the automobile industry in the days it was considered risky. Ironically, Morgan initially turned down the business!

Morgan was deeply entrenched in Wall Street, and when he died in 1913, a part of him lived on in other deal-makers. His son, J.P. Morgan, Jr. continued his legacy all the way into the 1930s period of reform, which essentially ended the House of Morgan's unquestioned reign over finance.

In Morgan's wake, a new breed of deal-makers emerged, partly mimicking Morganisms and partly improvising as they went along. Morgan partners George Perkins and his successor Thomas Lamont operated in this vein. Perkins was a picture of confidence in the Morgan tradition and helped stretch Morgan's influence to include big business, like wealthy national insurance firms.

Whereas J.P. Morgan had a disquieting physical appearance, and never let it get in his way, Lamont was the first of the image-conscious super-salesmen who came into power in the 1920s during Morgan, Jr.'s reign. Lamont was cool, literate, suave, and persuasive. But when Lamont tried to salvage America from the effects of the 1929 Crash, attempting to do so in the manner of J.P. Morgan, Sr. in 1907, it didn't work. He wasn't Morgan; this wasn't 1907; no private entity, no matter who headed it, could cure America's blues. America was emerging for the first time as a world power and no single financier could ever again be bigger than Wall Street.

Clarence Dillon emerged as a power on Wall Street about the same time as Lamont. The fact that new blood could operate on the same block as the House of Morgan reinforced the fact that the Morgan name no longer stood unchallenged. Dillon boldly took chunks of business away from Morgan and got away with it. In J.P.'s day this never would have happened, and if it did, Dillon immediately would have been crushed. Dillon prospered in later years, slicing himself bigger and bigger pieces of the pie as reform created more of an open market in the investment banking world.

Sidney Weinberg updated the Morgan attitude in the 1950s and became one of the most respected deal-makers in modern years. Weinberg taught modern investment bankers to be socially skilled networkers as opposed to the Morgan tradition that was more socially insular. Of course, Weinberg was also a visionary, detail-minded and a super-salesman. Combining business with pleasure became the vogue as Weinberg's formula continually worked to bring in deal after deal for Kuhn, Loeb.

Investment banker-turned-broker Charles Merrill also worked on updating some of the attitudes on Wall Street. Namely, he changed the way Wall Street viewed the little fellow. His goal was to bring Wall Street to the little fellow on Main Street, and he did it very well, creating America's largest brokerage firm and in the process a very potent and sometimes largest investment banking house. Starting in the 1940s, he set out to offer securities to the masses, opening Merrill, Lynch brokerage branches. Merrill became the first to tap into this new and abundant market, and later, many followed his lead, offering an array of accessible investment-related services to the unsophisticated investor. But none ever caught up to him.

Broker Gerald Loeb followed Merrill's lead and geared E.F. Hutton towards the masses. Loeb acted as Hutton's mouthpiece, making himself widely recognizable to the masses by cozying up to the press. In the spirit of self-promoters and used-car salesmen, Loeb knew the lingo so well that he could persuade almost anyone to invest in the market. While not a truly able investor or deal-maker, he sounded smooth to those who didn't know any better. Loeb got away with his gig quite successfully, because whatever he discussed or wrote was generally parlayed via mass marketing and popular periodicals to the little fellows who had paltry savings and almost no knowledge about the stock market. Loeb's success demonstrated the need for investment bankers to engage in public relations campaigns oriented toward convincing the little guy that "this" brokerage house could keep him plugged into the inside track on Wall Street. Of course, that track was really just a distribution channel for the investment banking arm of the brokerage firm to push its deals.

And that is what it is all about in the end. Large investment banking houses have become distribution arms to sell financial product to America. In what was once the realm of folks like Morgan, conceiving and constructing deals, today's investment bankers rarely control a deal the way Morgan did; instead they are reacting to the realities that the world is presenting and accommodating "deal flow" to what the world wants. Whereas the early investment bankers thought in terms of what was good for themselves and the world, today's investment bankers think in terms of what is good for themselves and their clients. Today's investment banking world is now cast into a realm of specialties: M&A (Merger and Acquisition), venture capital, IPOs (initial public offerings), etc.. But the original investment bankers did it all, blazing the trail for today's specialists, and in the process, literally making the market.

AUGUST BELMONT

HE REPRESENTED EUROPE'S FINANCIAL STAKE IN AMERICA

Like the **Rothschilds** before him in Europe, August Belmont helped transform America from a provincial and almost purely agricultural nation to a prosperous industrial country. But he wasn't your typical wheeler-dealer, speculating on the stock exchange or pioneering an industry for a fast buck; he preceded American industry. Instead, as the American agent of the House of Rothschild, the world's most powerful bank, Belmont for nearly 50 years was America's first link between investment banking and political lobbying. For the first time, finance met politics—and liked it! Belmont's Rothschild connections gained him prestige within the political community—and his political connections gained him business for the Rothschilds.

Belmont's success was initially a matter of good timing. Born in 1816 to poor Prussian parents, he started sweeping floors in the Rothschilds' Frankfurt house at age 14, by which time his bosses were already immensely successful. By age 17, he was supervising their Naples branch, handling a series of successful negotiations with the Papal Court. Now here's where the good timing comes in—four years later, while doing business in Havana, Cuba, Belmont heard that America was in the midst of a turbulent panic. So, at 21, he left Havana on the first ship bound for New York, arriving in the midst of the Panic of 1837 with fierce ambition and hordes of Rothschild credit. How many 21-year-olds do you imagine today would be entrusted with dispensing credit in what was then the equivalent of an emerging banana republic? But he was a Rothschild insider.

When he arrived, he didn't actually have any Rothschild money with him—just their name. But the name was so big that anyone and everyone extended him credit against his Rothschild connections and the faith that Rothschild money would follow. He immediately set up August Belmont and Company and began buying in a depressed market when no one else could. With the Rothschild name behind him, he was granted unlimited credit by folks who largely wouldn't have dared to grant each other credit. In essence he got America lending again. This provided the benefit of getting America to lend him the money to buy stocks, commodities, and bank notes, which stemmed the panic and shored up American banks on the brink of bankruptcy. Yet only he could do it, using America's faith in the world's largest private bank! As you would expect, this made him pretty darn popular.

With a razor-sharp wit and cultured background, Belmont charmed society with his accent, foreign phrases, and dapper looks. Short, stout with round features and bright, black, evasive eyes, he lured New York society to his doorstep. Within four years, Belmont's name was on the lips of every New Yorker. He was the city's leading investment banker and the hottest thing to hit society—and he was a Jew.

When he first arrived in America, Belmont sought to conceal his roots, like many other Jewish immigrants over the following 100 years. He changed his original surname—Schonberg—to its French equivalent (for beautiful mountain)—Belmont. Even in a rather tolerant land like America where so many had come to avoid religious persecution, most folks were down on Jewish money lenders. Still, as is true today, most of the folks who hated Jews the most probably couldn't recognize in Belmont his Jewishness—they were unfamiliar with it. And with a non-Jewish name he was ready to boogie among the best of bumpkins in New York's relatively unsophisticated "society." To New York society, he was a mysterious European who knew how to dress, decorate his mansion, throw a dinner party for 200, and even host a horse race, which came to be known as the Belmont Stakes (now part of the all-important-to-horse-racing "Triple Crown" with the Kentucky Derby and the Preakness). He even invented being "fashionably late."

The mystery man was also quite a Don Juan, who knew how to court the ladies. He had a certain sex appeal about him that the ladies loved—and the men hated. When he was done playing the field, he married a socialite, the daughter of Commodore Perry, and raised three boys and one girl. His second son, August, Jr., eventually took control of his father's firm and continued a family legacy like the Rothschilds'.

Belmont's life became intertwined with politics during the early 1840s, and from then on, his political kudos were endless—and with good reason. It was through his political connections and savvy that his loans for the Rothschilds were secure in a world where political instability was the rule rather than the exception. Belmont spent his life cultivating political connections and power—and therein is his importance to the evolution of America's financial markets. He is really the first to tie finance to politics in the United States. Politics was his insurance policy for the Rothschilds.

Belmont became a naturalized citizen and joined the Democratic party. In 1844, he was the Austrian consul-general in the U.S. for six years. In 1853, he became U.S. minister to the Netherlands and was active in the presidential election campaign that resulted in Pierce's election. He was the charge d'affaires of the U.S. legation at The Hague and later, minister resident of the U.S. at The Hague. Before retiring from politics in 1872, Belmont also served as chairman of the National Democratic Committee for four years.

In the face of the Civil War, Belmont temporarily switched loyalties to support Republican Lincoln in his fight for the Union, becoming the President's financial adviser. He was instrumental in obtaining foreign funds for the war effort, since at first neither the Rothschilds nor the English Government would support the Union. For years, Belmont funneled money into the U.S. Treasury by purchasing government securities for the Rothschilds.

By the time he died of heart failure in 1890, Belmont had built a solid bridge between European capital and a blossoming industrial America—and at the same time, he'd wed investment banking to politics. The Rothschilds, who had already discovered the importance of such a marriage a century earlier in Europe, could continue their dynasty in America via Belmont and his ties to the White House and Congress.

The fact that Belmont's life is highlighted by his social and political dealings stresses the fact that what he was doing as the Rothschilds' agent in America wasn't so much the pioneering of stock offerings or inventing corporate structures, because he preceded the heart of our industrial revolution. His role was primarily in government finance and the overall money markets which support the corporate world and without which there would be insufficient financial liquidity to support our wonderful capitalistic system.

EMANUEL LEHMAN AND
HIS SON PHILIP

ROLE MODELS FOR SO MANY
WALL STREET FIRMS

Charting the rise of Lehman Brothers, one of Wall Street's greatest investment banking houses, essentially traces the gradual emergence of a powerful, industrial United States. Beginning as cotton brokers in an agricultural society, the first Lehmans to arrive in America helped finance the Confederacy during the Civil War, and then turned to Wall Street to dabble in commodities well into the 1900s. It wasn't until second-generation Lehmans pushed for progress and bigger profits that the firm made its mark on Wall Street by financing the untraditional—retailing, textiles, mail order houses, and five-and-dimes—all of which had been shunned previously by bankers.

The legacy began in 1844 when Henry Lehman arrived in Mobile, Alabama—from Bavaria—and began peddling junkets from his wagon along the Alabama River. Within a year, he landed in Montgomery, where he hung his shingle, "H. Lehman," and sold glassware, tools, dry goods, and seed. In 1850, the general store paid the way to America for brothers Mayer and

Emanuel—and hence, "Lehman Brothers" was formed. With cotton being the number one commodity in the South, the sons of a cattle dealer soon became cotton brokers, accepting it at discount in return for their goods, then selling it for profit—turning a buck on both sides of the deal.

Since cotton payments usually took the form of four-month drafts on New York banks, Emanuel (30 years old and the family leader after yellow fever killed Henry in 1855) started a New York branch in 1856. In 1868, following the Civil War, which had put their business on hold, Mayer joined his brother on Wall Street, and together they re-established themselves as successful cotton and commodities brokers, obtaining a seat on the New York Stock Exchange in 1887.

The Lehmans became known on Wall Street as reliable, fair and fastidious brokers and slowly climbed the ranks within the Jewish community. Both were bright-eyed with full beards and tall foreheads; they usually wore silk hats, frock coats, and striped trousers—and looked almost identical, which gave them the appearance of being in two places at once. Good-natured and eager to do business, Mayer was the more aggressive, outgoing sales type who made contacts and continually drummed up business; Emanuel tended to be the long-term thinker and the more cool, cautious, and constructive of the two. It was said, "Mayer makes the money and Emanuel conserves it."

By the 1890s, both brothers were married and had sons old enough to bring into the firm. In that decade, three additional Lehmans joined the firm—Emanuel's son Philip, born in 1861, who would eventually take his father's seat at the head of the firm, Mayer's son Sigmund, and the late Henry's son Meyer. With new blood pulsing through the firm's veins, it expanded along with the infant industrial American economy. The Lehmans invested in new technology like automobiles and rubber, but still clung to the commodities business, trading in coffee, cotton, and petroleum.

Emanuel died in 1907—a month shy of 80—leaving in his place his assertive and aggressive 36-year-old son Philip. It was said "at anything he did, Philip had to win." With a sense of dignity and a sense of aristocracy, a restrained manner and intellectual brain, this Lehman unleashed his generation's quest for progress and abandoned the old ways instantly for a slice of the newly exploding investment banking business. He accomplished this primarily by hooking up with his best friend, Henry Goldman, before the Goldman Sachs partnership. (They toyed with creating Goldman and Lehman but instead decided on splitting the profits 50/50.)

Lehman and Goldman became Wall Street's hottest underwriting team, managing 114 offerings for 56 issuers. In their heyday, they introduced Studebaker in 1911; F.W. Woolworth in 1912; and Continental Can in 1913. One of their most famous coups was underwriting a $10 million loan for a growing mail-order house called Sears, Roebuck, headed by Goldman's distant relative. It was the first time a mail-order security had ever been on the market—a calculated risk, but one that paid off.

Out on their own, the Lehman Brothers continued their off-the-beaten-path format, underwriting early issues of airline, electronics, motion picture, and liquor stocks. They handled many of today's corporate giants, such as Postum Cereal, R.H. Macy and Company, Endicott-Johnson, Pillsbury Flour, Campbell Soup, and Yellow Cab. In 1935, they reorganized Paramount Pictures with **Floyd Odlum** and bought RCA's controlling block in RKO, when Wall Street involvement in the entertainment industry was unprecedented.

Why are they in this book? They sound like good solid investment banker types, but not radical revolutionaries. How is it that Emanuel or Philip might qualify as among the 100 minds that made the market? Pretty simple! They were the stereotypical role model for the Jewish investment banking firm. When I first came into this business there was still a strong sense of separation between Jews and Christians on Wall Street. One block of brokers was Christian firms with primarily Christian employees, and another was Jewish firms with primarily Jewish employees. Being someone who is of half Jewish descent and half Christian, I always found the split on Wall Street fascinating. The farther back in time you go, the stronger the split. Morgan ran a Christian firm, but he couldn't really have been Morgan without the presence of the Jewish firm, Kuhn, Loeb. Where is Kuhn, Loeb today? Nowhere! But the Lehman name has never lost prominence and is big on Wall Street today. While Kuhn, Loeb was more important in its prime, it couldn't maintain the continuity inherent to the notion of a permanent institution.

Lehman Brothers not only was at the heart of the Jewish New York financial and social circuit, but it also served as a role model after which dozens of firms patterned themselves. At its heart were the family members, who eventually hired outsiders to build a huge firm of partners who continued into the modern era. The pattern would be emulated by Goldman, by Bear Stearns, even by the great modern, famous, and recently infamous Drexel Burnham, to name only a few. There is today a long list of Jewish names on mastheads of leading investment firms, essentially all of whom followed Lehmans' model. I remember when I was a kid, before the long era of consolidation among investment banking-brokerage firms, that there were many more Jewish names on firms—again, all in the Lehman tradition. As the role model for Jewish firms, Emanuel Lehman and his son Philip will forever be held in high regard.

JOHN PIERPONT MORGAN

HISTORY'S MOST
POWERFUL FINANCIER

Back when Teddy Roosevelt was President, J.P. Morgan was probably the most powerful man in the world. A capital-conjuring wizard, Morgan erected a one-man central bank, financing his era's greatest mergers and saving America from perilous panic. His abrupt word was considered golden, and his formidable aura, almighty. For example, there is the legendary story of when an old friend's son solicited Morgan financing for a questionable venture. Morgan declined, but chuckled, "Let me offer you something equally valuable!"—and he took the young man by his side for a stroll across the New York Stock Exchange floor. Credit for the young man would never again be so available from so many!

Unlike presidents and royalty who have power bestowed upon them, Morgan earned his larger-than-life status by sheer will. Dogmatic and domineering, he had the brains to pull it off, selling securities, reorganizing railroads, and consolidating companies. Sure, he had a head start from his father, international banker **Junius Morgan**, but J.P. was the one who truly immortalized the House of Morgan by forming America's first billion-dollar corporation in 1901 and, as big daddy, rescuing the economy from the grips of the 1907 Panic.

Morgan, an undaunted capitalist, was deemed savior of the Panic. As excessive speculation and stock-watering caused companies to fail and banks to collapse, Wall Street turned to Morgan for hope. Working at his own pace amidst the terror, Morgan mobilized funding from friends and rivals to salvage what they could. He played the role of last-resort lender for troubled institutions, that is now played by the Federal Reserve System. Allowing the "unsalvageable" Knickerbocker Trust to fail, Morgan—with a big, black stogy cornered in his mouth—instead funded the near-failing Trust Company of America. Then, as stocks tumbled faster than the ticker could record trades, he turned to the Stock Exchange, which threatened to close. Within minutes. Morgan patch-quilted $25 million to keep it afloat. No problem for Big J.P.

With a protruding ruby-red nose, steel-gray hair, and blazing eyes set under black bushy brows, J.P. created a banking empire second to none. He wasn't particularly devious, although "the old man" knew a few treacherous tricks. Instead, he conducted business in his assured, gruff manner—succinctly and surely. He rarely changed his mind; once his word was spoken, he stuck to it. An old world gentleman, Morgan once secured a million-dollar loan in 15 minutes by announcing, "I'll take the loan."

Morgan's favorite style was corporate consolidation. It was efficient and neat. It crushed "destructive" competition and, above all, produced order from chaos. How he despised chaos! When you had a higher share of the market than all your competitors, you could pretty well do what you wanted with product prices. No chaos. During his heyday, he spearheaded such horizontal consolidations as American Telephone & Telegraph, General Electric, Pullman, International Harvester, Western Union, and Westinghouse. But he set his sight on steel for his most impressive deal. By 1901, U.S. Steel was capitalized at $1.4 billion in stocks and bonds—nearly half of which was water (goodwill in accounting parlance). It engulfed the entire steel industry and created hundreds of millionaires by paying steep prices for small, privately-owned companies.

En route, Morgan formed National Tube Company, and acquired American Tin Plate, Federal Steel, National Steel, and American Steel & Wire. He then focused on depreciating Andrew Carnegie's giant steel firm so he could buy it cheap. When Carnegie survived J.P.'s competitive tactics, such as attracting Carnegie customers to Morgan's steel, Morgan paid up, and Carnegie bailed out. Again in 15 minutes, J.P. agreed to pay $492 million in first-mortgage five-percent gold bonds. Underwriting syndicates took huge fees of $57.5 million—$11.5 of which went to the House of Morgan. Morgan, who suffered from emotional breakdowns and frequent headaches, was so gifted at creating fees for his firms that some people suspected his consolidations were mere fee-funnelers—not the strategic, cost-cutting market share mergers he intended them to be. Newspapers had a field day with the deal, much to

Morgan's chagrin. Word had it that God created the world, but "it was reorganized in 1901 by Morgan."

Born in 1837, J.P. entered the family business at age 19, working at George Peabody & Co. of London and gaining an impressive overview of international finance. He speculated successfully in coffee and Civil War gold and participated in the scandalous 1861 Hall Carbine Affair. In this exploit, J.P. loaned a colleague $20,000 to buy obsolete Hall carbines from the government at $3.50 each. He then resold them to Uncle Sam for $22 apiece!

Thereafter, he established his own firm, Dabney, Morgan, which by 1870 was ranked 16th among New York banking houses. Morgan ventured in railroads, first floating $6.5 million of Kansas Pacific bonds. Next, he sparred with pirates **Jay Gould** and **Jim Fisk** for control of the Albany & Susquehanna, absorbing their dubious ways—stock watering, blackmail, and political pole-vaulting. Whereas raiders Gould and Fisk wanted the line solely to loot it, church-going Morgan regarded the rails as an important form of transportation. By 1879, he was seen as a major railroad financier after successfully unloading William H. Vanderbilt's $25 million interest in the New York Central Railroad. His prompt, private handling of the matter won him a seat on N.Y. Central's board, admitted him to the upper echelon of railroad dealings and deemed him financial intermediary between American and overseas investors. The 1880s were a time for "Morganizing," whereby Morgan provided new capital and reduced fixed costs by reissuing securities at lower interest rates or converting bonds to stock, always earning an investment banking fee en route. Also en route, and to insure his investments, Morgan became a director of at least 21 railroads.

The House of Morgan completely saturated American finance, so when reform (triggered by the 1907 Panic) became fashionable, J.P. was an obvious target. His mergers, in particular, came under fire from President Taft and blood-thirsty reporters. Even Congress joined the game, initiating the 1912 Pujo investigation into monopoly finance, which featured Morgan as a suspected money trust kingpin. But while the old-timer successfully defended his life's work, his pride was mortally wounded. His kingdom and health in decline, arrogant and ornery Morgan died at age 75 in 1913, leaving a $77 million estate and $20 million in art.

No financier since has had the power Morgan wielded in his prime—not even close. He was power. Ironically, what he truly saw as power for good, the early 20th century's reformers saw as evil. Was the world better with Morgan's mergers or with the perilous price deflation of the 1870s and 1880s that led to the profitless need for consolidation? We could debate history forever, but the key in thinking about Morgan is that, more than any other person, before or since, he personified what the stock and bond markets are ultimately all about—financing or refinancing American business. It's one thing to worry about whether a given stock's price will rise or fall, but ultimately all the fluctuations come back to which businesses will get money in the future and which won't. The only person to attempt to rival Morgan's significance was the recent junk bond evolution of **Michael Milken** of the former Drexel Burnham Lambert. Milken was a revolutionary in finance, but despite creating a huge amount of refinancing via junk bonds, he never came close to the truly central role Morgan played in our entire economy. And Milken's legal problems and Drexel's bankruptcy insure for decades to come that Morgan will hold the title of history's most powerful financier.

JACOB H. SCHIFF

THE OTHER SIDE OF THE STREET

Jacob Schiff stood for a Wall Street different than **J.P. Morgan**'s. Sure, in Schiff's world, men still made millions underwriting loans that financed America's industrialization, and connections and integrity were still required to play the game. But Schiff and his crowd differed in one respect—they were the Jewish side of the Street.

Schiff reigned over Wall Street's number two investment banking firm, Kuhn, Loeb and Company, starting at age 38 in 1885, when the last senior partner retired. During the next few decades, he turned a mediocre firm into one to be reckoned with—one that financed the majority of America's greatest railroads, while J.P. Morgan & Company concentrated more on industries.

Known for his clear-headedness, fair-mindedness, honesty, and dislike for public attention, Schiff, like Morgan, never hesitated in business and completed even the largest of deals within half an hour. Schiff knew exactly what he wanted. But unlike the WASPy New Englander, Schiff, born in 1847, was raised in Germany, the son of a wealthy, prominent Jewish family. He moved to Manhattan in 1865 to follow in his father's footsteps—his father was a broker for the **Rothschilds.** By 1875, at only 28, he landed his Kuhn, Loeb position with fellow German Jews while marrying his boss' daughter, Theresa Loeb. His partnership in the firm was his wedding present, and from then on, Kuhn, Loeb continued to be a network of Jewish in-laws and blood relations.

While being a Jewish firm never really hindered Kuhn, Loeb, Schiff still had special decisions to make concerning his own heartfelt beliefs and business. For example, he had to face financing World War I in a businesslike way, even though he was torn apart inside between his homeland, Germany, and America's ally in the war, Czarist Russia, which was then persecuting Jews. As far back as 1904, out of intense hatred for Czarist Russia, Schiff had secured a $200 million loan for Japan while it was fighting the Russo-Japanese War. But in 1914, choosing sides wasn't that easy. If Kuhn, Loeb funded the Allied cause, Schiff felt he would be contributing to Russia—but if his firm refused to aid the Allies, it could be interpreted as being pro-German, which would be dreadful for business.

So, when England appealed to Kuhn, Loeb for a loan, his partners Otto Kahn and Mortimer Schiff (his son) offered a $500 million loan without collateral to England to aid the Allied cause. But when it came time for the boss to approve the loan, Schiff was forced to go with his conscience, instead of his usually objective business judgment. He agreed to the loan on one, impossible condition—that "not one cent of the proceeds of the loan would be given to Russia." This, of course, was impossible since England was allied to Russia, so the loan was turned down and Kuhn, Loeb became a dirty word on Wall Street for some time. It was only through Kahn's and Mortimer Schiff's personal contributions and public relations that the firm ever regained its enviable stature.

Being the number two firm under the House of Morgan also posed problems in the financial community—Schiff was required to prove his firm and himself in the eyes of Morgan. The test came at the turn of the century, when Schiff teamed with railroader **Ed Harriman** against Morgan and railroader **James Hill** for control of the Great Northern Railroad. In the end, after the battle culminated in a mini-panic called Blue Thursday in 1901, Schiff and Morgan compromised by forming a jointly-controlled holding company. From then on, their silent rivalry took on a tone of respect. Morgan not only gave Schiff his deepest respect—but considered Schiff his one and only business equal!

Not only were railroads the key to Schiff's respect from Morgan, but they also were the main ingredient in his success with Kuhn, Loeb. His experience with railroads, which began a few years before Morgan entered the scene, spanned some 40 years, during which he financed over $1 billion for the Pennsylvania Railroad alone. He courted the rails' business, where senior partner Loeb considered the investment risky, by befriending management, opposing speculators, and promoters and learning the ins and outs of the industry. His strategy paid off. Kuhn, Loeb was swamped with new clients, and soon they were regularly commanding fees of 10 percent—about $1 million in fees for floating and selling a modest $10 million bond issue.

Short, yet standing erect, the serious and strait-laced Schiff had compassionate blue eyes, a beard that later turned white, and a dapper, old-fashioned wardrobe. An avid reader and prolific letter writer, he was a homebody, unless he was visiting Europe. A dedicated family man, Schiff revered his parents, always carrying around their faded photos in his wallet. His most important reason for keeping the firm's high standing was his only son, Mortimer, who joined the firm in 1900 at 23 and later took it over when his father died in 1920—a little like what happened with the Morgans.

There are, and almost always have been, a lot of folks in the world who are hostile to Jews, particularly rich Jews in powerful positions. But when the pre-reformation Church made usury a sin, it carved, by default, a niche for Jews in money lending that evolved into the powerful position Jews maintained in 19th century investment banking. Just as the Jewish House of Rothschild preceded the Christian House of Morgan, the 19th century Jewish investment banking community was both disproportionately large and well established relative to its Christian alternatives and their respective population bases.

As the head and builder of America's premier 19th century Jewish invest-ment banking firm, Schiff perpetuated the Jewish presence in finance and propelled it forward in his sort of little-brother-to-Morgan role. Note that Schiff did not discriminate in favor of financing Jewish enterprises over others. He saw himself as an American businessman first and a Jew only incidentally. Along that line, he considered himself a "faith Jew" and not a "race Jew." He didn't like anything that fostered segregation. And so he would raise money among the Jewish community and finance without prejudice—and accordingly he and Morgan were often dealing side-by-side.

At a time when American investment banking was still heavily sucking money out of Europe to finance the evolution of what was then not much more than what we would see today as an evolving third world country, Schiff brought to Wall Street the counterpart function within the Jewish world of finance that Morgan did otherwise. Schiff is therefore almost as singularly important as Morgan. Without him, fewer enterprises, both Jewish and non-Jewish, would have been financed, and today we would all be a lot poorer for it.

National Cyclopedia of American Biography, 1916

GEORGE W. PERKINS

HE LEFT THE COMFY HOUSE OF
MORGAN TO RIDE A BULL MOOSE

J.P. Morgan rarely worried about competition—usually there wasn't any. But one day insurance executive George Perkins began treading in Morgan territory, underwriting foreign securities with his firm's vast resources. Certainly Perkins didn't wish to cross antlers with the almighty Morgan—he was just serving the interests of his firm. Just the same, Morgan was startled—then dumbfounded when Perkins committed his firm to a major German loan. That was way too close for comfort, so Morgan sprang into action, offering Perkins a Morgan partnership. Morgan never worried about competition—he just swallowed it up whole!

Perkins reluctantly accepted the partnership (after several offers) on one condition—that he be allowed to retain his vice presidency at New York Life Insurance. Morgan said, "Well, if you won't leave the New York Life, come along and join the firm and see if you can occupy that dual position. I don't think you can, but if you can, all right." And that was that. For five of his 10 years as a hard-working Morgan partner, Perkins acted as both Morgan partner and insurance king—what some later called a conflict of interest.

The charming, witty, and enthusiastic Perkins came to be known as "Morgan's right-hand man." He was tall, slender, and black-haired with alert dark black eyes and a get-down-to-business attitude. Born to a New York Life Insurance man in 1862, Perkins was a poor student who left school at 15 to clerk for his father. He rose up the ranks quickly and was well on his way to the presidency when Morgan knocked on his door. En route, Perkins revolutionized insurance sales, replacing the agency system with branch offices, and offered employees profit sharing.

Perkins brought to the House of Morgan a profitable alliance with New York Life that greatly extended Morgan's already-formidable power, influence and wealth. New York Life, and later, other giant insurance firms, served as a dumping ground for otherwise hard-to-place Morgan securities. In one four-year period, Morgan sold over $38 million worth to New York Life with Perkins acting as the go-between for both firms! The fact that he was both buyer and seller ultimately created a stir in the legal world. Sensationalized insurance investigations in 1905 eventually forced Perkins to resign from New York Life shrouded in scandal, but Morgan's relationship with the firm endured.

Besides his insurance dealings, Perkins remodeled U.S. Steel's internal structure and negotiated mergers to form huge trusts like International Harvester and International Marine. "I did not come to the firm of J.P. Morgan & Co. purely as a banker. My work with that firm was largely one of industrial organization." Indeed, if he had had more banking experience, maybe Perkins wouldn't have denied **W.C. Durant** backing for his plans to form General Motors. Durant, in his pitch to Morgan partners, had predicted a day when 500,000 cars would be sold yearly. Perkins commented, "If he had any sense, he'll keep such notions to himself if he ever tries to borrow money!" While a banker, Perkins was obviously no visionary.

Perkins was conservative when it came to money. He grew up poor and had been taught to scrimp. Though he died with over $10 million, he still carried an old leather wallet containing scraps of paper listing his favorite savings stories: Once he saved 10 cents walking to and from work instead of taking a streetcar; another time, he pocketed 15 cents by skipping lunch. And his lifestyle reflected his attitude. Perkins wasn't extravagant—instead of the usual millionaire toys, he'd splurge on a choice crate of fruit from a special orchard, and gave generously to charities.

Perkins left the House of Morgan at the close of 1910. **Thomas Lamont**, a partner who succeeded Perkins, once said he didn't leave by choice. Lamont claimed Morgan said Perkins was "a little second rate" on some deals, though Lamont never furnished details. Even the papers had a field day when he left. Some reported Perkins was speculating to control the price of U.S. Steel stock, though this was unlikely. Perkins wasn't the wild, speculative type. He was in Wall Street for results, not risky, unsure deals where he couldn't predict the outcome.

After his departure, Perkins devoted himself to Teddy Roosevelt's Progressive Party, serving as chairman of the Party's Executive Committee, and it was in this capacity that he gained his greatest fame. But his ties with Wall Street's most infamous firm hindered him and never allowed him the full trust of party cohorts. The notion of a former Morgan partner tied to the progressive movement is by itself interesting. The progressive movement, or any similar political upheaval, can't continue without the support of at least some turncoats from the other side. And that is what Perkins was, a turncoat who didn't trust free enterprise and the "divine hand" of capitalism to serve mankind. He spoke out on the day's business problems and believed workers should receive retirement benefits. That was fine, but he also believed competition should be replaced by cooperation; that large corporations properly supervised were more effective than small, competing firms. Not only would Adam Smith turn over in his grave, but so would I if I were dead.

Before he died at the young age of 58—the House of Morgan could do that to you—Perkins had a nervous breakdown, entered a sanitarium, and had a heart attack. He then died of brain inflammation in 1920. Married for 21 years, he left his wife, daughter, and son, George W. Perkins, Jr., who worked at rehabilitating European industry.

Perkins was a leader on Wall Street, but also a leader in the earliest phases of the process that finally led to taming Wall Street from its wildest days and leaving behind the world of heavy market manipulation and fraud as was done by so many of his contemporaries.

JOHN PIERPONT "JACK" MORGAN, JR.

NO ONE EVER HAD BIGGER SHOES TO FILL

J.P. Morgan, Jr. did that which is rarely done. He was successful in his father's field while dad was a national legend. Don't laugh! Most folks presume that having a super successful father is a big advantage. Not so! Think about it. We've had only two Presidents whose sons were particularly notable in politics. Sons or daughters of leading athletes rarely excel at all, and almost never in dad's field. The pressure is just too great for the normal human ego to take. Most sons of super successful fathers grow up emotionally damaged by their fathers' overpowering images. Among small-time business-types it's pretty common for lineage to help, but not in the big time. If your dad owns the local auto parts chain, it might help if you want to enter that field. But Morgan's father was arguably the most powerful man in the world, and how in the world does anyone fill in those shoes? Most sons would turn into alcoholics just worrying about what to say to the famous father at dinner.

While J.P. Morgan, Jr. was never more significant than his inherited position as head of the powerful House of Morgan, that was enough. His father, the almighty **J.P. Morgan**, had already created the most powerful institution in the world—bigger than Uncle Sam. J.P., Jr. made history by continuing the chain despite increasingly restrictive government regulations. While a lesser man might not have filled his father's shoes, "young Morgan" did.

"Young Morgan" called himself Jack. When his father died in 1913, Jack took over J.P. Morgan & Co. after a few days of mourning. It was no surprise—the 46-year-old had spent his entire life preparing for the day, continually egged on by his domineering dad. First, there was the elite New England prep school, then Harvard, marriage and a New York branch internship. Next it was off to the London branch, where Jack nearly faltered, falling prey to the wealthy brat-pack party circuit. But when J.P. Sr. hollered, dependable Junior came running back.

While his father financed railroad reorganizations, created the first billion-dollar corporation and could truly roll more money than presidents, so could Junior, whose forte was international financing during World War I. He handled French, British and Russian loans in the U.S. and once organized a 2,200-bank syndicate to float $500 million for England and France. He was equally vital in postwar financing, loaning $1.7 billion in reparations under the Dawes Plan. Because of his wartime activities, Morgan was nearly assassinated in 1915 by a German sympathizer objecting to Allied ammunition financing. Note that it wasn't Wilson the guy tried to kill—it made more sense to go after Morgan. The assassin managed to enter Morgan's Long Island summer mansion and shoot him twice. But Jack recovered. Later, his loans were the source of controversy when he was accused—via his loans—of influencing Wilson to enter the war on the Allied side. Morgan denied this. But private banking just wasn't what it used to be. That anyone should accuse a Morgan of anything was a sign of the changing times.

Standing 6 foot 2, with broad shoulders, big features, a bulbous nose, and piercing eyes, Morgan aged to closely resemble his father, both in physical appearance and personality. He adopted Morgan, Sr.'s gruff, monosyllabic speech, hatred for the press, conservative dress, and love for yachting. (It was because of his attitude towards the media that little has been written about him.) Like his father, he submerged himself in the firm, keeping to himself, batting at cameras with his cane—you've got to like a guy who does that—and running a thriving company until the mid-1930s, when Uncle Sam interfered.

"My special job is the most interesting I know of anywhere. More fun than being king, pope, or prime minister anywhere—for no one can turn me out of it and I don't have to make any compromises with principles," Morgan once said. His principles—"Do your work; be honest; keep your word; help when you can; be fair"—were the words he lived by. He was truly one of the very few forged from a cauldron of parental mega-success to have neither a rebellious bent nor an overwhelming fear of relative failure. Confident without being cocky, driven without being devious, Jack Morgan was a good man with high ideals. And he worked by his code of ethics. Unfortunately his idea of ethics and regulation didn't compare to what the changing times and the increasingly powerful Uncle Sam had in mind under the New Deal.

While Morgan always maintained that Wall Street—and private banking, in particular—could govern itself, Washington disagreed, particularly so after the 1929 Crash. While not irreparably damaged from the Crash itself, Morgan was still the very symbol of Wall Street power—the New Dealers went after Morgan and his firm with a vengeance. In many ways the Glass-Steagall Act of 1933 was aimed directly at him: It insisted that all broker-bankers, including the House of Morgan, choose between security underwriting and private deposit banking. With events beyond his control, and in a world very different from his father's, Morgan forfeited underwriting in 1934 to the newly created Morgan, Stanley & Co., financed by his partners and him as a separate firm.

But Uncle Sam was unrelenting. The Senate Banking Committee publicized that neither Morgan nor his partners paid income tax in 1931 or 1932, then promoted the firm's habit of offering new stock issues to select, powerful people at lower-than-market prices. Morgan quickly denied what was being insinuated—that in return for cut-rate securities, the firm received special favors. But meanwhile, the House of Morgan was on a downswing stemming from the Depression and would soon lose some $40 million on a defaulted **Van Swearingen Brothers'** loan. Morgan, financially comfortable, tended to ignore public opinion and do what he thought best.

Morgan, Sr. must have turned in his grave in 1940 when the government had its way—J.P. Morgan & Co., the banking entity, was incorporated and transformed to a state-chartered bank. The exclusivity was gone forever with 16,500 shares floated to the public in the open market. Sadly enough, J.P. Morgan, Jr. resorted to going public because of death and inheritance taxes that threatened the firm's capital as partners passed away. He reasoned that "so much of the capital is in a few hands, and those hands are elderly." J.P., Jr. was not happy with this move and slowly faded out of the picture. Private banking in America was dead. Soon so was Jack.

Remaining slightly active and still a director of U.S. Steel among other companies, Morgan turned to his yacht (the Corsair), his prize-winning tulips, and his father's library which was filled with rare manuscripts. But he succumbed to heart attacks and a stroke and died in 1943 at 75, just three years after the great private House of Morgan was turned into a public entity. Ironically, he died at the same age as did his father before him. Once more, he couldn't outdo dad, but in his case just keeping up was plenty good enough.

Whether Morgan's reputation would have flourished further under different, less restrictive political conditions can never be known. Sure, his father had reorganized the railroads, created the first billion-dollar firm and bailed America out of the Panic of 1907. But his father operated at the very end of the era of true free markets—a time when he could summon more money than the government could—and that granted him world-wide power. J.P. Jr., too, had his own impressive gig in international finance that had its own worldwide influence. Without his financing, the western war effort would have been much more difficult. But Junior had to contend with an onslaught of government regulations that, slowly whittled away at his operations. No man in finance ever had bigger shoes to fill than did J.P. Jr., and his strength kept the continuous presence of the House of Morgan a dominating feature on Wall Street through the Progressive era and into the New Deal. Dad couldn't have done better.

AMS Press, Inc.

THOMAS LAMONT

THE BEACON FOR A
WHOLE GENERATION

Thomas Lamont epitomized the cool, classic, well-bred and well-spoken House of Morgan partner during the 1920s and '30s. In many ways he was the perfect image of the 1920s. Silver-haired, slender, short, suave, and handsome, Lamont was polite and persuasive—impish, yet impressive—conservative, but with a flair. He was a salesman—perhaps the first super-salesman.

He wore spectacles, the very image of vision, and waved them as he spoke. He naturally created an image that made it impossible for others to separate style from substance when they looked at him. Many suspected he was the brains of the firm, but in the 19th-century sense of a man who could pick deals and sharpshoot them, he wasn't. He was a salesman and PR guy who made you so confident in him that you believed what he told you. When the press needed a quote from **J.P. Morgan Jr.** and his top investment banking firm, it was the costly-clad Lamont who whispered into the reporters' ears, firmly impressing upon them what Morgan wanted them to believe. A widely circulated quote in the Street crowd was, "Mr. Morgan speaks to Mr. Lamont and Mr. Lamont speaks to the people." From God's mouth to Lamont's ears, or vice-versa.

But during the notorious 1929 Crash, Lamont was on his own—Morgan was overseas. Keeping his head, as he always did, Lamont persuaded the public to keep calm—if only for a few hours. Using his greatest gift, his power of persuasion, Lamont reassured the public, telling his press buddies, "There has been a little distress selling on the Stock Exchange." He attributed the "distress" not to the economy, but to "a technical condition of the market." That was the understatement of the year—but enough for the moment. Lamont was at his most persuasive when he dealt in understatement and left the listener to wonder about the magnitude of the understatement. But after walking softly, Lamont needed a big stick.

So, he organized a syndicate, pooling $240 million from Morgan and other top New York bankers to support stocks and stabilize prices—much in the same way Morgan Sr. had bailed out America in the 1907 Panic. The market actually rallied based solely on his reassuring words! When the House of Morgan spoke, everybody listened, and it spoke through Lamont.

But the panic was bigger than the pool, bigger than 1907 and bigger than the House of Morgan—and words can only do so much. The pool's funds quickly dwindled, along with $25 billion in paper value. Later, when the situation was obviously beyond anyone's grasp. Lamont defended his attempts to calm the market, saying his "banking consortium brought about some order out of chaos and its modest operations served to calm a frightened public." That much was true—he had done his best, but in this situation, anyone's best wasn't good enough. Lamont had not been able to size up the situation as correctly as it had unfolded for the senior Morgan 22 years earlier. He wasn't an analyst the way the House's founder was. Had Lamont had that capability, he wouldn't have thrown good money after bad. Lamont was a salesman, a PR guy and all image—again, a little like the 1920s.

A director of U.S. Steel and various railroads, Lamont came to Morgan in 1911. Born in 1870 outside of Albany, New York, he was the son of a poor Methodist minister, and attended a posh prep school and Harvard via scholarships. Out of college, he became a reporter, then, when he felt business offered a better future, he reorganized a food brokerage firm, catching the eye of prominent Morgan partner Henry P. Davison. With this connection, it was only a matter of time before Lamont trained at the First National Bank of New York, then went to the House of Morgan at 40 in 1911. In a good-old-boys' network, 40 was still young. Today Wall Street is a much younger man's game.

Destined for the spokesperson's chair at Morgan, Lamont's diplomatic appeal saw him appointed negotiator of international loans. He organized the massive $500 million Anglo-French loan in 1915, and when America entered World War I, he served on the U.S. Liberty Loan Committee to help sell treasury bonds.

Between 1919 and 1933, Lamont remained the key figure in negotiating some $2 billion in foreign securities and floating them to the public. For instance, in 1920 he went to Japan as part of an international syndicate organized to help China finance development. Over the next few years, Lamont acted as a sort of diplomatic emissary—settling Mexico's debt, arranging a $100 million recovery loan for Austria, stabilizing the French economy and meeting with Mussolini to arrange a small loan. Lamont was ready and willing with a reassuring smile.

Despite his rigorous schedule, Lamont kept up with his writing, publishing several books and magazine articles, supporting a literary review, and purchasing the *New York Evening Post* in 1918 only to sell it four years later at a million-dollar loss. Despite his career and literary ambitions, Lamont married at 25 and raised three sons and a daughter. His son, Thomas S. Lamont, later tugged on his father's coattails, graduating from Harvard, then joining Morgan at 23 and making partner at 30.

As he grew older and became stooped—losing some of his spectacular appeal—Lamont, as usual, kept his head and good image even while scandal toyed with his spotless reputation. Because of the House of Morgan's clubby nature, Lamont had kept his mouth shut when his partner, George Whitney, came to him in 1937 for a million-dollar loan. When Lamont asked, Whitney told him the money was needed to buy back and cover up securities his brother, **Richard Whitney**, had misappropriated from "some customer." The "customer" was actually the New York Stock Exchange, of which Whitney's brother was president!

On the witness stand during an investigation a year later—as Richard Whitney's case went from bad to worse—SEC investigators slapped Lamont's hands for not telling them about the reason for the loan. Lamont said he believed his partner when he was told it was a one-time, isolated incident. The Wall Street club was like that. So, Lamont's reputation was far from tarnished—in fact, it was so dipped with gold that it was virtually impossible to tarnish. He was at the center of the closed-door and leather chair club—a no-questions-asked world.

When Morgan died in 1943, Lamont took over as chairman of the board. Being the first to follow in the chair of the senior and junior Morgan, by itself, would be sufficient to insure Lamont a position in financial history, but he played a more pivotal swing role. Decades of earlier financiers played the creative role that first built Wall Street. They pioneered means of financing: reorganizations, mergers, takeovers, raids, stock-watering and all the transaction and management oriented events you read about in the biographies of late 19th century and early 20th century Wall Streeters.

Lamont was a salesman and marketer—a man of image and style—who took a relatively mature but rough Wall Street "product line" and smooth-sold it to a world who felt reassured by his suave demeanor. Lamont was a man for his times. The unrealistic 1920s boom could not have been carried to the extremes it was had Lamont and men following his image not provided mid-America the reassurances that let them do crazy things. Lamont probably never saw this aspect in himself. He himself probably never saw the differences between substance and style that would have been so obvious to old **J.P.Morgan**.

Between 1920 and 1950, Wall Street changed from a world where ideas for deals and their tactical execution were the most important thing to a world; where selling became the most important aspect. Just as this world saw the old line firms fade, and the emergence of Merrill Lynch because it sold confidence to mid-America, it was a world that was steered by and modeled itself after the unflappable sales and image of Thomas Lamont. He in many ways blurred for all times the lines on Wall Street between substance and style. The significance of Lamont is that, when he died in 1948, he was followed by an entire era of an emerging national sales force on Wall Street, one that was largely modeled after him and his image. Since 1975 the brokerage world has changed from Lamont's model, heavily impacted by May-Day and its commission discounting and everything that flowed from it. But being the model for a quarter century of brokers is more than enough of a contribution to include him among the *100 Minds That Made The Market.*

CLARENCE D. DILLON

HE CHALLENGED TRADITION AND SYMBOLIZED THE CHANGING WORLD

In 1925, investment banker Clarence Dillon handed a $137.5 million check over to the owners of Dodge Brothers Automobile Company, buying the firm "lock, stock, and barrel." A picture of the check made front page in most papers across the nation and to most, it signified one of the largest cash deals ever consummated. But to Wall Street, the check signified much more than a cash deal; it represented Dillon's victory in a bidding war with J.P. Morgan & Company, an opponent no one in his right mind would have contemplated taking on in the past. To Wall Street, Dillon's check was a premonition of what was to come in the near future: a new Wall Street, one without absolute monarchy—and one with competition.

"The greatest thing in business, large or small, is competition. The element of keen competition, which is that intangible zest, the very essence of alert life, must be preserved in big operations, even if there is need of constant watchfulness to prevent machine-like, impersonal administration," said the head of Dillon, Read & Company about a year after his victory. He was talking of the corporate mergers that prevailed on Wall Street in the early 1900s, but perhaps on another level, he was talking about the big picture—one ruled by J.P. Morgan & Company, where room for new underwriters was non-existent—and how he had changed it.

Born in 1882 in San Antonio, Texas, Dillon was the son of a Polish merchant-banker. He received a good Eastern education and went on to earn an A.B. from Harvard in 1905 at 23. He changed his name from Lapowski to Dillon and headed into the business world, managing the Newport Mining Company with a classmate for a few years. After a two-year travel spree ending in 1910, Dillon acquired a half interest in the Milwaukee Machine Tool Company, became president, shaped up the firm, then sold it. In 1912, he entered the Chicago branch of William A. Read & Company, a moderate-sized New York investment banking house. Two years later he transferred to their main branch and in 1916, was made partner the same day Read was struck with a fatal illness that killed him six days later.

As head of what became Dillon, Read & Company, until his retirement in 1938, Dillon carved his niche in Wall Street by generally being conservative and cautious, considering only one deal in 10 and actually undertaking one in five. A Harvard classmate once said of him, "If Clarence Dillon wanted to buy a cow, he would read up everything on cows and before he closed the deal, he would know more about the animal than the farmer himself." And if a partner objected or expressed indescribable uneasiness about a deal, he dropped it like a hot potato in a fury of superstition.

In the early 1920s, the opportunist found a wide-open niche financing European businesses like public utilities and railroads. In 1922 he said, "Our opportunity lies in industrial Europe, and I might say that all Europe looks to us for help in this direction ... We will lend, but we will lend with care." Sounds like the exact reverse of what happened 50 to 80 years earlier when capital had been flowing into the U.S. from Europe with care—a sure sign of America's emergence in the 1920s as the dominant world power for the first time.

Dillon also specialized in loaning to foreign governments like Germany, Poland, France, and Brazil—and even gobbled up the royal Rothschild's slice of a $50 million Brazilian loan while they slumbered in drawn-out negotiations! A buck was a buck, and wherever Dillon found one, he grabbed it.

What enabled Dillon to even enter the same bidding room as Morgan in 1925 was his 1921 coup with Goodyear Tire and Rubber Company. With quick talking and quick fundraising—$100 million, to be exact—he bailed Goodyear out of receivership by negotiating settlements with its bankers, creditors, and stockholders.

The Goodyear deal landed him in the big leagues, but the Dodge deal left him in a league by himself—Wall Street underdog. His name and firm were on the tip of Wall Street's tongue. The *New York Times* even referred to him as the man "who outbid Morgan & Co. for Dodge Co." Business flowed in easily after that. In 1926, he was chosen to finance National Register's first public offering of 1.1 million common shares, the largest such offering then on record. It was completely sold out within a few hours!

Despite a few difficulties during the Crash, in which Dillon, Read's two investment trusts (totaling $90 million) took a great nose-dive, and a few more difficulties following the Crash, like the probing U.S. Senate Committee on Banking and Currency hearings, Dillon was able to keep the firm in the family. His son, C. Douglas Dillon, born in 1909, joined the firm after graduating from Harvard in 1931. He eventually became chairman of the board following service in World War II—and before serving as Secretary of the Treasury from 1961 to 1965.

Reserved, calm and courteous, Dillon was thin, handsome and well-dressed. Married in 1908, he was a well-rounded businessman. He bought a Bordeaux vineyard in 1934, served for 10 years as a trustee for Virginia's Foxcraft School, bred Guernsey cattle and poodles, dropped everything on Sundays for prayer, went fishing with his son, and loved photography, travel, reading, and music. A director of Chase National Bank, Central Hanover Bank, Dodge, National Cash Register Company, and Brazilian Traction, he died in 1979 at age 96 in Far Hills, New Jersey.

Dillon represented a changing of the guard. Tradition would not have allowed anyone to take on J.P. Morgan & Company and survive. Few would have had the gall to try, and **J.P. Morgan** would have had the power to crush the few. But times changed. First, it wasn't old J.P. Morgan anymore but his son. Second, America wasn't a wild and woolly pioneer country moving through the industrial revolution anymore; it was a world power—not yet fully recognized as such, but fully empowered and industrialized and financially sophisticated nonetheless. So, the playing field among financiers was more "level" than in the emerging earlier era when Morgan was absolute. Third, the 1920s was a time for risk-taking, and Dillon was the one ready to take the risk—challenging J.P. Morgan & Company. He felt no negative repercussions from it—rather he benefited from the notoriety.

In many ways, as a conservative investment banker who at the same time was risk-oriented enough to confront the source of traditional Wall Street power, Dillon was the personification of the changing of the guard on Wall Street to the new and modern era that would evolve in the '30s and '40s.

National Clyclopedia of American Biography

CHARLES E. MERRILL

THE THUNDERING HERD RUNS AMOK IN THE AISLES OF THE STOCK MARKET'S SUPERMARKET

Charles Merrill brought Wall Street to Main Street, urging the small investor with a spare thousand or two to invest in America's economy. While that wasn't the most original idea on Wall Street in the 1940s, Merrill was the first to do it on such a grand scale with such long-term success. When he knew he'd succeeded, Merrill rejoiced, "America's industrial machine is owned at the grass roots, where it should be, and not in some mythical Wall Street!"

Merrill tried out his idea during and after World War II, after already making his fortune in investment banking. He embarked on a huge, innovative publicity campaign with the purpose of courting the ordinary citizen, promoting the slogan "Bring Wall Street to Main Street." He advertised securities, printing easy-to-understand, full-page guides to investing in national newspapers. These guides brought in about 1,000 responses per day—and an army of small investors barraged the offices of Merrill, Lynch and Company. Still, in 1955, refusing to let up, Merrill and his firm held a "How to Invest Show" in Manhattan.

At the same time, Merrill revolutionized the inner machinations of the brokerage business, innovating by offering salesmen salaries instead of commissions and initiating a sales training program that was quickly adopted by other Wall Street brokers. He eliminated service charges, formed a company magazine, *Investor's Reader*, and became the first in the business to make full disclosures via annual reports of the firm's operations, holdings and investments of its partners. The results were phenomenal—by 1956, when Merrill died, his firm's active customer accounts numbered 300,000, and its assets peaked $500 million! The massive organization was the largest securities broker on every exchange; the largest over-the-counter dealer; the largest commission broker in every commodities futures market; and the fifth largest underwriter of corporate securities. Best of all, for him, Merrill had a 25 percent stake in the firm!

Born in 1885 the son of a Florida country doctor and pharmacy owner, Merrill started modestly, waiting tables while attending Amherst College in Massachusetts. He quit college after two years to edit a small-town Florida paper, then play semi-professional baseball. Eventually, he joined a Wall Street commercial paper house and was quickly promoted to head its new bond department.

A real go-getter, Merrill set up his own firm on Wall Street by 29 and later hooked up with bond salesman Edmund C. Lynch. Their underwriting and investment banking firm took off after they underwrote McCrory chain stores. By the 1920s, the firm's underwriting and brokerage business had expanded rapidly, and they were regarded as experts in their fields. Merrill Lynch customers included Western Auto Supply, Grand Union and other chains, but their biggest success was Safeway Stores. By 1953, Safeway was America's second largest food chain—and for some time, Merrill was its largest stockholder. As a sideline and pure money-winner, he launched the successful *Family Circle* magazine to be distributed in Safeways.

While other brokers were wrapped up in the great bull market of the 1920s, Merrill anticipated the 1929 Crash. In his company newsletter, he cautioned his customers to get out of debt. "We recommend that you sell enough securities to lighten your obligations, or better yet, pay them entirely." His foresight saved his customers an estimated $6 million! But depressed by a sagging stock market and the sorry state of the industry, Merrill got out of the brokerage business in 1930, turning accounts over to E. A. Pierce and Co. in order to concentrate on underwriting and individual banking.

In 1941 he returned to brokerage after his partner Lynch died, merging with other firms to form Merrill, Lynch, Pierce, Fenner and Beane. From the start, this was the largest brokerage house in the world with 71 partners in 93 cities—the perfect vehicle with which to try out his Main Street ideas. By 1956, after putting his ideas to the test, the firm had 104 partners in 110 cities and handled 10 percent of all trading on the New York Stock Exchange floor! *Time* considered Merrill Lynch, ironically, "a supermarket of finance."

Surprisingly, Merrill's success came despite a busy social life and even busier family life. A member of the international cafe society and avid tennis, golf, and bridge player, Merrill married and divorced three times.

Fathering one daughter and two sons, he married in 1912, 1925, and again in 1939 at age 54—divorcing a final time four years before dying from heart problems. Flashy, owning three luxury homes, Merrill loved champagne, good food, and obviously, women—but oddly enough, he left 95 percent of his $25 million estate to charity, setting up trusts for hospitals, churches, and colleges.

Charles Merrill filled an important role in the evolution of modern finance. Long before the industrial revolution, Adam Smith told us that capitalism would enrich everyone, of all classes, based on individual capability. In the 19th century, it looked as if capitalism might mainly enrich a small part of society and that Wall Street would reward only a small elite group of wheeler-dealers. But Charles Merrill arrived at a time when the little man in America (but not yet the little woman) would flourish into a thriving middle class. Passed by in the Roaring '20s, passed by in the Great Depression, and passed by during World War II, the middle class exploded on the American scene in the postwar environment. And Merrill was already there, pitching to the little guy to offer him the means to amass financial security. His approach to the common man was aided by the tremendous bull market that ran virtually non-stop from the late 1940s through 1965. And because of him and his philosophy and the bull market a lot of little people could retire in more comfort than their tougher and earlier lives could have allowed them to imagine possible. He truly brought Wall Street to Main Street in a fashion that has lived on for decades after him.

Dunn's Review, 1969

GERALD M. LOEB

THE FATHER OF FROTH—HE KNEW
THE LINGO, NOT THE LOGIC

There's nothing like drumming up business with a little advertising—that's exactly what E.F. Hutton was doing when it promoted its mouthpiece-broker, Gerald Loeb, during the 1950s. Loeb, whom *Forbes* once tagged "the most quoted man on Wall Street," became synonymous with the Hutton brokerage firm—and, not coincidentally, a flamboyant method of trading that generated brokerage commissions. Meanwhile, his visibility in the press was, as it often is, mistaken for respectability. To this day, years after his death in 1974, Loeb is remembered as one of the great brokers of that era. But the bottom line is this: he knew how to turn a phrase. Stripped of his catchy one-liners, provocative lingo, and superficial prose, what you're left with is a shrewd marketer who knew how to cajole the inexperienced investor and make a commission off it.

Loeb came along at the right time. The San Francisco native surfaced when Wall Street needed a lift, a new style—perhaps a mentor, someone they could trust. The 1930s had brought a clamp-down via strict legislation and the Securities and Exchange Commission (SEC). People were wary of investing in the volatile, post-Crash stock market, and public relations was in a shambles. Enter: Loeb. He had been selling bonds since he was about 20 and was known for his wide-eyed honesty. He made it well known that he quit his first job as bond salesman when he was told to push a bond he didn't believe in; the same went for his second job. He was on the side of the little people!

He soon found solace working for the venerable E.F. Hutton, and moved to the New York branch in 1924. After pushing up his sleeves and getting down to business, he was made partner five years later at the remarkable age of 30. Nobody was made partner in a major Wall Street firm in those days unless he could sell like hell—proof that Loeb could and did. His PR line, like that of many others of his day, was that he saw the crowd psychology and got out before the 1929 Crash when he found himself listening to the zany hot tips that filled the streets. He packaged himself as the perfect candidate to restore Main Street's faith in Wall Street. He did it well.

Reporters loved Loeb, as he lavished them with catchy quotes, news bits, and newsworthy speeches to groups like the Federation of Women Shareholders in American Business and the Bull & Bear Club of Harvard University Law School. But what secured his name in Wall Street history and skyrocketed him to fame was his 1935 mass-appeal book, *The Battle for Investment Survival.* The first edition—with a dozen printings and selling over 250,000 copies—contained 33 short, spunky, and intellectually-lacking chapters in 153 pages, such as: "It Requires Knowledge, Experience and Flair," "Speculation vs. Investment," "Pitfalls for the Inexperienced," and "You Can't Forecast, But You Can Make Money." Easy to read, superficial, intellectually inconsistent within itself, but fun, Loeb's book was what Loeb was all about—a lure to attract investors to him and to E.F. Hutton.

At a time when sure and steady value investing was gaining ground from **Benjamin Graham**'s 1934 work, *Security Analysis,* Loeb's philosophy seemed like a radical, refreshing approach to the market. In this self-appreciating book, which he pushed through a direct-mail marketing program after Dow Jones Publishers failed to unload enough copies, he advocated simple steps to speculating that promised spectacular results. "I say there isn't a good investment that isn't at the same time a good speculation." He urged his readers: "Detach yourself from the crowd;" don't look for small gains; "With the right issue, you should be able to double your money;" be careful not to over-diversify; and never hesitate to cut losses by selling the stock.

Selling stock was Loeb's favorite point. He advocated cashing in "some chips" each year and always having cash ready in case of an irresistible opportunity. Cutting your losses by selling a stock was a given, he said in a famous phrase, because "stocks were made to be sold." Selling and buying stocks at the drop of a hat were not just "advantageous" to the investor who didn't know any better, but they brought brokers—like those at his firm, E.F. Hutton—greater brokerage commissions. Loeb was simply taking care of his own. In fact, all of Loeb's philosophy was not just coincidentally parallel to that which generates high portfolio turnover and commissions on an account. What Loeb was selling to the mass market was good for him and brokers as a whole. Other brokers pushed his stuff in a circle where he promoted brokerage and brokers promoted him.

In case anyone was wary of brokers, Loeb did a meticulous job boosting their reputation. He helped transform the role of the broker into that of a professional, declaring they should not only study market trends and research company data, but become experts on taxation, real-estate, and insurance. How could you tell a good broker from a bad one? Simply look for these qualities: 100 percent honesty, a real code of ethics, genius, a flexible mind, appreciation of risks—not overly confident, unbiased, and unfettered, "on the ball" and the market must be his "first love." The reality was that most brokers, at Hutton or elsewhere, were salesmen, pure and simple—but Loeb helped romanticize them.

Born to a French wine merchant and an unlucky gold miner's daughter who both went broke during the 1906 earthquake, Loeb was eager, energetic and immodest. He looked like an egghead, with a perfectly round bald head, black-framed glasses and short, stubby hands and fingers. He married late in life in 1946 and had no children; instead he opted for the charity route to give him that well-rounded, caring appearance. He served the New York March of Dimes, Arthritis and Rheumatism Foundation, and created the Sidney S. Loeb Memorial Foundation in memory of his brother. All of his connections probably also promoted and reinforced his brokerage activities. His hobbies included photography, automobiles, and architecture. He wrote two more books in his time—*The Battle for Stock Market Profits* and *Checklist for Buying Stocks.* Neither is particularly worthy of your time. Nor do they have investment lore you can't easily find elsewhere.

But everyone was caught up in Loeb's gig—even he believed in his importance and how much others viewed him as important.

I remember one day, about 1972, when he invited my Dad, Phil Fisher, in summons-like fashion to lunch in San Francisco. My old man, then 65, was still just about the biggest name in the local investment community, then quite provincial. On a national level, Loeb was much more widely known then. Going into the lunch, my father was a bit apprehensive about what they would discuss since they had little in common, personally, professionally or philosophically. The early chit-chat carefully bypassed any deep or meaningful market discussion, and soon my father wondered why Loeb had concocted this contrived event. Suddenly, Loeb got to the point, laying it on the line—"Phil, who do you think are the best but largely unknown CEOs running new growth companies down the Peninsula?" My old man was a bit aghast, and for the life of him couldn't see a reason why he should share with Loeb the names of stocks he had worked hard to unearth. Loeb, of course, could publicize them and drive the stocks up, and couldn't naturally perceive why my father might not want to share such information with the great Mr. Loeb. But Phil Fisher was never interested in promoting his stocks and mainly preferred to keep them secret, figuring he could buy more later when he had more money and that the prices would take care of themselves. "Let's just get this lunch over with," was Dad's thought, and he changed the subject abruptly, and perhaps rudely. At the time I found it strange and small of my father. Loeb was, after all, a big name, and my father's few golden nuggets couldn't be all that important I thought. As the years passed, it became clearer to me, however, that Loeb's real investment contributions were negligible, whereas my father's, while capturing far less ink in their day, were fundamental and enduring.

In the test of time, a fundamental thinker's work may endure, but a PR machine like Loeb will quickly fade. The reason Loeb is important to the evolution of financial markets is that he was the 20th century's pre-eminent PR hog, and from him comes the important lesson that despite all the ink that was spilled around this man, there is no real contribution there of enduring value. As you look at the markets and what is said about them, it is always important to separate what is fundamental and new, or for that matter fundamental and old, from the kind of superficial sales-driven froth that Loeb and a nonstop stream of PR hogs ever since have delivered. Loeb was the personification of the saying that "you can't believe everything you read."

SIDNEY WEINBERG

THE ROLE MODEL FOR MODERN
INVESTMENT BANKERS

Sidney Weinberg, or "Mr. Wall Street," was a living institution on Wall Street for some 40 years. By the end of his 62-year career at Goldman Sachs, people visiting the firm would be escorted right by his office to see him at work as a special treat. His death in 1969 at age 77 even made the front page of the *New York Times* —quite an accomplishment for an investment banker. But shrewd corporate financing deals alone don't land a larger-than-life reputation on Wall Street—in Weinberg's case, it was his quirky, no-nonsense personality and fierce sense of duty. Serving a myriad of boards of directors, Weinberg mixed business with pleasure and business with politics, and before he knew it, a new Wall Street etiquette was born. In many ways he was the first of the modern investment bankers, combining shrewd finance with schmoozing, salesmanship, politics, humor, creativity, and trustworthiness. He is the model that many others have molded themselves after since the 1950s

Weinberg was Goldman, Sachs' lucky charm. He was touted as the best in corporate finance, his most notable deals including a 1956 sale of $650 million in Ford Motor stock for the Ford Foundation, then Wall Street's largest corporate financing project. Two years later, he pulled off another landmark deal, underwriting $350 million of Sears, Roebuck debentures in a market that was so soggy people doubted whether the debentures could be marketed at all. Weinberg pegged the market's mood and offered the debentures at a price yielding 4.75 percent, slightly above comparable offerings.

But brilliant financing has been done before and will be done again. He rose above the rest of the investment bankers with his personality and hard work, serving as many as 31 corporate boards at a single time. Unlike those who used the director's seat as a status symbol, Weinberg popularized the role of the working director. "The day of the stuffed-shirt director is over. Unless a man takes it as semi-public service, he shouldn't take on the assignment at all." He demanded that management circulate agendas and materials for directors to study beforehand and in 1933, laid out his "Ten Commandments" for directors. In his commandments, he required monthly meetings at a fixed spot; outside auditors' reports; data on sales, profits, and balance sheet changes; responsibility for corporate loans to officers, directors, and stockholders; and responsibility, along with stockholders, for agreeing on profit-sharing plans, among other rules now seen as commonplace.

Weinberg became an advocate for a responsible directorship after serving on McKesson & Robbins' board when its president, F. Donald Coster, defrauded the firm of $21 million and then killed himself. He always felt guilty for not having paid enough attention to see the scandal coming. That mistake cost the board a $600,000 "gift" to avoid possible litigation— $70,000 from Weinberg alone. "Boy, that was a lesson!" Afterwards, he always did his homework and was known as such a fair and conscientious director that requests for his presence on a board were received about once each week.

The "director's director" was fiercely—almost fanatically—loyal to the boards he served, which over the years included Ford Motors, Champion Paper, General Electric, General Foods (33 years), and Sears, Roebuck (23 years). Once, while a General Foods board member, he was served cheese other than Kraft. "Take it away!," he yelled to the waiter. "I won't eat it! Get Kraft!" The modest Scarsdale, New York house, where he and his wife raised their two sons, looked like a Sears showroom—that is, before he left the Sears board to join the GE board! The only company he found hard fitting in to his lifestyle was Champion Paper, and eventually, he made sure the Goldman, Sachs office stocked up with Champion stationery!

Weinberg was one of the first to loosen the stiff conduct barrier in board rooms, always ready with a snide remark to lift the tension. During one meeting, when directors sat in a circle of couches in an attempt at being casual—which clearly wasn't working—comical Sidney pushed his pile of documents off his lap and onto the floor, then fell to the floor to pick them up. He cried in "despair," "What the hell kind of corporation is this? Can't even afford a table!" Another time, when a company officer began reading off an endless list of numbers in a legal formality, Weinberg leapt to his feet when he couldn't take it any more and cried, "Bingo!" He had a way in board meetings that might have horrified his colleagues had they come from any other person.

The president of a large firm once said, "Sidney is the only man I know who could ever say to me in the middle of a board meeting, as he did once, 'I don't think you're very bright,' and somehow give me the feeling that I'd been paid a compliment."

Clearly, Weinberg was a character, and one of his more celebrated talents was getting people together. The keeper of a 300-name Christmas list that read like a volume of *Who's Who in American Industry*, he made schmoozing with fellow corporate captains common practice "because I put friendship first." Friendly and outspoken, he was said to be a mover who "got other people moving," according to another Goldman partner. He freely mixed business with pleasure—even going sailing with Boston investor **Paul Cabot**, though Weinberg was a landlubber who couldn't swim!

Weinberg basically institutionalized his network of friends in 1933 when he and Joseph Davies started the Business Council for President Franklin D. Roosevelt. It was his way of gathering some 60 of his closest contacts to make their views known to his other obsession, the government. In the following years, Weinberg matched dozens of friends with political posts in Washington—President Johnson asked him to recommend a few good men for his cabinet. By 1958, he was known as a one-man employment agency and a businessman's ticket to the capital. "There is a guy waiting outside right now," he said during an interview that year, "who is president of a multi-million dollar company. He's thinking of leaving and wants to know if I've heard of anything for him."

"Government service is the highest form of citizenship," Weinberg felt. "Men are better citizens for having served their country and community." The Brooklyn native's political involvement began in 1932 when he supported President Roosevelt's election. Years later, after fund-raising during World War II and Korea, Weinberg schmoozed with his fifth president, Lyndon Johnson. Considering himself "an independent Democrat and practical liberal," Weinberg was nicknamed "The Politician" by Roosevelt and was offered the ambassadorship to Russia, but declined. "I don't speak Russian—who the hell could I talk to over there?"

Looking a lot like a well-dressed kewpie doll standing only 5 foot 4 with rounded spectacles, Weinberg took the subway to work and was considered frugal. For recreation, he played tennis, handball, and golf. Occasionally, Weinberg would grab a few close friends and head for a Turkish bath, saying, "It's better than going someplace and drinking." At times he "went on the wagon" which implies that at other times he may have boozed too much.

Married twice—once in 1920 and again in 1968 (a year after his first wife died, to a photographer 30 years his junior)—Weinberg was proud of his family. He had two sons, each of whom followed in his footsteps: one became a Goldman, Sachs partner; the other, an Owens-Corning Fiberglas executive. Weinberg himself had come from a large family, one of 11 children born in the Red Hook section of Brooklyn to a struggling wholesale liquor dealer in 1891.

With only an eighth-grade education, of which he was very proud, he began his business career at 15 making as much as $10 per day by standing in line for depositors during the 1907 Panic. Next, he went to a Wall Street skyscraper, and, working his way from top to bottom, knocked on every office door asking for a job until he reached the Goldman Sachs office, where he was hired—as an assistant porter! Years later, Weinberg claimed that the well-polished brass spittoon displayed in his office was the one he polished as his very first task at Goldman Sachs. Weinberg made partner in 1927 ahead of others senior to him, he said, because of his personality, hard work, good health, integrity, character and an eagerness to go above and beyond what was required—his personal formula for success. It was a formula that would become standard for investment bankers from his time until the present. He was the role model for modern day investment bankers and, in that sense, played a key role in how modern day corporate finance evolved.

CHAPTER FOUR

THE INNOVATORS

SPECIALISTS WITH NEW IDEAS—WHAT MAKES AMERICA GREAT

The evolution of American capital markets has been a series of innovations, the product of more minds than could ever be recounted in a single book. It all started with a small group consisting of the Dinosaurs, which boldly staggered through unknown lands to make way for civilization and thus, future innovation. The Dinosaurs led America's agriculture-based economy into an industrial one. With every step they took, they set up the beginnings of a growing set of rules by which we operate today. For better or for worse, the Dinosaurs left a definable structure for future generations to improve upon and manipulate to their advantage. Which gets us to the Innovators.

The Innovators started working on the market system in the late 1800s. Wall Street was coarsely defined, and they set out to refine it. Most of the innovations were the result of personal ambitions, although a few of the more modern innovations evolved out of more community-minded efforts. Because of the Innovators mentioned in this section, the financial community has specialty stock exchanges, holding companies, access to market statistics, venture capital resources, conglomerates, and puts and calls.

The Innovators moved into a field of specialization, innovating whatever was at hand. "Lucky" Baldwin, for example, went to work on local finance, creating a specialty stock exchange decades after Dinosaurs such as Nathan Rothschild, George Peabody, and Junius Morgan strove to bring any dollar they could to America!

Lucky didn't like what he saw in San Francisco in terms of the stock exchange. He needed more money, quickly, to finance the booming mining industry in California. He achieved this by simply bucking the existing system and forming his own exchange. Though it didn't last forever and, in fact, was eventually merged with the very one he sought to rival, Lucky Baldwin impressed upon the financial community the need for regional funding that could readily be had through local, specialty stock exchanges.

General Georges Doriot innovated by offering America's first venture capital firm, purely dedicated to bringing new technology from the drawing table to market. Since Doriot's innovation, others have further refined venture capital, introducing specialized forms dedicated to individual industries and technologies. By the end of his lifetime, this widely regarded "Father of Venture Capital" was saddened to see venture capitalists using his ideas simply to make a buck for themselves and-to-hell-with the cause of furthering technology. Doriot would be further saddened today to see the twists that cause many venture capitalists to be labeled vulture capitalists. But that's only to be expected. Once you lay your idea on the line, anything can happen to it.

Innovations weren't always for the better—especially when they were concocted for reasons of greed. For instance, the last of the robber barons, Thomas Fortune Ryan, created the first holding company, which was later used to build unstable, corrupt empires in the 1920's public utilities industry. Charles Yerkes also offered a sort of double-edged innovation. He wed politics—corrupt politics—to business, gaining monopolies in streetcar railways by bribing city officials. Russell Sage, the brilliant market manipulator, was similarly greed-driven. He fathered puts and calls, originally to manipulate stocks and further his own profits as much as possible. Yet today, puts and calls, and subsequent specialty derivatives are a standard and almost indispensable part of the financial landscape.

Roger Babson probably also had his own future in mind when he innovated the market statistics and analysis industry. But motives aside, Babson pioneered newsletters and opened up an entire field of retail statistical information.

T. Rowe Price and Paul Cabot gave investors new ways of looking at and playing the stock market. Price was one of the early growth investors, picking sleeping giants like IBM as early as the 1930s, until they swelled into blue chips in the 1950s. Paul Cabot presented common stocks to provincial investors as an alternative form of conservative investing. Before his innovation, Wall Street was off-limits to an entire market of stodgy Bostonians. Cabot helped tap this market.

Finally, there are the corporate innovators who gave Wall Street new ways to build companies. Royal Little fathered conglomerates in the 1950s and '60s. Floyd Odlum built his empire in the 1930s, '40s and '50s via corporate raiding. Odium's was an innocent enough innovation, but like the game in which you repeat a sentence from person to person, when the 12th person repeats what he thought had been the original sentence...the first person could hardly recognize it.

Of course, these weren't the only men in this book who were innovators. J.P. Morgan was an innovator in many areas—for example, using Wall Street to create trust-based monopolies, but J.P. Morgan was much more than that. Jay Gould was an innovator of sorts—as the first to buy beat-up companies for cheap, fix them up and sell them back to the market at fancy prices. But he too was much more than that. Was not Joe Kennedy, as the first head of the SEC a form of innovator? Well, sort of; and you could say about the same of dozens of the minds represented in these pages. But the men in this section stand out for their innovations above and beyond all else. Were it not for their innovations they wouldn't be in this book, whereas Morgan, Gould. Kennedy and others would have been anyway. And yet their contribution was as great or sometimes greater.

Would the world rather have T. Rowe Price's growth stocks as a philosophy from which to operate, or the SEC? I'd vote for the stocks. Would the world now miss as much if Gould had never lived, as it would have without the introduction of venture capital? Again, I think we appreciate today the fruits of the pure innovator more than we commonly note.

More innovations have evolved since these men made their market impact. Yet today, things happen so fast that it's often hard to associate the innovator with the innovation. Who was the first to try his hand at discount brokering? No! It wasn't Charles Schwab; he was just the most successful at it. Who developed "primes" and "scores" and "program trading?" I don't know, and regardless, who did it matters much less than it used to when the innovations were giant steps away from the norm. Today everything moves so fast that we accept innovation as the norm rather than the exception. But that was never true in the world in which these innovators did their pioneering. Without their contributions, Wall Street would have evolved more slowly and differently than it did.

ELIAS JACKSON "LUCKY" BALDWIN

WHEN YOU'RE LUCKY, YOU CAN GO YOUR OWN WAY

When mining surpassed the pan-and-pick days and emerged into a laborious, capital-intensive process, mining stocks became all the rage out West. Thousands of mining stock exchanges attracted the cash that hired the men and bought the gear that unearthed the precious ore. Each time they struck ore, speculative frenzy ensued; everyone wanted in on the action—greedy crooks selling shares in nonexistent mines, hopeful clerks putting paychecks on the line and daredevil speculators risking their fortunes for a long shot. And the action was easy to find, as tiny ramshackle stock exchanges sprouted wherever ore surfaced—St. Paul, Missouri; Creede, Colorado; Laramie, Wyoming; even Eau Claire, Wisconsin—and died when the mines did. But not at first!

One of the earliest alternative mining exchanges was the San Francisco-based Pacific Stock Exchange, formed in 1875 by E.J. "Lucky" Baldwin. Ever the character, Baldwin exemplified the hot-headed, rough-and-tumble, won't-take-no-for-an-answer, shoot-from-the-hip California pioneer, speculator, womanizer, and everything else he could possibly be back then. But he was also important to American finance as our best representation of the specialty exchange creator who built a financial mechanism capable of drawing money from the east to the mines of the west where it could do productive "Main Street"-like work in places where there weren't any streets at all.

Anything but modest, he once told H.H. Bancroft in a turn-of-the-century interview, "Do you know, sir, I think I have done more for California, and am doing now more than any three hundred men it!" As a leading role model, in some ways, he did.

How he got around to starting a stock exchange was typical of Lucky. The story went like this: Being one of San Francisco's biggest speculators and, therefore, a member of the exclusive California Stock and Exchange Board, Lucky used to breeze in and out of the exchange every day to check his unpredictable mining stocks. One day, however, a new ore discovery prompted hordes of "outsiders" to try sneaking into the exchange to buy the profitable mines. So, new security measures required members to actually show their membership cards at the door to prevent non-members from gaining entrance. It just so happened that on that day, Lucky forgot his card—usually, he never needed it. But despite his don't-you-know-who-I-am routine, bureaucracy prevailed, and Baldwin was denied entrance to the exchange. The gall of them!

"By gad, I ain't been licked," Lucky said on more than one occasion. Aggravated and ticked off, to say the least, he vowed revenge—and it came in the form of the Pacific Stock Exchange (different from the present-day Pacific Coast Stock Exchange, formed in 1957). With a strong following among his former colleagues, he wooed more than 20 extremely prestigious local members away from the other exchange. Based on the prestige and power of the group he initially assembled, his exchange built momentum quickly, and rich mine promoters, successful operators and influential politicians scurried to join Lucky's new club, forking over the $5,000 fee and doubling membership.

In typical Baldwin style, he built a lavish, spacious Exchange headquarters complete with elegant mosaic floors and frescoes on the walls. If you're going to speculate, why not do it in style? After all, Lucky and his new clique felt they were giving "their full quota to the growth and development of the great mining interests of the coast" and were "helping most generously to extend the blessings of civilization into the wilderness."

As corny as it sounds, Baldwin wasn't too far off—he actually played a key role in transforming the West Coast from "wild frontier" to "civilized country" via a prosperous, competitive financial center. Back then, American money came from "back East." And Easterners were intrigued but afraid of the uncivilized west. In Lucky's time, transcontinental communication was only just starting as the first cross-country railroad and telegraph lines were completed. Cross-country finance was still years away—and mining couldn't wait that long.

By creating viable competition among the western mining exchanges. Baldwin brought to western mining finance a semblance of the benefits that competition accrues to any form of capitalistic endeavor—it attracted capital, kept things honest, built volume, kept prices competitive, and prevented the local "club" from taking excessive monopolistic advantage of whatever came out of the mines, reducing the risks that easterners who placed their money might be left "stuck with the shaft." On Lucky's heels was a phenomenal list of financiers who started exchanges in every two-bit town where ore was discovered. The lists of little mining exchanges in little towns—often two to a town—were truly staggering and almost incomprehensible. And this all brought mining finance to the mine, which brought the money, which bought the necessary labor and equipment to mine the ore, which built America into the most powerful country in the world.

By 1904, five years before his death, Lucky's Exchange was absorbed into the California Stock and Exchange Board, recombining it with the very entity it was created to escape. But by then it had accomplished its goal and role in the evolution of mining finance because the days of mining were essentially long gone in the California market.

Born in 1828, the son of an Ohio farmer-preacher, he was the oldest of five and grew up quickly. At 18 he married the neighboring farmer's daughter after winning $200 of honeymoon money at the racetrack. Baldwin settled down with his wife long enough to have a daughter and earn $2,000 as a horse trader. Then, at 25, he outfitted four wagons—two with brandy, tobacco, and tea to sell along the way—and headed into the Wild West at its wildest in 1853.

It took a certain type to want to settle in a relatively new land, but the Gold Rush was three years old and still booming, and packs of hungry wolves couldn't keep Lucky away any longer. Aggressive, energetic, bold, confident, and egotistical, he recalled, "You know, I think if a man is determined he can do anything; I was determined." Handsome even in his old age, with expressive features and mustache, a powerful gaze, standing 5 foot 10 and weighing 175 pounds, Baldwin did what it took to survive in San Francisco. He operated a grocery store, ran hotels, a stable and a saloon, built canal boats and when he reached San Francisco with his first wife, learned the brick-making trade and for four years provided the government with the bricks that built the Alcatraz fort—for a $2 million net profit.

A notorious gambler and womanizer (four wives, multiple simultaneous mistresses, and defendant in multiple "seduction" suits), Baldwin speculated and invested in real estate to turn a buck, and was one of the first ever to promote Southern California land. "I started with nothing, and I have been in every kind of business and succeeded in all. My greatest struggle was to get the first thousand dollars, not the first hundred," he said in 1892.

It's easy to see how a man like Baldwin despised the nickname "Lucky"— he felt there was nothing lucky about hard work and determination. Although there are several stories relating how he got his name, this one sounds as good as the next: Before sailing on a year-long journey on which he found his third wife, Baldwin told his brokers to sell off part of his substantial mine holdings. But when he sailed, his stocks were tucked away in his locked safe—and he mistakenly had the key in his pocket, so his brokers couldn't sell. Lucky for him—when he returned, the stocks he had wanted to sell but couldn't had risen to astronomical heights, making him about $5 million and "Lucky" overnight! We are all lucky that there were "Lucky" Baldwin and men that followed on his heels bringing finance to the local level when it was needed to build America's natural resource production.

National Cyclopedia of American Biography, 1907

CHARLES T. YERKES

HE TURNED POLITICS INTO
MONOPOLISTIC POWER

Charles Yerkes wasted neither time nor money while building his fortune. In 17 years, he seized Chicago's shoddy street railways, slapped a few surface improvements on them and sold them for millions in profits. When his victims discovered they'd been had, Yerkes revealed his secret with a laugh, "The secret of success in my business is to buy up old junk, fix it up a little, and unload it upon other fellows." That trick has resurfaced almost countless times on Wall Street. No one combined it with local power politics better than Yerkes. He was its master.

Born in Philadelphia in 1837, he started out quietly, opening his own brokerage firm at 22 and a banking house specializing in first-class bonds three years later. Financiers who start their own shops at such very young ages are usually extremely aggressive by nature, and Yerkes was no exception. At 29, he won himself a name in the financial community—and much of Philadelphia's bond business—by successfully selling a Philly bond issue at par value when the going rate was discounted by 65 percent.

But then Yerkes' luck soured—via the great Chicago fire of 1871, which not only ravaged Chicago, but wreaked havoc on the Philly stock exchange. Yerkes was caught overextended. So, when the City demanded its money from the sale of its city bonds, he came up empty-handed. Honest failure is never sufficient when politicians and the public are short-changed, and he who fails is always seen as a crook. Such was the case with Yerkes. He was sentenced to two years, four months on charges of embezzlement and served seven months before being pardoned.

Yerkes—with his soft-voice, pallid skin, and cold, dark eyes—was no ordinary ex-con. Crafty and ambitious, he emerged from prison just in time for the Panic of 1873. Having learned his lesson going long in the fire, he went short this time and cleared a cool million by covering his shorts as stock prices hit rock-bottom. Now he was prepared to shoot for the stars. But first he had to arrange his life in a fashion suitable for a wheeler-dealer. So, he dumped his wife and six kids to marry his long-time mistress, the daughter of a prominent Philly politician, and relocated to Chicago in 1882. Avoiding the stock market, he ambushed the "traction" industry and within four years controlled Chicago's north and west side streetcar lines.

Over the next 15 years, he expanded his empire by rebuilding existing lines, building an additional 500 miles of surface line, electrifying 240 miles of track and building the famous Chicago Loop (an elevated railway encircling the downtown area). His operations typically evolved around a tangled web of subsidiaries, construction companies, politicians and always watered stock. Whenever anyone was bold enough to challenge him by building an upstart streetcar line, Yerkes stayed cool until his prospective competitor had invested heavily in the venture—then he'd manipulate his competitor's stock, spreading damaging rumors on the stock exchange and initiating wild, far-fetched lawsuits. His competitors always succumbed.

The bigger Yerkes grew in Chicago, the less he did to accommodate the people who rode his lines. He ignored aging streetcar equipment and public convenience and safety, so that during the 1890s, Chicago newspapers overflowed with complaints about his system. His lines were notorious for filthy and unventilated streetcars, defective motors, frequent accidents, and double fares. When his shareholders questioned him about overcrowded cars, he snapped, "It is the straphangers that pay the dividends!" And although he controlled most of the city's lines in all directions, he refused to consolidate his holdings so that each separate branch of his system—within Chicago—could demand a separate fare! Yerkes was so indifferent to the public's safety that when pedestrians were struck by his streetcars, he made them sign release forms before being taken for treatment!

Calm and contemplative, Yerkes ignored his nasty reputation. Wearing a refined white mustache and expensive suits, he lived lushly, collecting art—including an Oriental rug collection surpassing the Shah of Persia's. He didn't care about anything except profits—and which woman he was wooing that night. Interestingly, now that he had married his former mistress, he found her boring and started a steady stream of love affairs.

Of course, mentioning City Hall would also raise one of Yerkes' well-manicured eyebrows—for politics was at the heart of his success. Yerkes' key technique in building his empire was political manipulation of City Hall, so that he could maintain a monopoly on the streetcar lines. Down that line, he needed to secure and control the public franchises for the use of city streets. Without the franchises., Yerkes' miles of track were worthless. He became a master at political corruption and legislative manipulation. City aldermen prospered under Yerkes' payoffs, and in turn, they voted him low-cost, short-term franchises and local laws advantageous to his system.

Yet Yerkes' blatant interference with politics ultimately led to his demise in Chicago. It all started when he became too greedy and secured a state bill renewing his franchises for a century without any payment to the city. Wher the aldermen prepared to vote to put the bill into effect in 1898, the city exploded with a grass-roots campaign against Yerkes. Reformers held mass meetings and marches against the pro-Yerkes legislation and against politicians who had voted for him in the past. The aldermen were warned that by voting in favor of Yerkes, they would in effect be committing political suicide.

On the night the bill came to a vote, City Hall was surrounded by thousands of protesters armed with guns and nooses, clearly signaling an end to Yerkes' reign. The angry crowd easily outweighed Yerkes' $1 million in bribes, and the bill was defeated. Within months, Yerkes' cronies were voted out of office for good and, within the year, Yerkes fled Chicago for London after unloading his system for a mere $20 million.

Yerkes seemingly ran out of steam after this. Estranged from his second wife, he went to London in 1900 and weaseled his way into its transit system by first acquiring one rail franchise for $500,000 and convincing the English shareholders to go electric. Yerkes and a syndicate later began revamping the London Underground—an $85 million project, after beating out **J.P. Morgan** for control of the rights, but stricken with Bright's disease, Yerkes died five years later on the brink of bankruptcy, unnoticed by his native land.

Everyone has always known that Chicago is a land where crooked politics long prevailed. But Yerkes teaches a more fundamental notion. He was among the earliest of Chicago's political wheeler-dealers. And he ran the simple scheme of combining finance with business via public utilities and political underhandedness. It is only in public utilities that you can monopolize commerce through political corruption. The realm of utilities is the purest place where business can be wicked with complete political protection. In other areas competition will always drive poor vendors from existence. Throughout the American landscape local utilities have been abused by sharp businessmen who used less sharp politicians as their tools. Yerkes was an early pure example of combining business with finance and politics that others could follow even into the late 20th century.

World's Work, 1905

THOMAS FORTUNE RYAN

AMERICA'S FIRST
HOLDING COMPANY

O ne of America's last great robber barons, ambitious Thomas Fortune
Ryan—known as the "great opportunist"—lived up to his prophetic
middle name and died one of the world's richest men in 1928. But besides
earning about $100 million—by hook or by crook, in industries like "traction,"
tobacco and insurance—Ryan created for America one of its most popular
corporate vehicles, the holding company.

Tall and distinguished looking, Irish-Catholic with blue eyes, a square face,
cleft chin, and forceful personality, Ryan was born in a small town in Virginia
in 1851. He came about forming his holding company in 1886, at the age of
35, while in the midst of building his Manhattan street railway dynasty. He
and a syndicate formed the Metropolitan Traction Company to hold various
operating companies and through it, buy up small streetcar lines, water stock,
then exchange the watered stock for more valuable Metropolitan stock. As
important as the holding company became to American financial history,
Ryan's initial success relied mainly on politics—the shady kind, that is.

"Mayors are his office-boys, governors come and go at his call . . . Tammany Hall is a dog for his hunting, and he breaks city councils to his money-will as folk break horses to harness," a muckraker once wrote of Ryan. Like Chicago's "traction" king **Charles Yerkes** before him, Ryan built his traction career on political corruption, bribing Manhattan politicos to tighten his grip on the City's street railway system. Politics played a key role in controlling street railways, for the right to use city streets had to be secured in the form of franchises via politicians. This game came easy to Ryan, for he entered the traction industry after serving as a general member for the famously-corrupt Tammany Hall in the 1870s. His Tammany connections, in fact, were what opened his eyes to the money that could be had in street railways.

Following a decade-long stint as a Wall Street stockbroker, Ryan jumped full force into traction in 1883, battling for control of one of the city's main franchises. He fought hard, bribing city alderman with thousands in cash and even more in stock in a firm he'd formed especially for the battle—but his competitor spent more. Within a year, however, Ryan—ever persistent and with the spirit of a rip-off artist—initiated damaging lawsuits and state investigations against his competitor, who finally succumbed to his dubious tactics. And when the legislature, tired of all the ruckus, annulled the franchise Ryan had fought so hard to win, Ryan turned around and fought the courts for two years more to reverse the annulment. When he played, he played to win.

Once he had formed Metropolitan, the holding company, he manipulated its stock by maintaining artificially-inflated dividends. He was among the first to teach investors that a very fat dividend can be a sucker's trap. En route he succeeded in boosting the stock to $269 in 1899, at which point he and other insiders unloaded the stock on an eager public.

Ryan retired from his traction interests, which encompassed all of New York City—including its subway system—in 1906, just before the great panic, selling out with a $50 million fortune. Of course, without him and his well-paid, powerful political connections to maintain his monopoly, his empire collapsed like a house of cards—leaving only his personal fortune in place. When the Metropolitan went into receivership, the receiver complained of missing proceeds from a $35 million bond issue. Mysteriously enough, $15 million was never accounted for—the other $20 million was traced to political graft! It is ironic that, with America's first holding company suffering political graft and finally bankruptcy, the holding company format would be used so many times thereafter, but it has been. And for that innovation we have Ryan to thank. You would think that would be enough for one lifetime.

But, instead of retiring, Ryan kept active in the business. Not only did he hold on to his immense fortune, but Ryan succeeded in doubling it—and as the exception to the rule, he doubled it in industries new to him, like banking, mining, public utilities and life insurance, to name a few. In most cases, when a successful financier switches fields, abandoning his forte, he winds up losing a bundle, if not his entire fortune, as in the case of **Jay Cooke**.

Ryan continued with the utmost confidence, winning big especially in the tobacco field. While still engrossed with traction in the 1890s, he helped organize one of the largest mergers of its kind—when "merger" literally was a new word—according to media accounts of the day. By merging three tobacco firms, Ryan helped organize the American Tobacco Company, capitalizing it at $25 million and eventually recapitalizing it again and again until it until it reached $250 million.

One of his more adventurous deals was investing in Belgian Congo mining—by invitation from King Leopold of Belgium. For his part in developing and financing an international firm to industrialize the rich African land, Ryan received a quarter of the firm's stock. When critics charged that the Congo firm was profiting off of human slavery, Ryan told a reporter in a rare interview, "I sleep like a baby." When in the Congo, do as the Congans do. A robber baron to the bone!

In his personal life, as in his varied business life, Ryan was not afraid to do exactly what he wanted, no matter what anyone thought of him. Insight into the man can be gained from the fact that he remarried in 1917, at age 66, a mere two weeks after his first wife died. This sparked a never-ending feud between Ryan and his eldest son, Allan A. Ryan, a stockbroker and president of Stutz Motors, who declared, "It is the most disrespectful, indecent thing I ever heard of."

Although trained by his father, the younger Ryan seemed to uphold better business ethics. But in the 1920s, whether out of pride or profit (it's unclear in historical accounts), he tried to corner Stutz, failed and ultimately declared bankruptcy. His father, Ryan senior, stood by and watched his son's failed corner and failed career with closed lips, closed checkbook and presumably closed heart. And when Thomas Fortune Ryan died, he left his wife and other sons well provided for, but poor Allan was left a pair of white pearl shirt studs.

Ryan left a fortune, the legacy of America's first holding company, and a nasty reputation. It is hard to see that he actually did much that was good for the world. As with his spiritual predecessor, Charles Yerkes, Ryan was a crafty capitalist who used politics to gain corrupt profits via the public utility format. Perhaps the greatest lesson to be learned from folks like Ryan and Yerkes is that they couldn't have done what they did were it not for our swallowing the notion that municipalities should have the right to control and regulate utilities in any regard. As Adam Smith always knew, competition would have been a far kinder master than either the politicians or Thomas Fortune Ryan.

RUSSELL SAGE

A SAGE FOR ALL SEASONS

Russell Sage, the brilliant market manipulator, was a man of maxims. "I made my millions from maxims, chief of which was the one my father favored, which went, 'Any man can earn a dollar, but it takes a wise man to keep it.'" Heeding his father's advice, Sage, like a dog protecting his bone, clung to his dollars through all financial seasons, prosperity and panic alike. Hoarding well over $100 million at his death in 1906, the wise old owl was the market's pillar of trust— Wall Street's sage for all seasons.

Shrouded in his trademark cheap, baggy black suits and frayed banker's vests, Sage made his fortune manipulating railroads, lending money at near usurious rates and pioneering the system of puts and calls, actually being the original inventor of straddles and spreads. A shrewd businessman, he used crafty convictions and strategic connections (which were sometimes bought) to squeeze the most from every opportunity. Born in a covered wagon in 1816, this poor farmer's son maximized his chances even as a kid—but when asked about his childhood ambitions, the humble millionaire said "About the only thing I made up my mind to early was that I would not be a poor man. I would succeed in whatever I undertook. I saw poverty around me and dreaded it."

Sage didn't see poverty for long. At 13—after working in his brother's grocery store in Troy, N.Y. for a year—he bought his first land. Ever fast-paced, after mastering the art of loaning friends money for a fee, Sage became a sought-after horse broker, took over his brother's grocery, then made a killing in shipping during a freak ice storm. Quickly learning the value of a dollar, Sage boasted, "If you take care of the pennies, the dollars will take care of themselves." At 21, already well-to-do, Sage entered Troy's city government, where he schemed his strategy for a future fortune in railroads.

In 1852, at age 36 and standing 5 foot 10, Sage was elected to Congress, where he not only loaned money to fellow legislators on a 24-hour basis, but discovered that the booming N.Y. Central Railroad needed his city's Troy & Schenectady line to expand. So, when the usually-profitable line's stock price mysteriously began to plummet, Troy turned to its favorite sage, Sage, who also happened to be a director on the line. At his urging, Troy unloaded the railroad for less than one-third its worth, $200,000—to a dummy company secretly headed by Sage! Secret double-cross! With steel blue eyes that screamed "No mercy!" Sage about-faced, slyly selling out to the New York Central for a cool $900,000 and a director's seat. Railroads came to be a favorite—but not exclusive—moneymaker for Sage, who commonly bribed state officials for valuable land grants. A little **Hetty Green**. A little **Jay Gould**. And a lot of Sage.

"If a stock is high enough to be sold, it is high enough to be sold short," was another Sage maxim. Turned out of Congress after two terms, he seized the market—wielding his fortune made in railroading, loan sharking and hoarding. Soon he became known as "the greatest stock trader who ever lived." Of course there have been lots of those, and they come and go with bull markets. Nonetheless, tucked inside a dingy, third-story office, operating from a swivel-chair originally owned by President Washington, Sage made as much as $10 million in one year exploiting his system of puts and calls— which he claimed helped out small brokers who wanted to operate on his huge credit.

It wasn't likely Sage ever had charity on his mind. He was unrelentingly cheap and miserly! Despite his great wealth, in the style of Hetty Green, he lunched for free daily on Western Union Telegraph's tab, where he was a director. He didn't spend any money on recreation, because he didn't have any: He idolized work and its fruit—money—for he had little else. He was childless despite two marriages. Market manipulation was his one and only game!

The only way to play the game, according to Sage, was to use calls to protect short sales and puts against long sales. He eagerly offered puts on stocks he thought would rise and calls on those expected to fall—for a hefty charge— because most of the time Sage rigged the stock on which he wrote options! In 1875, for instance, Sage bought **Cornelius Vanderbilt**'s Lake Shore Railroad at 72 anticipating a rise, sold calls to the extent of his holdings—he never overextended himself—and also sold puts! As Lake Shore dropped, Sage continued selling puts as large blocks were "put to him" between 52 and 55. When the rise came, he sold his stock at 62, securing profits for those with his put contracts and, of course, his greedy little self!

Sage may have been greedy—giving away next to nothing during his lifetime—but he wasn't stupid. This simple but now famous adage which he first uttered proved invaluable for him: "Buy straw hats in the winter, when nobody wants them, and sell them in the summer when everybody needs them." In his case, "straw hats" applied to dollars, and "summer" meant panic! A shylock to the end, Sage—again, like the miserly Hetty Green—granted loans during depressions, often saving the market with his sorely needed cash, but at a hefty price. He was well aware of the worth of his ready cash—as a rule, premiums rose with the urgency of the situation! When arrested in 1869 as part of a "usury ring," Sage pled guilty, but mumbled that he was only helping his fellow man! (He later got out of his jail sentence via connections.) Eventually, Sage avoided usury with calls: Instead of lending clients money to buy 100 shares at illegal rates, he got a put contract for the client, bought the block, protecting himself with the put when he sold them an overpriced call on the shares purchased. After all, there was no law limiting the price of a call!

While a business rogue, his personal life was not only lonely, but also relatively scandal-free. Yes, he was sued by a former cook who claimed Sage fathered her 25-year-old son, and yes, he was sued by a female painter who claimed he had been hanky-pankying with her instead of posing for his portrait, but rich men always have someone trying to smear them for money, and no, he was never found guilty of any of these charges. Sage stayed true to his calling which was to make money and to hell with the rest.

Years after a mad bomber attempted to assassinate the tycoon, Sage died in 1906, leaving about $100 million. Perhaps it was this simple saying—"Keep what you already have"—that prevented greed from blinding his cautious foresight and allowed him to glide through his last panic in 1893. Or perhaps it was fate that allowed him to narrowly miss the ruinous Panic of 1907!

In any case, Sage might have added to his list of maxims "Stay focused," for he rarely got sidetracked from his work. As in his famous "Buy straw hats in winter" quote, it was the contrarian in Sage that made him the enduring investor for all seasons that ended his career as one of the few of all time to die on top.

A guy like Sage makes you wonder if there isn't a greater meaning to life than just making money. Is there a point to being so wealthy when you have no friends, relatives, love or other and less non-greedy interests? It is scary the degree to which Sage is so similar to folks like Hetty Green and Jay Gould, who made and kept so much money, but who also gave so little of themselves to others around them. Ironically, when Sage died, his wife disseminated his fortune to countless charities. He must have turned over in his grave.

ROGER W. BABSON

INNOVATIVE STATISTICIAN AND NEWSLETTER WRITER

Inspired by Booker T. Washington's claim that specialization guarantees success, Roger Babson entered the stock market analysis field nearly a century ago when it didn't exist, and he had little, if any, competition. Over the next half-century, he created one of the first market newsletters, sparked an entire industry of both institutional and retail analysis, invented his own stock market index and from it, predicted the 1929 Crash.

Babson came up with the idea of setting up a statistical organization in 1900 at 25 while recuperating from tuberculosis, which abruptly ended his budding Wall Street career and forced him to stay in open-air quarters. Note that this notion was before statistics were well accepted: There was no GNP accounting, no broadly accepted stock market indexes, and very little in the way of reliable statistics in any form.

While on Wall Street, he noted that banks, investment houses and stock exchange firms each hired their own statisticians to gather statistics from bond houses. He figured he could do the work for all the firms himself more efficiently and more cheaply from his customized open-air New England home.

Four years later, after teaching himself to analyze and tabulate business reports, Babson and his wife of four years pooled $1,200 to buy a typewriter, an adding machine and some office equipment. Then, after securing eight subscribers at $12.50 per month, they formed the Babson Statistical Organization, Inc. (Later, he marketed a more detailed service for individuals as well as institutional investors that was eventually sold and became the basis for *Standard & Poor's*.)

Meanwhile, Babson—who in later years looked astonishingly like Colonel Sanders of Kentucky Fried fame—initiated his *Babson's Reports* newsletter while tucked away in Wellesley Hills, Massachusetts. Because of his bout with TB, his customized home and office featured open windows—during both summers and cold New England winters! His assistants—who didn't have TB when they started working for him—were made to work in the same conditions. They wrapped themselves in thick woolen blankets, wore bulky mittens and used tiny mallets with rubber pegs to strike the typewriter keys—truly hard to envision in today's modern world. While there is no clear record of his employee turnover, it must have been very high, indeed!

Through cold, snow, sleet and rain, *Babson's Reports* advised readers when and what to buy and sell. Amassing some 30,000 subscribers, he put forth a conservative investment philosophy and forecasted market trends via a weekly index based on Sir Isaac Newton's law of action and reaction. Affectionately calling the index the "Babsonchart," Babson said it evolved from his study of market transactions following the Panic of 1907. As a charted composite of agriculture, basic materials, manufacturers, transportation and trade figures, it tracked various forms of market activity and was "indispensable as a corrective against the tendency to follow surface conditions rather than fundamental trends."

"Our forecast of future events is based on the assumption that the law of action and reaction (Newtonian) applies to economics and human relations, en masse, as it applies to mechanics. Thus we assume that abnormal depression must follow abnormal activity; that lower prices must follow higher prices, or vice versa; and we as classes or nations must ourselves get what we give and must prosper as we serve," he explained. In essence he was saying: What goes up must go down and vice versa.

The Babsonchart was key to Babson's specific investment plan, outlined in his book, *A Continuous Working Plan for Your Money*. It called for a "complete, continuous, conservative and constructive" market strategy, including a three-way buy plan for profit, income and some for growth. Pious and persnickety, Babson preached to his readers to control themselves and resist the temptation of taking sinful short-term profits. "Success comes not so much by forecasting as by doing the right thing at the right time and always being willing to keep one's course prudently protected." Remember, he'd say, it takes years to build success! He even had his own set of stock market "Ten Commandments":

1. Keep speculation and investments separate.
2. Don't be fooled by a name.

3. Be wary of new promotions.
4. Give due consideration to market ability.
5. Don't buy without proper facts.
6. Safeguard purchases through diversification.
7. Don't try to diversify by buying different securities of the same company.
8. Small companies should be carefully scrutinized.
9. Buy adequate security, not super abundance.
10. Choose your dealer and buy outright. (Babson abhorred any type of margin or installment payment plans and, in fact, claimed he never borrowed money.)

Instrumental to any newsletter writer's existence today is keeping one's own name alive in the public's mind. Most of them are absolute PR hogs. In the good old days, Babson kept his name alive by writing countless magazine articles and an incredible number of books—about 40—many of which were constantly revised and reprinted. His name, in fact, occupies some three drawers in the Library of Congress card catalogue! Babson penned books like *Actions and Reactions*, an autobiography; *Business Barometers and Investment*, as well as obscure church-related treatises like *How to Increase Church Attendance and New Tasks for Old Churches*. Aside from writing, he fervently promoted hygienic products and tips via the American Public Welfare Trust; founded three colleges; conducted a publicized experiment in "industrial democracy," or profit-sharing, and ran for the U.S. Presidency in 1940 on the Prohibitionist Party ticket.

Babson never lacked for publicity, particularly just before the 1929 Crash. As early as 1927, he'd preached "Any major movement should be on the downward side" and advised clients to "hold their funds in good liquid condition" despite the booming bull market. His pessimistic sermons were largely ignored and laughed at until September 5, 1929 when he again repeated his prediction at his own New England Annual National Business Conference. This time, an advance copy of his speech was leaked to the press. Rumors spread and prompted wild speculation. **Jesse Livermore** gathered 30 brokers to sell short some $300,000 in stocks, betting on chaos. Legendary economist **Irving Fisher** was reserved for comment by newspapers to rebut Babson's expected speech and forecasts and calm the readers.

Sure enough, America was shocked by Babson's words: "More people are borrowing and speculating today than ever in our history. Sooner or later a crash is coming which will take in the leading stocks and cause a decline of from 60 to 80 points in the Dow Jones barometer. Wise are those investors who get out of debt and reef their sails." Radio programs were interrupted and presses stopped to relay his forecast. The news hit Wall Street like a bomb. Tagged "one of the world's greatest economists," "a famous financial prophet" and even, "the Prophet of Loss," Babson had started a mini-panic and what Livermore bet on came true. Investors became hysterical and started selling like crazy. After peaking at 386.10 just two days before, the Dow plummeted on heavy volume. **A.P. Giannini** was even interrupted from a board meeting to hear Transamerica stock was plunging!

Ironically, what temporarily saved the market—this time—was Irving Fisher's blind rebuttal: "I expect to see the stock market a good deal higher than it is today within a few months." Fisher's statement had the expected soothing effect on the public, and the market quickly rebounded. Livermore, even more quickly, covered his shorts and took his profits! Babson promised the rebound would only be temporary, but no one listened. When the Crash ultimately came, Babson called for "poise, discernment, judicious courage and old-fashioned common sense," but his words again fell on deaf ears.

Born in 1875 in Gloucester, Massachusetts, a descendant of a long line of seamen, Babson was an M.I.T. graduate of civil engineering, explaining his love for Newton. In his spare time, he taught Sunday school, collected and studied the works of Newton with his wife, gardened and collected old sailing maps, stamps and "good cheer" books. An oddball inventor credited with building the largest relief map in the world and a friend of Thomas Edison, Babson was obsessed with health, hygiene and diet, and never drank liquor or smoked. A stubborn and determined man with a lot to say, he lived—and worked—until dying in 1967 at age 92. And yet while he lived long, it is hard to envision him living well—that is having much fun, or allowing much fun in those around him. You can find many who count others in this book as their role model/mentor, but no one would see Babson that way. The exact reverse of the eat, drink and be merry mentality, extremely non-hedonistic, he was a classically rigid and stoic New Englander. In some ways he was simply a sourpuss.

And yet as an innovator, he was superb. While his books and articles were important, it was his innovations that changed the financial world. He was one of the first to offer statistical services and the first to make a go of it. He was one of the first of the newsletter people, and again, the first to make a continuing go of it. Either of these innovative contributions are enough to count him among the *100 Minds That Made The Market.*

T . ROWE PRICE

WIDELY KNOWN AS THE FATHER OF GROWTH STOCKS

L ong before it was in vogue to invest in promising new fields on the hope of catching the next hottest trend, Baltimore-based T. Rowe Price was holding tightly to "unpopular" picks as early as the late 1930s. It wasn't until a decade later, when he started realizing phenomenal results and established the T. Rowe Price Growth Stock Fund in 1950, that Wall Street took notice. Within another decade, thanks to Price and others, growth stocks swept the nation and became a major movement in Wall Street.

Before Price, what came to be known as growth stocks were overlooked because Wall Street regarded all stocks as cyclical—meaning they'd rise and fall with economic cycles. But Rowe Price was the first to see it differently. In 1939, he wrote, "Earnings of most corporations pass through a life cycle which, like the human life cycle, has three important phases— growth, maturity and decadence."

So he set out to use the phases to his advantage: "I figured that if we bought stocks whose earnings were growing faster than the economy, I could protect myself and my clients against inflation. The old idea of investing for the cyclical swings wouldn't do that." He claimed the least risky time to own a stock—if it first met his rigorous criteria—was during the early stages of growth. It was in those early stages that Price mustered up the nerve and foresight to buy into fledgling, unheard of firms like IBM, Coca-Cola, J.C. Penney, Dow Chemical, Monsanto, and Procter & Gamble, then hold on to them until they ultimately paid off.

Choosing the right firms to invest in was no easy matter for the hard-headed Price. Whereas money managers like **Benjamin Graham** opted for a quantitative approach in choosing stocks, Price denounced such pointed, mathematical approaches as being too rigid, leaving little room for unexpected bad news. Instead, Price sought the top one or two companies in up-and-coming industries which showed consistent unit growth and profits even through the down phase of a cycle. Then, he took into account the following guidelines, as described in John Train's *The Money Masters*. Price felt a firm had to have:

1. Superior research to develop products and markets.
2. A lack of cutthroat competition and apparent immunity from government regulation.
3. Outstanding management.
4. Low total labor costs, but well-paid employees.
5. Statistically, a 10 percent return on invested capital, sustained high profit margins, and superior growth of earnings per share.

It was time to unload a stock when it had "matured," usually after a decade. Price believed in holding stocks long-term, despite the fact that he was an impatient man. Obvious warning signs of a maturing stock are a decrease in unit sales, profit margins or return on capital, but Price also kept a lookout for the following:

1. Management changes for the worse.
2. Markets becoming saturated.
3. Patents expiring or new inventions deeming them less valuable.
4. Competition intensifying.
5. The legislative environment deteriorating.
6. Labor and raw materials or taxes jumping.

By the mid-1960s, he had a faithful cult-like following who adhered to the "T. Rowe Price approach," which included buying Price's favorite stocks— like Emery Air Freight and Fleetwood—dubbed "T. Rowe Price stocks." Yet, instead of being flattered, the egotistical contrarian in him grew increasingly worried. Suddenly, his "finds" were part of everyone's portfolios! To find virgin turf in which to ply his philosophy, he formed yet a third no-load fund called the "New Era" to invest in natural resources, real estate, and gold. By the late 1960s, with his philosophies and ideas becoming too mainstream for his own comfort, Price sold his interest in T. Rowe Price & Associates—which included the billion-dollar T. Rowe Price Growth Stock Fund. He got $2.3 million, which by today's standards is a measly sum for an investment management firm of that size and prestige. For his personal account, he cut back on his growth holdings and invested most of his newly-gotten capital in his "New Era" picks.

Price's preparations paid off in 1974 when growth stocks took a nose-dive, some falling 80 percent below their previous highs. His former firm, Price & Associates, lost a sack of money. They never heeded their guru's warnings and in fact, continued supplying their clients with over-priced "Price stocks." Although the firm didn't realize it, it had contributed to the slump by helping saturate the market with trendy growth stocks.

The great 1973–74 bear market made the mere mention of "growth" a taboo on the Street, as many investors panicked and dumped their holdings. For example, those who'd bought Avon at $130—a whopping 55 times earnings—now unloaded it at $25, a more reasonable 13 times earnings. Of course, Price—the king contrarian—realized that since growth stocks had fallen from favor, it was time to start buying them again, though not necessarily the same stocks that had so enthused everyone in 1972. So he bought, and his selections, like cable television, were successful.

Rowe Price was a sly one. This son of a Maryland country doctor, born in 1898, was a true professional and always looked out for his clients, believing, "If we do well for the client, we'll be taken care of." He was a great salesman who wore a flower in his lapel daily, and had the utmost confidence in himself—imperative in order to be a true contrarian. He was fiercely dedicated, with barely any friends or interests outside the office. Even his wife and children seemingly came second to his investing.

Thin, steel-gray haired, with a tuft of hair beneath his nose and wistful eyes beneath nerdy, '50s-style black-framed eye-glasses, Price was a Swarthmore College graduate who had studied to be a research chemist. His scientific training, however, opened his eyes to the opportunities in upcoming technology when conventional investors still kept faith in heavy industry and business cycles. In 1937, Price permanently shut the door on his personal evolution in chemistry to become an investment counselor. He then formed his firm, Price and Associates.

He was a strict disciplinarian, waking at 5 A.M. every morning even after retirement. Then he went about his day following a strict agenda, dutifully completing each task in exactly the order written and never undertaking tasks not listed on that day's agenda. "Mr. Price" was as selfish with his money as he was with his time. When his firm left its modest quarters for a gleaming new base overlooking the Baltimore harbor, Price—already retired but still working—stayed behind to share a more practical two-room office with his secretary of over 55 years. Though he wasn't a notorious tightwad, Price was never known for his generosity and stayed clear of the standard successful businessman's route—charity. Up until his death in 1983 at age 85, he stood by his staunch ways, and rarely went out of his way to do favors for anyone.

Rowe Price was remembered as an ornery-but-forgivable old guy. *Forbes* editor James W. Michaels (and my personal mentor in the *Forbes* organization) recalled in a Price memorial, "He would snap out with things like, 'You don't know anything, do you?' if I failed immediately to grasp some point he was making. But behind my back he said good things about me and this magazine."

As peculiar and narrow-minded as Price was, his contribution was phenomenal. He led a school of thought that blossomed into a huge, new philosophical investment wave that would evolve and endure for generations. Was he the father of growth stocks? Technically he wasn't the first to adopt the philosophy. [My own father was clearly using the growth stock approach on the west coast five years before Price, but Phil Fisher didn't write about it until many years after Price.] Price was the first to articulate growth stock investing in a format that the world embraced and emulated. And for that and his big splash with it, the investment world owes a debt of gratitude.

FLOYD B. ODLUM

THE ORIGINAL MODERN
CORPORATE RAIDER

Some 15 years was all it took for Floyd Bostwick Odlum to transform his $39,000 speculative pool into a $100 million corporate giant. He did it not by discovering growth stocks or establishing a new school of security analysis, but by snatching up undervalued post-Crash firms, often for 50 cents on the dollar, reorganizing them, then liquidating their assets and, with the cash, repeating the process over and over again. Hailed as the man who became a millionaire during the Depression and nicknamed "Fifty Percent" by **Sidney Weinberg**, the cool, collected, and understated Odlum contributed to Wall Street his own unique schtik, as important in recent markets as any investment philosophy—modern corporate raiding.

Odlum's Atlas Corporation began as a whim optimistically called the United States Company in 1923, when he, a friend and their wives pooled their money to join the 1920s bull market. Odlum had been working as a lawyer for a giant utilities firm, and with his knowledge, the pool set out to speculate mainly in utility securities. In its first year, U.S. Co. paid a 65 percent dividend; by the second year, its shares were worth 17 times their original value. In 1928, others were let into the firm, and the following year, it became Atlas Utilities Company with total assets of $6 million.

Somehow during the summer of 1929, Odlum smelled trouble. So he un-loaded about half of Atlas' holdings, sold a new $9-million issue, kept all proceeds in cash and short-term notes—and avoided the Crash almost al-together. Unencumbered by debt and with $14 million in assets, Atlas next adopted Odlum's inspiring takeover plan, starting with bust investment firms which littered the Street. The process of taking control of a firm and liquidating its assets took anywhere between three weeks and three years, but Atlas had accumulated so much capital that it was able to wait on potential profits for as long as it took to extract them. Wall Street sang, "Little investment company, don't you cry; Atlas will get you by and by."

Atlas Utilities became Atlas Corporation when hulking utility firms became the target of New Deal reform. Odlum, who'd befriended the New Deal program and even contributed to Roosevelt's election campaign, led Atlas through this era with great success. Atlas grew to require the services of 40 brokerage houses. Yet, as connected as Odlum was to Wall Street, he never saw himself as a Wall Streeter. He claimed he didn't understand the symbols on the ticker and couldn't "keep my balance if I watch prices." His method was simple: "You buy when the other fellow sells, and sell when it looks rosiest."

Tall, lanky and sandy-haired with sharp blue eyes behind horn-rimmed glasses, Odlum had a complacent smile, but quick, nervous movement and low-keyed, deliberate speech. He was known on the Street as ruthless, yet tactful; warm-hearted but discerning. He was a shrewd negotiator; it was hard to know what was going on in his mind when talking business. When making a deal, he'd sometimes fake boredom, plop his feet on his desk and look away from his visitor.

A chain smoker who usually drank milk and always avoided alcohol, red meat and raw fruit, Odlum liked bad jokes, squash, his Dalmatian—"Spot"— informal get-togethers and golf. He collected 19th-century landscapes and liked to think of himself as an artist—for relaxation, he'd sculpt clay but inevitably squeeze his works of art into lumps. By far Odlum's most famous quirk was doing business—via an extra-extended, snake-like telephone cord (another trademark)—while floating in his Olympic-sized pool at his Indio, California ranch. He soaked in his heated pool to alleviate his arthritis. When he hosted board meetings, they were also held in his pool. Directors, eager to accommodate Odlum's every whim, shed their three-piecers for swimming trunks and jumped in waist-high!

Once the New Deal got underway, Odlum's raiding machine abandoned his original orientation, which had focused on buying battered down holding companies, and instead shifted to the more direct investment thrill available in banks, railroads, motion pictures, department stores, real estate, and later, oil and mining. The stories surrounding his coups are endless. For example, he rebuilt the New York department store, Bonwit Teller, turning its management over to his first wife—the mother of his two sons—who divorced him in 1935 and continued running it anyway. That he didn't separate her from that function as part of the divorce is a telling statement about the man. As opposed to most men, he was obviously more able to separate emotional partnership notions from business relationships. He also reorganized Greyhound and made Madison Square Garden profitable. He sold Howard Hughes his controlling interest in RKO for $9 million five years after paying $3 million for it.

Eleven years after marrying record-breaking aviatrix Jane Cochran in 1936, Odlum bought control of Consolidated Vultee Aircraft, Convair, when the airplane industry had the post-war blues and Wall Street in general felt "making airplanes is not for Wall Street operators." Despite a loss of $13 million more than expected on certain commercial airline contracts, Odlum lifted Convair from its doldrums with the B-36 Bomber, which luckily became America's chief offensive weapon. Later, he sold out at the top, doubling the $10 million Atlas had dumped into the firm. Evolving from this experience, Odlum touted his rules for the successful "takeover":

1. Make the investment with fixed goals in mind.
2. Take over management.
3. Stay in until goals are reached.
4. When you leave, leave behind enough in the company for the next investor to turn a profit.

Born in 1892 in a Michigan Methodist parsonage, the son of a poor minister and the youngest of five, Odlum did odd jobs during his childhood—everything from picking berries, digging ditches, piling lumber, and tending celery to peddling maps door-to-door. His favorite story, though, recounts the time when a fairground's promoter hired him to race an ostrich against a horse. Young Floyd lost every race, but he got his fill of apple pie!

Odlum attended the University of Colorado at Boulder, studying journalism, then law. To afford tuition, he worked at the local paper, ran a student laundry, managed the dramatic club and women's opera, and, in the summers, operated four fraternity houses as tourist lodges. He never overlooked an opportunity. At the same time, he put in four years on the school debating team and became a star pole vaulter. He obviously had far more energy than most folks. In 1915, he earned his Bachelor of Law and breezed through the state bar exam with top scores.

Next, the ambitious lawyer ventured to Salt Lake City—to which he had a cheap one-way train ticket—and began working for the legal department of Utah Power and Light, a subsidiary of the giant New York utilities holding company, Electric Bond and Share Corporation. In Salt Lake City, he married a Mormon girl, and together, they went to New York when Odlum was promoted to that office. Odlum gradually climbed the corporate ladder, working on domestic utilities consolidations—and acquiring nervous indigestion.

The next phase for him is interesting because what went on was common then, but isn't now. He, in essence, held down two positions at the same time. In 1926, when Atlas' predecessor, U.S. Co., was well under way, Odlum was made chairman of its overseas subsidiary, American and Foreign Power. He was running his own newly created corporation, U.S. Co., at the same time he was remaining actively in the employ of American and Foreign Power—which today would be seen as a heavy conflict of interest. But he essentially did both on a shared basis until 1932, after which time he remained a board member of American and Foreign Power until the 1950s, which shows that they were perfectly happy with the relationship, despite the conflict.

Odlum died in 1976 at 84. Just three years previously, at 81, he made headlines talking about a $100 million condominium project he was planning on the site of his 732-acre ranch. The house where he'd lived for 34 years was slated to become the community's clubhouse—in fact, the famous pool where he had held submerged board meetings was drained, the art auctioned, and the furniture ready to be moved into another waiting mansion.

Art auctions and an empty pool sound awfully suspicious, but maybe Odlum was just getting pessimistic in his old age. That same year he'd told the *New York Times*, "Things, to me, have just gone to hell" and he expected a severe nose-dive in four to eight years. The reasons? Government deficits, inflation, and an overall disintegration of business ethics. Businessmen aren't "as much on the ball as earlier generations because they are too interested in golf courses, options and pensions instead of making money for their companies." Very old men usually feel that way, and today, they tend to feel that way about the same things that bothered Odlum. So, one lesson to learn from Odlum is not to take the pessimistic utterances of old men too seriously—it is their bias.

More fundamentally, Odlum demonstrated a precise art that others would follow, most heavily in the 1980s bull market. After the great discounting that occurred in the 1932 market, stocks sold in the public market far below what they could be dismantled for in the private market. He basically demonstrated the ability to arbitrage the value spread between the public and private markets. The flat market of the late 1960s through early 1980s, coupled with massive inflation, created another time period when stocks could commonly be bought for far less than the companies could be dismantled for in the private market, and folks came to re-enact Odlum's philosophy and tactics. Today, investors ranging from corporate raiders to the likes of money manager Mario Gabelli talk about "Private Market Value" as if it is a precise figure they can calculate. It will be fascinating to look back 20 years from now and see if they were able to do it with as much sustaining result as did Odlum, their predecessor.

PAUL CABOT

THE FATHER OF MODERN
INVESTMENT MANAGEMENT

Long ago, provincial, overly-cautious Bostonian investors liked to fashion themselves after the trustee whose rule it was never to invest in anything he couldn't watch from his office window. A little exaggerated? Maybe, but even today Boston has a fair amount of provincialness in its investment industry, and once upon a time, that was its overriding quality. But Paul Cabot did away with that narrow-minded mentality by investing in common stock at a time when it was thought fit for speculators only. Bonds had always been the wise, prudent and traditional choice of Boston investors, but Cabot, himself a stodgy Bostonian, only cared so much for tradition. Throughout his life he was a beacon drawing others to what has become the driving force in investment today, the world of institutional money management.

Cabot had always been a little different from his pretentious, severely polite, teeth-gritting friends. Once, while a director on the stuffiest and most influential board of them all, that of J.P. Morgan & Co., he came to a board meeting sporting a huge, glaring purple shiner and a cut on his brow. A fellow director commented that it must have been a fall while fox hunting. "Christ, no!" Cabot cried out across the boardroom. "Haven't any of you bastards ever been drunk?" During another Morgan board meeting, he asked the stiff General Motors guru Alfred P. Sloan, "How's it going?" When Sloan started spewing about corporate policies and his finance committee's activities, Cabot abruptly interrupted, "No, no! The hell with that! What I want to know is, when is it going to make some real dough?"

A blue-blooded Bostonian born in 1898, Cabot first rocked the investment world in 1924 by setting up one of America's first mutual funds, State Street Investment Company, with $100,000 and 32,000 shares. Within four years, the stock had risen from about $3 per share to about $24, and the fund had grown to $24 million. Of course, the early 1920s were phenomenal years for almost any type of investment—but Cabot's story isn't about his numbers. The fact that he'd created the now-common, third-party investment structure was revolutionary in itself, and he'd done it by putting his infant career on the line. If his mutual fund hadn't worked out, we never would have heard of Paul Cabot.

He did it by selling himself and what he stood for. Though he had his own mind, Cabot was still a Harvard man, a permanent fixture within the Bostonian "club" network, married with five kids, a tennis player, amiable—and he exuded common sense and respectability. Above all, he looked, sounded, acted, felt, and, in fact, was trustworthy—a familiar ruddy, Irish complexion, compact and padded body, gray tweed suits and vests, propped in a comfortable wooden chair behind a large, dark desk. Even in later years, when State Street Investments was housed in a modern skyscraper, Cabot's office boasted a few simple wooden chairs, a wooden coat rack supporting his wool coat and hat, a large bookcase, and an old pencil sharpener screwed to the inside of the door—nothing more. Cabot was in every visible way a product of the staid style inherent in the Boston of old.

At age 26, Cabot questioned his traditional, conservative Harvard education and banking experience when setting up his mutual fund, which invested in stocks from the start. Later he reflected, "When I started out in this business nobody believed in common stock, you know. People thought they were risky and exotic, unsuitable for a conservative investor. Bonds were the thing." Of course, as this book details, lots of folks had been deep in stocks for decades before Cabot came along, but less so in Boston, almost not at all among the common man in America and not at all in places where people didn't think of themselves as speculators. But Cabot went ahead with his plan, generally making out like a bandit by investing in stocks in which he doubled his investors' money.

Cabot didn't leave the old school completely behind when rethinking his strategy. For example, he could have made large, quick profits by joining 1920s bull pools, or even shorting stocks during the Depression, but that never would have worked in Boston—no one would have entrusted him with his money. And above all else, Cabot was trustworthy. He considered the quality of the firm he was investing in to be imperative, as were research, common sense, and risk-avoidance. "The most important quality is management that's able and honest. A hell of an easy way to get taken to the cleaners is by some goddamn crook like **Ivar Kreuger**. Then you want an industry that's prosperous and that's really needed." Essentially, Cabot was a realist. "First, you've got to get all the facts and then you've got to face the facts. Not pipe dreams." Ironically, Cabot personally invested his own money in high-grade municipals.

Cabot's style obtained the recognition it deserved while he served his alma mater, Harvard University, as its treasurer between 1948 and 1965. In Boston's investment community, being head of the Harvard Endowment was and still is a very, very big deal, and you wouldn't think Harvard would want to appoint a man like Cabot who went against the grain. But he had been successful at what he was doing, and Harvard wanted a piece of the action. And while Cabot was an innovator in Boston's investment community, he was still Bostonian through and through. Outside of Boston he would have been thought of as a staid fuddy-duddy. And while somewhat of an intellectual radical, he was so evidently trustworthy that staid Bostonians were willing to overlook radical traits in Cabot that they would have found abhorrent in most people and in any outsider.

Cabot broke tradition by doubling Harvard's holdings in common stocks to 60 percent of the total portfolio within a decade of taking over. That kind of allocation to stocks is very common in today's institutional pension plan, foundation, and endowment world, but in Cabot's day it was a new phenomenon—seen by most as risky—and a big part of what gave Cabot his reputation.

If you consider his 17 years in control at Harvard, asset allocation toward stocks in that spectacularly bullish period was at least as important as stock selection—particularly if you were to own mainly high quality issues as Cabot did. During those years the Dow Jones Industrials rose from about 175 to where it was just kissing 1000, and the heavy Cabot commitment to stocks made him a legend in his otherwise staid world.

Amazingly, when you consider the big bull market, Harvard's endowment grew only from $200 million to $1 billion, excluding capital additions—which works out to just under a 10 percent rate of return. That was OK, but not great, considering the bull market he rode. By today's standards 10 percent a year would not be considered good at all for a long-term rate of return during a bull market. But those were different times. Harvard was more than pleased, and the endowment world was revolutionized.

Cabot was not a great investor in the way a **Ben Graham** or a **Rowe Price** was. He didn't pioneer great stock selection ideas or generate record rates of return. What he did was infuse the stodgiest part of America's invest-ment scene with the excitement and long-term relative safety of American equities. It only could have been done in Boston, the then-stodgy capital of America, only by a Bostonian, and only by a trustworthy man. Cabot was the man. Endowments, foundations and pension plans will never be the same again. Following Cabot's lead they will always have a different and increased willingness to be conservatively aggressive, to seek higher returns, and to take equity risk. In this way, Cabot changed the world.

Through his mutual fund activity and his work for Harvard, he also represents the beginning of an industry—the third party investment management industry. Today, third party investment management—whether through mutual funds or independent account management firms—represents most of the money in stocks and bonds in America. There are more than 300 firms that manage more than $2 billion each, another 300 that manage more than $1 billion each, and more than 30 firms managing more than $10 billion each. It's a big industry. It is an industry based on due diligence and trust. Had guys like Cabot screwed it up way back when, the industry probably wouldn't exist today and certainly wouldn't exist in the present format. He was among its earliest practitioners, probably its first to be well-known and can be considered the father of the investment management industry.

GEORGES DORIOT

THE FATHER OF VENTURE CAPITAL

Getting the venture capital field off the ground four and a half decades ago was as risky as the new industries it would invest in. The task required a very special touch. Guts, confidence, drive, patience, resourcefulness and total dedication were essential, as were genius and creativity. General Georges Doriot had that touch and took up the challenge. He helped found American Research and Development Corporation (ARDC) in 1946, the first publicly-traded risk-capital concern to finance new firms by selling shares to the public. He staked both reputation and money in an effort to prove his idea was a viable method of encouraging economic growth and social progress.

A man with few critics, the Paris native liked to compare his role in creating and financing new firms to that of a doting father. He'd nurture start-ups—his most famous success story being Digital Equipment Corporation—from conception, through birth, well into young adulthood, until all he could do was "watch, push, worry, and spread hope." He pushed his "children," but was famous for not pressuring them. "When you have a child, you don't ask what return you can expect . . . I want them to do outstandingly well in their field. And if they do, the rewards will come. But if a man is honest in his efforts and loyal and does not achieve a so-called good rate of return, I will stay with him ... If I were a speculator, the question of return would apply. But I don't consider a speculator—in my definition of the word—constructive. I am building men and companies."

Instinctive and resourceful, Doriot was a harsh judge, yet his own best critic, a careful listener, subtle advisor, inspiring teacher, and amiable friend. Born in 1899 to an engineer who helped create the first Peugeot car, he graduated from Paris University in 1920, then went to Harvard Business School the following year to study then–brand-new "business administration." He remained at Harvard until retirement, becoming a professor of industrial management in 1926. He had one little side-jaunt. During World War II, Doriot served as deputy director of the Army's research, planning, and development program, rising to the rank of brigadier general. As in all his endeavors, he created quite a stir at the Pentagon by being himself—innovative, independent, and demanding. And for the remainder of his life he was known as "The General." Had one not known the facts, one might have suspected that he had fought with DeGaulle.

It's rare when an academician personally makes a difference on Wall Street, but Doriot was an exception. He brought with him a scholar's curiosity, a teacher's patience, and a general's determination, allowing him to freely experiment with his start-ups without getting disheartened if the profits didn't flow right away. He used to say in his thick Parisian accent, "Our aim is to build up creative men and their companies, and capital gains are a reward, not a goal." In fact, Doriot considered immediate success "dangerous." He insisted "it goes to our heads."

ARDC got off to a rough start losing with its very first venture—a degreasing gun. During its first eight years, ARDC had insignificant gains and moderate losses, but after 1955, it reported only gains. By 1966, with $93 million in assets, it was the textbook example of venture capital. Five years later, still under Doriot's reign, the firm's assets ballooned to $428 million with investments in some 46 companies.

Doriot's biggest and most dramatic success by far with ARDC was his initial financing of Digital Equipment in 1957. "Two young men came to us and said, 'We want to make modules.'" After making sure the two were his idea of "grade-A" men, he invested $61,400 in their idea. That year the firm consisted of "two men and a desk"; by 1971, it had over 7,000 employees and $147 million in sales. Founder and Digital head Kenneth Olson commented, "Doriot didn't rush to get Digital on the market. He truly wanted to generate something that would be useful for society."

Doriot financed Digital with loans repayable in installments, usually with options or warrants to buy stock. He protected his investment via ARDC's policy of purchasing voting control. This stipulated that the founders of the startup had to sell 78 percent of their firm to ARDC. If the firm were already underway, ARDC opted for less than 50 percent of its stock.

On the whole, ARDC fared well, but Doriot had occasional duds. For instance, the firm took a licking investing in Magnecord, Inc., a tape recorder manufacturer with management problems. Doriot, with his patience and cool, assured confidence, gave the go-ahead to buy $1.6 million of its stock, convinced the firm would resolve its problems—but it never did. Later, he defended his patience with iffy investments, saying, "If a child is sick with a 102 degree fever, do you sell him?"

Tall, lean, erect, with wavy gray hair, wispy mustache, and penetrating eyes, Doriot had a dominating presence. In the classroom, he'd constantly challenge his students, set high standards, question everything, and respond with polite sarcasm. "Always remember that someone, somewhere, is making a product that will make your product obsolete," was typical Doriot advice. His results as a teacher were often as good as any of his successes on Wall Street—many of his students became top Wall Street executives. "Doriot taught me the commitment and the sense of responsibility needed to succeed in business," said American Express Chairman James Robinson III. Former Ford chairman, Philip Caldwell, said, "I can still hear him saying, in his French-accented voice, 'Gentlemen, if you want to be a success in business, you must love your product.'"

Doriot gave venture capital his all until 1971, when he grew disgusted with what it had become. By this time, the second generation of venture capitalists had become money hounds, in it only for the buck, degrading everything he stood for and promoted. Venture capitalism was reduced to mere speculation, which violated his three basic no-nos by being financially, not management-oriented; impatient for financial rewards; and failing to understand the nature of technically-oriented firms. In ARDC's 1971 annual report, he wrote this melancholy prose: "... as speculative excesses increased, understanding and interest tended to disappear. Disillusionment and disenchantment usually follow periods when the true meaning of a task is ignored and forgotten. Venture capital seems to have shifted from a constructive, difficult task to a new method of speculation."

Doriot's brand of venture capital is very different from anything that exists today. He believed in the people first, the ideas second. He'd often say, "A grade-A man with a grade-B idea is better than a grade-B man with a grade-A idea," and "When someone comes in with an idea that's never been tried, the only way you can judge is by the kind of man you're dealing with." What he looked for in a good person was "resourcefulness, perception, courage, honesty with yourself, and a complete dedication to the business."

He arranged to retire in 1971 at age 71. When ARDC couldn't find a replacement for him, he arranged a merger with **Royal Little**'s Textron conglomerate. Since 1959, ARDC had been a Textron electronics division stockholder, and Doriot, a director. Long after his retirement, Doriot came to regret the merger, feeling corporate bigness stifled ARDC's creativity. (After his death in 1985, Textron sold the firm back to its managers.)

Aside from Wall Street and Harvard, Doriot loved photography and painting. Married in 1930, he and his wife lived on posh Beacon Hill in Boston. After his retirement, he channeled his still-high energies into heading the French Library of Boston. At 82, he said, "I don't watch venture capital today. I'm completely retired. Completely, absolutely, permanently."

It's hard to think of venture capital as ever being an earth-shattering concept. But before Doriot, new companies were brought into being by folks like Morgan, who amongst themselves, gathered the money to build a new corporation, then made it public—traditional capitalism. Doriot was the first to undertake modern venture capital, which has now become part of modern traditional capitalism. Like a Morgan, he was people oriented and saw the project only as viable as its people—but he was more than that. He was the creator of the concept of formalizing the start-up and nurturing of businesses as a business—to feed capital to entrepreneurs to foster rapid growth for our society and the new firm's products for consumers. It was his formula for success, and today's standard formula for breathing life into new industries and industry as a whole.

Dunn's Review, 1970

ROYAL LITTLE

THE FATHER OF CONGLOMERATES

In the 1960s Royal Little convinced corporate America that conglomerates were the best way to employ stockholders' capital. What he liked to call "unrelated diversification" avoided annoying, profit-exhausting business cycles, interference from the Justice Department and over-expansion during good times, followed by cutbacks during the bad. A decade later, the conglomerate was "one of the surest ways of having a faster growth rate than a normal single industry company can achieve."

"Unrelated diversification will beat any normal single industry company when it comes to return on net worth and cumulative growth rate of earnings per share of common stock," Little said before he died in 1987 at age 91. Yet he was the first to admit that what he did back in the '50s couldn't be done today, because prices are "just too damn high. Back then I was paying eight times earnings for what I purchased." Takeover artists in the late '80s typically paid 15 to 20 times earnings for acquisitions.

Little, who looked at personal extravagance as "a waste of capital that might otherwise be used positively," was the businessman's businessman. He lived simply and used to say, "People who run big business ought not to live ostentatiously." Genial, witty, communicative, charming, enthusiastic, and always youthful, he never took himself too seriously. He had a fierce respect for people and liked to be treated in the same manner.

Little's life illustrated that "one doesn't have to be an S.O.B. with a one-track mind to succeed in business," as someone once said in reference to him. Slim with bright blue eyes framed by glasses, Little shot river rapids, played tennis, skied, and even parachuted from an airplane at age 46! Married in 1932, he divorced in 1959 after raising two children. Soon after, he retired to pick up golf again—his wife had hated it—as well as sit on the boards of some 30 firms, run a small business investment company called Narragansett and take yearly photographic safaris all over Africa. "Unless a man can serve some useful purpose, he loses all interest in life. Those who just play golf die off."

Born in Wakefield, Massachusetts in 1896, the nephew of the famous consulting chemist, Arthur D. Little, Little graduated from Harvard and entered the textile business. At age 27, with a $10,000 loan, he started his own firm, Special Yarns, changing the name to Textron in 1944. While World War II brought major expansion, it opened Little's eyes to the fact that the textile world was too slow-moving, had too strong competition from specialty firms and was overly influenced by the business cycle. A few years later in 1952, he changed the company's charter to allow him to acquire firms outside the textile industry—and the first conglomerate soon was born.

Little acquired firms in electronics and aerospace, eventually selling off Textron's textile interests in 1963. By the mid-60s, Textron had some 70 different companies, covering some 37 different industrial categories. The firms Little looked to acquire were clearly stagnating, small, and the leading or second-best in their field. He stayed clear of companies competing in giant industries. "When you compete with the giants, you don't stand a chance."

From the numerous mistakes he made over the years—all of which are clearly and humorously detailed in his autobiography, *How To Lose $100,000,000 And Other Valuable Advice* —Little also learned to avoid letting personal interests sway his business decisions. In Little's case, it was golf—and this mistake happened later in life. Through Narragansett, which he'd set up three years before his retirement in 1959, Little financed All American Golf, a firm that planned to build a chain of Sam Snead par-three mini golf courses across America, but ended up in the rough. Never again would he let his personal taste influence his business decisions. While never very popular, or widely read, his book is one of this author's top 20 favorite all-time business books. Anyone who can expose his own mistakes has something going for him. But anyone who makes $100 million worth of mistakes and is still a success must have done a heck of a lot of right things, too. And it is very Little-like that he shows you his success through his failures. Most men would gloat about their success. Little didn't have to.

On the whole, Little was immensely successful. Textron became known prominently in the aerospace industry with four aircraft and aircraft parts companies, as well as Bell Aircraft, which became known for its helicopters.

In 1965, aerospace and defense comprised 35 percent of Textron's sales; industrial products, 20 percent; consumer items, like Hallmark cards, 16 percent; metal products, 17 percent; and agrochemical, 12 percent.

As far as running a conglomerate goes, Little said, "Most people do not realize that you have to depend on division managers. I have always made sure they had real incentives to do a good job." Textron division managers, often part owners of the firm, were given autonomy in running their firms and day-to-day operations. Interference from corporate headquarters, Little learned, only tempted people to look for opportunities elsewhere. So, he stayed out of their hair and, instead, kept score on the financials. "Don't try to tell them how to run the business," he declared. "You can't run a conglomerate from the home office."

Always humble, Little belittled his accomplishment of inventing the now-common corporate structure, the modern conglomerate. "All I ever did as a businessman was to bring men and money together. I was just extremely fortunate in some of the men I picked." Of course today, people are less enamored of conglomerates than in their heyday in the late 1960s. The conglomerate structure clearly subordinates management focus. It is hard for a small division of a big company to compete as intensely as a comparably sized independent firm where the firm's top managers carry an equity-owner's interest. Still, there have been a lot of successful conglomerates, and the structure and how to do it right came straight from Royal Little.

CHAPTER FIVE

BANKERS AND CENTRAL BANKERS

YOU CAN'T HAVE INVESTMENT BANKING WITHOUT BANKERS

The history of Wall Street chronicles the history of banking, because ultimately, the history of banking is tied to securities prices through both direct and indirect methodologies. Directly, there is an inverse relationship between interest rates and bond prices. Indirectly, this affects stock prices, too.

When the Federal Reserve decides to increase the money supply, it buys U.S. bonds, shrinking the bond supply. As the money supply increases, interest rates—sometimes referred to as the "price" of money (actually, the price of renting money)—are lowered. So now, if you had a stock and bond that both yielded 10 percent, for instance, the bond's price would rise so that its yield would decrease along with the interest rate to say 8 percent. The stock with the same 10 percent yield now looks a lot better than the 8 percent bond, and hence, it will be in greater demand than it was before, relative to the bond. The law of supply and demand translates this into higher stock prices. Thus, as the Fed loosens its purse strings, stock prices rise.

The bottom line is this: Central banking controls the money supply and thus, the interest rates, and interest rates very much affect Wall Street. Therefore, the following stories, which trace the histories of both banking and central banking, are key to Wall Street's evolution. It is like the relationship of the central nervous system to emotional feelings—it is all tied together.

Today central banking is a notoriously trustworthy concept. When you bring a $20 bill to the store, you trust you'll be able to buy $20 worth of goodies. Your short-term trust in the currency is absolute. But in the days before central banking was institutionalized here, currency was less than stable and the economy was much different. "Money" meant different things in different places and was seldom trusted universally.

Ironically, at its conception, central banking was anything but trustworthy. John Law, the father of central banking, was the epitome of flamboyance. He was a wild womanizer, outrageous dresser, and big spender who once slew a man in a duel over a shared mistress and was twice nearly hanged for it. Quite content to sleep with the wives of men with whom he did business, he was a born gambler who lived by his wits. In bringing the world central banking, Law sparked the infamous speculative Mississippi Bubble in France, which burst right in his face, leaving him a poor, lonely old man when it was over. But he changed the banking world forever.

Law left a legacy that would eventually reach the U.S. via Alexander Hamilton. Hamilton was another less-than-trustworthy character who was willing to take on the task of supporting the controversial concept of central banking. An illegitimate son, he took on a married mistress whose husband later blackmailed him, and in 1804 he was killed in a duel. Who would expect that someone with such a wild personal side would lead the American charge into today's staid field of central banking?

Nicholas Biddle, third in the legacy, actually was a trustworthy gent, but wasn't perceived as such in his day. Biddle was an aristocrat—wealthy when no one else was. He was intelligent, scholarly, handsome—and he single-handedly controlled the money supply. People were jealous and suspicious, and there was no way he could win their favor. So when the central bank he controlled went under in the Panic of 1837—after he retired—Biddle still bore the brunt of the blame and went down in financial history as yet another central banking scalawag. As a rich and sophisticated urban banker he made a great scapegoat for the eclectic populism of the Jacksonian era.

The condemnation central banking received in the Hamilton and Biddle eras was so devastating that it wasn't until the early 1900s that central banking could surface in the U.S. again; this time, in its present, staid and trustworthy form. And without modern central banking as we know it, Wall Street would be drastically different. First, to put the whole thing into play, the Panic of 1907 scared most folks into believing the U.S. needed a unified banking system. Few wanted to be dependent in the future on a single soul like J.P. Morgan, who might or might not be available and willing to bail America out should the need ever arise again. The question was how to do it. Paul Warburg had a plan, and it became the blueprint for the Federal Reserve Act of 1913, which created today's Fed.

In 1914, Benjamin Strong became the first to head the Federal Reserve Bank of New York, the largest regional bank in the system. He too was the epitome of confidence—dedicated, driven, even approved by the House of Morgan. Strong transformed the Fed into an influential force in world economic policy-making. Sadly, he died a year before the Crash; had he lived, the Fed might have performed less foolishly during the Crash, and the consequences might have been less severe.

Mild-mannered and flat-footed, George Harrison was left to fill Strong's shoes during the Crash. Following the course Strong probably would have taken, Harrison initiated an easy-money policy, pumping billions into the depleted money market and restoring some confidence in the market. It was the right thing to do. But Washington's decision to tighten the purse strings reversed Harrison's actions and led to drastic monetary contraction, imploding a serious recession into dire Depression. Harrison was not strong enough to lean into the wind and buck the political breeze, which is ultimately what the Fed is supposed to do at critical times. Still, Harrison is remembered for opening up the important relationship between the Fed and Wall Street in times of crises.

The middlemen between the central bank and Wall Street are the bankers. They provide the financing to buy the securities and determine the cost of financing via the Fed's current interest rate. James Stillman, Frank Vanderlip and George Baker headed Wall Street's biggest commercial banks before and during the Crash. Directly and indirectly they encouraged the 1920s bull market by involving their banks in securities underwriting and sales for 20 years or so prior to the Crash.

Personally eccentric, Stillman was a solid, conservative banker responsible for making National City Bank the largest commercial bank in the early 1900s. Too conservative to actually deal in securities himself, Stillman left his vice president, Vanderlip, with the money and influence to do so.

Vanderlip was a lot less conservative and, as a result, more willing to do what was previously considered taboo—to increase the bank's profits and influence by doing the things others wouldn't: more aggressive new account solicitation and mass securities sales and underwriting. He solicited new accounts with the fervor of a broker and gave the bank a personalized touch. An outgoing, dynamic salesman, he was one of the first to involve his bank in the securities business. This was so unconventional that it worked and, in fact, became all the rage with every major commercial bank. George Baker of First National personally capitalized his bank's securities affiliate in 1907 with his own $3 million!

Charles Mitchell and Albert Wiggin are the reasons why combining investment and commercial banking were outlawed in 1933. The heads of Wall Street's two biggest banks, they each expanded their securities affiliates to the point that it caused gross abuses of insider information, high-pressure, and deceptive sales tactics, and stock manipulation and wild speculation on the part of the banks! This continued through the Crash until the government interfered, inserting its New Deal Reformers.

Not all bankers were giants on Wall Street. There were underdogs like Natalie Laimbeer, the first notable woman banker on Wall Street who opened the door for other women to enter. And there was A.P. Giannini, who built up his San Francisco-based Bank of America and Transamerica empire by courting "the little fellow." In exchange for Giannini's achievement, Wall Street sent him a veritable time bomb, Elisha Walker, who attempted to dismember Giannini's organization. Walker returned to Wall Street without success; he just didn't have the grass-roots support Giannini had.

Ultimately Giannini was right. Banking is about the little guy, not the banker. It is providing intermediation between the masses with their small amounts of savings and borrowing needs and their counterparts, the large institutions with the financial credibility to be able to borrow and lend in big bites to build our industries and technologies. The banker is just the tool in the trade. But these bankers built the trade of banking, molding it over the decades into a format that at times accommodated Wall Street and at times made it bend.

It is impossible to separate banking or central banking from the evolution of Wall Street. Even today there is a move underfoot to allow the reuniting of banking and brokering under the same firm. If Wall Street is the way it is today, it is partly because of the way banking evolved. These are the leading bankers that drove a major part of Wall Street's evolution.

JOHN LAW

THE FATHER OF CENTRAL BANKING
WASN'T VERY FATHERLY

John Law didn't know the meaning of mediocrity—when he went after something, he went all out. When he rolled the dice, you knew the stakes were big. When a man lay dead—killed in a duel over a shared mistress—you knew Law was the culprit. And when France leapt from bankruptcy following Louis XIV's rule, to sheer decadence in just four years, you had to figure Law was behind it. This was the infamous Mississippi Bubble—and Law was its instigator! While this was quite a feat for the native Scotsman, who was twice nearly hanged for dueling, it wasn't really surprising. Law, a math whiz, had gallivanted all over Europe for 20 years in hopes of bringing to life his mastermind scheme: the central bank.

An attractive figure and outrageous dresser, Law fit in well in flamboyant times when wigs were in vogue and men rouged their cheeks. Born in 1671, the son of a goldsmith-banker, he worked in his father's counting house at 14 and studied banking principles in school. At 17, his father died, leaving him an estate and title—so, John Law of Lauriston set out to see the world.

After surviving the duel and two scheduled hangings because of it, Law—good at manipulating both women and cards—opted for what he expected to be a safer profession, banking. Living by his wits and profitable ploys, he gained banking knowledge while wooing bankers' willing wives. One woman, captivated by Law's lusty looks, led the rascal first to her bedroom and then to the heart of her husband's livelihood, his bank's international contacts, which later proved key to Law's fortune. With information in hand, Law sought new opportunities throughout Italy, Belgium, Scotland, and France—far from the banker's forlorn wife!

Constantly scrutinized by police envious of his licentious lifestyle, Law simmered down in Scotland, married, and observed his homeland's pathetic economy. The Scottish economy was broken by speculation brought on by a failed Central American expedition in which the entire country had invested (known as the Darien scheme), so Law figured this was the perfect place to test his theories. He advised the government to develop trade with capital obtained from taxing the wealthy, thus enhancing national wealth, but the Scots swiftly rejected this plan, and Law was out a test site. But not all was lost. When you don't get what you want, what you get is experience, and Law got a healthy dose.

After collecting his thoughts in pamphlets such as *Considerations on Legal Tender and Trade*, Law picked up his family and left for London to found a bank based on land. But when someone likened his "land-bank" to a "sandbank" in which the economy would surely sink with the changing tides of fortune, his system was doomed a second time. Meanwhile, Law made a killing speculating on the exchange, via his inside informants who leaked France's plan to melt down its currency to remake new coins laced heavily with base metal. Once again, Law caught the public eye and was forced to flee from police.

Ever smug, Law was finally called to France—where he was sure of success—just as the King lay dying in 1715. Assured of support from the new monarchy, Law proposed a royal bank to manage France's trade, collect taxes, and rid the country of debt—incurred by Louis' love of palaces, mistresses, and wars. If such a bright picture for such a bleak country were not enough to attract support, Law's promise to donate half a million livres of his own, should it not work out, pushed the deal right through, and in 1716, Law's "Banque General" began.

Capitalized at 6 million livres, in 1,200 shares, Law's bank performed the usual duties: issuing notes payable on sight to the bearer, discounting commercial paper and bills of exchange, accepting deposits from individuals and merchants, transferring cash or credit. But what made the bank outstanding was that its notes had fixed value, unlike state notes valued at a quarter of their face value. His currency grew so popular that by 1717, the government made taxes payable in bank notes, causing a boom in note issue and raising state credibility by absorbing much of its depreciated coin. Everyone began to prosper, including Law, who was hailed on the street, "God save the King and Monsignor Law!"

But trouble brewed—though it seemed quite the opposite at first—when Law was asked to find further use for the vastly depreciated state paper. Perhaps overly confident, Law formed the Mississippi Company in 1717 to mine treasures that supposedly awaited explorers in America—like a gigantic emerald requiring 22 men to seize it! Forgetful of his homeland's ruin via the Darien scheme, Law obtained exclusive trading rights over the Mississippi basin and capitalized the firm (a separate entity from the bank) at 100 million livres in shares of 500 livres apiece. A giant publicity campaign claimed "savages exchange lumps of gold and silver for European manufactures." An old soldier, who had been to the area, claimed the stories false; but he was shipped off to the Bastille before arousing too much suspicion!

Heady with confidence, Law charged ahead with his firm, buying the government's tobacco monopoly for a generous amount, delighting the stockholders. He bought the right to coin money for nine years. He successively bought rights to collect salt mine and farm taxes, the East India Co., and a Senegalese slave-trading firm. By 1719, he had a virtual monopoly of France's entire foreign trade—and stock prices were skyrocketing! To keep the ball rolling, Law upped capital to get controlling interest in each new concern, issued over a million new shares on the market at 500 livres each and declared 6 percent dividends for the next year. To absorb the abundant amount of state notes, he refused payment in specie, while enthusiastic crowds paid up to 5,000 livres for shares worth one-tenth that sum!

Meanwhile, few efforts were made to develop Mississippi—and even fewer people were willing to go. So, prostitutes, beggars, and vagrants—about 400 couples forcibly matched—were swept out of French prisons and tossed into Law's lark, the Mississippi. At the same time, the Laws were treated royally. High-ranking folk flanked to Law's house, paying enormous bribes just to have their names announced, though Law would see few of his flock of visitors. One woman had her coach driver head into a wall in order to attract John Law's attention, if not his sympathy. There wasn't a woman in Paris who wouldn't do anything to get her hands on Mississippi stock—and Law took advantage of the fact often! It was sheer bedlam and sheer decadence. There was massive trading and gambling—anything to squander money! Even household items were produced in silver and gold.

As the speculative bubble escalated and company stock was feverishly traded at 40 times its original value, Law—noting the drain on specie—declared a gold premium and debased the currency. But the government forced Law to unite the bank and company—even though the bank's capital was scarcely large enough to cover its own notes. So Law forbade anyone to own more than 500 livres in specie and tried to call off bank loans, but the bank was insolvent by August, 1720. Panic ensued when he tried to lower the price of stock, causing wild crowds—the same that once revered him—to throng at bank doors, inciting a stampede that killed 15. Still confident, Law retorted, "You are all swine!" and retreated to one of his country estates in hopes of being recalled. But that never happened. His property confiscated, Law was forced out of France, accompanied by three soldiers for protection—his wife was forced to stay.

Retiring to a cheap Venice flat and relying on gambling for a meager income—high stakes were no longer feasible—Law yearned for his French system and wrote *Comparison of the Effect of Mr. Law's Scheme With That of England Upon the South Sea Company*, about the English version of the Mississippi Bubble.

When Law's flat froze for lack of fuel—and fuel money—he donned thin-soled slippers, sauntered to the local gambling hall and returned with funds and a cough that led to pneumonia. He died one week later in 1729, alone—but not forgotten. To his death, he was hounded by those after the "secret" to his system.

Of all the unique individuals in this book, none would so well form the central character for a titillating movie as Law. His complete inability to separate his business risk-taking from his personal lifestyle made him colorful, bigger than life, and, thereby, more effective in his radical endeavors than more staid souls might have been. Had he been personally more conventional or conservative, he might well have avoided the boom-bust cycle that eventually proved his undoing. Yet, at the same time, had he been more conventional and less ready to push life to the limit, he probably wouldn't have had such ultimate impact on finance—an impact that was simply staggering! As much as any modern Federal Reserve Chairman would hate to admit it, Law is the father of central banking everywhere around the world. From the impish ways of this wild womanizer and his to-the-limits lifestyle came the seeds which would grow into the unendingly conservative and conventional presence which is today's central banking.

ALEXANDER HAMILTON

THE GODFATHER OF
AMERICAN FINANCE

S ome people think all central bankers should be shot. Alexander Hamilton
actually was—killed deader than a doornail by Aaron Burr in an 1804 duel.
Hamilton was more than political. His impact on our financial markets, in a
spiritual sense, is epic. And yet the man's life is immensely ironic. Imagine that
the spiritual godfather of our present day Federal Reserve System, our central
bank, should have lifted his ideas almost straight from the seminal thinking
75 years earlier of the scandalously profligate European central banker and
scalawag, **John Law.** Where is the irony? Hamilton himself was an illegitimate
son!

But before lying cold on the ground due to Burr's bullet work, Hamilton
laid the groundwork for America's economy, financial markets and even our
industrial revolution. Without him or his equivalent, everything that came in
the 19th century economically would have been impossible.

Leaning on Law's legacy, he almost single-handedly created the wildly controversial Federal Reserve-predecessor, the Bank of the United States (B.U.S.),
establishing the country's credit and advocating strict tax policies. Known as

our economy's Godfather and America's first Treasury Secretary, Hamilton was a visionary, coddling capitalism and foreseeing the evolution of predominantly agricultural America into what it would become decades later—a great industrial nation and again, decades before the industrial revolution.

Hamilton's most impressive task, forming the B.U.S., came from his 1789 proposal boosting public credit. Following the Revolutionary War, America owed some $79 million. American credit was shot—and ambitious Hamilton dictated fiscal policy as Treasury head. So, using debt instruments as a foundation for credit, Hamilton called for payment of the entire war debt—foreign, domestic, and state—through a program of foreign loans, customs duties, wartime Continental dollar refunds, and uniform currency circulation via a national bank. His plan was based on the notion that public debt would benefit the economy and, in turn, the people—straight out of Law's earlier European notions.

Inevitably, though, folks found the central bank concept controversial—not surprising since it had already taken a severe beating in Europe tied to the disastrous results of the central bank-fostered South Seas Bubble and the Mississippi Scheme (see John Law for further detail). Liberals condemned a government-chartered bank as unconstitutional. (In those days they called liberals what we now call conservatives, and what we call liberals now they called "federalists." Hamilton was a federalist, Jefferson was a liberal.) But Hamilton convinced former army-buddy President Washington of the B.U.S.'s key role in America's fledgling government.

"This general principle is inherent in the very definition of Government and essential to every step in the progress to be made by that of the United States," he urged. Hamilton envisioned a bank making loans to the Treasury, depositing government funds, circulating a uniform, elastic currency, aiding in tax payments, and stimulating trade and labor via commercial loans. Although a staunch supporter of Uncle Sam, Hamilton demanded a privately-run B.U.S. By 1791, the bank was operating just as he had hoped. Chartered for 20 years, it was capitalized at $10 million—$2 million of which was subscribed by the government via foreign funding. The remaining $8 million in B.U.S. stock was bought by citizens who oversubscribed within an hour!

Prior to the B.U.S., speculation in America was almost nonexistent. It was universally thought appropriate to invest in land or ventures which might add to the future common good of society; but to buy covetously pieces of paper for resale at higher prices seemed, to most upstanding folks like Thomas Jefferson, to be greedy, nonproductive, and vaguely un-Christian.

But Hamilton sparked a flurry of speculative activity based on his promise to refund drastically depreciated Continental dollars to establish America's credit. Savvy, in-the-know greedsters scrambled to purchase "Continentals" cheaply from those ignorant of Hamilton's intentions (news traveled slowly). They then traded them with the government for substantial profits. Both Continentals and B.U.S. stock provided outlets for America's first true financial speculators. (By the way, those speculators, including Hamilton's assistant secretary of the Treasury, William Duer, culled nice profits via insider information.) This separation from those who previously operated in land, Treasury bonds and joint stock companies marked the fountainhead launching of our financial markets. The markets then set the stage for our emerging bond market, followed by our stock market, all of which were necessary and preparatory to our Industrial Revolution.

Note that our Industrial Revolution lagged behind England's by over 50 years. Ever wonder why? The main reason is that when theirs began, we didn't have the financial markets here to finance the previously unimaginable magnitude of industrialization that burst forth upon the world. Hamilton's actions laid the early seed for their evolution. He could see what was going on in England and saw no reason it couldn't flourish here as well.

Masterminding his plan for America's economy, Hamilton also established a modest mint to eliminate foreign coinage such as Spanish dollars. Coinage of cents and half-cents would also enable poor folks to make small purchases. With his B.U.S. and mint underway, Hamilton set out to unleash America from the hand-to-mouth survival aspects and constraints imposed by its purely agricultural society. Clearly a man ahead of his time, he preached industrialization feverishly, convinced of its benefits for the economy and population. Combining farming and factories, he proclaimed, would create an independent nation by decreasing imports, enhancing population by attracting immigration and employing more workers—including women and children. In that regard he may have even been a spiritual father of feminism. As to whether he was a brute for helping to create a system that would later exploit child labor, he would have thought not.

Born on a British West Indies island five miles in diameter in 1755, Hamilton was the illegitimate son of Rachel Faucette Lavien, who lived with his father, merchant James Hamilton, for 15 years until he picked up and left. (John Adams often called him the "bastard brat of a Scotch peddler.") Young Hamilton began working for a sugar exporting firm in St. Croix at 13. Four years later, his boss was so impressed with his work that he sent the boy to attend Kings College (now Columbia University) in Manhattan. Exploitation of child labor in an early industrial world? It wouldn't be possible if all children had half the heart of Hamilton.

This tough, self-made master predicted new cities would arise to house factories and workers and act as additional markets for farmers, thereby eliminating overproduction. To create the system, Hamilton, the capitalist, favored government backing of entrepreneurs to encourage risk-taking.

Mired in irony, this illegitimate son took a married mistress of his own, whose husband later blackmailed him—the only black spot on his otherwise life-long distinguished character. As to his fatal duel with Burr? We leave that to the many conventional history books, or any encyclopedia, all of which can adequately tell the tale. The lesson of this man's life is simply that it takes an environment that tolerates speculation to allow for the financial markets—to allow for the industrial world in which we live. Maybe another lesson is: Don't be a central banker if you want a long, healthy life.

NICHOLAS BIDDLE

A CIVILIZED MAN COULD NOT BEAT
A BUCCANEER

Y ou can say this about central bankers: They evolved in a steady stream
from scalawags to refined and restrained statesmen. The original central
banker, **John Law**, was wild. Then came **Alexander Hamilton**, an illegitimate son. Nicholas Biddle was the third important central banker in the
evolution of Wall Street, but he was as strait-laced as they come. He was well
bred, well-spoken, intelligent, handsome, and patriotic. For such a proper and
scholarly type, he defended central banking amazingly well, despite its some
what ragged public image. Biddle almost created for us a permanent central
bank, similar to today's Federal Reserve, but 100 years before America could
permanently institutionalize the concept.

Biddle's struggle began in 1823, when he became the third president of the
Second Bank of the United States at age 33. Born in 1786 to a prominent
Philadelphia family, he graduated from an Ivy League college at 13, married
an heiress, studied law, served diplomats overseas, edited the Lewis and Clark
expedition journals, and served as a state senator and a director on the Second

Bank's board before he became its president. But nothing could have prepared him for the battle he was about to face.

At the time, the Philadelphia-based Second Bank of the United States had a virtually nonexistent public image—its first leader had perverted its power for political purposes. Its second leader, in trying to reverse the damages, called in too many loans too quickly, causing branches to close. This was definitely not a user-friendly bank.

Biddle tamed the Bank to serve the Treasury, commercial banks and the financial community, performing most duties of today's Federal Reserve. Within six months of his election as president, business loans increased by over $2 million, though he was picky with loan applicants, sometimes refusing loans to friends. He maintained high standards when it came to the bank, making an "invariable rule" not to borrow from the bank himself and not to endorse discounted notes at any institution. He was a creative banker, but on a day-to-day basis, he was fiercely conservative.

The Bank sustained the national economy most importantly by issuing and regulating a national paper currency. Through Biddle's regulation of the money supply, the Bank could regulate supply rates of domestic and foreign exchange and guide state banks with their issues of money, pleasing the government. Without this concept. Wall Street as we know it today could never avoid tremendous boom-bust cycles. Even the people came to like the bank, since its money was good throughout the entire U.S. Both Biddle and the Bank, which by supplying credit eased America out of its 1825 financial strain, enjoyed popularity for a few years. But just when it looked as if his struggles were over, politics poked its ugly head into the picture—via President Andrew Jackson's election.

Jackson hated and distrusted all banks—especially Biddle's and his paper money. So naturally, he couldn't sit still while the Bank thrived. He initiated wild accusations that the Bank was not only unconstitutional, but also an irresponsible monopoly using public funds to enrich a few wealthy men. By the 1830s, Jackson was fighting an all-out war on the Bank, which annoyed Biddle—he had voted for the man!

Biddle, perhaps being too rational, and assuming that a similar rationality permeated Washington, thought he could easily win the battle. He appealed for the Bank's re-charter four years before it was to expire—mistake number one. Though most of the government supported his cause, Jackson had the power to veto the charter—and did. But Biddle didn't buckle. Instead, he began contracting loans. Jackson, in turn, halted government deposits at the bank. Then Biddle contracted more loans and Jackson withdrew all government deposits. Mistake number two—he took on the President! Biddle felt that he had to try for the sake of central banking, but his effort failed and left the U.S. in a credit crunch known as Biddle's Panic.

Based on the faith and deposits of creditors, banks cannot withstand a continuous stream of negative publicity, and nothing can generate more negative publicity than a fight with a President, even if the President is obviously wrong. Dwindling faith in the Bank, coupled with the loss of its federal charter, caused deposits to decrease by $17 million (27 percent) within a year. En route, the central currency collapsed while money rates climbed, firms failed, wages dropped, and unemployment rose. The whole situation left people with a bad taste in their mouths—an impression that maybe Jackson was right and maybe the Bank was too powerful. Of course the Bank didn't disappear. It was now a big "regular" state bank. Biddle relaxed the Bank's "tight" position, and even without government deposits, loans reached their former level the next year.

But every good central banking story has at least one twist. Biddle's continuation of the Bank via state charter in 1836 operated under the title: The United States Bank of Pennsylvania. At the same time, because of Jacksonian policies and the suspension of specie payments, the Panic of 1837 hit. Biddle wielded his new weapon, the U.S. Bank, and almost single-handedly swept America out of panic—for a while. Using the bank's resources to restore market prices, he provided the means for payments and collections. He formed a syndicate to corner cotton, since its price was then crucial to the American credit abroad. His plan worked, and his cotton pool earned an $800,000 profit! Feeling pretty good about himself, and justified in his prior banking activity by the panic's course of events, he then resigned from the bank at 53, believing it safe and secure. But a second and later corner failed, and the bank lost $900,000, which ultimately led to the bank's closure!

It is important to note that the Panic of 1837 led to one of the very largest and longest economic declines of American history. Basically the economy moved downhill steadily until 1844, ironically, the year of Biddle's death. A seven-year decline makes it the second longest recession in America's history, exceeded in length only by the decline of the 1870s and early '80s. It is hard to tell how bad the decline was in magnitude. Records were poor then, and it would be virtually impossible to quantify differences, for example, between the primitive economy then and the more sophisticated post–industrial revolution recessions and depressions that would later occur. But it was clearly huge and created a very bad impression in the public's mind.

The U.S. Bank's failure reflected badly on Biddle—and on central banking. Someone had to be blamed, and Biddle bore the brunt of it. He died in public disgrace—but financial comfort, which only fueled the public's hate for him. Because of all this bitterness associated with Biddle and the second central bank, central banking didn't make another comeback for almost 100 years. While you can't measure the significance of what never happened, the absence of a central bank during that period, in this observer's mind, cost Wall Street and America a great many times what was lost in Biddle's Panic.

JAMES STILLMAN

PSYCHIC HEADS AMERICA'S LARGEST BANK

Reporters might have had a field day with James Stillman, had he allowed himself the spotlight, but because of his responsibilities—heading a national bank—he kept to himself. Too bad—he would have made great headlines—"Banker Believes He Is Psychic." When Stillman looked at a man with his impenetrable dark brown eyes, he claimed he could read the man's mind and that a sixth sense detected truth from lies. While his "sixth sense" probably was mere keen observation and ability to listen, Stillman gained the reputation of an omniscient banking god. Men trembled in his grave presence as he transformed an insignificant bank into a major powerhouse that rivaled the House of Morgan.

Despite many idiosyncrasies, Stillman was ultra-conservative in running Manhattan's National City Bank. A banker has two customers: depositors and borrowers. He was a depositor's banker rather than a borrower's banker. When he took over in 1891 at 41, the impeccably-dressed Stillman, wearing a large, square-cut emerald ring on his right hand, steadily took the safe road of conservative lending practices. In this manner, he increased the bank's surplus cash on hand, increasing its credibility. Thereby, he reasoned, merchants could feel safer depositing with him. And they did—in droves.

The strategy derived from his stubborn pride. In his beginnings in banking, he somehow couldn't get himself to do the one thing all salesmen must do to get business—to ask for it. Asking "for the order" is basic to selling. But Stillman thought it tacky. Frank A. Vanderlip, a vice-president at Stillman's bank commented: "To get a good account for the bank, Mr. Stillman would have risked his life, but he never would have stated his purpose in words . . . the convention was that no one could, with dignity, ask for an account."

Within two years, after making a killing loaning millions during the 1893 panic, his integrity paid off—deposits nearly doubled. National City Bank had become the largest commercial bank in New York with the greatest cash reserve in America. **Thomas Lawson**, in a fit of jealousy, once called it "Stillman's Money Trap." Of course, it wasn't the underwriting powerhouse that the House of Morgan was.

A real cold fish, Stillman was nicknamed "Sunny Jim" by his competitors at Morgan. The dour mustached banker was so dedicated to National City that he rid himself of all distractions, including his wife. He had no need for her. To Stillman, women just got in the way. He used to say, "Never consult women, just tell them." So, after 23 years of marriage and five kids, Stillman, without remorse, shipped his wife to Europe to avoid a sensational divorce suit (or, as a former servant once said, to avail himself of the children's attractive nurse). Whatever the reason, when the social circuit discovered his wife's disappearance, Stillman concocted rumors of a supposed drug habit and mental illness. He then forbade her to contact their children, and forbade the children to ever mention their mother—one of the rare times he ever spoke to them when they were young.

With such a dour demeanor, you'd expect Stillman to be more like robber barons **Daniel Drew** or **Cornelius Vanderbilt**, ruthlessly profiting and using people and property. That was true in his personal life, but not in business. What saved Stillman from a ferocious reputation was the required civilized nature of commercial banking. Prissy-neat, composed, and quiet, he was a banker, and kept his emotions and eccentricities under wraps during business hours, so few paid much attention to him—that is, until he associated with the big names and bigger deals.

His first big-name deal was backing the Union Pacific Railroad for Morgan rivals Kuhn, Loeb and **Edward Harriman** in 1897. As the possessor of America's largest cash reserve, National City Bank was perhaps the only bank, outside of the House of Morgan, capable of financing the required $45 million. This rankled kingpin **J.P. Morgan** for years, though the two later made amends when their respective railroad interests were combined in 1907 (see **James Hill** for further explanation).

Amazingly, for being in such a cutthroat business, Stillman never made long-term business enemies. He had two related rules:

1. "A man is never so rich that he can afford to have enemies. Enemies must be placated."
2. "Competition must never grow so keen as to wound the dignity of a rival man or institution."

But business bonding could be based on his willingness to subordinate his family. For example, Stillman expanded his business to include investment banking, underwriting stocks for the Rockefeller clan. To secure the relationship, he arranged to marry off both his daughters to Rockefellers. Women, after all, weren't worth much to Stillman and were easily sacrificed to move further on the chessboard of life. For the Rockefellers and Harriman, he bought undigested stock issues at depressed prices, participated in the Rockefellers' bull pools and manipulated stocks, running up their prices, then unloading them on the public—all the standard stuff of the day. Ironically, he never bought stocks for his personal account. In good conservative-banker style, he owned only bonds of companies with solid personnel, future prospects, and earnings potential.

Born to a New England cotton merchant, Stillman began his career at 16, bypassing college to work for his father's firm. He later took over the firm and earned millions, with which he bought a Newport, Rhode Island mansion and a yacht—all the necessary possessions of a rich young Wall Streeter of the era. More important, those millions, coupled with his respectful, quiet demeanor and ability to listen, earned him a spot on the Chicago, Milwaukee and St. Paul Railroad board of directors. It was there that he first met fellow director, William Rockefeller, who was undoubtedly the key to his consequent success.

After dabbling in railroads, Stillman was vaulted to a director's seat at National City Bank where Rockefeller was a major stockholder. He was soon its president. Stillman knew he had made it to the top when, in 1894, the U.S. Treasury unexpectedly called on Morgan for $50 million and Morgan turned to Stillman for aid in putting the deal together! When the big guy turns to you, you must be pretty big yourself.

Ironically, another milestone in Stillman's life was again helping Morgan—this time in bailing Wall Street out of the 1907 Panic. While Stillman was overshadowed by Morgan, he was influential in the bailout, advocating support of the weaker banks via the stronger ones. Two years later, Stillman—a director of 41 firms—retired as president of National City Bank. For the remainder of his life he lived in France. He died in 1918 of heart disease the same year National City's assets first reached $1 billion. An important point to note, and the only sign of potential family closeness in Stillman's life, was that National City reached the $1 billion mark under the direction of his son, James A. Stillman.

Stillman was a quirky character during his banking career. For example, he felt it was so important to keep bank affairs secret that he kept his papers under the protection of a secret code and cipher key held exclusively by his vice president, **Frank Vanderlip**, and himself. When he traveled, Stillman never parted from the valise in which the code was kept secure.

But at home, he was absolutely eccentric. He shaved three times a day and took an hour to dress. He was vain about his small feet, which he thought were refined. He nibbled at meals, ranked each dish by percentile—and flew into a rage if the rating was too low! At breakfast, he sometimes returned dozens of eggs to get the four that met his standards!

As for his psychic concoction and claimed ability to read minds, well, it doesn't take the world's shrewdest person to notice obvious traits—just a perceptive one. The mind reading schtick may have just been PR that Stillman cooked up to intimidate flaky borrowers. It is unlikely such a successful conservative banker actually heard voices in his head—that would make him crazy and prone to do crazy things during work hours. My guess is that, a little like a would-be Sherlock Holmes, he just observed well and drew astute conclusions. For example, Stillman used to claim that men wearing pompadours were vain and crafty—well, he was probably right, but that doesn't mean he was psychic. Bankers who don't take the time to notice things like hair cuts, body language, and say, shifty eyes are easy targets for a bad loan—Stillman wasn't.

AMS Press, Inc., 1916

FRANK A. VANDERLIP

A ROLE MODEL FOR ANY WALL STREET WANNA-BE

Frank Vanderlip never expected to become a great banker. Born on an Aurora, Illinois farm in 1864, he supported himself with everything from machine shop work to newspaper reporting until the age of 33. It was then, after a stint as a financial editor, that he was appointed assistant to the Treasury Secretary. From then on, his financial genius flourished. Highlights from his career include financing the Spanish-American War while at the Treasury and building Manhattan's National City Bank (today's Citicorp) into America's largest commercial bank by 1919. He was innovative, creative and, most important, bold enough to put his then-revolutionary theories into action.

To get to a position where his ideas could make a difference took ambition and a strong dedication to his work. After about four years with the Treasury, during which he floated a $200 million Spanish-American War bond, Vanderlip caught the eye of National City Bank President **James Stillman**, who saw in Vanderlip a hard and dedicated worker like himself. In a biographical *Saturday Evening Post* piece titled, "From Farm Boy to Financier: My Start in

Wall Street," Vanderlip admitted, "I did not play. I never have learned how to play. I would go abroad, but always with a driving purpose to find out more about the currents of world commerce."

Vanderlip's drive paid off. In 1901, looking like a typical banker—distinguished, bespectacled, and mustached with his hair parted in the middle—he became Stillman's protege and the bank's youngest vice-president. Here was his opportunity to shine. National City was then a modest, old-fashioned bank run according to Stillman's quirky beliefs—a man like Vanderlip with new, imaginative ideas could make it a world power!

He first set about building City Bank by soliciting new accounts, which doesn't sound too revolutionary, but it made a world of difference for the bank's assets. Stillman was too timid to solicit new accounts, instead relying upon City's solid reputation to attract customers. Vanderlip, on the other hand, felt a solid reputation should be flaunted, so he solicited new accounts with pride. Though it was considered unorthodox, Stillman never raised an eyebrow, because Vanderlip got results. In his first year, Vanderlip pulled in 365 new accounts—"one for every day of the year!" The savvy whipper-snapper said proudly, "Before I finished with the bank, deposits of $20,000,000 had been increased until they could be written in the form of an incredible sum of money—$1,000,000,000!"

Vanderlip also brought City Bank into the investment field, beginning with government bonds. Previously, the bank had rejected such business—and the commissions that went along with it. So Vanderlip organized the National City Company, a general bond firm that earned as much are the bank itself! "This, too, was a thing no national bank had done in that period. It was a thing the private banking houses wished we would not engage in." (Ultimately, in the 1930s during **Charles Mitchell and Albert Wiggin's** era, Uncle Sam would come to the same conclusion.) Later, he put out a monthly circular explaining and advertising City's government bond business, which became a sort of voice for City, since Stillman never said a word regarding the bank.

Living in upstate New York with his wife and six kids, Vanderlip led City Bank into foreign markets, paving the way for today's American investors. He stimulated foreign trade and international financing while lobbying to change regulations preventing banks from opening overseas branches. As a result of his efforts, he helped author the Federal Reserve Act of 1913, and the next year, City Bank became the first American bank to open a foreign branch in Buenos Aires.

Although he violated just about every banking taboo initiated by Stillman, Vanderlip did well for the bank—and Stillman respected that. So when old-school bank officers complained about Vanderlip to the boss, the boss simply said (while secretly chuckling), "I can't control that young man." Vanderlip said, "There was a tinge of pride in his voice when he said that. Largely I did what I believed was proper and helpful, using my own judgment, which was what he wished me to do, for he wished me to grow."

Vanderlip, bank president since 1909, resigned in 1919 due to a falling out with his board of directors. His 1937 *New York Times* obituary repeated

Wall Street rumors that the board blamed him for large losses suffered in foreign ventures, specifically in loans to Russia, which had just undergone its revolution. Other rumors blamed Vanderlip for too-rapid expansion in areas that weren't ready for it. Both Vanderlip and the board denied all rumors, and the agreed-upon reasons for his leaving were ill health and a needed rest.

But rest wasn't on Vanderlip's agenda—he kept busy until his death in 1937, plunging into everything from foreign policy to repealing prohibition. Vanderlip traveled extensively throughout Europe and Japan after his resignation, advocating an end to American isolationist policies and urging friendly relations with Japan. Later he organized the Citizen's Federal Research Bureau to investigate graft. He had been away from the business world for eight years when he joined a Wall Street firm as a special partner, dabbling in automobile stock and making $3 million. Vanderlip also dabbled in real estate with two of his sons, including Frank A. Vanderlip, Jr., reconstructing slums in upstate New York and developing Palos Verdes, California. Vanderlip died at 72 of intestinal complications.

He was an aggressive salesman, a corporate builder, a world-wide visionary, a good "deal" man, a devotee of civic duty—even at the federal level—and a family man. While every single thing in his business life didn't work out perfectly, most worked pretty darn well, and Vanderlip is perhaps most representative of the kind of quiet yet dramatic success which is possible in the financial world where a break with convention becomes convention if it is truly conservative and makes money. For anyone with a flair for finance, Vanderlip is a good role model to compare with the bad role models of flamboyant hedonists. Those who tailor their personal and business lives to Vanderlip-like style rather than that of a **Jim Brady** or **F. Augustus Heinze** will improve their odds of success, whatever their initial financial and mental assets.

GEORGE F. BAKER

LOOKING BEFORE LEAPING
PAYS OFF

Remember the tortoise and the hare? The hare, recklessly speeding and blindly confident, raced ahead, but then fiddled around and napped, while the tortoise crawled on sluggishly to victory—as the hare dozed. Sometimes it pays to move slowly but surely. George Baker operated much like the turtle: patient and persistent. Baker was the driving force behind New York's First National Bank from 1877 until his death in 1931, always relying on his faith in the American economy and always optimistic. In an era plagued with wars and panics, Baker withstood the worst by being prepared—and looking before he leaped.

Stout, with muttonchop whiskers, Baker became a venerable N.Y. banker—and occasional business associate of **J.P. Morgan**—because of his surefooted, reliable manner, and squeaky-clean character. After his death, even the *New York Times* noted his "unchallenged" personal integrity "in days when scandal walked unashamed in the street." No wonder he was considered an "old-fashioned" banker! Equally characteristic of Baker was his silence, perhaps explaining why his fortune far exceeded his fame. Asked once to wield his power in support of a particular cause, Baker declined, acknowledging, "I do have a lot of power so long as I do not attempt to use it."

Born the son of a Troy, N.Y. shoe-merchant-turned-state legislator in 1840, Baker began his banking career at 16 after finishing school, clerking for the N.Y. state banking department for seven years. His financial flair raised the eyebrows of John Thompson, a N.Y. financier looking to form a bank in 1863 when America needed funds to finance the Civil War. Invited to join the venture, Baker, 23, invested his entire $3,000 in savings for 30 bank shares, a teller's position and seat on the board of directors. Immediately, the bank undertook the lucrative business of selling government bonds to finance the Civil War, a task that provided the bank with a firm foundation for credit. Just two years' time saw the First National become America's largest underwriter of government and corporate bonds—and Baker, the bank's acting leader. In 1869, he married, insisting that he and his wife live on half his income, in order to invest the rest! Later, they raised three children, one of whom—George, Jr.—followed in his dad's exact footsteps.

The first feather in Baker's cap came in 1873, when leading bankers, Jay Cooke & Co., failed, causing a run on banks. Threatened with the closure of the Wall Street-quartered First National, Baker kept his cool—amidst failing banks and closing factories—and kept the dollars flowing, claiming a panic could be cured if banks paid out their reserve. "When we stop paying it will be because there isn't a dollar in the till, or obtainable." From then on, Baker never panicked—he instead vowed to never sell out any borrowers and to constantly accumulate profits in good times, in order to glide through the bad. He declared, "It is cheap insurance to keep strong!"

By 1877, Baker, 37, was First National's president, which he remained until becoming board chairman at 61. The bank netted $750,000 that year and declared dividends of up to 60 percent. Stockholders rejoiced, particularly Baker, who had been steadily increasing his bank holdings! Unabashedly supporting the profit motive, he boosted dividends steadily over the years and increased bank surplus and capital regularly.

Meanwhile, as was then all the rage, Baker invested in railroads—joining syndicates, acquiring control of run-down lines, then improving and selling them for profits. He rejuvenated the Richmond and Danville line (later, the Southern Railway system), bought for $51 per share in 1882, and sold seven years later for $240. Of course, before buying anything, Baker religiously attended inspection tours on the line and afterwards, if new owners went broke, his group rebought and reorganized the line. In 1896, Baker—quite railroad-savvy—bought out the Jersey Central for $30 per share and sold at $160 to Morgan, who then transformed it into the Reading line. Being consistently successful in his ventures, Baker and his golden touch were often sought by company boards—in fact, he served on over 50 (about half of which were railroads), including Morgan's U.S. Steel and several competing N.Y. banks. His key to success? Carefully take the long view, build up a property as an investment and never milk it for short-term, speculative profit!

George Baker ruled the First National with an iron fist—with foresight and constructive planning. Some said that Baker was the bank, as the two were seemingly inseparable. In his dark attire and flat-top derby, he handed over to his bank more than $3 million of his own in 1907 when capitalizing the First Security Co., a holding company for securities held by the bank. His nerves of steel assured the bank's strength during panics—which led to others' strength as well. During the 1907 Panic, for instance, he met with J.P. Morgan each night in Morgan's library-turned-office to plan the economy's bailout.

But the 1929 Crash caught Baker off-guard or unaware. At 89, he was somewhat set in his ways and refused to heed his son's warnings to liquidate overvalued stock, saying that the young just "didn't understand." As with almost everyone of his generation, his over-70-years' experience told him that an advance in market value was followed by a decline, and then by another advance to a higher level. (Later, Baker came to realize that "every time is different.") So, while his securities tumbled, Baker remained optimistic about a quick recovery, though he supposedly admitted at a U.S. Steel board meeting in 1930, "I was a damn fool." Continuing to operate on the premise that "It is better to wear out than to rust out," Baker remained First National's chair right up until the very end at the ripe old age of 91, leaving some $73 million, mostly to his son, though in his last few years about $22 million had gone to various charities. Reputed to be America's third richest man in his heyday, Baker found solace in giving to the Harvard Business School and the Red Cross, among others; hence his later reputation as a man with "the hardest shell and the softest heart."

While 91 is a ripe old age by anyone's standard, it is not inconceivable that Baker's life was shortened by the tragedy of the Crash; he caught pneumonia and died in his sleep. The magnitude of the Crash may have dampened his otherwise optimistic spirits. Most of the biggest fortunes ever built were assembled as Baker's was, through slow, careful planning. Perhaps the lesson is that, while it pays to be a long-term investor and builder and not be shaken from the good things you own due to fear of economic downturn, it is also wise to be watchful and wary for the rare secular turning points that catch society unaware. Baker may have been the tortoise, but it wouldn't have hurt him any to be able to cut and run.

AMADEO P. GIANNINI

TAKING THE PULSE OF WALL STREET OUT OF NEW YORK

When fire swept through San Francisco following the 1906 earthquake, local legend has it that one man leapt ahead of the flames to salvage his bank's currency and securities. Quickly loading the goods on two vegetable wagons, A.P. Giannini galloped across his smoldering hometown eagerly distributing loans that helped rebuild the city. At 36, the son of Italian immigrants was at the very bud of a magnificent banking career. In the years to come, until his death in 1949, Giannini controlled over 500 chain banks from California to New York via what later became the worldwide Bank of America.

Standing 6 foot 2, weighing over 215 pounds with white hair and mustache, Giannini became a true banking legend in the 1920s, when his original Bank of Italy—barely salvaged from the fire—grew by leaps and bounds. Riding the coattails of California's booming movie, oil and real estate industries, A.P. made one acquisition after another, seeking to build the first nationwide branch-banking system. He was a true visionary, placing San Francisco on the map as a financial center for the first time since the Gold Rush, and revolutionizing banking. "The bank of tomorrow is going to be a sort of department store, handling every service the people may want in the way of banking, investment, and trust service." A proud man—and never greedy—he wanted his system for reasons other than fame and fortune: He wanted to help "the little fellow." Whereas Wall Street catered to the elite few, the Bank of America served millions of customers—"the little man who needed a little money." And rather than fill the pockets of "twenty thousand small unit bankers," he sought "a more general distribution of wealth and happiness."

A.P. was California's hero, resembling the little fellow he often spoke of—but on a grander scale. He was affable, fair, empathetic, enthusiastic, and a local boy, living in small town suburban San Mateo. Born in San Jose, he began working for his stepfather's San Francisco produce firm in 1882. Just 12, he worked from 2 a.m. until schooltime. Seven years later, despite a poor education, he made partner. At 31, he was married and rich enough to retire. Instead, this bundle of energy dabbled in banking, opening his first bank in 1904 with $150,000 and three partners. Based in a remodeled tavern in San Francisco's Italian district, North Beach, the bank served primarily local merchants and working men. Using then-unorthodox methods—soliciting depositors on the streets, displaying eye-catching ads, and pioneering small loans—Giannini's bank proved successful. Convinced (by the numerous bank failures of the 1907 Panic) that big banks were safe banks, he built the first statewide chain, operating 24 branches by 1918.

Ever resourceful, Giannini financed his branches as easily as he operated them. He simply sold stock in holding companies, then used the capital to buy stock in future branches—and those always came to him on his terms. Never a major stockholder in his firm, Giannini first formed the Bancitaly Corp., which invested in American and European banks, then replaced it with the Transamerica Corp, in 1928. Merely by coincidence, but perhaps ironically, the two tallest buildings in today's San Francisco are the Bank of America Building and the Transamerica Pyramid. Giannini was an expert pyramid builder of his own. In many ways, this guy was a visionary of finance. Whether it was a little truck farmer's inventory or the water system for Northern California, whether a local stock brokerage firm or a statewide chain, Giannini financed California, and he did it locally.

By 1929, his empire exceeded 400 branches, with resources exceeding $1 billion. Most important, Giannini built it all on his own, always taking two steps at a time—staying one step ahead of Wall Street. Whereas Wall Street took control of America's railroads, and en route much of the west, Giannini's efforts, for the most part, kept control of California businesses within state lines, breeding the spirit of entrepeneurship that is central to capitalism and that has also been successful. On Giannini's heels, following his structure of localized finance, came an unprecedented state growth rate, such that today California's economy is actually larger than England's.

At a time when major corporations almost always had Wall Street's seal of approval, Giannini's phenomenal success wasn't exactly applauded in New York, especially when Bancitaly invaded New York's banking scene. Wall

Street was so bitter, in fact, it sent a representative to seek revenge and raise hell within Giannini's organization. **Elisha Walker** succeeded Giannini as Transamerica chairman in 1930 and right away began dismembering the firm, distributing severed branches to his Wall Street allies at severe losses to Transamerica! When he realized what was happening, A.P. charged out of retirement, armed with supporters. The Giannini camp gathered enough proxies to oust Walker and salvage the remains of his empire. Despite Wall Street shenanigans and new government monopoly regulations, Giannini kept on as strong as ever. Not even the Crash got in his way, as the Bank of America won the bid to finance the massive dam-building projects under A.P.'s new friend and co-supporter of the masses, Franklin Roosevelt.

Always modest, A.P. made way for his equally modest son Lawrence Mario Giannini to run the firm after he was certain his empire was again sturdy. The chairman of the board, who had announced "retirement" at least twice before, said in 1936, "I'll stand on the sidelines in a fatherly sort of watchfulness, the family watchdog ready to growl at any sign of danger from without and ready to bark at you if I find any turning away from the ideals on which the institution was founded." Starting as a clerk with his father's firm in 1918, at 24, Mario—largely responsible for the bank's overseas facilities—made senior vice-president in 1932, president four years later and took over when his father died.

A.P. Giannini was one of America's greatest bankers, applying the age-old concept of national banking to today's society. While bankers and businessmen may remember him for his holding companies, marketing strategies, bold expansion, and sure-fire success secret ("Enjoy your work and bypass part-time ventures"), the customers surely remember him for his magnetic personality. There is perhaps no other banker who ever received a steady stream of fan mail. Contrary to his New York rivals, he cast aside the heavy wooden doors of the House of Morgan to work out in the open—both in his office and publicly. Unlike other bankers, he saw between 50 and 100 visitors per day—mostly "little fellows"—and spoke freely to the press in his loud, crackling voice. He preached, "Avoid the speculative, grow with your work and have less worry and more fun out of life!"

A key point to remember about Giannini is that even when Wall Street was more clubby than it is today, a person with a vision and an independent streak could make good without selling out to the club. Scandal-free his whole life, loving his work and loving his customers, Giannini represents the best of banking in terms of its ability to bring power to people who otherwise wouldn't have had it. Once Wall Street pulsed from New York only. While today it pulses around the world, every bit as much outside of New York as in it. Giannini was a key part in taking the pulse to California, and keeping it there.

Oh, by the way, when he died he was worth only $600,000. He had given the rest of it away. I guess he knew he couldn't spend it in heaven.

PAUL M. WARBURG

FOUNDER AND CRITIC OF MODERN
AMERICAN CENTRAL BANKING

When Paul Warburg arrived in America from Germany in 1902, he viewed our banking system as archaic and desperately in need of reform. It was scattered, disorganized and unable to withstand the demands of a growing industrial nation. Serious-minded and determined, Warburg set about promoting a plan derived from his native Europe—central banking. About a decade later, the investment banker saw his efforts pay off in the passage of the Federal Reserve Act of 1913, which created our current central banking system, the Federal Reserve. En route, Warburg was at times ballyhooed as the "father" of the Federal Reserve System and as the foremost banking authority in America.

Born in 1868 to a family of bankers, Warburg grew up the sad, picked-on ugly duckling of his family. To compensate, he dove into his books with a fury, studying banking, and eventually became a confident, scholarly banker—with an inferiority complex. At age 23, he joined the Hamburg firm his great-grandfather had founded 70 years earlier, M.M. Warburg and Company. Eleven years later, he left the family firm to marry the daughter of recently deceased American banking giant Solomon Loeb. He promptly joined his wife's father's former firm—the infamous and almost all-powerful House of Kuhn, Loeb.

As an investment banker, the visionary Warburg floated major railroad bonds and government issues for Japan, Brazil, China, Argentina and Cuba. But as a concerned citizen, Warburg became obsessed with reforming American banking, writing pamphlets, courting editors and speaking to anyone who would listen—at the time, mostly banking scholars. In his detailed, two-volume 1930 history of the Fed's creation, called *The Federal Reserve System*, Warburg said one of the banking system's major defects was its lack of leadership. The book, written mostly in the late 1920s, was perfectly timed to coincide with the largest economic debacle of modern capitalism. The system was so loose and decentralized that, when financial calamity struck, he predicted there would be no governmental or private authority to assume leadership. He claimed no one "had the actual power to put on the brakes if the car were moving too fast and heading for the precipice." By 1932, everyone would know he was right, whether they knew who he was or not. By most modern accounts, the Fed actually worsened the Great Depression.

But originally, at the turn of the century, Warburg and his plan for reforming banking had three counts against them. First, bankers were reluctant to admit there was a problem in need of attention; second, they were dubious of central banking; and third, as a relative newcomer to America, Warburg's criticisms were not welcomed. Warburg recalled that, at the time, central banking critics worried that a centralized system would inevitably fall into the hands of either the government or Wall Street. Enemies of central banking tended to fall onto one side or the other, either friends of Wall Street and enemies of government, or proponents of governmental regulation and enemies of the Street. So neither side would pledge its support.

What finally swayed everyone concerned was the Panic of 1907, and just as Warburg had previously predicted, there was no leadership to prevent the resulting calamity. Yes, **J.P. Morgan** stepped into the breach to bail out the world, but had this old walrus been unable or unwilling to do so, everyone knew there was no one else with the power to prevail in a time of madness. Soon afterwards, Warburg had the ear of bankers and politicians alike, and his plan quickly gained momentum.

A kindly man, with a sad face, dark complexion, walrus mustache, partially bald head, and a penchant for writing sad poetry, Warburg drew up an initial blueprint for a "United Reserve Bank of the United States" from which legislators drew up, in part, the Federal Reserve Act. Although Warburg would have opted for a central bank with regional branches, he gave his blessing to the Americanized version consisting of a dozen regional banks governed by a central board.

The only gripe he had with the newly-created Fed was that the President was granted the ultimate power in choosing heads of the Federal Reserve Board. Warburg, like all central bankers preceding him, felt politics represented "the gravest danger confronting the system." He feared politics would ultimately taint the Fed's independence and turn it into "the football of politics" so that a "splendid instrument of protection might thus become an element of dangerous disturbance." What would result would be disastrous: "A Federal Reserve System turned into a political octopus, a national Tammany Hall, would infest not only the counting houses but every farm and hovel in the country." Still true!

Warburg was able to keep his eye on the Fed when President Wilson appointed him one of five original board members and vice-chairman. One account said Wilson wanted him to serve as chairman, but Warburg, being as modest as he was, would accept a position only as high as the vice-chairmanship.

Serving on the first board was an incredible responsibility, and Warburg did not take it lightly. He retired from his immensely profitable Kuhn, Loeb position and resigned from various directorships to concentrate on his work. Since the Board united the regional banks into one central bank, Warburg felt its members had the job of upholding its integrity and keeping it free from special interests, especially politics. Sadly, after his four-year term ran out during World War I, Warburg felt the heat of resentment as a German-born American in a prestigious position. So, he resigned his position in 1918, declining assured re-appointment. Of course, that didn't stop him from staying active in finance. Only 50 years old, Warburg returned to the private world, creating no headlines but specializing in international banking, while keeping abreast of Fed issues by serving on its advisory council until the mid-1920s.

A year before the 1929 Crash, insightful Warburg predicted gloom and doom to follow what he called an "orgy of unrestrained speculation." This, he predicted, would "bring about a general depression involving the entire country." Wall Street, still high from a bull market, laughed at his prediction—for a while, anyway. While Warburg could have bragged, "I told you so," he chose his characteristic, constructive route and campaigned for further interdependence within the Fed and closer cooperation among its banks.

Warburg was a man way ahead of his time. He was probably never understood, because from day one the Fed had a political tone to it that Warburg never wanted. Still, his impact on America's financial markets via the creation and early direction of the Fed is immense. A lesson is to be learned from Warburg. The Fed would be more effective if it were stripped completely of political appointment and meddling. With the problems the banking system has recently gotten itself into, aided by political meddling, we should all wish the Fed were free to do its job better, leaving us with a better banking system. Warburg would have liked that.

Brown Brothers

BENJAMIN STRONG

HAD STRONG BEEN STRONG THE
ECONOMY MIGHT HAVE BEEN, TOO

Despite barriers of all kinds—ill health, a tragic family life, political rigmarole, and volatile economic times—Benjamin Strong became one of America's greatest modern-day central bankers before his untimely death in 1928. He headed the Federal Reserve System's New York branch when the Fed was still an unproven concept, and with it, created an influential force in world economic policy-making during the 1920s.

Strong was a man of many achievements. Born in upstate New York to a modest family, central banking was in his blood. His great grandfather had clerked for **Alexander Hamilton** at the beginnings of central banking in America. Strong started out working his way up Wall Street's rungs managing bank trusts. Then, seven years before reaching his Federal Reserve post at just 42 in 1914, Strong assisted **J.P. Morgan** in reviving the American economy during the fierce 1907 Panic. Because of his ties with influential Morgan partner Henry P. Davison and his position at Bankers Trust Company, he was chosen to head a small committee deciding which banking institutions were worthy of Morgan money. Typically, Morgan ignored details, and instead relied on Strong's bottom line in making decisions.

The Panic of 1907 boosted Strong's reputation among Wall Street's banking community, and he was well on his way to a Morgan partnership. He was perfect for the job—tall, handsome, intelligent, well-liked, alert, dedicated, relentlessly driven—and he had Morgan's blessing. Strong was also good friends with Davison, so when the Fed was created and Davison was called to help pick its head, Strong's Morgan partnership was permanently put on hold in favor of the Federal Reserve post.

But Strong, like much of Wall Street, objected to the Fed's structure and refused the appointment at first. The system was structured so that the regional banks answered to directors sitting in the heart of bureaucrat-land, Washington! Strong, a central banking history buff, knew this would inevitably lead to political influence, which in turn would lead to the system's demise. But eventually, because of Davison, he relented, accepted the position, and dedicated the remainder of his life to central banking.

Strong had little else going for him; his home life was literally a tragedy. It started out wonderfully. He married in 1895, had a girl and two boys, moved to Englewood, New Jersey where he made his Morgan connection and did the suburban social circuit with his wife. It was a wonderful 10 years—until his wife killed herself (while weakened by childbirth, one source said). Davison took the Strong children into his own home, and two years later. Strong married a woman 15 years his junior. They had two daughters, but this time, his wife left him in 1916 with the girls, and they divorced in 1920.

Even more heartbreaking, the same year his second wife abandoned him, Strong contracted tuberculosis. It attacked first his lungs, then his larynx and kept him away from his desk for more than a third of the 12 years remaining to him. He offered to resign at least twice because of his health, but his directors refused to hear of it, for Strong "was" the Fed—even while in his sickbed.

When Strong wasn't bedridden, he was hard at work building a powerful Fed. He often visited European central bankers, soliciting their combined cooperation to give the central banks a stronghold on international monetary matters. He devoutly believed such matters were up to the central banks—not the governments. "Central banks should deal only with central banks, not with foreign governments." While that is a commonly accepted concept today, it was a groundbreaking notion then, at a time when most classical economists believed that each country was its own economic island. [As I demonstrated in my second book, *The Wall Street Waltz*, this concept was never true.] Yet it survived in the common mind until fairly recently. Strong saw through the economic island notion long before almost anyone else. Had the world understood then what Strong knew, much of the 1930s Great Depression could have been avoided simply by worldwide monetary cooperation among central banks in providing liquidity.

At the time, however, Strong's ultimate goal in working for cooperation was to lift Europe from its postwar financial doldrums—he knew the Fed couldn't do it alone. Sometimes working with his best friend, Bank of England

Governor Montagu Norman, or a pool of central banks, Strong helped stabilize Belgium, Italy, Romania, Poland, and France. Often, Wall Street financiers participating in stabilization loans would wait for Strong's approval before even thinking of floating a loan. He surprised everyone, particularly Wall Street, in making the Fed internationally influential during the postwar period.

As instrumental as Strong was in furthering central banking in international economics, he became more infamous for restoring England to its former $4.86 parity in 1925—and the events which followed this feat. The Fed and the House of Morgan, both at Strong's prompting, fed England $200 million and $100 million, respectively. Meanwhile back in America, Strong sponsored an easy-money policy, reducing the discount rate from 4 percent to 3.5 percent. Low discount rates in America, Strong figured, would stop the continuing outflow of England's gold, thereby defending the pound's new position.

His actions helped restore international liquidity, but by 1927, skeptics blamed his easy-money policy for increased stock market speculation. Strong's easy-money policy had lowered interest rates, and in turn, the price of call money, which then triggered increased securities purchases. In one year, from 1927 to 1928, brokers' loans soared a record amount from $3.29 billion to $4.43 billion! The market boomed in 1928, and by the time the Federal Reserve Board raised the discount rate up to 5 percent (Strong was too ill at this point to make decisions), it was too late. Interest rates zoomed from 8 percent to 12 percent, but people didn't care how much they shelled out for the borrowed money—the profits they anticipated would more than make up for interest charges!

From this point on, Strong's health prevented him from contributing to the Fed's policies. Pneumonia, influenza, shingles, and a damaged nervous system continuously knocked him to his knees. Shortly before he died, he wrote a friend, "Facing the past, honestly, I wonder that I am alive. When I review or catalogue what I have had to cover—the inside of the Bank, the Board, Congress. Governors' Committees and meetings, Treasury, Foreign banks, complicated plans, all the personal equations, our unruly members, hostility, illness—it's a mental high-speed cinema which staggers me—and in its experience has or had nearly finished me."

By October, 1928, he was dead at 56. He had been operated on for an abscess due to diverticulitis and seemed to recover, but a week later he suffered a relapse and died from a severe secondary hemorrhage. Shortly before he died, he had said with prescient insight, "I do not think the problem is necessarily one of security prices or of available volume of credit, or even of discount rates. It is really a problem of psychology. The country's state of mind has been highly speculative, advancing prices have been based upon a realization of the wealth and prosperity of the country, and consequently speculative tendencies are all the more difficult to deal with."

For a fighter like Ben Strong, death must have been much more agreeable then it would have been had he lived to face the stock market crash incapacitated and unable to do anything about it. What Strong would have done in the face of the booming market of 1927 and 1928 will never be known—the luck of the draw drew him from power and placed it in the hands of **George Harrison.** Had Strong been given the chance, he might have been able to lessen the fall, especially when you consider his psychological insight. As the market crashed, a healthy Strong likely would have loosened the monetary coffers to cushion the blow, and as the event was worldwide, he would have Strong-armed his foreign central bank buddies to do the same. The world-wide depression could have been much lighter.

GEORGE L. HARRISON

NO, THIS ISN'T THE GUY FROM THE BEATLES

Mild-mannered spot-spoken and affable central banker George Harrison got things done his own way at a time when things were as frenzied as they get—the 1929 Crash. This was Harrison's time to shine, and he did, working hard behind the scenes—everywhere but the doted-upon Stock Exchange floor. As a long-time deputy governor of the Federal Reserve Bank of New York, he wasn't the likeliest to become the hero of the day, but he earned the honor while helping ease the load on America's stressed-out economy. Because Wall Street was so much more powerful then than it is now in relation to non–Wall Street financial institutions, the head of the New York Fed was also more powerful then than now. In those days, Harrison was essentially the entire power of the Fed.

"The day after the market crash of October 24, I knew there was going to be a huge calling in of brokers' loans and a complete breakdown. Actually, loans were called in on the part of others than banks to the extent of $2,200,000,000. No money market could stand that." So Harrison leapt into action as best he could, since he walked with a cane after a childhood accident.

At first, he joined in the secret meetings held underneath the Exchange trading floor by Morgan partner **Thomas Lamont** along with other top New York bankers who pooled $240 million to shore up sliding stocks. But that money wasn't nearly enough to do the trick, and some New York Stock Exchange firms teetered on the edge of bankruptcy while brokers leapt out skyscraper windows. They all shared Harrison's fear of a calling in of all bank loans. The bankers met again, and this time Harrison spoke up. "The Stock Exchange should stay open at all costs. Gentlemen, I am ready to provide all the reserve funds that may be needed to permit the New York banks to take over the call items of out-of-town banks if my directors agree." That's about as bold as bankers ever get.

Harrison used open-market operations to ease the load on New York's commercial banks, allowing the Exchange to remain open even in the face of unbridled selling. This meant the Fed purchased Government bonds the banks were unloading, creating book entry credits for the bank with a swipe of a pen, and pumping much-needed currency into the New York money market. Since the Fed wasn't supposed to bail out ruined speculators, Harrison got his board of directors' approval late that night and began operations early the next morning, immediately buying $160 million worth of Government bonds.

Harrison bought $100 million chunks of the securities each day, putting the banks "in money"; he increased their credits at the Reserve Banks, enabling some $4 billion to be pumped into the depleted money market. Liquidity was preserved and pre-Crash interest rates, too—he had saved the banking structure. Harrison also lowered the rediscount rate, from 4.5 percent to 3.5 percent over the following months. His short-term "easy-money" policy, together with the open market operations, saved the banks immediately after the Crash and restored as much confidence as possible in the marketplace in the short-term. It set the stage for the stock market rally that ran into the spring of 1930.

Of course, over the long term the world was going over a financial cliff, and no one was capable of stopping it. Harrison and the Fed would later receive flak for what he and it had done—first from Washington, where there was still fear of the notion of central bank intervention and where they thought his easy money policy excessive, and most recently from monetarists who didn't think he did enough. Washington's then-conservative view that frowned on central banks and loose money soon led the Fed's Board of Governors back to a restrictive policy that would cause the money supply to actually shrink in a reversal of Harrison's thrust—and that actually made the Depression far worse than it otherwise would have been.

But Harrison's actions were big and generous for the day. This wasn't J.P. Morgan of 1907 acting for his account. This was a man with fiduciary responsibilities and a board of directors. And he was acting on behalf of an institution that was only 15 years old and still held in high suspicion, without benefit of the trust and power of today's Fed.

Harrison's actions set the precedent for later cooperation between the Fed and Wall Street. During the Panic and stock market Crash of 1987, Fed

Chairman Alan Greenspan pumped money into Wall Street, preventing the market from continuing implosion. Harrison must have been cheering from his grave, because this time, in somewhat similar circumstances, it worked perfectly.

While the 1929 Crash may have been the hallmark of Harrison's 20-year stint with the Federal Reserve Bank, he had plenty of other achievements of which to be proud. He was instrumental in stabilizing the dollar during the early 1930s, when Roosevelt—far from being an economics genius—began buying up Europe's gold. Eventually, Harrison, a "sound money" man, convinced the president to stop his buying, allay the Europeans and leave the dollar alone.

Harrison also saw the Fed through two world wars. Following World War I, he acted as a sort of diplomat, extending the Fed's credit to stabilize war-ruined countries' currencies. Prior to World War II, he once again initiated open market operations—this time to keep the price of Government securities from dropping, and thus, to restore confidence in the government.

A San Francisco native, Harrison graduated from Yale in 1910 and Harvard Law School in 1913. He clerked for Supreme Court Justice Oliver Wendell Holmes as a reward for extraordinary scholarship, then moved to the newly-established Federal Reserve Board as assistant general counsel, later becoming general counsel. By 1920, at 33, he was chosen as deputy governor of the New York Fed, becoming head honcho in 1928 (six years later, a title change formally named him president).

A pipe smoker and golf, chess and poker player, Harrison later resigned from the Fed to head the long-time–Morgan-controlled New York Life Insurance Company in 1941. Some speculated Harrison had been a Morgan pawn all along and this $100,000-a-year job was his reward. Sounds to me like bologna from petty critics. There is no hard evidence to that point. In any case, Harrison sparked New York Life into action, greatly expanding the number of policyholders and their average policy costs. Under Harrison, the firm delved into group insurance and began writing accident and health policies for both groups and individuals. During a decade when overall economic growth had been at most, moderate, Harrison boosted the company's assets from $2.869 billion in 1940 to $6.895 billion in his last year with the firm, 1953.

Ultimately, though, Harrison represents the first link between our central bank and intervention at a time of Wall Street panic. And that is quite enough to be included among the *100 Minds That Made The Market*.

The Woman Citizen, 1925

NATALIE SCHENK LAIMBEER

WALL STREET'S FIRST NOTABLE FEMALE PROFESSIONAL

It used to be that a woman contributed to Wall Street by either supporting her husband's budding business career, mistressing a mogul's many desires, or screening a boss's calls—but by 1925 a woman named Natalie Laimbeer broke through the barriers that had held women back and began the process that led to today's world where women are steadily building their presence on Wall Street. A widowed socialite, Laimbeer chose banking in which to make her mark, and within a few years, she became the first woman bank officer at one of Wall Street's largest and most conservative commercial banks. While **Hetty Green** was powerful on Wall Street long before Laimbeer, Green was both exceptionally weird and a market operator for her own account. Laimbeer was a professional, and in that regard, she trailblazed the path for decades of women to follow.

Laimbeer wasn't really looking to make her mark on Wall Street. After her second husband, a Wall Streeter himself, died in a car accident in 1913 that left her a semi-invalid for a while, she decided to go to work. Her husband had left them financially well-off, but she wanted to keep her children in the grandeur to which they were accustomed—after all, the Laimbeers were an integral part of New York Society.

During World War I, the New York City native volunteered in the U.S. Food Administration devising plans for canning food, and later lectured about home economics and the usefulness of electricity in the kitchen. The fact that

Laimbeer "had never done a stroke of work as a wage earner," as the *New York Times* quickly pointed out, never seemed to deter her. She was driven.

"Charm of manner, a quick smile, a pleasing personality, and amiability will take you far, but not unless backed by brains and ambition," Laimbeer later said. And she should have known—by 1919, she was off to a promising start in banking. Though she never prepared for a business career—or any career, for that matter—Laimbeer's interest in finance was rooted in her childhood, when her grandmother would take her to the bank and let her clip coupons from bright orange bonds. Later, at 15, she collected $25,000 in dimes for the American Red Cross to help finance construction of a Cuban ice plant!

Her first position in banking was mainly a clerical one, as manager of U.S. Mortgage and Trust Company's women's department. Back then, women clients were as rare as women in top management, so women's departments were formed exclusively to take care of the few female clients that existed. It was Laimbeer's job to take charge of all the business done by women in the bank, granting secured loans and opening new accounts for them. Within six months, she was appointed assistant secretary in charge of their Manhattan branches' newly organized women's departments.

By 1925, Wall Street's largest bank, National City Bank, offered Laimbeer its first executive title (assistant cashier) ever given to a woman, and she took full charge of its newly established women's department. While a handful of other women held similar titles, National City was the most prestigious, and the last top Wall Street bank, to permit women to the ranks of bank officer. Ironically, while the *New York Times* realized the significance of her achievement as front page news, it chose to focus on her ties with society and the way her new office was decorated to suggest "home rather than an office," rather than detail her banking achievements or describe her business acumen.

"(Women) are on trial," Laimbeer said. "They feel they must do twice as much as is demanded of them to hold their own in the world they have set out to conquer." Although she swung the doors open for women on Wall Street and, in other traditionally male-dominated fields, it would be decades before women were truly accepted in the industry. Even now it isn't clear that they are really accepted. But, way back then, Laimbeer worked at keeping the doors open for other women by co-founding the Association of Bank Women, part of the American Bankers' Association, for female banking executives.

"I believe that the greatest development in any future phase of banking will be the development of the woman power in banks." The group had 110 members in 1925. In those days, banking and investment banking were inseparable (**Charles Mitchell**, for example), so when a woman like Elaine Garzarelli grabs headlines these days for her market views, she owes a lot to the pioneering legacy left behind by Laimbeer and those who followed.

Laimbeer's position lasted only briefly, as her health forced her to resign in 1926. Instead of fading into the woodwork, however, she again grabbed hold of the reins as a pioneer in financial writing. Between 1928 and 1929, she was editor of the financial pages for *The Delineator* and often contributed to the *New York World*. She died in 1929 in New York of a heart attack.

CHARLES E. MITCHELL

THE PISTON OF THE ENGINE THAT
DROVE THE ROARING 20S

Investment banking had long been considered the turf of private banking firms like the House of Morgan when Charles Mitchell came along—and maybe it was better that way. But Mitchell cared not for tradition. He was young, gutsy, self-confident, a fighter, and daring enough to invade the holy territory, taking a huge chunk of it for his budding National City Bank empire back in the 1920s. With outrageous expansion, however, came even more outrageous abuses—and by 1933, the commercial-investment banking combination, then inherent in every major bank, had to be dismantled by Uncle Sam.

No doubt about it, Mitchell had a magnetic personality. Tall, heavy-set with broad shoulders, a handsome smile, and a bold jaw, he was ambitious, forever energetic, and popular—even those who disagreed with him liked him. Born in Chelsea, Massachusetts in 1877, the son of a merchant-mayor, the 39-year-old liquidated his own small investment banking firm to reorganize National City Bank's "banking affiliate"—the National City Company—in 1916. Just five years later, Mitchell seized the presidency of both the Company and the Bank.

The banking affiliate was the key to Mitchell's success, as well as his ultimate undoing. While private bankers like Morgan and Kuhn, Loeb had long combined investment banking and simple deposits and loans, the independent commercial banks where the little man on the street banked got into the investment banking game only later, in the early 1920s. National City Company was the vehicle through which National City Bank and Mitchell sidestepped the law to operate in securities—since by law, banks were not supposed to do so.

It was the first of many dubious activities National City embarked on under Mitchell, but the profits poured in. Not surprisingly, it sparked a whole wave of banking affiliates across the country—including **Albert Wiggin**'s Chase National Bank—subjecting the little man on Main Street to the risks of having his bank's solvency tied to security prices! At first this setup seemed like a good thing. A lot of bad things seem like good things when prices are rising. By the mid-1920s, a great deal of investment banking business was secured by banks. National City alone, by decade's end, was pumping out between $1 to $2 billion in securities annually!

Being ambitious, Mitchell wasn't content simply to underwrite bond issues, so he transformed the Company into a veritable securities factory, pushing stocks and bonds on Bank depositors and any sucker his sales force could get its hands on. And with quantity, went low quality—Mitchell floated and sold $90 million in Peruvian bonds that ultimately defaulted, even though Peru was a known risk. As long as the issue sold, Mitchell could wash his hands of it. Note that it is far different and easier for an investment bank to move successfully into commercial banking than for a commercial bank to move safely and well into securities. But Mitchell was not your typical prudent banker.

Selling was the name of Mitchell's game, and his sales force reflected it. An extraordinarily persuasive salesman himself, he hired hundreds of pushy salesmen, then fueled them with pep talks and cutthroat sales contests. The contests were based on a point system—the more risky an issue, the more points a salesperson could rack up if he unloaded it!

That pressure, of course, trickled down to the customer, as revealed by testimonies during the U.S. Senate Committee on Banking and Currency hearings in 1933. Case in point: A sickly little man named Edgar Brown had $100,000 secure in U.S. bonds when he was lured into a Company branch office by a clever ad claiming to "keep you closely guided as regards your investment." Not knowing much about investing—except that it was the hottest game around in the 1920s—Brown was told his U.S. bonds were "all wrong," and consequently, his salesman's "capable hands" had him leaving the office with a colorful array of Viennese, Chilean, Rhenish, Hungarian, and Peruvian bonds. In fact, the salesman told him, these bonds were such a great buy that it would behoove Brown to invest further.

Brown was persuaded to borrow—conveniently from the mother bank—and wound up with $250,000 in dubious bonds. When the bonds declined, he complained, and they switched his bonds to a rainbow of stocks (particularly National City Bank stocks). When the stocks fell, he requested that they sell out his position. The entire office of salesmen gasped, ran over to Brown, surrounded him—then convinced him he was being entirely foolish! Brown again foolishly listened, and when the Crash came, it wiped out all of his speculative shallow holdings, leaving him plumb broke. Desperate, he applied for a loan at National City Bank—but they turned him down flat in a cold form letter saying he had insufficient collateral!

Mitchell's game blew up in his face during the post-Crash, reform-hungry period that swept Wall Street. He became a principal target of the sensational-ized 1933 Senate hearings, despite the $3 million debt he ran up in an attempt to support National City stock during the Crash. On the stand, he shocked the nation—and even Wall Street—with tales of National City's million-dollar salaries and its role in speculative copper stock pools and stock manipulation. It was also revealed that Mitchell had avoided $850,000 in income tax in 1929 via wash sales—that is, he claimed a $3 million loss by selling 18,000 shares of bank stock to his wife at a drastically and falsely reduced price. He faced criminal charges, but escaped with having to pay back the taxes plus stiff fines.

Just five days after his testimony, Mitchell resigned from National City, and soon afterwards, the Glass-Steagall Act began dismantling the entire system he had made popular, divorcing commercial from investment banking. Mitchell, meanwhile, worked his way out of debt by setting up his own investment counseling firm at 56 in 1934 and, becoming board chairman of an investment banking firm (Blyth) the next year. He died 20 years later at 78 of circulation problems, leaving behind a daughter and a son and a largely reformed Wall Street.

Mitchell was a pushy salesman at just the time Wall Street needed restraint. Had Wall Street had a little more self-restraint just then, it might not have suffered governmental restraint via regulation. Mitchell became a symbol of what was wrong on Wall Street and a scapegoat for all of Wall Street's abuses—beyond those his salesmen actually executed. And there is a lesson here throughout history; whether via Mitchell or, more recently, Mike Milken (who actually got nailed for only a very tiny fraction of his huge volume of transactions). The lesson? A little restraint goes a long way. Yet another lesson to learn the power of salesmanship. Even after a terrible public image via very public congressional hearings, Mitchell—the master salesman—could sell his way to a very secure and prominent future on Wall Street. Perhaps more poignant than "A little restraint goes a long way" is the amendment: "A little salesmanship coupled with a little restraint goes a very long way."

ELISHA WALKER

AMERICA'S GREATEST BANK
HEIST—ALMOST

The Bank of America was almost stolen in 1930. It could have been the greatest bank heist in history—the mighty B of A tugged from the ground its founder stood on! While the "heist" never worked out, its mastermind, Elisha Walker, still goes down in history for giving it a mighty good try. And the timing is important to the evolution of financial history.

It all started when **A.P. Giannini**, the San Francisco-based bank's aging founder and head of its huge holding company, Transamerica Corporation, started shopping for an investment firm to expand his multimillion dollar banking empire. At the time, Giannini had—by choice—absolutely no ties with Wall Street, but he was in the midst of going national and hoped to go international. He had grandiose plans for his baby—and Wall Street resented that.

On Wall Street, Giannini thought he had found what he was looking for in 49-year-old native New Yorker Elisha Walker, head of Blair and Company, a blue-ribbon private investment banking firm that was right behind Morgan and Kuhn, Loeb in influence. Walker was considered an up-and-coming star on Wall Street, but most important, Giannini liked him. A father of five, Walker seemed agreeable to the Italian Californian who was used to big Italian families. Almost overnight a deal was struck, and Blair was adopted into the Transamerica "family."

At that instant, Walker's keen mind began to spin—and Giannini should have run! A rising star, Walker figured, could rise a lot more quickly and maybe even make a few bucks at the same time by securing Transamerica for his Wall Street cronies, who would love to Wall-Streetize its Main Street methods. So, Walker went along with Giannini's vision for Transamerica, cozied up to the higher-ups and eventually took over the firm when Giannini retired a year later in 1930. That's a pretty darn big move for an outsider to any corporation in just a year. But Walker was superficially complimentary. "I can promise that we will do our best to try to follow in the footsteps of Mr. Giannini," he said, secretly crossing his fingers behind his back. "I am not in this for (my) individual gain but for the good of the company."

Using America's wilting economy as an excuse (which may have been a pretty darn justifiable one), Walker immediately cut Transamerica's dividend, a serious no-no in Giannini's eyes, especially during panicky times. But Walker got his way—he was chairman of the board now. Next, under Walker, real estate mortgages were sold to a Morgan-affiliated life insurance company, abandoning old customers. Earnings and financial prospects appeared worse than previously expected (which may have just been a sign of the times). As a result, the stock fell from about $50 a share to under $30, cutting the firm's worth in half! Gradually, tension grew between Giannini and Walker, particularly when Walker refused to defend Transamerica stock against a bear raid.

Walker recklessly sold Transamerica assets left and right without stockholder approval at cheap prices to hungry Wall Streeters, of all people! For example, he was quick to cut loose the firm's New York branch banks, earning brownie points with the Wall Street bigwigs who resented Giannini's presence on Wall Street—mainly because Giannini hadn't brought them business and, in fact, had taken some away.

With customers alienated and stockholders ignored, the bank just wasn't what it used to be under Giannini—and this unnerved the thousands of stockholders who placed their trust and savings with the bank and its founder. So, just as Walker probably expected, stockholders began selling their stock. Transamerica stock plummeted, later hitting an all-time low of about 2! Now Walker could easily afford to buy stock, which he did, becoming the largest individual stockholder in the firm. This horrified Giannini, who never owned large blocks in his firm, but instead controlled the firm through thousands of little investors who trusted him and gave him their proxies.

Bit by bit Walker dismembered the gigantic firm, taking Transamerica further and further from the goals to which he had pledged his allegiance just months before. Giannini was outraged and denounced his successor's plan as a premeditated conspiracy spearheaded by Morgan. The "corner (J.P. Morgan & Co.) never liked our substantial interest in leading companies, nor our going into Europe for business and issuing travelers checks which Banker's Trust (a Morgan bank) strongly objected (to)."

Giannini came out fighting, waging all-out war with Walker and his Wall Street backers. Whenever a battle like this takes place, history almost guarantees a Wall Street victory—such was the case for **Robert Young, Sam Insull** and **Charles Morse.** Giannini's case looked equally gloomy since he was nearly broke—remember, he had never been a major stockholder in Transamerica, and the ever benevolent Giannini had given away to charities a lot of the money he had amassed. But what he had that Walker did not was stockholder support, which proved key in the end. Also, it was difficult for Walker to find Wall Street allies in the dismal Depression days of 1932.

Walker, portrayed as the Wall Street "racketeer," out to swindle his stockholders, proved powerless against Giannini's popularity with the people and the press. The battle finally culminated in a sort of popularity contest at the 1932 stockholder's meeting. Walker was voted out of Transamerica when Giannini won the majority of proxies by a landslide. Walker and his supporters were immediately ousted from what was left of Transamerica. And Walker was never heard from again in California.

Hated in San Francisco, Walker fled back to his friends in New York, where his brownie points paid off—he was made partner at Kuhn, Loeb, remaining there until he died at 71 in 1950, tucked away in relative obscurity in Long Island. The good old boys took care of their own. Yet, after the Giannini fiasco, Elisha Walker was never really a force to be reckoned with again.

Transamerica is basically his only claim to fame. Wherever you see his name in a book, you're sure to see Giannini's soon afterwards—and right on his back.

Here is an instance where the typical top Wall Street executive—Republican, Yale and MIT-educated, energetic, confident and connected—is beaten by the little people's champion. Surely, this was a sign of the times. Walker represented Wall Street before the 1930s when Wall Street almost always got its way. Almost no one survived its disapproval before Giannini—but by the 1920s, a few clever entrepreneurial types were trying. Insull and Young tried, but in the end they failed without Wall Street's financial backing. Giannini was one of the first to succeed in dethroning a Wall Street club-king without sharing the victory with equally powerful Wall Street allies. Though it was a very close call, Giannini's successful attack on Walker was symbolic.

The 1930s whipsawed America's vision, making Main Street clearly more important than Wall Street and in many ways separating them for the first time. Just as Glass-Steagall separated commercial banking from investment banking and brokering, and just as the 1940s saw the emergence of Merrill Lynch as a giant based on its championing of America's little investors, the failure of Walker in the Giannini/Walker battle was perhaps the first major symbolic ripple of the shift of power from Wall Street to Main Street and its emerging "little" people that would dominate the financial world for the next 40 years, ended only by the 1980s reappearance of leveraged mega-raiders.

ALBERT H. WIGGIN

INTO THE COOKIE JAR

Albert Wiggin is a great example of why Uncle Sam passed the Glass-Steagall Act (Banking Act of 1933), which separated commercial banking from investment banking. Prior to the act, the two functions were literally attached at the head, like a pair of Siamese twins, sharing top management, their lifeblood—customers, and even insider information. This made it fairly easy for clever, greedy folks like Wiggin—and there were plenty like him—to take advantage of their positions.

Once called the "most popular banker in Wall Street," Wiggin headed Chase National Bank, having built it into the world's largest commercial bank by 1930. Simultaneously, he headed Chase's investment banking affiliate, Chase Securities Corporation, giving him full access to valuable insider information regarding Chase's stock deals. Had Wiggin not acted on this information and used his prestigious position for his own personal profit, he might well have gone down in history with his prestige intact—but Wiggin simply couldn't resist dipping his fingers into the cookie jar.

Although the calm, reserved and business-minded Wiggin appeared to run the bank conservatively, he had a wild speculative streak that consumed him when it came to his personal finances. Sometime during the mid-1920s, he got his shady operations underway by forming six personal, family-run corporations—such as his Shermar Corporation—to use as speculative vehicles while keeping his identity under wraps. Speculation wasn't by any means illegal, but he certainly didn't want his name tainted by its flamboyant nature! Wiggin was, after all, internationally respected and an important member of Wall Street's banking elite, who frowned on that sort of thing.

So, while keeping his activities as secret as possible, Wiggin made it common practice for Chase Securities to cut his personal firms in on its own maneuvers, like stock pools. By itself this was neither illegal nor immoral, but it represented the start of his path to problems. For example, when in 1928 and 1929 Chase Securities joined a Sinclair Consolidated Oil pool run by celebrated market manipulator **Arthur Cutten**, Wiggin's Shermar Corporation was also cut in.

The pool bought about a million shares of Sinclair stock at $30 per share, then waited to unload them at falsely-inflated prices while Cutten manipulated the stock. The stock sold so well that the pool was able to dump an additional 700,000 shares on the public—at prices ranging between $35 and $45. In all, the pool realized some $12 million in profits! Chase, with a 15 percent cut in the pool, received about $1.8 million while Wiggin, under his corporate name Shermar. received 7.5 percent, about $870,000—not bad for simply being who he was! And no one was the wiser. Again, this was not illegal then, and since he put his money equally with everyone else's in a risky venture, it was not particularly immoral, but it was the beginning of his secret deals.

Those who were wise to Wiggin's operations were wise enough to keep their mouths shut. Wiggin was highly regarded in Wall Street—and exposing him as a speculator instead of a pious banker just wasn't considered a courteous thing to do in the community. Furthermore, the shrewd and calculating Wiggin—who never left anything to chance—strategically planted the bank employees who knew of his activities on his firms' "phony" boards of directors. That way, they were intimately associated with his affairs and, thus, couldn't rat on Wiggin without condemning themselves!

By far Wiggin's most horrendous act was speculating in his own bank's stock—during the 1929 Crash! In just the three months surrounding the Crash, using his Shermar alias, Wiggin sold over 42,000 shares of Chase stock short, reaping some $4 million when he covered his shorts. Again, no one suspected a thing. Outwardly, Wiggin appeared the same reserved and respectable banker had always been, and he even joined in a ballyhooed banker's consortium led by **Thomas Lamont** to support stock prices. Ironically, the spotless reputation of the consortium's members succeeded in calming the market for a very short while, but of course, the Crash was too much for anyone to handle. The more the market—and Chase stock—declined, the more Wiggin continued to sell short! It is an obvious ethical violation of a fiduciary relationship to be head of a company, and supposedly doing your best to protect your stockholders' interests, while you short the stock.

Meanwhile, Chase Securities had its own pool aimed at supporting the bank's stock. So while the affiliate conveniently poured money into Chase stock to keep it temporarily afloat, Wiggin relentlessly sold short—even selling 5,000 shares to the pool itself! Of course, at every point along the way he knew exactly where the bank's buy orders were placed so he could place his short sales accordingly. Absolutely merciless!

Topping it all, Wiggin wasn't even speculating with his own money—but with Chase's! The bank was naturally generous with loans to Wiggin's corporations, sometimes forking over $5 million in one week—which Wiggin gleefully used for speculation. Now that by itself is a clear ethical violation. Banks aren't supposed to lend money to their own officers on a non-fully-disclosed basis. As you will recall, it was that same indiscreet fiduciary breach that drove Bert Lance from President Jimmy Carter's administration.

Anyway, no matter how generous the bank was, Wiggin continued to take advantage of it. In December 1929, he borrowed $8 million to cover his shorts in Chase stock and earned $4 million! By this time, he was a long way from his beginnings in simply participating in hidden but honest speculations. His scruples were nowhere to be found, and Wiggin next dodged the income tax on his gain by juggling the stocks among his wife's and his own corporate accounts, so that the stocks sold short were never actually traded in his name. This was to be his final undoing.

Wiggin's wheelings and dealings finally came out during the U.S. Senate Committee on Banking and Currency hearings, which began in 1933, immediately following his resignation from Chase. His resignation had ironically been much celebrated. He received a whopping $100,000 per year pension and multitudes of praise for his selfless dedication. "The Chase National Bank is in no small measure a monument to his energy, wisdom, vision and character," wrote new management. Actually, Wiggin's Swiss bank account—if he had one—was a much more fitting monument.

When Wiggin took the stand, remaining his dignified, aloof self, but looking a little haggard, all of his dealings were revealed and his reputation decimated. Ferdinand Pecora, counsel for the Senate Committee, recounted Wiggin's more memorable testimonies in his book, *Wall Street Under Oath*. Wiggin, for instance, refused to use the word "pool" because of "that feeling" it provoked. He also refused to apologize for his dealings in Chase stock, saying, "I think it is highly desirable that the officers of the bank should be interested in the stock of the bank."

After his testimony, Chase washed its hands of Wiggin, and he resigned his pension. Because his tax dealings were also aired during the hearing, he was charged with defrauding the government of taxes and ordered to pay back over $1 million in back taxes and penalties. He fought the case for three years all the way to the U.S. Supreme Court but ultimately lost, settling for an undisclosed amount in 1938.

Wiggin lived out the rest of his life in obscurity away from the financial community with his wife, whom he married in 1892, and two married daughters. Note that in more modern times he almost certainly would have gone to jail. But in those days you just didn't put Wall Streeters in jail. He died at 83, in 1951. By the time he died, Chase Securities had been long dismantled.

Wiggin suffered from the same basic problem that more recently put Ivan Boesky and others in jail. He failed to separate in his mind short-term greed from what was good for him in the long run. Morals are easier than crooks can ever envision. In the long-run, greed and morals go together, hand in hand. Had Wiggin always placed his stockholders' interests above his own, this otherwise capable man would have died rich and respected by all. Instead, by placing his own short-term greed above his beneficiaries' good, he lost everything. Crossover crooks, who begin in respected, powerful positions and then start abusing their power, rarely set out to be bad guys. Like Wiggin, they do a few simple and relatively harmless deals and, slowly over time, one step at a time, evolve into worse and worse abusers of privilege. Wiggin taught America that every fiduciary relationship is a potential conflict of interest and should be handled by all with awe and a complete lack of secrecy.

CHAPTER SIX

NEW DEAL REFORMERS

NO BETTER THAN THOSE THEY DESPISED

The New Deal Reformers led the 1930s stock market regulatory revolution, which most notably created the Securities and Exchange Commission (SEC). They were politically ambitious and power-hungry bureaucrats who consecutively influenced our financial market system via legislation and enforcement. In that regard they made the market what it is today.

The Reformers initially arose from the rubble of the 1929 Crash and ensuing Great Depression, which left America economically afraid and generally suspicious of any free market system. What was once viewed as routine—such as speculation, pools, insider trading, borrowing on margin, and combined investment and commercial banking—was now eyed as abusive and near-criminal, if not in fact illegal in all instances.

Crowd mentality blamed tough times on speculative abuses. Politicians promoted reform—declaring new regulations and legislation aimed at permanently eliminating the abuses. But this widely held platform, on which generations of reform was later based, was flawed.

It is totally unclear how the financial markets would have evolved had the reformers been contained, but the markets would have evolved somehow, and clearly differently than they have. And it is also unclear that we ever needed reform in the manner that it occurred.

First of all, contrary to public opinion, the Great Depression was not an adverse reaction to 1920s speculation. While almost everybody believes (and believed then) that speculation was to blame, it simply isn't true. The world always needs a scapegoat for what it doesn't understand and can't rationally explain. And the rich and greedy make a villainous image that is emotionally and often morally easy to believe in.

But, the fact is that the Crash and Great Depression were worldwide events that began abroad and eventually were imported into America. Second, the whole mess worsened here because of our own central bank's dismal monetary policies and tactics. The Federal Reserve shrank our money supply by 30 percent from 1928 to 1938. Few serious students of economics believe 1929's aftermath would have been nearly as severe as it was had the Fed loosened the monetary reins instead of tightening them. Some believe the upshot would have been no worse than what happened after 1987's market plunge of comparable magnitude (when the Fed acted with greater wisdom and tactical capability). Finally, the Great Depression was a clear worldwide reaction to government-mandated trade barriers here and abroad. Was 1920's speculation to blame for the 1930s? No! The government was. It is ironic that Uncle Sam thought it was its job to blame business and then apply the curative for abuses created in Washington, D.C.

So, it's hard to know if we ever really needed regulation in the form in which it evolved. First, legislation aimed at reform makes little difference in alleviating the strains of a worldwide downswing. Second, as a shield against fraud, regulation makes an even weaker weapon. There has never been a shortage of con men and bunko artists, before or after the 1930s reforms. There will always be abuses and abusers, and the more laws there are, the more clever will be the folks who try to get around them. Who's to say that abuses are purely negative (as you'll see perversely in reading about Crooks, Scandals and Scalawags)?

The government always seems to somehow believe that if it weren't there to keep us honest, we'd all swindle each other. Not true. Without The Reformers, our markets would have evolved—they just would have evolved differently. Yes, some folks who were swindled probably wouldn't have been. But then again, others who were swindled probably wouldn't have been had the SEC not been there. In some ways, the SEC and governmental reform provide a false sense of security for many folks that makes them vulnerable to abuse. Those folks, for example the victims of penny stock operators and current Ponzi schemes, would clearly be better off had regulation not lulled them into believing that bunko artists aren't still widespread. Lefevre correctly foresaw that point in the *Saturday Evening Post* in 1934.

Had The Reformers been heeled by a different political leash, the markets would have evolved in ways we can never fully fathom now. It just didn't happen that way. Clearly there would have been more self-regulation and self-regulatory authorities, and there probably would have been more state regulatory effort if there had been less federal effort. It would have been different.

But in some ways it would be the same. Ultimately—via Adam Smith's "invisible hand"—competition is the real regulator of the markets. Without it, as we have recently seen in Eastern Europe, government falls apart. It is competition in the financial markets that eventually weeds out those who perform poorly in favor of those who do well.

Ironically, the Reformers themselves were real pieces of artwork. Winthrop Aldrich, Joseph Kennedy, James Landis, and William O. Douglas were overzealous and extremely ambitious for personal power—extracted through politics. E.H.H. Simmons wasn't. Yes, he was also reform-minded. But as their predecessor, he was urging self-regulation to control fraud as early as 1924. Once the Crash came (while he honeymooned), the ignorant public was embittered and out for blood, and his gentler ways were never again seriously considered.

Aldrich helped draw up the Banking Act of 1933, which divorced commercial from investment banking. The very bank he headed became the first to adhere to the banking reforms when he dissolved its profitable investment banking affiliate, setting the example for the rest of Wall Street. Was that a good idea? Apparently not, because we are undoing his handiwork now. And, as with all other regulators, Aldrich ultimately sought to use the prestige earned from his regulatory efforts to seek the more lofty political position as Ambassador to England.

Kennedy was a scumball and ambitious social climber who ended up—guess what—also as Ambassador to England. This is the guy that married the mayor's daughter and cheated on her mercilessly while playing almost every financial scam that would soon be declared illegal. Contributing to the Democratic party, he bought social prestige and Roosevelt's favor. After putting in a year as the SEC's first chairman, he became an Ambassador to England, schmoozed with political bigwigs and watched three sons climb the political ladder—very high.

His successor, Landis, used his SEC position as the pendulum from which to swing back and forth between prestigious academic and public administrative positions. Yet en route he committed and was convicted for tax evasion, did time and was barred from practicing law. He might have done better as a con artist. It will always be unclear whether or not he committed suicide.

Finally, after serving as the SEC's third and most active chairman, super-ambitious Douglas was appointed to the Supreme Court! This liberal darling was also a womanizer who prided himself in personally mixing Roosevelt's martinis and marrying a series of ever-younger wives. There's little doubt Douglas used his position to catch the eye of Roosevelt and assure his own future; with no formal background or experience in business, economics or Wall Street, he did so with little thought as to whether or not what he was doing was good or bad for the economy's long-term future.

Did any of these egocentrics have much of an impact on our market system? Sure! Did they contribute more than a Charles Dow, a Charles Merrill, or a Ben Graham? No way! Despite all their basically well-meaning attempts to discourage aspiring crooks, regulation doesn't hold a candle to the impact of competition in the long run. Regardless, had we gone without the Reformers, there's no telling how our markets would be operating right now. Better? Worse? Who knows for sure? I certainly can't know because I can't back-seat-drive history. It's a matter of opinion at best, but it certainly would have been different without them. For that reason, the Reformers are among the *100 Minds That Made The Market*.

E . H . H .   S I M M O N S

ONE OF THE SEEDS OF TOO
MUCH GOVERNMENT

The stringent federal regulations that bombarded Wall Street and left crooked opportunists reeling in the 1930s were partially the result of an ambitious antifraud campaign initiated by E.H.H. Simmons. During a record-breaking six-year presidency of the New York Stock Exchange (NYSE) between 1924 and 1930, Simmons crusaded for a new, more trustworthy Wall Street to replace the old one, which had included unscrupulous speculators, swindlers, and fly-by-night bucket shops.

The nephew of straight shooting railroader **E.H. Harriman** (from whom Simmons got his initials), Simmons firmly believed that Wall Street was no longer able to clean its own house and that to protect the American economy, he and Uncle Sam first had to protect its investors. He advocated, "Crooked business is the worst enemy honest business has." It was a heartfelt view, if a naive one.

"If I could reach all the investors of America—and who is not an investor nowadays?—I would try to impress upon them the menace of the bucket-shop keeper and the security swindler," he wrote in a typical, heartfelt editorial in

1925. In his first year as president, the private and moral-minded Simmons recruited Chambers of Commerce and newspaper editors nationwide to help him inform the uniformed investor of the typical swindler's actions. He himself wrote articles, gave speeches, and courted politicians, advocating stricter laws and stricter enforcement. Too often, he said, politics played a role in acquitting popular stock market criminals of crimes.

Simmons aimed much of his attack at bucket shops, which gave investors virtually no chance of winning profits, yet had been accepted by society as a virtual institution. Wild plunger **Jesse Livermore** made his first million via bucket shops in the early 1900s, but he was the rare exception—most folks lost heavily. (See **Livermore** for a more detailed description of bucket shops.) Simmons called the buckets "a civic, moral and economic cancer" that went undetected. Bucket shops were so common and entrenched in society back then—like off track betting is now—that people and law enforcement officials seldom saw them as a menace. And although Simmons carried on about them for a good decade, it wasn't until 1934 that the Securities Exchange Act outlawed them.

Fake stock promoters—like those selling stock in phony gold mines and underwater Florida land—also got the boot from Simmons. He worked with state and federal authorities to eliminate such crooks and boldly encouraged fellow stock market members to turn in suspicious colleagues. "The honor of the institution and the honor of its members must be maintained at all times. That can best be done by obeying and conforming to the rules of the Exchange," he declared.

Simmons was basically your average old-fashioned policeman who liked to see justice served and who happened to work on Wall Street. He was born in Jersey City, New Jersey, graduated from Columbia in 1898 and bought a stock exchange seat in 1900. He became a partner in a brokerage firm, Rutter & Cross, and became a governor on the exchange in 1909. Thereafter, he rose rapidly, becoming exchange vice president in 1921, then president in 1924. Married and widowed twice, he was popular with members of the exchange, the press, law officials, and investors who looked to him as someone they could trust.

In turn, the NYSE grew rapidly. Under Simmons' leadership, the exchange underwent its greatest expansion in history with sales exceeding all previous records. Much of that was owed to the booming market of the 1920s. But regardless, he expanded the Exchange's physical facilities, adopted a new ticker system, increased membership by 275 seats and broadened its ties with foreign stock exchanges. London deemed him the "busiest man in the world" because when he vacationed in the city, he always ended up studying its financial works.

The stock market was everything to him, but ironically his presidency ended without the glitz and glamour you might have expected. Sure, there were still the appreciative ceremonies and all, but Simmons left his position after being absent from the exchange during the 1929 Crash. At age 52, he had been honeymooning in Honolulu when the market crashed, leaving vice president **Richard Whitney** in charge as acting president. What Whitney did with his temporary power vaulted him into the presidency the next year—and Simmons back into private life. This didn't reflect badly on Simmons—he, in fact, returned as vice president of the exchange a few years later.

Simmons died at age 78 in 1955. During his lifetime, he kept his private life as discreet as possible, though he was never able to hide his fierce values and moral code. His high ethics were characterized in a speech he gave up-and-coming stock market trainees one day in 1926. Urging them to dedicate themselves to their jobs, as menial as they might seem, Simmons said, "It really means the satisfaction and the contentment which comes from having done your job well, having measured up to requirements of your conscience and having accumulated for those dependent on you a competence which will make them comfortable. . . ."

He called for intelligent effort and warned against "living only for the moment." A visionary, Simmons cautioned, "Do not bind your intelligence to your desk and your thoughts to your books . . . let your thoughts and your intelligence go outside and look over the world and study the situation and see how you can improve."

It's easy to see why Simmons saw peril in a freewheeling capital markets system that allowed market rigging to prosper and why he fought to change this. But it's harder to see why he didn't foresee the risks to business of governmental intervention. As stated earlier, he claimed, "Crooked business is the worst enemy honest business has." In looking back on it today, one wonders if he wouldn't have realized that while crooked business is a peril, excessive government is a far worse enemy.

WINTHROP W. ALDRICH

A BLUE BLOOD WHO SAW RED

Banker Winthrop Aldrich was the antithesis of the back-slapping good ole boys who dominated Wall Street until the early 1930s. He was the kind of banker who walked with "stiff, cold strides" straight to his desk—without meandering through the office; the kind of banker who frowned on long lunches unless important business needed discussing. Since he had no desire to play their game, he lacked the heart to preserve it. So, in 1933, as the financial community recovered from the 1929 Crash and ensuing Depression, Aldrich dealt the fatal blow to the "fraternity," calling for the separation of commercial banking and investment banking. His drastic points of reform were incorporated in the landmark Glass-Steagall Act, or Banking Act, of 1933—one of the bigger feathers in the New Deal administration's cap, which led to the abolishment of Wall Street's century-old, elitist banking fraternity.

Reserved, distant and fiercely moral, Aldrich used to say, "I never smile south of Canal Street." (Wall Street is, of course, south of Canal Street—implying that he never smiled on Wall Street.) A descendant of Mayflower pioneers, he was born in Providence, Rhode Island in 1885. The son of an influential senator and the tenth of 11 kids, he graduated from

Harvard Law School in 1910 at 25. The fact that his sister married John D. Rockefeller, Jr. helped him gain entrance to prestigious Wall Street law firms, and his marriage to a prominent Manhattan lawyer's daughter in 1916 all but guaranteed his success.

Content with his flourishing law career, by chance or by Rockefeller's blessing, Aldrich became president of Equitable Trust Company when its president suddenly died. "I'm not a banker," he protested, "I'm a lawyer"—but to no avail. With an uncanny memory, calm rationale, and sharp, quick mind, he made an excellent banker. So, when Equitable merged with Chase National Bank in 1930, he became Chase's new president. Here, Aldrich began to clash personally and ethically with Chase chairman **Albert Wiggin**, who was rather flamboyant with Chase's capital.

Where Wiggin believed in investing his bank's funds in speculative securities via a securities affiliate—as was common back then at large commercial banks-Aldrich insisted on a more conservative approach. Once the onslaught of the Great Depression engulfed America, he won support from other concerned directors who suddenly saw events more to Aldrich's conservative way of thinking than they had before. With their support, he ousted Wiggin and finally succeeded him as chairman in 1933 for the next 20 years.

"It is impossible to consider the events which took place during the past ten years without being forced to the conclusion that intimate connection between commercial banking and investment banking almost inevitably leads to abuses," Aldrich once said. Immediately, he set out to shake up the banking industry with his own brand of New Deal reform—he began dismantling the system. (Further description of this system and how it worked can be found in the chapters describing National City Bank chairman **Charles Mitchell** and Albert Wiggin.) The existing system allowed major commercial banks to take advantage of the wild 1920's bull market profits via insider information, interlocking directorships, a virtual monopoly on major security underwritings, and a ready-made market—bank customers—on which they dumped their securities. Aldrich found the system preposterous, and, to the horror of folks like Wiggin, Morgan and other back-slappers, he came out publicly against it.

Somber-faced with cold, disapproving blue eyes, Aldrich cried, "The spirit of speculation should be eradicated from the management of commercial banks." In his famous speech made March 8, 1933, he surprised his colleagues by calling for sweeping reform in the banking industry. After previewing the not-yet-passed Glass-Steagall Act, he decried it as not being drastic enough! Aside from separating commercial from investment banking, which the act already called for, Aldrich's demands included:

1. Any partnerships or corporations taking deposits must abide by the same regulations as commercial banks.
2. No firm dealing in securities can accept deposits.
3. No officer or member of a partnership dealing in securities may hold office in any bank (and vice versa).

Every one of Aldrich's points was aimed at reducing the banking fraternity's hold on the capitalist system. Under his say, speculative ventures would be eliminated in commercial banks, and insider information would be harder to obtain. The third point, for example, would forbid a J.P. Morgan partner from holding a director's seat on the Chase National Bank board. In the past, the Morgan director and Chase board might have shared insider information regarding any clients they might have had in common and used it to their own advantage.

Ironically, Chase, the very institution Aldrich headed, violated every one of his outrageous reforms. So, courageously, he began adapting Chase to his list of new rules—and his shareholders readily went along with his game plan. He gleefully dissolved the Chase securities affiliate and removed its investment banking department, except for the handling of government securities. Not once throughout the entire ordeal did he attempt to win acceptance from his peers or a pat on the back from his opponents. It was full speed ahead, regardless of what anyone thought: Wall Street hated him with a vengeance, and the Roosevelt administration fully encouraged him. Aldrich got the red-carpet treatment at the White House and was able to see his suggestions go down in the history books.

In his 20th year as Chase chairman, Aldrich severed his business ties to accept the ambassadorship to the Court of St. James for four years. After struggling with the relationship between America and Great Britain, he returned to the States in 1957, and threw himself back into business, managing his and the Rockefellers' financial affairs. Aside from banking and finance, Aldrich found the time to serve on the International Chamber of Commerce and dabble in a handful of other civic affairs. He was a celebrated philanthropist involved with seemingly every charitable organization ever created including various hospitals, the New York branch of the Girl Scouts, Tuskegee Institute, and the American Cancer Society. He headed World War II's largest relief effort—the Allied Relief Fund—and would later receive honorary degrees from Columbia, Georgetown, Harvard, Colgate, Brown, and several other universities. A world traveler who wintered in Nassau, Bahamas, Aldrich was survived by five daughters and one son when he died—while still quite active—in 1974.

You can't reform a group if the entire group stands opposed to the reform—in that case, all you can do is put the whole group in jail. To reform a group, you have to split off factions from the group who will act as the leaders for reform. This is what Aldrich did. From his blue-blooded background he wasn't money-hungry like many of Wall Street's self-made moguls. His whole background, from birth, to law school, to Rockefeller connections was more oriented toward preserving position than building it. To Aldrich, moral rectitude was the correct path to preserve his position. At the time he was correctly reading the direction of the political winds. Without Aldrich you wouldn't see the "reformed" securities and banking industries in the format in which they currently exist.

JOSEPH P. KENNEDY

FOUNDING CHAIRMAN OF THE SEC

When you think of Joe Kennedy, you recall his legacy of political giants. What Wall Street notes, however, is a speculator who kicked and scratched his way to some $500 million—and the perks that went with it, like a well respected name. But what the "Street" should remember is his role as the founding chairman of the Securities and Exchange Commission (SEC).

His story starts with his scrambling for millions—the kicking and scratching part. Kennedy was unrelenting and unscrupulous, a womanizer, and social climber who was often in it for his ego. Whether it was taking a mayor's daughter for his wife or contributing to a President's campaign till in return for a political appointment or two, Kennedy had a fistful of strategic moves that took him wherever he wanted.

His drive was always a matter of pride. The carrot-topped son of a popular small-time Boston-Irish politician wanted admittance to Boston's high society—which was, of course, impossible for a person of poor background. Perhaps that was why he wanted it so much—because it was so out of reach. This hunger produced a driven man who allowed nothing to get in the way of his ambitions. So, as a Harvard grad who almost played pro ball, Kennedy stormed into banking via his father's political connections. By age 25, in 1913, he was America's youngest bank president at a small bank his dad had formed.

Kennedy was charismatic. And when he was happy, you knew it. A wide grin showed off his voracious teeth, and his bright eyes crinkled through round spectacles. With his dynamic and amiable personality, freckle-faced Kennedy made a sprawling network of contacts that brought him a variety of jobs before he landed on Wall Street. First, he married well, winning the Boston mayor's daughter. Then he ran a local pawnshop, dabbled in real estate, managed a Bethlehem Steel shipyard, served on a utility's board and, finally, managed a brokerage office for Hayden, Stone and Company (long ago merged into Shearson).

In 1923, Kennedy struck out on his own—"Joseph P. Kennedy, Banker"—and quickly established himself as a lone wolf on the Street, though he also worked with syndicates. Without conscience, but with a shrewd mind, Kennedy would "advertise the stock by trading it." When the public bought in, he pushed up its price and sold out; and then Kennedy sold short as the stock drifted back down to its normal price. He was a manipulator of unusual skill. Kennedy once told a friend, "It's easy to make money in this market. We'd better get in before they pass a law against it!"

In a maneuver typical of Kennedy but unusual for most folks, Kennedy once returned a favor to a Yellow Cab executive when Yellow Cab stock was in the midst of a bear raid, having dropped from 85 to 50. Acting as the stock's sugar daddy, Kennedy set up shop in the Waldorf-Astoria running a shoring-up operation which he warned his friend could cost as much as $5 million. The Waldorf was a convenient location for his unending string of floozies. There he installed a ticker tape, and from his bedside, bought and sold Yellow Cab, using various brokers to conceal his position. He pushed the stock below 48, up to 62, down to 46, then stabilized it at 50 to confuse the bears. En route, instead or costing $5 million, it cost relatively little, and Kennedy claimed a hefty take for himself.

Always manipulating public relations to his much-loved family image, he said with false innocence, "I woke up one morning, exhausted, and I realized that I hadn't been out of that hotel room in seven weeks. My baby, Pat, had been born and was almost a month old, and I hadn't even seen her!" Such was the demeanor of the father of a future U.S. president. Pat probably never noticed her father's absence, but poor Rose must have wondered where hubby was and what he was doing. Presumably it wasn't merely the Yellow Cab stock operation that exhausted him in that bed. A few months later, when Yellow mysteriously plummeted again, it was Kennedy who was blamed by his former friend for the decline—and threatened with a punch in the nose! The presumption was that Kennedy, with his knowledge of the stock and its market, stepped back into the market and drove it down via short selling. No one ever knew for sure. But it's possible.

Befitting his personality—that of a social pariah—Kennedy took on Hollywood, where few Wall Streeters had ventured prior to the 1920s. During his cinematic stint, he financed a movie-theatre chain. He later sold it to RCA for half a million and made two films, including a costly silent flop with actress-girlfriend Gloria Swanson. While Swanson actually ate the losses, Kennedy basked in free publicity, laughing off his million-dollar loss. What he really lost was a girlfriend, and there was always another one of those to be had.

In 1928, in a move of uncanny vision, Kennedy unloaded his movie securities for $5 million (to help create RKO) and did likewise for his other securities in preparation for hard times. With amazingly good timing, Kennedy said, "Only a fool holds out for the top dollar," and when the Crash hit, he was able to watch the market from a safe distance, keeping his fortune intact. In the 1929 Crash, while he held stocks that were hit, they were offset for by an equal number of short positions that rose in value. The Crash left him unscathed. There is a legend, which he probably promoted at the time, that he sold short heavily as the market crashed and made a killing. Not true—merely legend. His short sales were a hedge, and he did not profit in a material way from the Crash. He maintained.

Meanwhile, he took stock of his life. Now that he had made his pile, he wanted to make it respectable. But he wasn't actually too successful at it. It would be up to his sons to truly salvage his reputation, which was far from sparkling. But he tried. He started out the only way he knew how—he made more connections. But this time he went straight to the top, courting presidential hopeful Franklin Roosevelt by oiling his campaign fund with more than $150,000, which was a lot for those days. Of course, you never can have too much money, and as the Kennedy and Roosevelt families grew closer, Kennedy borrowed Roosevelt's son to secure prestigious English Scotch franchises just before Prohibition was repealed. And, he was somehow allowed to ship in the booze for "medicinal" purposes before the law was actually appealed! This is the period of Kennedy's life when he was tagged a "bootlegger," which was neither terribly material to his wealth or life, but it was to his image.

When Roosevelt was elected, the mid-1930s became the self-proclaimed "President-maker's" favorite years. He was picked by Roosevelt and elected to chair the newly-established Securities and Exchange Commission. Democrats shrieked at Kennedy's selection as an abomination. They figured he would do nothing to hamper the activities of his old friends on Wall Street. It was an appointment likened to letting the wolf out to guard the sheep. But Roosevelt was satisfied with Kennedy's promise to stay out of the market—and, the President mused, he "knows all the tricks of the trade!" Roosevelt supposedly muttered something to Kennedy's detractors to the effect that, "it takes a thief to catch a thief." Surprisingly, the charming Kennedy won over his harshest critics in his one year at the SEC, diligently outlawing most of the methods he had used to amass his fortune. Supposedly Kennedy's knowledge of how to manipulate stocks was central to the New Deal version of how to reform the securities industry. Realistically, I think he was picked as a pay off for his efforts and money on Roosevelt's behalf, and I haven't seen any evidence that his SEC functioning was more than perfunctory.

Still, Kennedy's SEC stint did much to scrub up his image. That allowed Roosevelt to move him on to a more prestigious position—U.S. Ambassador to Great Britain—just what the doctor ordered for an Irishman who grew up with a chip on his shoulder!

As World War II ended, with the Roosevelt world gone and with Kennedy older and slower, he turned again to business, but this time focused on real estate. His prime purchase was the world's largest commercial building, Chicago's Merchandise Mart—which he bought in 1945 for $13 million and 20 years later was worth $75 million, throwing off more than $13 million of cash annually. Various estimates of his net worth in the mid-1960s place it on the high side of $200 to $400 million.

In some ways the 1960s had to be the high point of his life as son, John, was elected President. But it was also the end, emotionally and physically. His heart started giving him problems and he suffered a stroke in 1961. Later, John's death was like a cloud over his heart. A series of heart attacks left him incapacitated for the first time in his life. Robert's assassination in 1968 couldn't have helped. He died the next year, after funneling his fortune into intricate trust funds for his children and grandchildren to avoid Uncle Sam's take.

Kennedy was an enigma. A social climber, womanizer, mad scrambler, market manipulator, movie mogul, government regulator, Ambassador, real estate tycoon, and President's father. He is very hard to summarize briefly. But whenever I think of Kennedy, I think of the many things he did in early eras that were taboo in later ones, and his ability to adhere to the social and legal mores of the day. You have to be reminded by the founding chairman of the SEC to honor the law. You have to also be reminded by Kennedy's evolving lifestyle and business style that what is legal and acceptable today may be very illegal 10 or 20 years from now. Staying flexible is a requirement for surviving in the financial markets.

JAMES M. LANDIS

THE COP WHO ENDED UP IN JAIL

A hard-nosed, hard-driving and hard-drinking law professor-turned-securities regulator forced a resistant Wall Street to prepare for drastic change following 1929. As a main architect of the Securities Act of 1933 and one of its first enforcers, James MacCauley Landis defined and directed that change and helped shape a new, regulated, and reformed Wall Street.

A chain smoker and workaholic who drove too fast and drank too much, Landis typified the staunch, serious, and overzealous policeman out to get his man. Standing 5'7", with thinning hair, tight lips, and big jowls—a real sour-puss face—he wore dowdy, rumpled suits and kept his hands stuffed in his pants pockets. Gulping black coffee and smoking two packs of Lucky Strikes each day, he was nicknamed "Cocksure" Landis for his self-assured arrogance and inability to take criticism.

Known as an independent thinker, Landis was called to Washington from his Harvard professorship and Cambridge home to help draw up the Securities Act in 1933. He wrote tough enforcement provisions, including making non-compliance of a subpoena a penal offense. He called for fines and prison terms for all parties involved with fraudulent securities sales, from company directors to underwriters and lawyers. Landis also devised a "stop order" that allowed the commission to freeze an issue if its paperwork looked suspicious. The legislation was a hit with the reform-hungry New Deal crowd and its popularity vaulted Landis into upper-crust capital circles. But back on Wall Street, the press said Landis symbolized "a New Deal brain-truster with somewhat radical tendencies and an inclination to go off half-cocked on high-sounding but impractical reforms."

Impractical or not, most of Wall Street adopted the new Securities Act which went into full effect on July 7, 1933. That day, 41 firms filed statements with the Federal Trade Commission (FTC) Securities Division, the first agency to carry out the law. Together, the firms paid out $8,000 in registration fees to issue $80 million in stock after 20 days. It was the beginning of a new Wall Street—and Landis remained in Washington to make sure it stayed that way.

In 1933, just as he prepared to head back to Harvard, Landis was appointed to the FTC by President Franklin Roosevelt. He worked day and night—even keeping a cot in his office—to develop the rules and regulations that carried out the Securities Act. That year, he prevented or suspended 33 illegal issues. In 1934, when a senator's amendment created the Securities and Exchange Commission (SEC) to replace the FTC, Landis was named to that, too. He wrote most of the SEC's first opinions while serving under the first SEC chair, **Joe Kennedy**.

A year later, on the day before his 36th birthday in 1935, Landis took Kennedy's place as the $10,000-per-year SEC chairman. He promised to uphold Kennedy's cooperative stance with Wall Street as much as possible, while vowing to prosecute all stock frauds. For instance, he expelled stock operator **Michael Meehan** from three major stock exchanges on charges of manipulating stocks via "matched sales" in Bellanca Aircraft. The liberal press hailed him! Years later, he'd say, "The Securities and Exchange Commission has to be both a crackdown and a cooperating agency, depending on the circumstances. I don't think we have soft-peddled anything."

More than prosecuting individual violators, however, Landis was left the task of deconstructing what was then "the" corporate way of life—the holding company. The controversial and much-hated Public Utility Holding Act of 1935 called for giant holding companies to divest themselves of all subsidiaries not geographically or economically linked. Trying to be Mr. Nice Guy and still uphold cooperation between government and business, Landis "suggested" the holding companies "voluntarily" divest themselves. But Wall Street hated him, and perhaps not without reason. All basic notions of capitalism are based on freedom, which at its most extreme means anyone can do anything, and pressure from Washington was restrictive and therefore threatening to Wall Street, which for 100 years had been the citadel of freedom in finance. The holding companies fought the law all the way from inception to passage, so they weren't about to voluntarily divest themselves of anything without a major legal battle.

Landis chose to convince them with a big splash—to make an example of the world's largest utility holding company, Electric Bond and Share Company. First, he gave the company one more chance to register with the SEC by December 1, 1935. No luck; Electric Bond wouldn't budge. Then, two days after the deadline passed, the firm's president personally visited Landis to declare it would sue the SEC! That was when he struck: As the smug president strolled out of Landis' office, Landis picked up the phone and put down the meter to start a lawsuit he had prearranged before his visitor had arrived—before Electric Bond could get its suit started. Landis won. By January, 1937, the courts backed the SEC and demanded the holding companies comply with the legislation. Landis triumphantly declared the losers had "cut their own throats."

By 1937, Landis was tense and weary, with little family life to speak of. His wife regularly attended Washington social functions on her own. If someone asked for her husband, she'd reply, "What husband?" The marriage was crumbling, and he'd neglected his two daughters. His obsession with his work and booze was costing him his health—he suffered a series of bouts with influenza before the doctor demanded a lighter workload.

As much as he disliked the idea, Landis resigned in 1937 to return to Harvard Law School as dean. Unfortunately, he lingered in his SEC position—as a favor to Roosevelt, skipping a needed vacation—long enough to catch flak for that year's deep recession. Stock prices hit the lowest they'd been since the Great Depression, and the New York Stock Exchange president openly blamed the SEC. Landis retaliated, blaming the crisis on speculators who had returned to the market because of New Deal prosperity. What's better—prosperity with a few crooked speculators or depression with no opportunity but everyone on the up and up? Sort of makes you wonder if Landis didn't like it better with the world in depression.

Landis was remembered politically as a realist who didn't expect rapid change. By drafting and adhering to legislation, he expected reform to evolve gradually. He felt regulation was a process that would occur naturally—without harm to the economic process—if not made uniform and rigid.

For being such a careful and patient planner, Landis had an extremely erratic life. Besides his SEC career, at one point or another he: Had his own law practice (Joe Kennedy was his number-one client); served as Civil Aeronautics Board chairman; reorganized and directed the Office of Civil Defense; authored a few books on law; served on the National Power Policy Commission; campaigned for President Roosevelt's third term; and for a while, became active in local school politics. His love life was no less hectic. While married and working at Harvard, post-SEC, he fell in love with his married secretary. They eventually both divorced their first spouses and married each other.

Born in Tokyo in 1899, the son of Presbyterian missionaries, Landis came to America in 1912 to attend private school. By 1921 he worked his way through Princeton University as a justice of the peace and he received a law degree from Harvard in 1925. After clerking for the prestigious Supreme

Court Associate Judge Louis Brandeis, he landed at Harvard as an assistant professor of law and made full professor at 26, the youngest in Harvard's history. From Harvard, he embarked on his Washington career.

Landis died in 1964 at age 64. He was found face down in his 40-foot-long swimming pool at his 10-room Westchester, New York home—with traces of alcohol in his blood. Although he swam every day, it was rumored—falsely—that he'd committed suicide. Just days previously, Landis had been suspended from practicing law in New York State for a year because of a year-old conviction on income tax evasion. Imagine that! The head cop breaking the law. In 1963. Landis pleaded guilty to failing to file Federal income tax returns for the years between 1956 and 1960; he received 30 days in prison and paid some $92,000 in back taxes and fines. He didn't mean any harm, he'd said—he was just too busy. One doubts if the firms and people he pressed in his securities regulation career would have gotten very far with him had they used the same excuse.

Is the world a better place with all of the securities regulations that Landis helped put in place? Most folks assume so. But I don't think anyone can tell. The world is so fundamentally different now, almost 75 years after the first New Deal securities legislation, that it is impossible to say how the securities world would have evolved had the Roosevelt administration and Congress blinked five times, looked the other way, and avoided securities regulations until the securities markets naturally returned to higher prices. One could argue, as the New York Stock Exchange did, that prices might have returned to 1920s levels much faster with the presence of the SEC. But who knows? The world is what it is, and it is partly what it is because of the serious role Landis took in playing cop to Wall Street.

Current Biography, 1950

WILLIAM O. DOUGLAS

THE SUPREME COURT JUDGE ON
WALL STREET?

I t's ironic that 36 years as one of history's most controversial Supreme
Court Justices all but obliterated the memory of William O. Douglas as
the third Securities and Exchange Commission chairman. His SEC term was
the very thing that vaulted him to the Court in the first place. As SEC chairman
for 19 months between 1937 and 1939, Douglas sparked a "revolution in
financial morality." He picked up where **James M. Landis**, his predecessor,
left off and made his one of the most ambitious chairmanships in the SEC's
history.

Douglas, like the leading liberal he was, immediately denounced the
stock market as a "private club" with "elements of a casino." Despite early
1930s legislation—like the Securities and Exchange Act, which he called "a
nineteenth-century piece of legislation"—Douglas sought to make the market
still more accessible to the public and free from insider abuse. A deep hostility
towards "the goddam bankers" drove him to incite more competition among
investment banking houses in order to prevent banker monopolies. He also

followed through with Landis' enforcement of the Public Utility Holding Company Act and attempted to consolidate SEC enforcement of the over-the-counter markets. Not all his attempted coups worked out, but he was able to build a coherent, workable policy for the next generation of reformers. Douglas said he made the effort out of concern for "the preservation of capitalism." Yeah! Right! And the government is here to help you too. It is very hard to be concerned about capitalism and see bankers as "goddam" all at the same time.

A political liberal, Douglas was born in 1898 in Maine, Minnesota, the son of a poor Presbyterian minister who died early in Douglas' life. His mother moved the family to Washington where he almost died of infantile paralysis. From then on, he was sickly and weak and threw all his energy into school work. Recovering from his physical condition by challenging himself to climb mountains, he pushed on in his studies to graduate from Idaho's Whitman College in 1920, paying tuition earned with migrant farm work during the summers. Eventually, after a brief teaching stint, he hopped a New York-bound freight train with hobos and enrolled in Columbia Law School. Three years later, at 27, he graduated second in his class, joined the prestigious Columbia Law faculty, briefly worked for a high-powered Wall Street law firm, then moved to Yale in 1928.

Between 1929 and 1932, Douglas worked with the Department of Commerce on producing various financial studies, like one on bankruptcy reorganizations, a topic that grew popular during the Great Depression. Soon, he became known as an expert in financial law, and in 1936, was appointed to the SEC under **Joe Kennedy**, its first chairman. Although he seemed distant and shy around strangers, both Kennedy and President Franklin Roosevelt took an immediate liking to Douglas, and he quickly became the President's "adviser, friend and poker companion." He prided himself on mixing Roosevelt's martinis. Wall Streeters probably thought he was practicing to deliver a different form of elixir to Wall Street.

A year later, Roosevelt offered him the SEC chairmanship. Douglas took office at a time when Wall Street was particularly vulnerable: One of its most well-known heads, New York Stock Exchange President **Richard Whitney**, had just been convicted of embezzling some $3 million—a scandal that dealt the financial district a severe blow on top of the worst economic conditions since the Depression. Douglas emphasized his leadership would "be a period of action."

Douglas succeeded in creating more "action" than came from Kennedy's cooperative approach with business and Landis' steady, patient negotiations. He exploited the political implications of Whitney's conviction and demanded the NYSE reform itself, or the SEC would do it for them. He demanded more than superficial change. Within hours of Whitney's expulsion from the Exchange, he said, the "reorganization of the Exchange should not be a mere sham but thoroughgoing and complete in actual fact. The former philosophy of Exchange government should be abandoned not merely on paper, but in practice."

Whether Douglas was capable of carrying out his threats of overhauling the NYSE, himself, was questionable, but the Exchange didn't want to find out, and it carried out his demands. It added a 13-point Douglas-driven reform program including frequent and detailed audits of member firms; the banning of brokers doing business with the public from maintaining margin accounts; the establishment of a 15:1 ratio between broker's indebtedness and working capital, and a new requirement forcing members to report all uncollateralized loans to other members.

In the case of over-the-counter stock market regulation, Douglas tried his best. However, the 6,000 or so O.T.C. brokers and dealers operating in 1938 were not ready to be gathered centrally, and Douglas rightfully felt it "impractical, unwise and unthinkable" for the SEC to try to regulate directly the sprawling, independent agents. He was able to keep them somewhat in line, though, with his famous line: "Government would keep the shotgun, so to speak, behind the door, loaded, well oiled, cleaned, ready for use, but with the hope it would never have to be used." Whether Douglas actually ever had such a weapon "behind the door" was questionable. Author Robert Sobel believed that, like Kennedy and Landis before him, Douglas lacked the money, staff and power to actually carry out his threats—but his points had been well taken.

In 1939, when Justice Louis D. Brandeis resigned from the Supreme Court, Douglas asked his friends to lobby Roosevelt for his nomination. "Somewhat later," he recalled, "I got a phone call from F.D.R., and, when I got to the White House, I thought he was going to draft me as chairman of the Federal Communications Commission, which was then in terrible trouble. He teased me a bit for five minutes and then offered me the Court job." Douglas was confirmed by the Senate by a vote of 62 to 4—at 41 becoming the youngest Justice since 1811, with the dissenters thinking he was a Wall Street reactionary! During his stint on the Court, the *New York Times* said Douglas "championed the right to dissent." Before retiring in late 1975, he wrote important decisions in bankruptcy, rate-making, mergers and securities law.

Douglas, an ardent free-speech advocate, was later criticized for publishing an article about conservationism in *Playboy*, speaking out against the Vietnam War and condemning the government for what he called its witch hunts for Communists in the 1950s. Even his personal life was condemned, as he was married four times to progressively younger wives. His first marriage, during which he had two kids, lasted from 1924 to 1954 and his second, nine years. His third marriage was to a 23-year-old in 1963. In 1966, less than a month after divorcing number three, he married a 23-year-old blonde-haired, blue-eyed college co-ed at age 67! I guess he really was liberal. By the way, that was two years before he got his pacemaker installed!

Some say all of his regulatory success regained investor confidence and paved the way for the post-World War II, 1950s bull market. Others, particularly Wall Streeters of his day, thought all his actions just beat the devil out of anybody's urge to speculate, which paved the way for the doldrum markets of the 1940s. It depends on with whom you talk. Liberals saw Douglas as a champion who busted the bad guys—and conservatives simply saw him as a liberal scalawag. Who knows how his four wives saw him. This author tends to believe that laws have a big impact on Wall Street in the short to intermediate term, and only cosmetic impact in the long term. Douglas clearly made a big impact. Do we still feel it today? That is less clear. Yet someone had to finish off the Democratic Party's initial assault on Wall Street, and Douglas was just the man to do it.

CHAPTER SEVEN

CROOKS, SCANDALS, AND SCALAWAGS

THE ULTIMATE POSSESSORS IN THE SCHOOL OF HARD KNOCKS

Crooks, scandals, and scalawags are good. Con artists of all forms offer us a sort of perverse education. They are a key ingredient to avoiding stagnation and achieving a constantly evolving Wall Street, for without them we would never learn the often-costly lessons of excessive greed and blind trust that prompt change and reform. In the way a child learns not to touch a red-hot stovetop, the stock market has learned—sometimes over and over again—to be skeptical of just-too-good-to-be-true investment opportunities and the people promoting them. Because the root of all swindles, greed, is inherent to human nature, Wall Street will never lack for its share of con artists and con games, regardless of what drastic measures Washington might think it's taking. So, rather than condemn such swindlers, we can easily learn from their stories.

Initially, it is hard to see the good in a con. Just think of the victims—a widow swindled out of her retirement savings or hard-working parents who bet their kids' college fund on a lost double-your-money sure-fire deal. Tear-jerkers? Well, maybe—but for most folks seeking to double their money overnight, all they suffer is a slight financial hit, a bruised ego, and a loss of faith in humanity.

A con just might teach them something about what they did wrong in the process of getting conned. Even more important, and more likely (since many folks can't learn from their own mistakes), it might teach the victim's relatives, friends, neighbors, peers and co-workers. For every victim, there are a good many observers learning lessons. And these folks are the beneficiaries of the con artists' finesse. When they tuck their newfound experience and lessons under their belt and go on with their lives, they will have learned to be a lot more skeptical and, if they're wise enough, a little less greedy—a lesson everyone can afford to learn.

Swindles and con games dot the entire time-span of stock market history. Looking back on the 1800s, you might view some of the Dinosaurs like John Jacob Astor, Daniel Drew, and Cornelius Vanderbilt as con men, but whether they actually were considered con men in their day is questionable. Each operated via deceptive methods that are today highly illegal and unethical. But then, their methods were widely accepted as the norm, simply because there were no securities laws. Their actions set the precedent for the most fundamental beginnings of modern stock market ethics. As Drew introduced the notion of "watering" stock by selling new shares in firms he controlled without disclosing that they were new shares, he took a first deceptive step toward teaching the masses to watch out for "insider" manipulation. While the lesson is never fully learned by everyone, look at all the standard practices that have been adopted in the last 150 years to keep the playing field level. Without the crooks and con artists, ethics would never become engrained in our capitalistic financial markets. But it does.

By the time the many scalawags featured in this section came to crime or near-crime from the 1920s to 1950s, there clearly was an ethical agenda to follow and one that was becoming irregularly more stringent as the years passed—it's just that these hombres chose to ignore the rules. Charles Ponzi, Ivar Kreuger, Samuel Insull, Michael Meehan, Richard Whitney, Lowell Birrell, Walter Tellier, and Jerry and Gerald Re—they all either bypassed and evaded laws or discovered a niche, as the Dinosaurs did, where there were no distinct laws. And every one of these folks generated a backlash of ethical or legal reform.

For example, Charles Ponzi, whose name is now synonymous with illegal zero-sum pyramiding schemes, was the first to bring the con game to Wall Street in the late 1910s. He promised his victims a 90-day rate of return that was just too good to be true. Indeed, it was too good to be true, and while suckers placed their money and trust in him, Ponzi used some of the money to pay back phony interest payments to the investors while placing the rest of the money in his personal bank accounts! With the first fat interest payments made, he used his unaware victims as references to sell more suckers on his scheme. His method, not terribly complicated, became a role model for modern scams that is commonly repeated in some form or another to this day. Today we see a similar variation in the common chain letter. Yet today, most folks know that Ponzi schemes are a sucker's game.

As Yogi Berra said, "Sometimes you can see a lot just by looking." Yet many people, overcome by greed or fear, often choose not to look when it comes to their finances. Two men who became caught in scandals and en route gave us some permanent debt lessons, were Ivar Kreuger and Samuel Insull—who both built debt laden pyramid-style empires that toppled when they grew too top-heavy in the early 1930s after the Crash decimated assets. Both were blamed for the fall and the millions in losses it represented to investors. But as their empires toppled, they ripped off investors, and the scandals that ensued show the perverse power that forces men beyond their normal moral bounds when huge amounts of debt backfire on the borrower. We again see those lessons in many of the backfiring leveraged buy-outs of the 1980s. But the lessons were already there, for anyone to see who wanted to look.

Michael Meehan blatantly ignored the power of a young SEC in the mid-1950s. So when he continued doing what he had been doing in the 1920s—manipulating stocks on a visible scale—he became the first to be nailed by the SEC. What an honor!

Richard Whitney's con game was embezzlement in the mid-1930s. Nothing new or different about the crime, but its context—right within New York Stock Exchange walls—absolutely shocked Wall Street in what was its juiciest scandal ever. Suddenly folks realized that if as well-placed a broker as Whitney could be a crook, no position of power or prestige assured ethical conduct, and you could only insure that you wouldn't be taken by swallowing a heavy dose of financial skepticism.

In the 1940s and 1950s, Wall Street was no stranger to scandal. Lowell Birrell unloaded worthless securities on insurance companies, where the SEC had no authority! Walter Tellier mass produced worthless penny stocks, promoted their irresistible price, and mercilessly flung them on the public via high-pressure sales tactics. Jerry and Gerard Re gave stock specialists a bad name that subtly exists to this day by selling illegal, unlisted stocks at their American Stock Exchange post.

In each case, immediately following exposure of the scandals, a wave of reform swept the market, eliminating more and more loopholes in the laws. The violators were either tried on various charges and jailed or acquitted. Others fled to Rio, another killed himself and some were never seen or heard from again. And the victims? Yes, they were stung, but people learn from situations like these. Were it not for this bunch and others that have followed in their footsteps, our greed and trust might otherwise go unchecked. And for this eye-opening service, they must be included in *The 100 Minds That Made The Market.*

CHARLES PONZI

THE PONZI SCHEME

I'm sure Charles Ponzi wasn't the first ex-con on Wall Street, but he was the most successful. He succeeded in making his name synonymous with "swindle" after his great get-rich-quick scheme was exposed as a fraud! En route, he managed to rip off hundreds of investors of millions by juggling capital from investor to investor, creating a rip-off often replicated today—the "Ponzi Scheme."

Born in Italy, Ponzi had the most atypical background of anyone in this book—guaranteed. Not only was he poorly educated, which so many had to overcome back then, but he worked as a laborer, clerk, fruit peddler, smuggler, and waiter until the age of 42, when he decided to try finance. A smug little man just over five feet, Ponzi was good-looking, slim, dapper, self-assured, and quick-witted—but it was his smooth talking that truly brought his character to life.

He began his scam in early 1920 with $150 in advertising, setting up Old Colony Foreign Exchange Company and claiming to pay 50 percent interest in 45 days and 100 percent in 90 days. Ponzi had great timing—it was the onset of the Roaring 20s, when people had a little spare cash to spend and were willing to take what looked like a good chance. With a super-salesman's flair he talked up a storm, making his deal sound riskless.

Ponzi proposed to pay such horrendous premiums on people's investments by purchasing International Postal Union reply coupons overseas. Then, by manipulating foreign currency quotations, he would redeem the coupons elsewhere, where the currency was inflated.

Everyone sent him money—stockbrokers, their clerks, widows, heiresses. The money flowed in, first in drops, then in buckets once the newspapers caught on and publicized this newly-discovered financial genius. At first the money was stuffed into desk drawers in Ponzi's little Boston office, but then it started coming in at a rate of over $1 million per week! Bills flowed from the tops of wastepaper baskets, then covered the floor ankle-deep! There was an endless flow of cash—plenty with which to pay off eager investors.

An endless flow of cash was just what Ponzi needed to pull off his scheme, for the more money that came in, the more in debt he became. He wound up paying his first investors with money from later investors and later investors with money from even later investors, and so on. But as long as the money kept coming, he kept paying what he promised—and that perpetuated the cycle.

Realizing he had stumbled onto a good thing, Ponzi started planning for branch offices and talked of creating a string of banks and brokerage houses. He bought controlling interest in Hanover Trust Company, made himself president, then bought a large house and servants. He even gained control of his former employer's firm and fired his former boss! He was great at spending money—but as his investors later found out, he wasn't actually investing it. He was robbing Peter to pay Paul.

While crowds followed him, chanting, "You're the greatest Italian of them all," the Boston district attorney's office and the *Boston Post* embarked on their own quiet investigations. Ponzi was just too good to be true. It was then, by mid-summer of 1920, just a few months after he'd gotten started, that it was discovered that only $75,000 in reply coupons were normally printed in any given year—and that in 1919, only some $56,000 in coupons had been printed. But Ponzi had taken in millions. He couldn't possibly have spent the millions on reply coupons that hadn't been printed. Yet few stopped to think that through. The next step in his demise was the *Boston Post*'s revelation that, under an alias, Ponzi had been involved in a remittance racket in Montreal 13 years earlier.

As rumors started to spread, which could have sparked a panic among his "investors," Ponzi simply upped the ante—and his talk. He denied the charges and promised to double the interest payments! Through early August, the money continued to flow into Ponzi's pockets, even though the *Boston Post* declared him insolvent. Two weeks later, Boston learned that Old Colony had no assets—and had liabilities of over $2 million! In only eight months, Ponzi had taken in some $10 million and issued notes for over $14 million, yet less than $200,000 was ever recovered from his accounts.

What did Ponzi do with the money he bilked from investors? Not much! He lived high, yes, but there is no evidence that he actually accumulated any hidden riches. A lot of it was simply sent back out to the early investors, who didn't actually lose anything. Like a modern day chain-letter, it is the people putting up the money at the end who suffer. Ponzi probably didn't figure that his money machine would break down as soon as it did, and being the first, may not have even fully understood that it would have to break down eventually. He may have believed he could go on reshuffling people's money forever. In any case, one of the main victims in this scheme was Ponzi himself.

Ponzi pleaded guilty to charges of larceny and using the mail to defraud. Whatever his intentions, and whatever his level of financial sophistication or lack thereof, he was clearly a con man. While on bail pending appeal, he sold underwater lots in Florida, making another small fortune before going to prison for 12 years for the coupon scam. When he got out in 1934, he was immediately deported to Italy where he said, "I hope to open either a tourist agency or a hotel. My American connections make me particularly suitable for this sort of business." He did neither. Instead, he joined up with the fascists, gained government clout and was made business manager for LATI Airlines in Rio De Janeiro. Presumably this attempt at an honest living didn't go well. He ended up making a meager living teaching English in Rio. He died there in 1949, partially blind and paralyzed from a blood clot on the brain. To show how far the great swindler had fallen, note that he died in a Rio charity hospital ward with $75 he had managed to save from a small Brazilian government pension.

The Ponzi Scheme is a standard feature in modern mass fraud. Whether it is the infamous chain letter that almost everyone has received—promising great wealth for everyone—or various of the recent insurance frauds that have promised people high and safe annuity income when in fact there has been little or no business behind the promoters (a la ZZZZ Best, Baldwin United, or Equity Funding), the Ponzi Scheme is unlikely to fade from society as long as our strongest feature, basic freedom, endures. Foolish investors will always do themselves in by being too greedy and chasing returns which are unrealistically high. In some ways you could look at Ponzi as a slimeball form of greedy humanitarian—by fleecing the ignorant greedy, he and his kind regularly reteach society the old saw that bulls make money, and bears make money, but pigs get slaughtered.

SAMUEL INSULL

HE "INSULLTED" WALL STREET
AND PAID THE PRICE

Many a picture has been painted of Sam Insull—swindler, simpleton and genius among them. But scapegoat seems the most probable. During the 1920s, Insull knew electricity, turned it into a convenient, profitable commodity, then got zapped by his own voltage after he tried to take on Wall Street. When his multibillion-dollar electricity pyramid toppled, resulting in millions of losses to investors, he was microscoped from top to bottom and blamed—basically because big figures were involved. Everything he had accomplished for the industry, and for that matter, for America, via his role in the evolution of electricity, was forgotten—and he was branded a crook who cheated an unassuming public.

Insull built a lot during his lifetime, but what he didn't build—namely, Wall Street banking connections—cost him his empire. What he had going for him were a few basic good ideas, one of which was building a large consumer base for electrical power in order to naturally cut rates and increase profits. Eventually, his electricity firms, with $2.5 billion in assets, served

4.5 million customers—nearly 10 percent of America's power in 1930! Rates were reasonable and profits, immense. So far, so good.

In building upon his idea, Insull needed constant funds to increase power generation. Thus, he formed his first holding company, Middle West Utilities, in 1912, raising money through stock sales and then using the money to expand operations—not line his pocket. Financing rarely posed problems for Insull—but here's where he went wrong. Instead of appealing to first-line Wall Street investment banks like the House of Morgan and building strong relationships with them, he used local Chicago banks for loans and local, small-time investment bankers to underwrite security issues. Why go all the way to New York for money? The answer is simple. Staying local works fine when things are going your way, but not so well when times are tough, either because the economy is bad or because of a firm's own internal problems. Top financing sources can sustain a firm in tough times and may do so if the firm has built a solid relationship with them. Schlocky financing sources do not have the capability to finance anyone in tough times.

Unfortunately, as Insull later learned, when his pyramid-based world got large enough, with enough debt, so that it was easier to topple in tough times, it was also a valuable target for the first-line financiers to attack. The same folks he should have built ally-like relationships with saw his weakness as an opportunity to exploit. **J.P. Morgan Jr.**, long mad at Insull for not using his services, eventually got even.

Sober, hard-working, confident and born in 1859 to a poor minister, mustached Insull came to America from London at 21 to work with his idol, Thomas A. Edison, never having enough time to marry until he was 40. (Then he married an actress and had his son, Sam, Jr., who later came into business with him.) Though Insull's thick cockney accent was barely understandable, he served as Edison's personal secretary and business manager for years. At 30, Insull was picked to head Edison General Electric Company, but four years later, when J.P. Morgan took over the firm in organizing General Electric, Insull was left behind. Morgan factions claimed Insull borrowed too much—so you can see why the House of Morgan never came to mind when Insull sought funding!

Not easily dismayed, Insull bought into a small electric firm, vowing to make it the largest electrical power station in the country, which he did via expansion within two years. Middle West Utilities, his holding company, came next, multiplying Insull's power in his adopted hometown, Chicago, where he loaned money to good customers and supported local senatorial candidates. He became one of Chicago's most prominent citizens—until his empire began to slide.

Because of his holding-company structure, Insull owned minority interests in each holding company. So when Cleveland banker **Cyrus Eaton** on one side, and the House of Morgan on the other, began battling each other for large blocks of lucrative Insull securities, Insull got worried, puffed on his cigar double-time and figured the only way to defend his stocks from raiders was to build a pyramid which intertwined his assets! Though he knew little of stock operations, he believed that—through pyramiding—he and friends could control all of his companies by exchanging their utility holdings for stock in one major, all-encompassing holding company.

In 1928, he created Insull Utility Investments "to perpetuate existing management of the Insull group of public utilities." Insull, who used to love staring out his office window watching the city lights come on, turned over his and his associates' holdings to IUI, in return for controling interest in IUI. IUI stock was floated to the public at $12 per share and closed at $30 on its first day of trading—and within six months, $150, one of the original hot initial public offerings. Likewise, all the other Insull companies within his pyramid went berserk—one went from $202 to $450, and Middle West, from $169 to $529!

Insull didn't like such an overly optimistic market, which sent his personal fortune—on paper—to $150 million. He figured the bubble had to burst. But, while waiting, like everyone else who hangs around a cookie jar, he couldn't resist taking just a few. He took advantage of the speculative binge by refinancing Middle West Utilities, splitting its stock 10-for-1 and retiring its debt. Then he formed another top pyramid company intertwined with IUI, hoping again to put control of his empire out of reach of outsiders. But his pyramid was too big and was now a prime target for Wall Street.

Weakened by the 1929 Crash and forced to continuously defend his securities from raiders, draining cash and credit, Insull was forced to borrow some $48 million including some from the now not-so-friendly New York banks like Morgan—using his stock as collateral. So now he not only had reached his hand into the cookie jar, but he had it stuck in there. When the market collapsed again in 1931, while Morgan men intentionally sold short Insull securities, his stock finally gave way—and the bankers took their collateral. When further credit was denied by all, Insull's top firms went into receivership and he was left holding the bag.

Insull was wanted for mail fraud and embezzlement, along with his son on some charges. But he had fled Chicago for Europe, supposedly for relaxation, according to his generous biographer Forrest McDonald. I doubt he ever relaxed. As he travelled throughout France and Greece, the government tried to extradite him. Romania offered him a cabinet level position as head of electricity, which he was lucky or smart enough to turn down. Ultimately, the Turkish government arrested him in Istanbul as he disembarked a cruise ship. Extradited to the U.S., he was tried and, though acquitted on all counts, his reputation was ruined, and he died a broken man—a scapegoat.

There are a great many lessons to be learned from Sam Insull's life. First, note many folks assume that if they are major movers in industry, they can conquer Wall Street, too—as per Insull, few succeed. Main Street is straightforward, and Wall Street is tricky. Second, debt is always dangerous, but if you can't master Wall Street it's doubly dangerous. Third, if you're going to borrow big money and sell stock, it really is worth it to pay the price and build relationships with the top financing firms—partly so they won't turn on you later and eat you alive, particularly if you owe money. Debt is both Wall Street's carrot and its stick.

And finally, there is one little irony from Insull's life I relate to personally. Insull wanted to retire in the early 1920s. Had he done so, he would have quit a rich hero instead of ending up years later with a crook's reputation. Why didn't he quit? He finally decided to hang on long enough to turn his empire over to his son. That decision cost him his reputation. (I started in life working for my father and decided it was kinder to him and easier on me not to put him in that position.) If a son or daughter is good enough, he or she will rise to the top anyway, outside of the father's firm, or after the father is gone, without being handed the reins in a privileged postion. The father should depart when it is natural to do so and hand the reins to the best manager possible, family or not. If the offspring does it on his or her own, he will feel better about himself and never doubt his capabilities in terms of rising to the top. But Insull took the often tried and unnatural approach of handing his world to his son, and en route, hung around too long. It cost both his son and him everything but their lives.

IVAR KREUGER

HE PLAYED WITH MATCHES
AND GOT BURNED

Matches. They're cheap, readily available, necessary—and the basis for one of the most intricate and profitable financial schemes of the 20th century. Swedish Match King Ivar Kreuger masterminded a world-wide scheme in which he essentially borrowed money from Americans to loan millions to European countries in exchange for their match franchises. At his pinnacle in the late 1920s, he controlled 75 percent of the world's match manufacturing—a virtual world monopoly! Ultimately, a lack of liquidity, too many secrets and careless mistakes led to his demise, so in 1932 he shot himself in the chest to avoid public scrutiny. Once hailed as a financial genius, historians still wonder whether he was a pioneer, crazy, or just a crook.

Key to Kreuger's plan was his appearance, his facade. From the beginning his goal was to gain the confidence of American lending sources on Wall Street. With gray-green eyes, pallid, porous skin, and a pursed mouth, he met Wall Street's every expectation of a respectable businessman. He knew that if he looked and acted right, he would be granted credit. Kreuger appeared impeccably-dressed in expensive, yet uniform suits, accompanied by a cane and dark hat to cover his balding head. He was quiet but well-spoken, cultured, well mannered, and mildly forceful. He courted Wall Street, eventually winning over top investment bankers who forked over hundreds of millions to his supposedly solid firm—at a time when a hundred million mattered. But they didn't know he was a phony, full of contradictions.

After his death, Wall Street's vision of the reserved, respectable Match King was shattered. To start with, Kreuger was plagued by multiple black-mailings for reasons unknown. Probably at least some of them were his many mistresses—he had one in almost every major European city and kept over a dozen on regular allowances! And that wasn't all. Kreuger, who had his first love affair at 15 with a woman twice his age (his mother's friend), kept a little black book filled with women's names—each had her own page detailing her personality, likes and dislikes, how much she cost—and whether she was worth it!

He kept drawers full of expensive brooches, cigarette cases, gold purses, watches, silks, and perfumes for his one-night stands. If he tired of one, he tossed her an envelope filled with stocks! Kreuger remained a bachelor, he said, because marriage and the honeymoon required "at least eight days, and I haven't got time."

His business practices, a later audit revealed, were equally shocking. He alone supplied the figures for his books, juggling numbers in his head even as his Stockholm-based holding company, Kreuger and Toll, went international. Kreuger conducted business through his own accounts to eliminate or create assets and liabilities and shift them from one firm to another.

Like his books, Kreuger made acquiring match factories and franchises an art form. Typically, to seize a factory, he would sell his own better-quality matches in the targeted factory's locale at current prices, taking the market away from the local source without price-cutting. Then, once he had hurt the local source, he sent phony "independent" buyers to make ridiculously low offers on the factory, which would discourage the owners. Afterwards, when the offers had been rejected, he came in with his own better offers, which now seemed good to the owners. Once the factory was seized cheaply, he would again drop the quality of matches in the local market.

Franchises were secured by loaning countries like France and Germany millions at good rates for long periods, thereby securing long-term match franchises. An occasional bribe or two to the right official sometimes pushed agreements along. One of his greatest coups was loaning France $75 million at five percent after World War I, when American financiers like the House of Morgan were tightening their purse strings. He also bought hefty amounts of French bonds to stabilize the falling franc—and secure for himself a French match monopoly! After bribing necessary politicians, the deal was approved in 1927, and he got a 20-year franchise—which would last longer than he would.

To keep confidence in his firm secure, Kreuger made sure his securities always paid high dividends. Sometimes, he quietly bought shares in one of his match companies, then sold them for profit to another company within his trust, inflating their value, claiming a profit en route and enabling him to declare higher dividends. For fear of losing Wall Street's confidence, high dividends were paid right until the very end, even when Kreuger could barely afford them. Each time he issued stock in his firms, the stocks' worth was always based on exaggerated business volume. That is to say, he commonly cooked the books. He was said to have inflated earnings to the tune of $250 million between 1917 to 1932!

Born in 1880 and trained as an engineer, Kreuger worked as a bridge builder, a real estate agent and a steel salesman before realizing, "I cannot believe that I am intended to spend my life making money for second-rate people." In 1908, he formed Kreuger and Toll, an architectural-real estate firm, and five years later its subsidiary, United Match Factories, taking over two match manufacturing factories his father and uncle owned. Within four years, Kreuger, who ate little, believing it made him lazy, swallowed Sweden's largest match firms. He built a vertical trust whose securities were considered golden.

Throughout his career, Kreuger remained outwardly charming, but towards the end, his inner, eerie coldness began to seep from beneath his facade. He grew nervous. His smile weakened to the point of numbness. His handshake grew clammy. He spent money impulsively, collecting things like leather suitcases, canes, and cameras rather than art, as was customary among millionaires. And he spent money—lots of it—in desperate speculative deals that might right his desperate situation. That speculative trait is common among crooks in deep trouble.

The 1929 Crash was the beginning of the end for Kreuger. While his securities survived the crash relatively well, he had lent and borrowed too much—and the Crash caused a tight money flow. Instead of cutting back dividends or pulling in loans to conserve cash, which he felt would have sparked fatal rumors, he forged ahead on what auditors called "an orgy of financial ventures"—the most famous of which was his counterfeiting scheme. He had 42 Italian government bonds and five promissory notes printed, representing $142 million. As soon as he received them, he locked himself in his private top-floor Stockholm Match Palace and forged the names of Italian officials, spelling one official's name three different ways to make the securities look "authentic." Later, his accountants entered the phony bonds in the books.

By March, 1932, Kreuger had fallen apart at the seams. He had a nervous breakdown, couldn't sleep, answered imaginary telephone calls and door knocks, fumbled for answers regarding nonexistent cash balances and finally, transferred money and securities into relatives' names. He wrote a couple of notes, one of which said, "I have made such a mess of everything that I believe this is the best solution for all concerned."

Then, in his business-like fashion, Kreuger lay down on his bed fully dressed, unbuttoned his pin-striped jacket and vest and with his left hand held a handgun, purchased the day before, to his silk monogrammed shirt. He pulled the trigger and died almost instantaneously.

The Match King swindled some $250 million from American investors before his kingdom toppled. Yet he managed to build and operate a highly-leveraged empire that lasted some 15 years. In many ways the 1929 Crash was only incidental to his story. As a basic crook and swindler he probably would have ended up in the same place before long anyway. You can't keep a debt-driven phony house of cards standing forever. No one ever has. He is just one more of the many wild and extravagant, womanizing Wall Streeters who was doomed to failure by his greater love of fast money and the things it would buy, than of the actual processes of investing, owning and running businesses.

RICHARD WHITNEY

WALL STREET'S JUICIEST SCANDAL

It was October 24, 1929—Black Thursday—when the tall and arrogant Richard Whitney, Wall Street's best-known broker, strode across the New York Stock Exchange floor to the U.S. Steel specialist's post and uttered the most famous phrase in Stock Exchange history, "I bid 205 for 10,000 Steel." Stock prices were imploding and Steel could be bought for under 200, but by bidding what the stock was last sold for, Whitney breathed much-needed confidence onto the floor that day. People figured if Steel wasn't sliding, maybe others wouldn't.

Equipped with millions from a Morgan consortium, Whitney continued buying other blue-chip stocks, always in huge amounts at the price of the previous sale. Within minutes he racked up some $20 million in orders, and then the market rallied—for a while. "Richard Whitney Halts Panic," read the headlines.

Overnight, fame found Whitney, the acting president of the NYSE. The press reported his every move, the New York Stock Exchange post where he uttered his first famous bid was retired from the floor and ceremoniously presented to him, and then Whitney was elected president of the Stock Exchange.

He literally became Wall Street's voice and respected statesman. Whitney had a magnificent reputation to uphold.

He had a great time with his new role. All his life—at Groton, then at Harvard—he knew he was destined for something big. The son of a Boston bank president, Whitney was impeccably connected and a born leader. Handsome, broad-shouldered, and well-dressed, he inspired confidence.

A member of Manhattan's most exclusive clubs, he lived expensively with a wife, at least one mistress, town house, country house, prize-winning livestock—lots of big bills. Once, on a whim, he gave his barber a trip to Florida for keeping quiet while shaving him. Spending $5,000 per month on living expenses during the Great Depression, Whitney was among the crowd everyone gossiped about—and he loved every minute of it!

But what the papers overlooked—until it was too late—was that Whitney couldn't afford his lifestyle. While he came out of the Crash with "increased faith in this marvelous country of ours," he also came out of it poor. Years later he said he lost $2 million in the Crash. But he never had any large personal fortune to fall back on. His firm, Richard Whitney & Co., had high overhead and serviced a small, elite clientele, mainly J.P. Morgan & Co. It grossed more prestige than money—annual profits amounted to only $60,000. (In the Morgan tradition, Whitney was an elitist and preferred not to have anything at all to do with the public—let alone handle its brokerage.)

So what does a big spender do when he's shy cash? In Whitney's case, he plunged into the market, hoping to recoup his position. There were several deals—all far-fetched. He invested in the Florida Humus Company, which experimented with peat humus as a commercial fertilizer—he would have done better to invest in real organic fertilizer. For a four-term NYSE president, he was surprisingly easy to sucker. To make matters worse, Whitney didn't know to cut his losses—instead he let them run, buying further and further into big schemes that were going absolutely nowhere.

By 1931, his firm's net worth was about $36,000, excluding over a million he had personally borrowed from his brother George, a Morgan partner. It continued downhill from here—he borrowed from J.P. Morgan & Co., again and again from his brother, and then he fell further, borrowing from lesser brokers, from floor specialists, and from anyone on the exchange floor who would lend money against his prior great reputation. But folks in general didn't realize the extent of his borrowing.

Whitney remained optimistic, taking faith in applejack (a backwoods-style booze) of all things! No, he didn't hit the bottle—instead he prepared for Prohibition's repeal by taking over a chain of New Jersey distilleries. In 1933, he and a brokerage partner organized Distilled Liquors Corporation to make "New Jersey Lightning," which they thought could become America's next craze. While he waited for the craze to catch on, Whitney talked his creditors into extending his loans and borrowed still more from people he barely knew. Banks, at this point, were of no use, for he had no collateral.

When repeal became effective, Distilled Liquors, which he bought between 10 and 15, jumped to 45. Had Whitney sold out he could have paid off everyone but his brother and worried about George later. But he had gambler's fever and bad judgment, and, thus, held on. Predictably, Whitney's luck soured as Distilled Liquors lagged for a lack of buyers. The more it sagged, the more Whitney scrounged to support the stock price—just barely above $10.

He was desperate now—if the stock declined, his outstanding bank loans would be called in for deficient collateral—and a desperate man does desperate things. In 1936, having run out of suckers to borrow from, and as word of his finances spread, Whitney became a swindler. Still treasurer of the New York Yacht Club, he took over $150,000 in Yacht Club bonds to fraudulently use as collateral against a $200,000 bank loan. He had gotten away with a similar scheme in 1926 when he "borrowed" bonds from his father-in-law's estate and replaced them three years later, with no one the wiser.

All rationality gone, Whitney embezzled the New York Stock Exchange Gratuity Fund (a multimillion dollar mutual-benefit arrangement for the families of deceased members). It was easy. He was one of its six trustees and its broker. So when the Fund decided to sell $350,000 in bonds and buy a like amount of another bond issue, Whitney sold the bonds, placed the orders on the new ones, bought them, but then instead of delivering the new bonds to the Gratuity Fund, he took the bonds to a bank as collateral for a personal loan! He repeated this scam over and over again, and within nine months, the fund was missing over $1 million in cash and bonds!

By 1937, the missing securities were discovered by the Gratuity Fund trustees. They asked for their property, and after a few days and a cockamamie story about paperwork delaying delivery, Whitney returned the loot by the seat of his pants. The seat of his pants, meanwhile, was actually his brother George, who himself had to borrow the money from fellow Morgan partner **Thomas Lamont.** During a later investigation, George Whitney said, "I asked him how he could have done it . . . and he said he had no explanation to offer."

Finally, the Exchange got wise to Whitney, dug into his books, and discovered his shady deals. But even then, he had hope. He reasoned with the Exchange and promised to sell his NYSE seat in return for dropped charges. "After all, I'm Richard Whitney. I mean the Stock Exchange to millions of people." In the end, completely oblivious to what was right and wrong, Whitney withdrew over $800,000 in customers' securities from his firm's account and within four months, gathered some $27 million via 111 loans. He literally approached strangers on the Exchange floor, even prior enemies, holding out his hand and asking for money!

The *Nation* summed it up when it said, "Wall Street could hardly have been more embarrassed if J.P. Morgan had been caught helping himself from the collection plate at the Cathedral of St. John the Divine." Whitney got five to ten years at Sing Sing and an injunction banning him from the securities industry forever. During sentencing, he looked haggard, his hands twitched, and he blushed when he was called a "public betrayer."

The aftermath of Whitney was even more pathetic. During his prison sentence, Distilled Liquors went bankrupt and his prestigious U.S. Steel specialist's post, where he made his famous bid, was auctioned off for five bucks. Fellow inmates called him Mr. Whitney and sought his autograph—Whitney always obliged. A model prisoner, he was paroled in 1941, then stayed with relatives. For a while, he managed a family dairy farm in Barnstable, Massachusetts, then dropped out of sight permanently, and died at 86 in 1974 at his daughter's home. His brother repaid all his debts.

As Stock Exchange president, Whitney not surprisingly fought against government-guided stock market reform, calling the Exchange a "perfect institution." He said members had the "courage to do those things which are right, regardless of how unpopular they may be for the time being," and thus, were capable of policing themselves. This was obviously quite untrue and ironically, we have Whitney to attest to the fact. It kind of reminds me of an old carpenter who once told me, "A good gate keeps 'em honest."

Historical Picture Service, 1936

MICHAEL J. MEEHAN

THE FIRST GUY NAILED BY THE SEC

Mike Meehan wasn't unusual, but he helped create a crazy time in the 1920s, and afterwards he helped introduce a new form of fear into Wall Street—fear of the SEC. Crafty and high-strung, the redhead manipulated stocks so skillfully that flappers, secretaries, and shoe shine boys, eager to make a quick buck, clamored to buy his high-climbing stocks. Once they bought in, Meehan sold out—and almost overnight the stock deflated back to its original value. Meehan made between $5 and $20 million in deals like this, yet ultimately, like the Roaring 20s, he fizzled out—after 1930s anti-stock manipulation laws outlawed his flagrant methods. Lacking the foresight and flexibility to change with the times, Meehan was the first, and one of the biggest traders ever to be expelled from the New York Stock Exchange by the SEC and died with hardly a notice from Wall Street.

Born in England in 1892, Meehan grew up in Manhattan, attended public schools and became a messenger boy. A real go-getter, he next worked selling theater tickets in a tiny, Wall Street-based ticket office. By age 19, chubby Meehan was scrambling to get the best seats on Broadway for powerful Morgan, Lehman, and Goldman Sachs partners, guaranteeing his future with every ticket he sold. Six years later, in 1917, his influential clients helped him get a seat on the Curb Exchange—and from there his success was rapid. By 1920, he'd saved the $90,000 needed to buy a NYSE seat, quit the ticket agency, and launched M.J. Meehan and Company.

Meehan's timing couldn't have been better, and his firm took off with the 1920s' bull market. He quickly became the darling of the financial community, specializing in Radio Corporation of America stock (RCA) when it was first listed on the exchange in 1924. A super-salesman, respected Meehan made RCA one of the market's hottest issues, manipulating and promoting it among the common public. High-strung, hard-working, and all smiles, he forked out over $2 million for eight Stock Exchange seats—more than any other firm at the time—and dealt in such a large volume of stock that he was able to take in $15,000 per day in RCA stock commissions alone.

As RCA's specialist, Meehan was hired to oversee speculative pools, which were responsible for driving the non-dividend paying stock from about 85 in 1925 to its peak, 549, in 1929. One pool, which included such industrial heavy-weights as **John Raskob** and Charles Schwab (the "steel" Schwab, not the modern-day discount broker), traded a million RCA shares, which then stood at 90. Meehan manipulated RCA in his usual way—trading heavily to create the illusion of activity, driving the price to 109. The pool sold out and left the stock to deflate to 87. For his part in the coup—which took little over a week—Meehan pocketed half a million, and the pool, $5 million.

Meehan enjoyed the good life right through the 1929 Crash—for him, very little changed during the ensuing Depression. Before the Crash, he took up residence at Manhattan's posh Sherry-Netherland Hotel, lined his office walls with calfskin-bound Shakespeare and opened nine branch brokerage offices, including one in uptown Manhattan and others aboard Cunard luxury liners! Generous with his money, he gave each of his 400 employees a full year's salary as a 1927 Christmas bonus. After the Crash, Meehan closed a few branch doors, but later managed to buy his son a $130,000 NYSE seat for his 21st birthday. Rumors that he had lost his shirt in the Crash were not true.

But if Meehan learned nothing from the 1929 Crash, Uncle Sam did—and the government did something about it. A Senate banking committee was launched to look into pre-Crash stock-rigging practices—and soon the word "pool" became a dirty word that no Wall Streeter dared utter. The Securities and Exchange Act of 1934 was passed, outlawing pools and stock manipulation practices—the very things Meehan had built his reputation on! But whether he was still too busy having a good time or just unconvinced that Uncle Sam meant business that Wall Street really had changed, Meehan completely ignored the new laws and jumped back into the market, using his trademark, flamboyant trading methods.

In 1935, Meehan set out to manipulate Bellanca Aircraft via what was known as "matched orders"—actively buying and selling the stock to give the appearance of a rising stock on high volume. This creates the illusion of heavy trading, when in fact one small group is trading the stock among themselves in order to sucker in the public, who in their own greedy way, believes they've found a hot number. The public buys the stock en masse, pushes the stock up further, then the pool quietly sells out its position. Meehan got his usual spectacular results—within a few months, he was able to move Bellanca from $1.75 to $5.50 and hold it there while he and his colleagues dumped hundreds of thousands of shares on the public. Once he concluded his pool operations, the stock fell back to its original price—and only then did he discover that Uncle Sam meant business.

After a long series of ballyhooed hearings (Meehan, after all, wasn't considered a criminal by anyone except the government), the SEC decided to make an example of Meehan and expelled him from every exchange he belonged to—the New York Stock Exchange, the Curb Exchange, and the Chicago Board of Trade. It was the first action taken under the anti-stock manipulation section of the Securities Exchange Act, and it profoundly changed an awed Wall Street. Meehan, too, was shocked—so shocked that he checked into a sanatorium, some say to gather his nerves together, others say to avoid the law. Meehan died suddenly in 1948 at 56, leaving his wife and four kids moderately wealthy—despite his failure on Wall Street.

Prior to the Securities Exchange Act, stock-rigging and pool operations were legal and rather old-hat for Wall Streeters; it was hard for anyone—especially Meehan—to think of them as being illegal. Meehan's friends, in fact, defended him, saying his actions were "the kind that made him the toast of trading circles in the Coolidge era." But times change, and so do laws, and you must obey the laws. Governments tend to implement harsh new laws by making harsh examples of a few offenders to deter the broader masses—and Meehan was one of those examples.

As a 1920s speculator, Meehan was successful, but not so noteworthy as to be included in this book. Putting brokerage offices in ocean liners is hardly innovative finance. He did nothing in a positive sense to further the evolution of Wall Street or finance as a whole. But he did get busted. And he was the first of a breed in that respect, and he gave us all, even those of us in the profession who aren't even close to breaking a law, a very healthy respect for the SEC's power. Times change, and being flexible on Wall Street, whether to market trends, new industries—or as in Meehan's case—to social demands and evolving laws, is a necessity.

Life, August 10, 1959

LOWELL M. BIRRELL

THE LAST OF THE GREAT
MODERN MANIPULATORS

How the son of a smalltown Presbyterian minister and Methodist missionary grew up to become one of Wall Street's most ruthless, devious and colorful manipulators is anything but a mystery. Birrell was a clever, money-hungry and exceedingly charming young lawyer when he stumbled upon an irresistible "fool-proof" way to beat the market. With an impeccable memory that recalled every clause and comma in the SEC provisions, Birrell began illegally dumping unregistered stock on the market at exaggerated prices via an elaborate network in exchange for legitimate stock and cash. When the SEC finally caught on to him almost 20 years later, Birrell was said to have "wrecked more corporations, duped more investors and engineered the theft of more money than any other American of this century." The SEC conceded he was "the most brilliant manipulator of corporations in modern times," which certainly should be enough to make him among the masterful minds that made the market what it is today.

Birrell maneuvered his first crooked deal in 1938 at 31. He borrowed money from a millionaire cigar manufacturer's widow to buy control of a Brooklyn brewery that made Fidelio beer—but it wasn't the beer that interested him. Birrell converted the brewery into a holding firm that he used in later deals by merging it with other firms. And that wasn't illegal. But then, to finance acquisitions, he issued a stream of richly-priced stock never registered for public sale; and to get around legislation, Birrell and his buddies held the stock as a "long-term investment," but actually dumped it on the market for cash.

Six years later, Birrell maneuvered a complicated insurance scam in which he loaded a group of his own insurance firms with overvalued securities ... just like **Jay Gould** and **Jim Fisk**. The scam got underway in 1944 when he used watered brewery stock to buy Claude Neon, Inc., a neon lights maker listed on the Curb Exchange (which preceded the American Stock Exchange). Again, he wasn't at all interested in the firm's products; he was after its prestigious Curb listing which made its stock easy to water and then market with few questions asked. Right away, Birrell had Claude Neon issue hordes of stock with which he bought control of several small insurance firms, an industry in which the SEC was without jurisdiction.

A shady insurance veteran helped him set up a firm that "selected" investments for his group of insurance companies. For this service, the firm took 25 percent of all the companies' net income. That is, he was siphoning money away from the firms he controlled. But the real scam was this: Birrell bought heaps of cheap securities at market prices, sold them to Claude Neon at inflated prices, then had the insurance group buy them from Claude Neon for the portfolios he controlled. As the portfolios appeared to skyrocket in value, the insurance firms took on more business—and Birrell's cut ballooned. If that is in the slightest confusing to you, note that really top-notch swindles have always been confusing—that's what makes them work. Birrell was a master at swindles confusing enough to fool everyone.

Birrell got away with this for about five years until his board of directors questioned the value of the stocks they'd been sold. By 1949, Birrell was found out and forced to relinquish control of the insurance portfolio. But he wasn't prosecuted, presumably because his board wanted it kept quiet. While Birrell was no longer in formal control, the companies themselves were good for one more scam. In 1953, he initiated a similar insurance scam via his newly acquired United Dye and Chemical Corporation, a maker of logwood dyes listed on the New York Stock Exchange. He watered United's assets, bilked the firm of some $2 million in the process and within two years sold out.

Birrell was like a virus that feeds off its host's blood. By sucking the lifeblood from the companies he controlled, he maintained a decadent lifestyle. He had a Manhattan suite, an apartment in Havana, and his ultimate party headquarters—a 1,200-acre estate in Bucks County, Pennsylvania, complete with slot machines that rarely paid off, a baby elephant he fed Scotch, and a shiny red fire engine he'd bought for one of his three wives. There, beside a seven-acre manmade lake built to house his yacht, he'd host two- and three-day orgies based on booze, and the most expensive call girls. He was used to having his way—and he'd happily pay whatever his way cost. After all, money came to him easily. Only once was he let down when a model refused his $1,000 offer to strip in front of a pack of reporters and shower in oil gushing from a Birrell well.

When he wasn't partying in Pennsylvania, Birrell usually kicked up his heels with Manhattan society. Standing 5 foot 8 and weighing some 200 pounds with a puffy face, Birrell was not handsome, but his roguish qualities bedazzled friends and lovers alike. He dressed in expensive, custom-made blue suits and talked up a storm. He slept no more than three hours a night, and was famous for catnapping in telephone booths and on nightclub tables! He'd drink 'til the wee hours, but was always alert and ready for business by 9 a.m. the next morning. You could say he was born ready.

Born in Whiteland, Indiana in 1907, Birrell graduated from Syracuse University at age 18, then from University of Michigan law school at just 21. He worked for a prestigious New York law firm for five years, then went out on his own to discover Wall Street after helping reorganize and refinance some local firms. Instead of following the same respectable route, where he may have ended up a legend in his own right due to his tremendous intellect, Birrell shot for the stars and wound up swindling anyone he could. Some of his more wretched endeavors include swindling land from his elderly, widowed next-door-neighbor, and deviously gaining control of his wealthy dying friend's fortune. Nice guy.

But by far his grandest scam was the Swan Finch Oil-Doeskin swindle, for which he was indicted on 69 counts of grand larceny, income tax evasion and stock fraud and accused of stealing $14 million in stock from two firms. Like all Birrell deals, this one was confusing. It featured interlocking directorates, dummy accounts, overvalued stock and a host of other devious deceptions meant to circumvent SEC laws. As early as 1947, Birrell had acquired Doeskin Products, a listed corporation, by selling it $2 million in overvalued securities, then using the proceeds to buy out the controlling stockholders. In essence, he bought it with its own money! When other stockholders complained of the dubious debentures, issued for a company called Beverly Hills Cemetery—of Peekskill, New York—and sued, Birrell was forced to pay back a measly $200,000. Compared to $2 million, that was peanuts.

In 1954, he took control of Swan Finch Oil Corporation for a song—and with it, gained trading privileges on the Amex. This way Birrell could trade through Swan Finch stock without disclosing financial information. With his dummy companies in place, Birrell floated about two million shares of newly created but unregistered "watered" stock to build the firms up (see **Daniel Drew** for the original deployment of this technique). Swan Finch, which was at the time a maker of industrial oil and grease, then acquired gas fields, uranium mining leases, a grain storage terminal, and finally stock of Doeskin Products, which Birrell already controlled. Then he promoted the conglomerate to the public through a series of five sensationally successful ads in the *New York Times*. Ultimately, what started as an obscure concern with 35,000 shares of common stock barely worth $1 million became a popular firm, with over two million shares worth over $10 million.

Swan Finch became one of the success stories of the 1950s bull market, or so people were led to believe. Once the stock caught on, Birrell found all sorts of devious ways to indirectly unload his stock on the public, such as selling the stock to various brokers who in turn sold it on the market. He also sold shares via dummy Canadian accounts and hired the notorious Amex stock specialists, **Jerry** and his son, **Gerard Re**, to unload stock on the Amex trading floor. His most ingenious route was putting stock up as collateral for $1.5 million in loans. When he defaulted on the loans, as was planned all along, the moneylenders then sold the shares to the public.

In early 1957, Swan Finch's tremendous stock activity finally caught the attention of SEC investigators, and almost immediately the courts ordered an injunction preventing the illegal stock distribution. When he was subpoenaed in October, Birrell did a disappearing act, leaving his third wife behind for a Havana-bound airplane. He remained in Cuba until Fidel Castro took over and at that time, flew to Rio de Janeiro, Brazil, which had no extradition treaty with Uncle Sam. Rio police, however, thought they had a famous American criminal on their hands and held Birrell in jail for 89 days for traveling with a falsified passport. Police ultimately let Birrell free to live as he always had—ostentatiously, after discovering just how much cash he had to spend!

Birrell chain-drank vodka-sodas and danced the samba. He spent his nights in Rio's top nightclubs, spending $200 a night on food, drink, and women. One night he even entertained the warden of Central Prison while officials prepared a futile deportation case against him. Somewhat paranoid, Birrell hired off-duty police officers as his bodyguards, carried little cash, and conducted business from public telephones. After all, Brazil wasn't just his vacation hideaway; it was a land full of opportunity. "It's like being a hungry kid in a candy store; you don't know which box to pick from." He dabbled in tourism, as he grew nostalgic for America, exported gemstones and castor oil, imported cattle semen, and patented a wooden balancing toy.

In 1964, Birrell returned to America as he always said he would. He was kept in prison for 18 months while Uncle Sam prepared its case, using the hordes of files they'd seized from his abandoned office back in 1959. Ultimately the case fizzled when a judge ruled that the evidence—Birrell's files—was seized illegally, without a specific warrant, and Birrell escaped further prosecution—and headlines. It was not the finest moment for the SEC, securities regulators, or for that matter, the general public. After that, Birrell dropped out of sight.

In the 19th century none of Birrell's tricks would have amounted to much. He would have been just another manipulator and would have had to slug it out with peers who knew how to play rough. But in the 1950s, he was the last of a vanishing breed. The last of the big-time manipulators. With luck we will never see his kind again. Yet, whether it's Robert Vesco, Barry Minkow or a host of other, lesser con men, Lowell Birrell stands as the biggest and the best modern example to remind us to always be looking over our shoulders for crooks.

The Bettmann Archives 1956

WALTER F. TELLIER

THE KING OF THE PENNY
STOCK SWINDLES

U nsophisticated investors didn't stand a chance against Walter Tellier
and his band of boiler room bandits. High-pressure sales tactics and
grade-A sucker lists fueled Tellier's well-oiled machine, which churned out
millions of worthless, irresistibly cheap "penny stocks" in exciting, "sure-
fire" opportunities like uranium mines and Alaskan telephone circuits. When
Tellier was finally caught and the gig was up, investors were left about a
million in the hole and rocked by yet another Wall Street scandal.

Originally a cosmetics salesman from Hartford, Connecticut and born about
1900, Tellier peddled securities in the middle of the great 1920s bull market.
When the 1929 Crash hit, he relied on the buy-now, pay-later plan to attract
salaried workers with meager savings and big dreams. By 1931, his outstanding
salesmanship paid off—Tellier was able to start his own firm with a couple of
thousand bucks distributing various issues for Wall Street brokerage houses.
Two years later, one of the houses he worked for suggested he open a New
York branch. He did, and business boomed, so he closed down the Hartford
office and moved to the Big Apple to specialize in wholesaling securities to

brokers. No sooner was he settled in his new office, than he was indicted on conspiracy charges and mail fraud—but this case was later dismissed.

Soft-spoken yet aggressive, Tellier laid low, selling securities legally (presumably), making moderate money until the 1950s bull market—of which he took full advantage. He began pumping out penny stocks to freshman investors, a new market recently rediscovered by Wall Street and loved for its wide-eyed enthusiasm, gullibility, no-questions-asked loyalty, and hope for miracles. Guys like **Charles Merrill**, and much of Wall Street, loved these investors for the commission-based opportunity they represented—and served them well. But Tellier touted miracles by the dozen—miracles for only fifteen cents to a half-dollar per share! Tellier served these guys too, like a baked pig with an apple in its mouth.

The validity of his "miracles" is one story—one that you can read about in any of the sources listed below—but his method of dumping them on the public is a much better story. Tellier didn't invent boiler rooms, but he made fine use of them, as described in the book, *The Watchdogs of Wall Street*. Boiler rooms were no different from any con game, except they were out to swindle in the name of Wall Street! Typically found in dingy lofts, several flights of stairs from any outsider's view, the rooms themselves were furnished in a makeshift fashion with boxes for benches, propped-up plywood as conference tables, cramped cubicles with telephones for the con men, harsh bare bulbs, and cardboarded windows. The victims on the other end of the phone line assumed they were talking to one of America's top financial leaders from one of those plush Wall Street offices.

The men who made the boiler rooms boil were often hardened criminals who'd served time for serious crimes; entry-level positions were filled by college kids looking to pay for tuition. Ties and shirts tossed aside in the sweltering heat, the "coxeys" or entry-level swindlers, made first contact with customers, calling from lists of potential suckers. Some had already received Tellier's direct mailings so they were familiar with Tellier's name when they received the call. To make the initial good impression, the coxey would say he was calling "from Wall Street," then proceed to make wild claims about the penny stocks. "Mr. So and So, just make a small purchase and you'll see what we can do for you." This call might bring in between $50 and $100.

The lists would then be forked over to the "loaders," the more experienced cons. It was their job to find out how much their target was really worth—that is, if he mortgaged his house and borrowed from every friend and family member. If the person held blue-chip stocks, the loader talked him into selling them for a Tellier issue. Finally, "superloaders" or "dynamiters," the highest-paid and most persuasive in the scam, could convince their target to steal if necessary to buy a hot stock! They'd slyly confide "hot" tips they "just learned from the floor" or "picked up in the board room."

Amidst the cigar smoke and cigarette butts, boiler rooms in 1956 alone parted tens of thousands of suckers from some $150 million. And the cons were well taken care of for their efforts: A sales manager might take $150,000 from managing one boiler room, and one loader once made $75,000 in six months. While the boiler rooms pumped out the goods, Tellier was busy twisting securities laws to protect himself and not his victims, as in the case of the full disclosure provision of the Truth in Securities Act of 1933. In this case, the law allowed an issue to be exempt from full registration if it sold for under $300,000, which ironically was ideal for penny stock scams. So, of course, his issues typically totaled $295,000.

He also plunged into advertising, promoting his issues on radio stations and in major dailies, like the *New York Times*. His print ads featured a coupon to clip and send for more information—a seemingly innocent promotion that in reality supplied his boiler room staff with names and addresses. Later, it was said Tellier sold his infamous sucker-lists to an investment advisory firm after the government nabbed him.

But until he was nabbed, Tellier walked with his head held high and projected the utmost respectability. At North American Securities Administrators conventions—filled with the very officials who were supposed to police Tellier-type activities—he threw lavish cocktail parties that became the highlight of the conventions. He became a respectable family man living in lush Englewood, New Jersey—home of Morgan partners for years. He joined the Westchester Country Club (where he sold some stocks to clubhouse employees), lavishly furnished his office and drove a Cadillac. Slightly balding, Tellier was very conscious of appearances and dressed to impress.

By 1956, he was impressing a federal grand jury with his utter disregard for SEC regulation. Despite his claim that he was "the most investigated person in the world" because of his prominence in the penny stock industry, the next year, Tellier & Company was closed down, and Tellier was barred from trading in stocks in New York and New Jersey, where most of his victims lived. He was charged with fraudulent stock promotion practices in the sale of uranium and Alaskan telephone securities that swindled investors out of about $1 million. During his trial, he tried to bribe a government witness with $250,000 but was unsuccessful. In 1958, he received a four-and-a-half-year prison term and an $18,000 fine. After that, the king of penny stocks was never heard from again.

In most penny stock scams there is a consistent phenomenon: The brokerage firm carrying the issue is the only place where you can buy or sell the stock. This lets the firm control the market. For example, in a usual securities deal, there is a syndicate put together by the lead underwriter, and the syndicate members each carry a piece of the overall deal. Then, various syndicate members agree to "make a market" in the stock after the deal is complete by competing against each other to buy and sell the stock. In this and every other market, it is competition which insures honesty. In a regular market you can buy a stock from dealer X and sell it through dealer Y. And if you don't like X or Y, there are also dealers U, W, and Z. But in a penny stock scam there is no other market. There is no syndicate on the original deal, and there is no after-market of competitive brokerage firms—only the guy who stuck you with the stock in the first place. So when he sells it to you at $1.50 one month, you may find you can only sell it back—to him—for a quarter the next month. There is no place else to go, no competition for your stock.

Another trick of penny stock guys is to break up the country, or even a state, into geographies. In some of the areas, they start selling the issue. A few months later, they start buying it back at a fraction of the price, while at the same time, selling it in another geography to a new set of suckers at a much higher price, often even higher than the original offering price. They tell this new second set of suckers that the stock has been going up since it was issued—because it is so hot. Tellier pioneered all of these methods via the boiler room.

Tellier led the penny stock scam phenomenon, and it has replayed almost nonstop ever since, and largely in the same form as when Tellier did it. The main difference recently has been that the boiler rooms look just like standard brokerage offices and the crooks have learned how to dress. Dressing like a businessman and being able to scam face-to-face increases the image of respectability and lets you get away with bigger swindles. Tellier should have been smart enough to see this, but he was the pioneer, and every industry gets better with practice.

Whether it is Robert Brennan advertising his New Jersey-based First Jersey Securities scams on national television, any of a host of penny ante Colorado-based scam masters, or the new "king," Meyer Blinder, and his devoted army of arm twisters (also in Colorado, and now, having been driven out of America, pulling the same scams overseas), the penny stock arena has evolved into one of the prime places where out-and-out crooks work their magic in the modern securities world. Tellier would be proud.

Drawing by Jesse Fisher

JERRY AND GERALD RE

A FEW BAD APPLES CAN RUIN
THE WHOLE BARREL

Stock specialists "make the market" for the stocks they represent: They bring buyer and seller together and supervise trading on the harried trading floor. Forbidden from selling to the public, they keep the market stable and liquid—balancing supply and demand—by buying securities for their own account if buyers are scarce, and selling their own shares when sellers are few. In essence, they not only orchestrate the "auction" that is a stock exchange, but from time to time participate in it as buyers, and seller, to keep it moving along when it hasn't enough active participants naturally. It's a prestigious position, fundamental to running the stock exchange. What's required of specialists is detailed technical knowledge and a keen ability to judge the value of securities and pick up on pricing trends. But most importantly they must have respect for and maintain silence regarding their insider knowledge.

They must have integrity.

The father-and-son stock specialist team, Jerry and Gerald Re, lacked integrity. For years, between 1954 and 1960, they unloaded illegal stocks on the market, paid kickbacks to brokers who helped them, bribed reporters who played up their stocks, acted on inside information, operated via dummy accounts and bilked unsuspecting investors—including the American Stock Exchange (AMEX) president!—in the biggest stock swindle in decades. And all this almost as if the SEC had never been born.

The Res dumped over a million illegal shares on the market by taking advantage of their prestigious roles. They rigged markets, took over $3 million for themselves while selling investors some $10 million of illegal securities, and according to formal charges, defrauded investors in transactions totaling $13 million. "Everybody knew there was something smelly in Jerry Re's corner of the floor, but only in general," said one specialist. When the SEC finally cracked down on the Res in 1961, it marked the first time in the Commission's near 30-year life that it took action against a stock specialist. When I was first in the investment industry, folks used to wisecrack that the main requirement to be an AMEX specialist was a criminal background. They were joking, whether they knew it or not, about the Res.

The son of Italian immigrants and born in 1897, Jerry grew up with street smarts and little formal education in Manhattan. In the streets, he discovered the Curb Market—then operated on financial district sidewalks rain or shine, snow or sleet, summer or winter. In 1920 he bought a Curb membership and, 20 years later, he was a prospering specialist, husband and father with solid social connections. Short, stocky and bug-eyed, with a large nose, booming voice and jolly laugh, Jerry was an amiable guy who liked schmoozing (and swindling) with anyone who mattered in the Big Apple—city politicos, baseball stars, senators, judges and restaurant owners. He grew rich and prominent, wintered in Boca Raton with influential friends, bought a summer farm in upstate New York and maintained an apartment in Greenwich Village.

Jerry had become something of an institution on the trading floor by the time the Curb became the American Stock Exchange in 1953. So, automatically, he became the premier AMEX stock specialist, specializing in some 17 stocks. His son Gerald, born in 1923, joined the Curb Exchange in 1944 and, over the years, had become a major part of their specialist firm, Re, Re & Sagarese. The junior Re, who looked like his dad, wasn't as bold as his father, who thought they should be given a medal for what they'd been doing. More soft spoken, Gerald once said, "My Dad and I are very proud of our reputation down there as good specialists and maybe we carry it to the nth degree, but we try to stay on top of all our situations and do whatever we can."

The mastermind behind their illegal activities was seemingly Re Senior, who probably remembered such far-fetched schemes from his younger, pre-SEC years. In fact, Jerry never acknowledged the reformed marketplace and his duty to adhere to the new rules. For instance, he illegally supported price declines and once told the SEC, "Our success has been where people come to us and want to give us stock because they know we will support their stock. We will buy twenty, thirty, forty, fifty thousand shares of stock. We are not afraid of doing it."

Indeed, the Res often bought large blocks of stock from top corporate officials or major stockholders who wanted to sell but didn't want to depress the stock price in the market. So, insiders sold stock to them at discounted prices, then the Res had the task of unloading the stock on the public at much greater prices and in smaller increments. Sometimes, they did this via "long-term" investors to avoid registering the sale with the SEC, or they gave the stock to a dozen or so different brokers to disguise their interest in the stock. Sometimes the senior Re even offered brokers "ten cents a share under the table" to push a stock (in very large volume of course); then they'd meet uptown, where'd he'd make payments in cash. A specialist had never been busted by the SEC, so the Res probably thought they would never be accosted.

Their list of violations was a long one. They ignored what became standard bookkeeping procedures and practiced "painting the tape." Painting the tape is an outlawed practice whereby stocks are shorted on the books at the exchange by borrowing shares and at the same time putting them up for sale. "Dummy" accounts then buy up the stock (thereby avoiding the risk involved in covering the shorts), making the stock appear to be active—when the transaction was really entirely fictitious. The trades had never actually happened but were just paper shuffling within the specialist's books. The Res also accepted discretionary orders, key to manipulating a stock price. With these orders in place for "friends and relatives"—obviously fronts for the Re themselves—they could make purchases at crucial moments to give the stock a lift, again making the stock appear more active than it really was. Stuff straight out of the 1920s.

When they were finally found out, the SEC expelled them from the AMEX and revoked their brokerage licenses. They were brought to trial on charges of manipulating the market to expedite the sale of $10 million in Swan Finch Oil stock between 1954 and 1957. Their own lawyer said that defending them would be a waste of time (implying that there was no way they could get off). During the ensuing trial in 1963, through which the SEC tried to regain the public's shattered trust in the securities industry, the prosecutor paraded 76 witnesses and used a series of 3.5 × 6-foot charts to tell of the intricate, round-about routes used to pump illegal stocks onto the market. When the Res, ages 66 and 40, were touted as swindlers and labeled as mere puppets of Swan Finch Oil king **Lowell Birrell**, Birrell responded from his Brazilian exile, "That is ridiculous. They were no small fries. They handled a great deal of stock." I'm sure the Res were ecstatic to get the incriminating endorsement.

Ever since the Res scandal, there has been suspicion of the specialist function. There has also been suspicion of the AMEX. The AMEX has never regained the prestige and position it once had, suffering continual pressure and competition from both over-the-counter markets (which as dealer markets have no specialists) and the more prestigious NYSE. Condemnations of specialists ran rampant for a while, culminating in the claims best articulated by author Richard Ney that Wall Street was a game rigged for the benefit of specialists.

Jerry Re was an exception. There has been little else to buttress the arguments of the specialist-bashers. Yet folks like the Res and their more recent counterparts involved with violations of insider trading rules form the continuing basis of why the SEC can't turn regulation of securities markets over to the industry itself. And in that way, by their singular bad example, the Res helped make the market what it is and will be. One bad apple can ruin the whole barrel.

CHAPTER EIGHT

TECHNICIANS, ECONOMISTS, AND OTHER COSTLY EXPERTS

WITCH DOCTORS OF WALL STREET

Technicians, Economists and Other Costly Experts operate by one of two motives—they either empower you or empower themselves. Those empowering you offer tools or lessons you can learn to use on your own so that, as you go forward, you are more powerful than you were before; those empowering themselves sell you something intangible, like their reputation or forecasts, but without the underlying support and reusable lessons that have lasting impact for you.

W.C. Mitchell, John Magee, and William P. Hamilton empowered others, not themselves. Dealing in statistical and technical information, they provided followers and readers with the know-how to further their knowledge on their own—without charging directly for the expertise. Hamilton, for instance, as a pioneer of "technical" stock market analysis, empowered people through hundreds of *Wall Street Journal* editorials that explained how to use the Dow Jones Averages to forecast the future. Mitchell, as a statistical pioneer, did much of the work that led to modern economic and financial statistics everyone uses today. While Magee wrote books, believe me, the royalties off financial book sales are pretty paltry. And in them he laid out his vision in a clear fashion anyone could learn.

By contrast, Evangeline Adams, William Gann, R.N. Elliott, Robert Rhea, and Irving Fisher were interested primarily in empowering themselves. If they had some sort of gimmick or stock market "secret," it was kept private unless some sort of fee was involved, usually in the form of a newsletter subscription rate. And then it was sold only in a format that others couldn't really grasp; to employ it would always require the great guru himself (or herself in the case of Evangeline). Rhea, for example, unlike his more generous guru Hamilton, proclaimed himself the expert Dow Theorist and sold his personal word on how the theory worked in his newsletter. But a lot of his writings were vague and his methodology unclear. Two people looking at the same chart and, having read Rhea's methodology, might come to completely conflicting views on the same stock—simply because a lot of Rhea was simply inside Rhea and inaccessible to the masses.

Those empowering themselves are easiest to spot, because they make a living by keeping their names alive, creating a ballyhooed reputation when there is little to ballyhoo. Generally, they are publicity hounds and, often, rich from their efforts. Irving Fisher, for example, was a typical economist, no better than any other, when he began constantly and adeptly promoting himself. With great academic credentials and strong academic contributions in monetary theory, Fisher couldn't cut it when it came to real-world predictions. But despite several wrong calls, he made it to the ranks of "the world's greatest economist" and, consequently, grew wealthy. In the 1920s he was heavily visible, continually forecasting economic boom. He missed calling the 1929 Crash and then, after the turn, he dug his heels in further, saying that good times and higher prices were immediately ahead. Ironically, he died poor by putting his money where his big mouth was during the Crash and Depression.

Evangeline Adams empowered herself by becoming one of the first newsletter quacks, publishing and selling stock market picks for a fairly steep price during the 1920s bull market. She already had a spiffy reputation as a fortune teller, so promoting her role in the market was that much easier. Her gimmick—astrology—was so elusive, so vague, so dubious that it would have been impossible to actually teach others her trick. So, she willingly reaped the benefits of her more-entertaining-than-profitable newsletter.

William Gann sold his newsletter to market a theory he created that was too complex for most to follow on their own—a gimmick almost as novel as Adam's. Selling something clients can't easily do on their own is also comparable to selling something as intangible as an inflated reputation—it is pure self-empowerment. Even to this day folks market themselves as latterday interpreters of Gann, but there is no clear body of knowledge that is consistently employable by Gann fans.

R.N. Elliott never personally sought to empower himself by hawking his cyclical stock market theories . . . those who resurrected him did! From out of the blue in the early 1980s, Elliott's obscure name and theories popped up in books, financial magazines and customized newsletters, and those responsible for the publicity eagerly took advantage of his new-found popularity. Again, like the others, Elliott's theories are too vague and mumbo-jumboish to be employed with much precision, and again, his fans argue among themselves as to how to interpret things based on his theories—it is all self-empowerment.

Not everyone involved in the stock market system is out for his or her own interests. As mentioned above, W.C. Mitchell empowered others by sharing his years of intense research on business cycles and market indices. Had he wanted to, with the respect he had garnered, he could have hawked mumbo-jumbo but was above that kind of activity. John Magee offered as easy an explanation of charting as is possible, available to anyone free of charge in most libraries. Hamilton presumably could have made a pretty penny selling his knowledge through a newsletter that contained subjective forecasts similar to Rhea's—but he didn't. When you look at the ever present nationwide menu of experts selling services, the first question you should ask yourself about any one of them is: "Does interacting with this expert leave me more able to act on my own afterwards, or simply hook me to the guru du jour?" If you don't get something more than a forecast, the guru's fee is often too costly.

Of course, there are exceptions. Yet, for the most part, they are rare enough to be the exceptions that prove the rule. Numerous studies show that economists' forecasts, as a group, are very wide of the mark (for a good introduction to these studies see David Dreman's *The New Contrarian Investment Strategy*). There are no studies pointing the other way.

Still, individuals are always unique. Consider the economist John Maynard Keynes, whose economic theories were widely hated and bad-mouthed by conservatives then and now. Yet he was an economist who could actually trade stocks successfully, while founding his radical theories. The weight of his trading success makes him more credible than conservative theorist Fisher, who couldn't put his theories into practice. Somehow, Keynes was vastly more "real world" than Fisher. Another great exception was Edson Gould. For most of his career he was a completely obscure forecaster who was almost uncanny in his accuracy. He was no self-promoter and never boasted a gimmick or even his own predictions. Ironically, he went all but unnoticed until he was practically dead himself, when he was "discovered" as an old market seer in his 70s.

There are always exceptions proving any rule. Life is full of quirks, and Wall Street is no different. For the most part, financial gurus aren't worth the price. Most of them are either phony or nebulous. The real "value added" which any one of them may offer is best measured by looking at whether, from his or her teachings, you can empower yourself to move better through life on your own than you could have before your interaction began.

WILLIAM P. HAMILTON

THE FIRST PRACTITIONER OF
TECHNICAL ANALYSIS

I t was no fluke when journalist William Peter Hamilton decided to de-
vote his life to the development of the Dow Theory. He felt there were
definite reasons for market movement, reasons that could be predicted fairly
accurately—using Dow's theory. He once said, "The stock market is the
barometer of the country's and even the world's business, and the (Dow) theory shows how to read it." From the early 1900s to his death in 1929, Hamilton
studied, explained, developed and asserted the Dow Theory to provide a foundation on which future generations could build—and technical analysis would
thrive.

The Dow Theory is based on the belief that the stock market always reflects
three distinct movements:

1. A primary trend of four or more years.
2. A secondary reaction of about two weeks to a month.
3. Day-to-day fluctuations.

The primary movement has been compared to the tide of the ocean; the secondary reaction has been compared to the waves, which sometimes sweep up on the beach despite an ebbing tide or fall back despite a rising tide; and the daily fluctuations, to ripples and splashes that are unimportant by themselves, but must be considered in the whole picture. The primary trend was said to be bullish when the average of one high point tops those of previous points—just as the tide is said to be rising when waves peak one another.

"It admits highly human and obvious limitations. But such as it is, it can honestly claim that it has a quality of forecast which no other business record yet devised has even closely approached," Hamilton said. One of his most important contributions to the Dow Theory was simply putting it to work in making forecasts in popular *Wall Street Journal* and *Barron's* editorials. Forecasting was something **Charles Dow** rarely did, but maybe should have—since Hamilton compiled an impressive record. Applying the theory between 1900 and 1921, he forecasted the Panic of 1907, the sluggish market preceding World War I and a bear market in 1917—in all, six major bull and bear markets.

His most famous prediction was an October 21, 1929 *Barron's* editorial titled, "A Turn in the Tide," which gave "a distinctly bearish warning" to investors right before the Crash. While he'd indicated an end to the great 1920s bull market three times since 1927, this time the signs were unmistakable. On September 3, the Dow Jones Industrials hit a high of 381.17 and the Railroads, a high of 189.11. Within a month, the Industrials declined 56 points, and the Railroads, which usually fluctuated very little, fell over 20 points. "The severest reaction from the high point of the year had just one month's duration. In view of the nationwide character of the speculation, this seems a dangerously short period to infer anything like a complete reverse in public sentiment." Three days later, panic swept across Wall Street on what became known as Black Thursday. A few weeks later in October, he died.

Born in England in 1867, Hamilton described himself as "an incurable newspaper man." Sporting neatly combed hair, mustache and spectacles, he went into the news business at age 23, working in London and throughout Europe. In 1893, he covered the South African Matabele War, then remained in Johannesburg as a financial writer. He was an eager reporter and believed "the man on the desk must know as much and more about the news he handles as the reporters who write it." At age 32, Hamilton came to Manhattan and joined the *WSJ* in 1899, working closely with Dow. Nine years later, working for **Clarence Barron**, he took over as editor of the editorial page and held the post until his death at 63. In 1921 he became executive editor of the newly created *Barron's*.

En route, Hamilton wrote *The Stock Market Barometer* in 1922, explaining the Dow Theory in detail. It began as a newspaper assignment but blossomed into a 278-page doctrine for Dow theorists. Successful and controversial, it gave the theory much-needed exposure, since many were still dubious of it.

Hamilton also revised the theory, saying that both the Railroad and Industrial averages must corroborate each other before any prediction for a change in the market can be given. He was the first to "make a line" in the same way that more modern technicians create "support" and "resistence" lines on stock charts that are supposed to represent floors and ceilings for stocks. When stock prices fluctuated within a narrow margin and stayed within his "lines," there was little being indicated except that stocks were being accumulated or distributed. But it was unclear at that time as to which was the case, accumulation or distribution. The buying and selling seemed relatively in "equilibrium." It was only when the two averages broke out of their lines and rose above their high points that this action foretold a bullish outlook on the market; when the averages fell below the high point, it was a bearish sign, since the market had obviously been saturated.

"The market is a barometer. There is no movement in it which has not a meaning. That meaning is sometimes not disclosed until long after the movement takes place, and is still oftener never known at all."

Hamilton's role in journalism, while great, is not sufficient to include him among the minds chronicled in this book, but his role in creating technical analysis as a field is more than sufficient. Some people think and others do. Dow thought and created an index and pondered it. Hamilton put it to practice as a workhorse. He was the first serious practitioner of the art of forecasting future stock action based on precise prior action. Ditto for his forecasting of the economy based on the market. It is a well established fact that the market is among the better leading indicators of the economy, even if imperfect. At a time when no one was watching it in that regard, it was certainly a better economic forecaster than it is now when so many market mavens fixate on the market's every move. Hamilton was not just an intellectual pioneer, but he was also ready to put his ideas and reputation on the line, in print, where others could ridicule him. They were never able to.

National Cyclopedia of American Biography, 1936

EVANGELINE ADAMS

BY WATCHING THE HEAVENS
SHE BECAME A STAR

The Roaring 20s were crazy, and naturally everyone wanted his personal piece of the action and the big fat profits that went with it. Some invested cautiously with their meager savings, others speculated their already-large fortunes making them larger—but whether rich or poor, smart or stupid, experienced or fresh, most looked for a system that would guarantee their success. Scores of clever promoters eagerly provided myriads of "unbeatable" systems. Some promoted the premise that no bull market would break in a month without an "r" in it; another depended on sunspots; yet another went by moon cycles. At least one self-appointed market guru claimed he had the ultimate inside information—from God! There was even an Oyster Theory that predicted the market would peak during oyster season. No theory was crazy enough; each had its own following. There were enough suckers for every kooky system concocted.

By far the most famous nontraditional investment system was that of Evangeline Adams. Touted as a descendant of President John Quincy Adams, Evangeline had some 125,000 subscribers to her 50-cent newsletter in which she predicted future market activity. The truly rich and famous regularly sought her services in her Carnegie Hall studio. **J.P. Morgan**, steel magnate Charles Schwab, movie star Mary Pickford, even England's King Edward VII were among her clientele. Her catch? Fortune telling!

Adams may not have paved the road for women in the investment business, but for a while she made Wall Street stop and listen. Already a famous fortune teller by the turn of the century, she apparently wasn't able to predict the great bull market of the 20s in advance, but by 1927 she knew a good thing when she saw it and jumped into the act—and her fame skyrocketed along with the bull market's last legs upward. She was adored by investors and got rich from marketing her prophecies. Her monthly newsletter—tagged "a guaranteed system to beat Wall Street"—predicted stock activity via the changing positions of the planets. For $20 per reading, she would predict where the Dow Jones Industrials would lead. The more she charged, the more popular she became! Some 4,000 fans wrote her daily asking for their future in the stock market.

Hailed as "the wonder of Wall Street" and "the stock market's seer," Adams stocked her studio with all the props of a respectable broker's office. First, she presented herself in her trademark, business-like black suit and spectacles in keeping with her stern mouth, confident voice and shrewd, serious manner. In the waiting room, fur-coated women and well-suited men milled about, chatting in unison about their stocks and bright futures while waiting for their individual consultations. A ticker tape machine dutifully hummed out quotations and copies of the *Wall Street Journal* were displayed prominently. The walls were lined with paintings and photographs of her most famous clients—King Edward, Schwab, Pickford and, of course, Morgan.

Morgan held a special place in Adams' heart and vice versa. He supposedly swore by her after loaning her $100 million when she said his rising sun, Aries, was favorably positioned. Legend has it he profited well from the loan and, afterwards, took her cruising on his yacht to conduct "scientific investigation" into her miraculous powers. Results from the "investigation" were never uncovered!

Adams' accuracy wasn't astounding, but that didn't stop people from acting on her predictions. In a bull market people will believe anything. Indeed, when she predicted a "violent upswing" on February 15, 1929, she enjoyed a violent upswing in her subscriptions. In May, 1929, she predicted the month's breaks with precision, but on Labor Day, on her radio program, she claimed "the Dow Jones could climb to Heaven." That had to be one of her more famous lines, since she managed to blurt it out during a Friday evening, holiday-weekend rush hour, when countless commuters had their car radios turned up.

When the Crash finally came, she was said to have pinpointed the market's pre-noon peak 24 hours in advance. That Black Thursday evening she was forced to hold mass sessions to accommodate the long lines out her door! Will the market recover? Is it worth hanging on to my stocks? Should we cover our margins? People were panicky and sought refuge in Evangeline's holy words—and she didn't let them down. Adams consoled her followers, assured them the market would rise, pocketed the fee and that night, when her broker told her she was $100,000 in the hole, she told him to sell out her position first thing in the morning.

Born sometime between 1868 and 1872 in Jersey City, Adams was educated in Andover, Massachusetts. She studied astrology, and in 1899, she became a star when she predicted a certain disaster: Her horoscope told her she should go to Manhattan on March 16, 1899. So, she checked into the Windsor Hotel and that evening consulted the stars of the hotel owner. "I hastened to warn him that he was under one of the worst possible combinations of planet conditions, terrifying in their unfriendliness." The next day the hotel burned to the ground, taking with it the owner's family. Fortunately, somebody, probably she, remembered to tell the papers of Adams' incredible foresight, making Evangeline a household name—particularly in prominent social, political and theatrical circles.

Rather matronly looking, she was married in 1923 to a former astrology pupil. She kept her name in the news by making major predictions. She guessed the duration of Lindbergh's first transatlantic flight correctly within 22 minutes, predicted Rudolf Valentino's death within a few hours and foresaw the 1923 Tokyo earthquake within a few days. In 1914, she won a court case that had challenged her legal right to practice astrology as her profession. A fan of the occult, Adams penned several books on astrology and her autobiography, *The Bowl of Heaven*, in 1926.

She died in 1932. Evangeline Adams demonstrated two simple principles. First, if you predict enough wild and crazy things and publicize the few that come through, folks will remember the hits, never notice the misses and attribute your successes to knowledge or technique rather than luck. Second, in a bull market people are desperate for any "sure thing," no matter how harebrained it is. She was an obvious quack with no real investment knowledge. While less extreme than Evangeline, other quacks are ever-present. There is never a decade when major quacks don't find some success in the popular press predicting the ups and downs of Wall Street—and always with an extreme, dramatic flair.

Finally, Evangeline could be seen as the mother of astrology as it is applied to the modern stock market. It is hard to imagine anything sillier, but remember your P.T. Barnum—there are always plenty of suckers. Even today there is a small contingent of quacks successfully peddling useless investment services to the public via astrology. Some people never learn.

Laura Gilpin, 1938

ROBERT RHEA

HE TRANSFORMED THEORY
INTO PRACTICE

Robert Rhea took an unrefined Dow Theory and whipped it into an updated, defined, and systematic guide to the stock market, sparking theory into practice. In doing so, he converted **Charles Dow**'s rather abstract ideas and **William Hamilton**'s applications into "a manual for those wishing to use it as an aid in speculation." When he died in 1939, he left an accessible theory and devout Dow descendants to continue his legacy.

Born in Nashville in 1896, Rhea had a father who owned a Mississippi River boat line, loved the stock market and went boom and bust several times. While still in school, his father handed him Hamilton's dense *Wall Street Journal* editorials and told him "to master them or get spanked." Though no easy task for a teenager, young Rhea eagerly complied!

After a short college stint, he followed in his father's footsteps, starting his own river boat line, which nearly sank his old man's. Rhea kept his profits stuffed inside his pants pocket until dad advised him to send the cash to Wall Streeter (and author) Henry Clews for safe stocks. In return, Rhea received 10 shares of U.S. Steel, bought at 14—and he was hooked on the market just like his father, regularly eyeing his stocks in the *WSJ*. Next, he caught some bad luck—i.e., tuberculosis—but recovered enough to enlist in the Air Corps in 1917, only to have his airplane crash. The crash caused a piece of propeller to pierce his lung, leaving Rhea bedridden, an invalid, for life.

Where most people's lives might have ended here, Rhea's just began. Basing himself in Colorado Springs, he researched economic trends as his only form of recreation, "offsetting the pleasures enjoyed by more fortunate men." He worked so intently, he found he forgot his pain, and was so tired at the end of the day that he could sleep more easily at night. Through exhaustive studies of the Dow's action, Rhea theorized the Dow was the only reliable method of forecasting market movement—a theory he felt was worthy of his life's attention.

Rhea's bedroom became a veritable statistics factory as he churned out averages and constructed Dow charts, which became vitally important to traders adhering to the Dow Theory. Rhea himself dabbled in the 1920s bull market, basing his buys on his chart with generally good results. He later recalled: "Either the Dow theory or just plain luck caused me to buy a few stocks at the proper time in 1921 and prevented my owning any during the final stages of the 1929 uprush. Moreover, either the Dow theory or luck caused me to carry a short account of small proportions during the two years after the crash. Thus my study has paid dividends. ...."

By the late 1920s, he was a highly regarded Dowist. So, when Hamilton, the current Dow expert, died a few weeks after predicting the 1929 Crash, Rhea replaced him as the "high priest" of the Dow Theory. *Barron's* published some of his "notebooks" that year, but people pined for more. Rhea then penned *The Dow Theory*, which was at first panned by publishers. When no one would accept his "white elephant," he published it himself in 1932. The book is Rhea's most famous work, selling an astounding 91,000 copies in its first six years.

Rhea's fascination with and sheer awe of Dow and Hamilton are reflected in the book, which includes Hamilton's 252 *WSJ* editorials that initially gave form to Dow's ideas. Handling the theory with kid gloves, Rhea made a point of protecting it from the scorn of unlucky speculators. "Perhaps the greatest danger in the application of the theory to speculation in stocks lies in the fact that the neophyte, having beginner's luck, may arrive at correct conclusions several times and then, thinking that he has discovered a sure method of beating the market, read his signals the wrong way. Or, what is even worse, he may be right at the wrong time. In either of these events, the Dow theory is usually blamed, when the fault lies within the trader's impatience." (Actually, this type of disclaimer—the old don't-blame-the-theory, blame-the-interpretation line—became a sort of motto for modern technical analysts like **John Magee** every time their forecasts were off.)

Rhea never said practicing the Dow Theory was easy—it just took a little patience and a lot of understanding. "The Dow Theory, like algebra, is not readily understood after a mere casual reading of a textbook on the subject." Nor is it "an infallible system for beating the market. Its successful use as an aid in speculation requires serious study, and the summing up of evidence must be impartial. The wish must never be allowed to father the thought." He felt any trader with ordinary market sense and the experience of having gone through a complete market cycle should be able to succeed 70 percent of the time. A few points Rhea suggested remembering when testing the Dow Theory are:

1. They profit most from Dow's Theory who expect least of it.
2. The Theory is no sure method of beating the market, and no such theory or system will ever be devised.
3. Trading based upon an impartial reading of the averages as implied by the Theory will net frequent losses, but gains will outnumber them to a reasonable extent.
4. Do not try to work the Theory too hard.
5. Do not try to inject innovations until they have been tested over the 37-year record of the averages.
6. Do not try to trade with thin margins and Dow's Theory at the same time.
7. If the Theory is worth following, then study it—learn to form independent opinions, checking them against those of others who have learned to use Dow's methods through several bull and bear cycles.
8. Do not allow your position in the market, or current business statistics, to influence your reading of the averages.

Apparently enough people were willing to try it out, as fan mail piled up at the foot of his bed. Before Rhea knew it, he had a loyal following for his advice. Unable to answer the letters individually, he sent out notices in the mid-1930s saying that if and when he had anything to say to his public, he'd mimeograph it and send it to whomever wanted it. But he didn't say it would be free. By 1938, his bedroom was bustling with 25 assistants who helped him churn out *Dow Theory Comments* to 5,000 subscribers, each shelling out $40 per year. Dubbing himself the Dow Theorist, he appears to have decided to capitalize financially on his position as heir to the Dow/Hamilton legacy.

Like Hamilton, Rhea had a few successful calls, such as predicting the bottom of 1932's bear market within a few days and forecasting the 1937 bear market and 1938 bull market. But Rhea's public career in terms of continuous investment advice offered in his newsletter was too short to really measure his efficacy. His health was lacking. He was down to the use of one lung and had heart problems, finally dying in 1939 at age 52. His relatively large circulation base came to him in a hurry, yet received his commentary for only months.

In some ways, a little like Marilyn Monroe or John Kennedy, Rhea's image became enhanced by his early death. Had he lived and stubbed his toe in public through continuous advice, the Dow Theory approach might have faded fast, but his death left his record in an unassailable position, and for decades investors would take the Dow Theory more seriously than they now do; even today it receives no inconsiderable attention. Just before he died, he turned the newsletter over to a junior partner, Perry Griner, who continued the Dow Theory legacy by promoting the concepts of Dow, Hamilton and Rhea. But unlike Rhea, Griner and subsequent Dow Theorists were never able to push the concept into new territory or make it bigger or more powerful than it had been before. The fact that folks have read Rhea and followed the Dow Theory for 50 years after his death is a testimony to him and clear evidence of his impact on the market.

Yet, at the same time, he was a newsletter writer who was never really proven over time. The folks who have picked up his banner over the decades have had no shortage of material to work with, and Dow Theory as interpreted by Rhea is now accepted as a fully applicable theory. Sadly, their advice hasn't been as rewarding as Rhea might have hoped. Perhaps the same fate would have followed had Rhea lived and been able to stub his own toe. While the Dow Theory has moved and shaken a lot of people and markets over the decades, the test of a theory lies in how well it transfers from practitioner to practitioner and decade to decade. By this standard, Rhea's work didn't quite meet the market. In recent decades, in my estimation, the Dow Theory people have done truly terribly, often making very backward market calls.

Rhea was one part visionary, refining Dow's and Hamilton's ideas. He was also part newsletter writer and, the subscribers to his newsletter legacy, as with most newsletter subscribers, haven't gotten one iota out of it in my estimation. The big benefit always goes to the writer, which brings us to the lesson of Rhea's life—writing about the theory in periodicals and books and making it generally available, empowers the reader. Authors of financial periodicals and books get darn little money from it—only prestige, respect and name recognition—and only to the extent they give their readers something to use on their own when they put the page down. But newsletter writers typically sell conclusion and entertainment and get lots of money for it. They typically don't empower the reader to continue on his or her own way. Be skeptical of newsletters because few if any are worth their high prices.

IRVING FISHER

THE WORLD'S GREATEST ECONOMIST OF THE 1920S, OR WHY YOU SHOULDN'T LISTEN TO ECONOMISTS—PARTICULARLY GREAT ONES

Economist Irving Fisher left an abundant amount of work in mathematical economics, the theory of value and prices, capital and monetary theories, and statistics. Indeed, it seems almost as if he were touted as one of the great economists simply because he had a lot to say. He wrote at least 10 major books and taught at Yale for over 35 years. But credentials don't always mean you're right. In fact, in Fisher's case, credentials allowed him to be wrong in a number of his major hypotheses—like the 1929 Crash—and then spring back with revised jargon after the fact. Clearly, Fisher's greatest contribution to Wall Street was his own negative example which should stand as a permanent warning to all concerned with financial markets and economics to steer clear of what economists have to say. Since Fisher's day all kinds of studies have demonstrated that economists are wrong more often than right.

During his lifetime, Irving Fisher, who died at 80 in 1947, campaigned for scores of issues—both economic and social. He was known as a social philosopher, crusader, teacher, inventor and businessman. He was an advocate of fanatically strict health and hygiene rules, Prohibition, world peace, and eugenics (which is a kind of racist notion of societal self-improvement through genetics). He explored econometrics, probably knowing that the easiest way to gain recognition is to explore a brand new field. Fisher even got to schmooze with five presidents, so that he, in a **Bernard Baruch**-like way, promoted himself by becoming known as an adviser to presidents. Fisher liked to indulge in self-acknowledgment and built up his credentials to make it easy.

In the world of economics, he is most noted for his early work in monetary theory, which has more recently been replaced by monetary theory from "the Chicago School" of economists. It is often ironic to Wall Streeters that Fisher is still held in high regard by economists and economic historians. Wall Street historians often see that as a form of condemnation of economists and economic historians, proving they don't know anything. Fisher clearly didn't when it came to forecasting. And if an economist can't forecast correctly, what good is he?

His biggest blunder, beyond a doubt, came with the 1929 Crash and ensuing Depression. Fisher spent many evenings in 1928 preaching permanent prosperity and never once saw the Crash coming. He even denied it as others started predicting it, as pointed out in a satirical *Outlook* Magazine article. On September 5, 1929, Fisher asserted stock prices were not too high and insisted there would be no crash.

"There may be a recession of stock prices, but not anything in the nature of a crash . . . Dividend returns on stocks are moving higher. This is not due to receding prices for stocks and will not be hastened by any 'anticipated' crash, the possibility of which I fail to see." In October, he countered **Roger Babson**'s insightful doom-and-gloom prediction with the claim that the market had reached a permanently high plateau. About a week before the Crash, when the market started to sputter, he dismissed a sharp break as a "shaking out of the lunatic fringe that attempts to speculate on margin." Perhaps it was he who was on the lunatic fringe.

On October 23, Fisher found the "public speculative mania" to be the least important reason for the long bull market. He still refuted Babson's expected 60 to 80 point drop in the Dow Jones barometer, unless it was accomplished by shakedowns of 5 percent to 12 percent, followed by recovery. (The Dow Jones later showed a 48 percent decline!) When his blunder became quite obvious after Black Thursday, Fisher would sometimes attempt to rationalize it by saying others had been equally misled. Modern economists run the same number. If they are all equally wrong, they consider themselves justified by each other.

Shortly after the Crash—but long before the market continued over the cliff in 1930 and bottomed in 1932—Fisher quickly penned *The Stock Market Crash And After*, gathering up all his goofs in one embarrassingly obvious, tidy collection. It is one of the best reads ever because it shows how completely bass-ack-wards-wrong the world's leading economist(s) can be. It is a marvel in rationality by negative inference. You learn from it what never to believe (and you can find it in major libraries).

Fisher's book detailed a glorious vision for the immediate future in chapters such as, "The Hopeful Outlook," "The Dividends of Prohibition" and "Remedies and Preventives of Panics." He listed government and private "remedies and preventives of panic" that together would help save the "market from further disaster."

Fisher even went so far as to call the 1930 depressed stock market "one of the most wonderful bargain-counters ever known to investors." He claimed that "in spite of the tremendous harm that has been done to common stocks during the panic of 1929, investment trusts have made it safer to invest in common stocks than ever before." He concluded his book by saying, "For the immediate future, at least, the outlook is bright."

Fisher could not have been more wrong, and soon the immediate future grew very dark, especially for his own personal finances. Unfortunately for him, he followed his own advice! He wound up losing forever the fortune he had made from inventing a visible card index system. He did so by investing his last million in Remington Rand stock after the Crash. He bought the stock on heavy margin for $58 per share, thinking he was getting an amazing bargain ... later, it plunged to $1, and he lost his shirt.

Fisher never recovered financially and constantly had to borrow money from his family until the day he died—quite a testimony for the guy supposed to be the world's greatest economist. On his deathbed—after getting swindled for the last time by an obvious con artist—Fisher likened himself to a shoemaker who made fine shoes for everyone except his own barefoot family.

His son, Irving Norton Fisher, wrote a 1956 biography of Fisher, *My Father, Irving Fisher*, and in it, rather comically plotted his father's wealth by the cars he drove. In the early years, there were a Dodge and a few Buicks. When finances soared, there was a chauffeur-driven Lincoln, a swank La Salle convertible, and a Stearns-Knight. When the market hit rock bottom, wiping out Fisher's finances for good, the hot cars disappeared and a Ford reappeared. His last car was a used Buick bought in 1938!

With gray hair, a mustache and goatee, and round spectacles, Fisher looked the part of the intellectual. Born in 1867 in New York's Catskill Mountains, Fisher was the son of a Yale graduate and minister. He worked his way through Yale as a tutor, earning in 1891 a Ph.D. in economics—the first doctorate in pure economics ever awarded by Yale. Two years later, he married the daughter of a wealthy Rhode Island family and began writing furiously. When folks marveled at the amount of work he churned out, Fisher said he simply followed his formula: Delegate what can be delegated and stay healthy. He became completely paranoid about his health after contracting tuberculosis in 1898. After recovering, he avoided tobacco and alcohol, followed a regimented diet, and became obsessed with the Prohibition movement—perhaps further proof as to why you shouldn't listen to economists if you want to make money in the financial markets.

Times change. Big names come and go. Technology evolves, and society grows bigger. Americans grow ever more prosperous each decade. And economists keep forecasting. "Often wrong but never in doubt," economists are injurious to your financial future. Folks tend to believe their forecasts, which are rarely correct, particularly at important turning points. Irving Fisher was the first of the big name economists to be taken seriously by the marketplace and the first to blow it in public. He started a trend. The markets have listened to and then rejected a never-ending stream of economic witch doctors ever since. Personally, I'm always embarrassed when folks ask me if I'm related to Irving Fisher. But I'm always proud to say no.

WILLIAM D. GANN

STARRY-EYED TRADERS "GANN" AN
ANGLE VIA OFFBEAT GURU

William Gann looked to the stars—via astrology—for the calm, focused, and meditative frame of mind he needed when studying the stock market. His complex and New Age–like trading method, concocted in the 1920s, demanded undivided attention, as it was based on a hodgepodge of mathematics, philosophy, mysticism, and the laws of nature. While many Wall Streeters found Gann's system too weird for their liking, this author included, he has long been a guru to offbeat market traders, almost always technicians, who feel themselves truly connected to the inner workings of the market through Gann's teachings. Feeling free of the conventions of both fundamental and technical analysis, Gann's followers continue, 35 years after his death, to giggle and mutter Gannisms, and glance back and forth at each other with that we've-got-a-secret look that is almost cultish.

Born in 1878 the son of a Lufkin, Texas cotton rancher, Gann grew up respecting cotton and other commodities markets. After making his first trade in cotton futures—and winning—his curiosity, open-mindeness and knack for math led him to the stock market at age 24. Within a few years, he was well known in Texas; local papers even published his cotton forecasts. But looking to the stars even then, Gann left his home for New York and a larger audience in 1908.

Operating from his Wall Street office, Gann made a modest splash working as an analyst, stock market letter writer and stockbroker until 1919. So, he was at least part salesman, which is important to note as you watch the progress of his life and the image that developed around him. In 1919 he began his own advisory firm, put out his own newsletter called *Supply and Demand*, operated a chart service, researched markets and began writing his first of eight books that would make him a cult figure in Wall Street. Organized, dedicated and thorough, he published *Truth of the Stock Tape* in 1923, followed by *Wall Street Stock Selector* in 1930, which laid the foundation for his system.

The Gann Theory primarily identifies the best times to buy and sell by determining major and minor market trends and pinpointing where changes could occur. In formulating his theory, Gann relied on the re-enactment of the past, feeling that time changes but people do not. "Times and conditions change and you must learn to change with them. Human nature does not change and that is the reason history repeats and stocks act very much the same under certain conditions year after year and in the various cycles of time."

Among his "Rules for Trading in Stocks," as listed in his 1949 work, *Forty-five Years in Wall Street*, Gann urged investors to determine the trend of the Dow Jones via his other rules. Once the trend is established, he suggested buying and selling three weeks into an advance or decline and on five to seven point moves. (Note that five to seven point moves then, when the Dow was at 175, were much more material than today with the Dow at several thousand.) After buying a stock, to reduce risk, Gann repeatedly reminded the reader to place a stop loss order 1, 2, or 3 points below its cost. "When you make a trade you can be wrong," he says, and a stop loss greatly reduces risk.

In another trading checklist of 24 "never-failing" rules, Gann suggested the following:

1. Divide capital into 10 equal parts and never risk more than a tenth of it on any one trade.
2. Never overtrade.
3. Never let a profit run into a loss.
4. Do not buck the trend.
5. Trade only in active stocks.
6. When in doubt, get out, and don't get in when in doubt.
7. Never buy just to get a dividend.
8. Never average a loss.

"Everything in existence is based on exact proportion and perfect relationship. There is no chance in nature because mathematical principles of the highest order lie at the foundation of all things," Gann said. He was a numbers guy—obsessed with mathematical relationships and ancient Greek,

Babylonian, and Egyptian mathematics. Gann claimed he could pinpoint early trend reversals on the basis of his hundreds of charts—daily, weekly, monthly, quarterly, and yearly charts—for stocks and commodities from 1900 to 1955. His charts revealed a bull market was coming, for example, when prices rose, leading to a pull back and another rally, which then formed a higher bottom than the previous one.

At the heart of Gann's intellectual contribution to Wall Street is the notion of Gann "Angles" which are constructed to measure "support and resistance lines" and to determine trends. There are few heavy traders who don't pay attention to Gann Angles, either because they believe in them, or because they know that so many other traders believe in them. If a Gann Angle is crossed, it might generate a "crowd" reaction among traders. Gann Angles are based on the theory that time is as important to market movement as price. This is somewhat similar to the teachings of **R.N. Elliott**. The actual techniques of constructing Gann Angles are relatively complex to describe, but easy to do, and can be accomplished with nothing more than paper, pencil, a simple ruler, and very simple math—enhancing their appeal to a large mass of followers.

Technically, this whole notion is seriously flawed (as is the work of Elliott) by the fact that all Gann's stock market efforts were aimed at forecasting major moves in the Dow Jones Industrials. Anyone who has really studied how a price-weighted index like the Dow works knows that you can't make accurate forecasts for any price-weighted index without being able to forecast future stock splits—which most of these people never even think about because they don't think about how the index works. However, there are often periods when there are no stock splits within the Dow, and when this is the case, Gann's concepts might apply. Whether or not Gann Angles have any validity, many traders believe they do and they are an ever-present concept among the minds of traders both on the stock exchanges and the commodity markets.

Thin-lipped and stern-mouthed, with a sharp nose and oval spectacles, Gann, always clad in spiffy duds, was intrigued with people's attitudes and behavior towards the market. In his books, he preached his own market etiquette: "Do not trade or invest if motivated by hope, greed or fear. Always be in a good frame of mind ... Pay close attention to your health ... Take a lot of time off." He felt time off was crucial. Actually, that sentiment is quite common among technical traders. "If things are going well, take a nice, long break ... Go on a vacation if you can. If things are not going well, then this is another reason to stop everything and take that break or vacation. But, when you get back, study as hard as possible." He took his own advice, wintering in Miami and finding inner peace through astrology.

Aside from his moral stance and far-out connection to the stars, Gann was pretty run-of-the-mill personally. A fellow of the Mark Twain Society, he lived well, but often pinched pennies, presumably saving it for his family after his death. He wasn't particularly generous: He only gave after having been given. Some say he was simply cheap—stingy. Once, while mowing his lawn with an electric mower, he ran over the extension cord and severed it. Not being a handyman, he had an associate fix the cord and, in return, told him, "I know

you're long on soybeans. You'd better be out of them before the close today."
From that point in 1948 on, soybeans were on a steady decline, for the next
25 years. Did that really happen? Who knows? It is all part of the unprovable
Gann legend built on spectacular public market calls, his ability to promote
himself and the market's insatiable need to have a guru who really "knows."

It is the combination of these three that made Gann. He had no provable
public record of accomplishment in the market the way a **T. Rowe Price** or
Ben Graham did. His actual market performance is quite obscure, so no one
could really prove he was or wasn't a great market tactician. His followers are
people who are ready to take him on faith. He published and promoted his
books and newsletter; en route he built the legend of his perfect market calls.
To do so, he probably knew he needed obscurity to hide the imperfections
that plague even the best market timers. Yet to folks who need a holy grail
to trade the market, Gann is perhaps still today the most holy of the holy.
Few aggressive traders haven't studied Gann, and while the realm of Gann
devotees is not limited to quacks, almost every quack I've ever seen has Gann in
his quiver of quackisms. While Gann's mathematical methodologies are quite
primitive by modern computer driven standards, they still feel good to the
trader who works with paper, pencil and calculator and wants to follow only a
relatively few number of indicators. They are particularly exotic and mystical
to those looking for a magic key to unlock the wealth of Wall Street—and
there is never a shortage of people looking for just that.

Unfortunately, Gann's writings bear the telltale tag of the self-promoter.
Far from humble, ever bragging, never copping to mistakes, his writing sounds
very much like the earlier version of the modern self-promoting newsletter
writer. He claimed, for example, that he wrote not because he wanted the
money or the glory but because folks begged him to, and because he wanted
to "give to others the most valuable gift possible—KNOWLEDGE." The
style and motivation seem phony to this long-time author.

Gann retired from serving clients in 1946—44 years after he went into the
business, but didn't quit trading until 1951. He died four years later at age 77
in Brooklyn, leaving behind his wife, son, and three daughters. It is unclear
how much money he left. Gann fans maintain he was fabulously wealthy when
he died—all based on his market profits. Skeptics scoff and ask for proof and
they see whatever money he had as coming from clients who were suckered in
by his PR. This author has no way of knowing for sure whether Gann was truly
what his devotees believe him to be, or a quack. Perhaps he was something in
between—a heavily self promoting self-seller who had some skill and intuition
and was a good—but not great—Wall Street "outsider." Regardless, merely
by the size of his rather underground-like following of fans fully 35 years after
his death, and the degree to which Gannisms still flow out of trader's mouths,
Gann qualifies among the *100 Minds That Made The Market.*

WESLEY CLAIR MITCHELL

WALL STREET'S FATHER OF MEANINGFUL DATA

Wesley Clair Mitchell was anything but your typical dime-a-dozen economist who constantly makes superfluous, inaccurate forecasts and does whatever it takes to get media attention. Just the opposite, modest Mitchell stayed behind the scenes of the economic world, working hard to provide the numbers and facts which were previously unavailable— yet needed—to decipher the economy. When he died in 1948 at 74, he left behind a legacy of index numbers and statistical information gathered by the National Bureau of Economics Research (NBER)—which he helped organize in 1920. Today the NBER is the official body that determines when recessions have begun and ended.

To the economic community at large, Mitchell may best be known for his life-long, exhaustive research on business cycles, which formed the basic business cycle model used by macro-economists even today. Where others put forth pretentious explanations and verbose hypotheses, Mitchell backed his theories with cold, hard figures. Ultimately, in his 1913 landmark book, *Business Cycles*, he was the first to realize business cycles weren't natural, but systematically generated by-products of the capitalist system. Because of his work, "business cycles" became a common phrase—replacing "commercial crises"—and the financial community came to appreciate the ebb and flow of our economy and the degree to which much of it could be quantified and measured.

Born in Rushville, Illinois in 1874, the eldest son of a country doctor and farmer, Mitchell joined the University of Chicago's first class. Here, he was surrounded by intellectuals like fruitcake economist Thorstein Veblen and pragmatist philosopher John Dewey, who—together—had a profound impact on Mitchell's thinking. He worked on his father's farm during the summers. In 1899, he earned his doctorate, summa cum laude, and the following year, began his academic career at his alma mater. Throughout his life, Mitchell also taught at the University of California at Berkeley and Columbia University and helped found the New School for Social Research in Manhattan. Despite his impressive credentials, Mitchell never truly dedicated his life to academics—it always came second to his economic research.

Relentlessly driven, forthright and methodical, even when recording daily events in his diary, Mitchell always said he'd "rather be at work than to be talking about it." But with his occasional free time, Mitchell was surprisingly flexible—he'd read a mystery book, work with wood, write letters, go camping, and climb mountains with his wife. A family man. he loved playing with his grandchildren.

"Clair" to his friends and family, Mitchell was first and foremost an economic toolmaker, inventing the technical instruments needed to conduct massive research projects. His statistical expertise set a new standard for analyzing mass observations over time. His charts and tables, which showed an economic society in action, set a new standard for presenting results. His obsession with index numbers stemmed from his belief that they provided detailed information on price fluctuations; very important to Wall Street.

Mitchell was less an economic hypothesizer than a tool vendor. Before him, there was very little in the way of index numbers for a Wall Streeter to look at when considering the economy's impact on the market—few economic analysis tools available to Wall Street about Main Street.

His numbers spoke for themselves and carved the foundation for the interplay of economic and financial thinking that would underlie the works of economists like **Irving Fisher, John Maynard Keynes** and all our modern economists—the realization the stock market itself is a powerful leading economic indicator. Without Mitchell and his work, all "top-down" investment managers would operate radically differently than they do today. (Top-down managers comprise most of the financial players today; they assess the economy, then use those conclusions to assess the markets and decide what stocks to own.) Mitchell was fundamental to all subsequent economic and top-down financial thinking. Without him, it wouldn't exist.

Were it not for the National Bureau, Mitchell's advances in economics might not have been recognized as widely as they were. Upon its inception, Mitchell regarded the Bureau as an experiment where he could live his dream—"a program of critical research." During the 25 years he served as its director, organizing an enormous database of statistics on the American economy, Mitchell and his staff centered their research around long-term problems like the nature and causes of business cycles; the measurement and analysis of national income, and the sources and processes involved in the formation of capital. Results were presented in a no-nonsense fashion—without "convenient rationalizations." Rather, Mitchell assumed the role of instigator. His work would consistently lead to more questions and, in turn, more research.

His work was never-ending. After World War II, for example, Mitchell lobbied to preserve the statistical work gathered and to further new research started during the war. Three days after the Armistice, he boldly requested not only to retain his small staff, but also to hire a dozen more staff members to capture the knowledge regarding price movements that were then flooding the economy.

Rosy-cheeked, yet stern and serious looking, Mitchell spurred the economic community into furthering his intense quantitative research, replacing untested generalizations with verified knowledge. We can thank Mitchell for what we know today about national income, prices and price series, investment, money markets, and business cycles. Just as **Charles Dow** and **B.C. Forbes** demonstrated the importance of news information in the investment process, Mitchell demonstrated the importance of overview information in the investment process. Without "Clair" Mitchell, we would know little today about Wall Street's ties to Main Street.

British Information Service, 1948

JOHN MAYNARD KEYNES

THE EXCEPTION PROVES THE RULE I

Countless sources praise the father of post-Depression economics, John Maynard Keynes, and his keen comprehension of the capitalist system. But perhaps the best example confirming him as the dean of economists lies in his little-known personal investment record—namely, in securities markets, where he speculated successfully for about 40 years. Rather than relying on insider information, "hot tips" or market-timing devices, he had his own quirky system that basically defied whatever the mass populace was up to at the time. A contrarian in temperament as well as in the market, Keynes relied on courage and self-confidence to win himself a bundle, boost the world's faith in stock markets during the 1930s and 1940s, and prove himself the exception, rather than the rule.

Sure, other economists have tried to apply their beliefs and predictions to the market but, for the most part, professional economists have been worse than terrible in trying to deal with the financial markets. When I was a college kid, I was vastly impressed by Milton Friedman's philosophy that the test of a social science was whether it was able successfully to predict the future. That made and makes sense. On this basis, economists, as a group and consistently within the group, get an F- for a grade. Strangely, the world keeps listening to economists and their forecasts but, as per **Irving Fisher**, they're just terrible at forecasting and, more importantly, at predicting financial markets.

But Keynes succeeded where other economists always failed: He made a killing in the years following the Crash. By contrast, the leading economist of the 1920s, Fisher, blundered time and time again in the market, most notably during the 1929 Crash and Great Depression, losing everything he had and living the rest of his life on money borrowed from relatives.

Born in Great Britain in 1883 to an intellectual and cultural family, but a modest one just the same, Keynes started dabbling in securities in 1905 at age 22. Fourteen years later he became a serious operator—self-taught, speculating in foreign exchanges with good results. In 1920, however, he lost it all—including funds family and friends had entrusted to him—when the tide turned and the currency markets went against him. But by then he was hooked to the game.

Keynes quickly took a loan from a friend and an advance from one of his early works, *The Economic Consequences of Peace*, and plunged deeper in the same positions that had just wiped him out! Within two years, he paid back his "moral debts," and went from over 8,500 pounds in debt to over 21,000 pounds in profit. By 1945, the year before he died, he had amassed the equivalent of about $20 million in 1990 purchasing power. That's an annual compounded growth rate of 13 percent during a time when inflation was practically nil, so that the real rate of return was really quite high on a sustained 25-year basis. Few investors can match his record over those years.

Keynes refused to say he had a "strategy," but instead claimed, "My central principle of investment is to go contrary to general opinion, on the ground that, if everyone is agreed about its merits, the investment is inevitably too dear and therefore unattractive." Later, in 1938, he put forth "that successful investment depends on three principles:

1. A careful selection of a few investments (or a few types of investment) having regard to their cheapness in relation to their probable actual and potential intrinsic value over a period of years ahead and in relation to alternative investments at the time.
2. A steadfast holding of these fairly large units through thick and thin, perhaps several years, until either they have fulfilled their promise or it is evident that they were purchased on a mistake.
3. A balanced investment position, or, a variety of risks in spite of individual holdings being large, and if possible opposed risks (e.g., a holding of gold shares amongst other equities, since they are likely to move in opposite directions when there are general fluctuations)."

Keynes' typical portfolio consisted of large holdings in just four or five securities, going directly opposite to the old assumption that you should "never put all your eggs in one basket." He once wrote to a colleague, "You won't believe me, I know, but it is out of these big units of the small number of securities about which one feels absolutely happy that all one's profits are made . . . Out of the ordinary mixed bag of investments nobody ever makes anything."

In 1931, for example, Austin Motors and British Leyland represented some two-thirds of his holdings. While some might have looked upon this as terribly risky, Keynes felt confident in knowing that he knew more about each of his few stocks than he could have known had he invested in a rainbow of securities. Knowing all about your securities, he said, was the best way to avoid risk in the first place. "I am quite incapable of having adequate knowledge of more than a very limited range of investments. Time and opportunity do not allow more."

Unlike Irving Fisher, Keynes used his techniques to make a killing during the Depression. In the years between 1929 and 1936, when many operators called it quits, he multiplied his net worth by 65 percent via stocks that sold at bargain prices. That wasn't too hard to do: You just had to be calm and cool enough to roll with market fluctuations and not panic. For example, in 1928 he owned 10,000 shares of Austin Motors at 21 shillings apiece. The following year, they were worth five shillings, but Keynes refrained from selling until the next year, when he was able to sell 2,000 shares at 35 shillings each! He also found a bargain in the big utility holding companies, which bottomed out in the mid-30s after utility magnate **Samuel Insull's** empire collapsed. Sald Keynes, "They are now hopelessly out of favor with American investors and heavily depressed below their real value."

Perhaps the most contrarian aspect of Keynes' operating style was leveraging his portfolio to the hilt; this meant death to many speculators during the Depression. In 1936, when he was worth over 506,000 pounds sterling, his debts were some 300,000 pounds sterling. In later years, however, Keynes reduced his margin debt: After 1939, it averaged about 12 percent of his net assets, as compared to more than 100 percent in the early 1930s. He used maximum debt when it fit, and in less advantageous times, he didn't.

World renowned for his classic 1936 work, *General Theory of Employment, Interest, and Money*, Keynes tried to make use of his revolutionary theory in the market—but he knew it was his uncanny ability to pick quality stocks, rather than his ability to time the market, that made him successful. The market was too unpredictable—yet he used that to his favor. "It is largely the fluctuations which throw up the bargains and the uncertainty due to fluctuations which prevents other people from taking advantage of them."

Standing a formidable 6 foot 1 (with stooped shoulders later in life), with large lips and a mustache, Keynes' disdain of the public was a product of his aristocratic, intellectual upbringing. Both his parents were professors at Cambridge University in England; his father famous for authoring an early major economic textbook, *Scope and Method of Political Economy*. Young Keynes attended Eton, then Cambridge—riding on his parents' coattails. He soon found a place for himself, counting classical economist Alfred Marshall, as well as literary giants like Virginia Woolf, among his circle of friends. A vicious debater, Keynes was known for his candid talk and combative nature when discussing economics. Yet, otherwise, he was soft-spoken, an art collector, a great Lord Byron fan, and a ballet fan—leading to his marriage to a Russian ballerina in 1925.

After Keynes and his *General Theory*, economic thinking in America and around the world was changed forever in a revolutionary and nonlinear way that no one could have anticipated. But that isn't why Keynes is in this book of financial market makers. No, there have been lots of folks who were important to economic theory and implementation. But they couldn't make investments work, and Keynes could. Just as he was a radical in economic theory, his success in the markets demonstrates the fact that only a radical economist could ever be successful in the markets. Therefore, most folks should shut their ears to the utterings of conventional economists on anything that relates to financial markets.

R . N . E L L I O T T

HOLY GRAIL OR QUACK?

Ralph Nelson Elliott, author of the "Wave Principle," was one of those marginal Wall Streeters rarely heard of while alive. Some 20 years after his death, however, his work was resurrected and adopted as the base investment philosophy for a sprinkling of contemporary promotional newsletter types who declared it a lost treasure, claiming themselves possessors of the lost grail and therefore worthy of attention. There is much in Elliott's work that is interesting, but there is also enough bunk to prevent it from ever becoming seriously accepted by top money managers. Yet, for a period of time in the 1980s, the Wave Principle seemed to be working in almost uncanny fashion, and it gained credence, primarily among newsletter writers, stockbrokers and business writers. This newfound recognition vaulted Elliott's otherwise-forgotten theory into Wall Street's history books and its calculating practitioners into a new school of technical analysis that became wildly popular from 1984 to 1988. Today, the Elliott Wave Principle is again losing ground and its devotees often maintain it is being kept hush-hush—a valuable "secret."

Since the theorist skirted fame while alive, little is known of him personally. His obscurity argues, although not perfectly, against him. We know he was agnostic and, judging from his work, leaned towards mysticism like **William Gann**. Reportedly an accountant, Elliott was said to have been a telegraph operator in Mexico before coming down with an illness that forced him to return to his native California. During his three-year recuperation, he was only physically capable of rocking in a rocking chair on his front porch. So, to keep his mind active, he turned to a topic he knew nothing about—the stock market, covering Dow's work extensively. "Gradually the wild, senseless and apparently uncontrollable changes in prices from year to year, from month to month, or from day to day, linked themselves into a law-abiding rhythmic pattern of waves." The Wave Principle emerged in 1938 and was published in *Financial World*, but it attracted little attention, as did its more comprehensive 1946 follow-up, *Nature's Law*.

The overall Elliott cycle spans some 200 years and contains cycles-within-cycles ranging in length from the 50-year-or-more Grand Super Cycle, to the 15- to 20-year Supercycle, to the smallest hours-long unit, the "Sub-Minuette." Identifying the correct cycle depends on forming dozens of charts to visualize the patterns. "To maintain a proper perspective," he wrote, "the student should chart at least two and preferably more broad averages, using the weekly range, the daily range, and the hourly record, and showing the accompanying volume." Once the current cycle is correctly identified, investors will see where the market is going next, based on the typical Elliott Wave pattern.

The typical Elliott Wave is complex and difficult to describe without charts and illustrations. In addition, there are multiple nuances in practicing it and plenty of exceptions to the rules. In general, Elliott felt the "cyclical behavior is characterized by two forces—one building up and the other tearing down." Thus, each sub-cycle consists of eight distinct movements— five upward waves and three downward, called "impulse" and "corrective" waves. Author R.C. Beckman described an Elliott Wave as follows: "Beginning with an upward cycle, Elliott discovered three ascending waves which he called 'impulse' waves. Each of the first two 'impulse' waves was followed by a down wave which he called a 'corrective' wave. The third and final 'impulse' wave was followed by a wave which acted to correct the entire upward cycle, and this correction wave itself consisted of two downward 'impulse' waves interspersed by one upward corrective wave." You got that? No sweat—almost no one else did either.

Inherently, Elliott Waves are so subjective and intangible that only the high priest gurus of the religion will lay claim to perfect knowledge of them—and even they argue among themselves. It is very lucky for the modern-day Elliotters that he is long gone, so he can't be among the arguers. Since it is all very complicated, and most folks will never get a believable handle on the Elliott Wave, it is a perfect vehicle for the purveyors of Elliottness to sell you their knowledge of the holy grail. You don't have to know all this baloney—just buy their newsletter for $169 a year and be saved. For the resurrectors of Elliottness, it was a perfect theory to sell—nebulous, long-term, (so short-term forecasts can be either accentuated or downplayed relative to the long-term) and, best of all, its creator wasn't around to argue with them about what it all meant.

Those who adhere to the Wave Principle believe it offers the only consistent explanation of stock market history. Foreseeing continued progress and stock market growth, they claim the theory pinpointed the general rise in stock prices from 1857 to 1929, the setback between 1929 and 1949 and the upsurge between 1949 and 1972. But if it was so great, why then didn't Elliott's few direct students bother to continue the tradition; one of them, Garfield Drew, mentioned Elliott's work on just two pages of his 350-page book!

Critics of both fundamental and technical persuasion say Elliott concepts are stretched to accommodate Elliott conclusions, and the theory itself is confusing and inaccurate. In a *Barron's* piece, Steven J. Warnecke blasted the theory out of the water, labeling it full of "misapplied number theory, unclear concepts, conflicting statements and mysticism." He said a basic conflict within the theory is that it categorizes itself as scientific, yet the charts themselves are open to heavy interpretation.

This author believes Elliott had an interesting but inaccurate idea. Here is the problem as I see it: Technically, the Elliott Wave can't and won't work with the indexes available. While it is seldom appreciated, correct index construction is as important to the implementation of a charting-based technical approach as the approach itself. Elliott makes very long range, precise forecasts based on charting single indexes. But to do that you need an index which is internally highly consistent over long periods. The Dow Indexes, for instance, which are the ones most commonly applied to Elliott, can't work with the Wave because it doesn't predict stock splits. Any price-weighted index, like the Dow, is so sensitive to stock splits in the intermediate to long-term, that if you have a technical system based on the Dow without the ability to predict splits, it's hopeless—the stocks themselves, or any portfolio based on them, will behave very differently than does the index. If this happens, what good is a precise forecast? (If none of this makes sense, you might enjoy and benefit from 20 minutes with the "Indicator Series" chapter in Frank Reilly's wonderful textbook, *Investment Analysis and Portfolio Management*, published by Dryden Press).

Technically, the only common form of index construction sufficiently stable in the long-run to be compatible with Elliott Wave forecasting is market-cap weighted indexes like the Standard & Poor's 500. The catch is they aren't old enough to capture the very long-term historical perspectives in which Wave fans deal.

Elliott was just a guy with an interesting theory that is very hard to apply. Were he still alive, he would be just another market junkie with an oddball approach, as he was throughout his lifetime. To a large extent, the fame of Elliott is due to the fact that he is conveniently dead, so folks can push his guru-ness without him screwing up their marketing of him. Imagine how-many quack religious leaders would be screwed up if Jesus walked and talked among us on a real world daily basis to tell us all where our interpretations of him are incorrect.

The fact is that the financial market is always full of folks selling magic elixirs to naive buyers. This author believes that there is an over-concentration of quack sellers in the newsletter market, but that they exist in almost every part of the financial world, including the supposedly sophisticated large institutional world where academics often dress up unrealistic mumbo jumbo as "academically verified" (one of your basic oxymorons) and then sell it. Elliott provided the financial world with one of its major underground quackisms, and a lot of money has been allocated based on his thinking without much thought on the part of the allocators. We have all heard since we were kids: "You can't believe everything you hear." Elliott indirectly teaches us that this slogan has double validity when what we are hearing has a fee attached to it and comes purveyed by a Wall Streeter.

Forbes, Jan. 15, 1977

EDSON GOULD

THE EXCEPTION PROVES
THE RULE II

Market technician Edson Gould always laughed at the idea of having a significant influence on the stock market, but his predictions were the most precise around. He pinpointed major bull markets and prophesied bottomed-out markets as if he had his own peephole into the future. But in place of a crystal ball and wacky off-the-cuff schemes, his were smart, intensely researched and time-tested theories that made him a legend in the investment community.

A small, shy man, Gould graduated from Lehigh University intent on becoming an engineer, but in 1922 joined Moody's investment service where he immersed himself in research. He became obsessed with finding the one factor—over and above economic and monetary conditions—that sparked the market. "I carried indices back 100 years and more and soon you discovered that no matter how much you knew about fundamentals, you still didn't get very accurate stock market answers."

A Dixieland music lover and a banjo player, Gould first looked for his answer in the harmonics of music, then in quantum physics—with no luck. Finally, he found his answer at the New York Public Library in Gustave LeBon's 19th century book on mass psychology called *The Crowd*. "It brought me the realization that the action of the stock market is nothing more nor less than a manifestation of crowd psychology. With this insight, an apparently irrational stock market became comprehensible." Gould concluded that stocks sell at the price they do "not because of any systematic evaluation of their real worth, but, rather, because of what the mass of investors think they are worth."

After heading Moody's economics department through the 1930s, followed by a stint as Smith Barney's research director, Gould made his niche in writing and began writing a bimonthly market letter called the *Wiesenberger Investment Report*. In the 1960s, he founded the publication that vaulted him to fame a decade later called *Findings & Forecasts* with a pricey $500 subscription price tag (the equivalent to about a $2,000 newsletter today) and a scant 2,500 subscribers (the equivalent to about $5 million per year in total annual subscription revenue at today's value)! Each bimonthly report typically began with an easy-to-read intro, then plunged into technical text accompanied by charts, historical comparisons, statistics and plenty of colorful metaphors. For example, instead of saying the market will rise quickly, he'd use the phrase "jet takeoff." But no matter how witty the prose, Gould's cult following clearly worshipped him for *Findings & Forecasts'* content. His record was uncanny. Just as the market recovered from the sharp decline of 1962, Gould predicted that the Dow Jones Industrials would rise 400 points and the great bull market of the last 20 years would end in 1966. He was right. Then he predicted that Wall Street was in for eight years of trouble beginning in 1966—right again.

Gould's biggest break came in 1963 when he noted that the bull market of the last 20 years "was a dead ringer for the bull market of the 1920s." But, although their velocity was the same, the current bull market was lasting three times longer than the 1920s bull market, which lasted eight years. Thus, he predicted, the 1960s bull market would end in 1966—24 years after it started!

More recently, in October, 1972, when the Dow Jones industrial average stood at 940, Gould prophesied it would top 1040 by year's end—it did so in early January, 1973. Three market days later, on January 16, he whipped up a "special sale bulletin" urging his readers to sell, believing 1067 was the end of the bull market that started in 1970. Within the next two years, the market plummeted nearly 500 points.

How did Gould reach his magical conclusions? He used several tools, including his insight on psychology in the form of his "Senti-Meter." Calculated by dividing the Dow Jones Industrials Average by the aggregate annual dividends per share paid by the 30 companies in the average, the Senti-Meter is a ratio of stock prices to their dividends—or more simply, "the price investors are willing to pay for one dollar's worth of dividends." Gould explained, "The more confident they are, the more they'll pay; the more worried they become, the less they'll pay." I covered this indicator in my second book, *The Wall Street Waltz*, and it is still an amazingly accurate long-term forecaster, but it doesn't explain Gould's shorter-term precision. For that you have to look to crowd psychology.

"Basically, the market is shaped by human emotions, and those emotions haven't changed in thousands of years," he firmly believed. In order to prevent his own emotions from shaping his predictions, Gould personally avoided the stock market like the plague. "It would interfere with my objectivity. If I were personally invested, I couldn't keep my cool when the market was soaring or collapsing." Sure, he used to invest—but that was way back in the 1940s, when he made money investing in railroad securities. Besides, he said, "for the long-term investor, real estate is probably far better than the stock market!"

Gould, oddly enough, became famous only in his 70s when his new publisher, Anametrics, decided to promote Gould and his surefire forecasts. Operating from a Wall Street office and his modest 35-acre farm in Pennsylvania, Gould kept up his work until retiring in 1983—at 81! He died four years later, leaving behind his wife, two sons, a daughter, a legend and a forecast.

The forecast, first made in November 1979 with the Dow Jones under 850, was for a super-bull market of almost unprecedented proportions. It was issued first as a special report entitled, "The Sign of the Bull" and called for what seemed at the time a wildly over-optimistic Dow Jones Industrial level of 3000 in ten years. Ironically, ten years and eight months after his prediction, the Dow Jones peaked at 2999.75. He is probably smiling from his grave and probably would have called the peak in advance were he still here. One of the very best market timers of all time and the exception proving the rule that no one can time the market, Gould stuck to the major trends, forgetting the little in-between wiggles and jiggles—yet he called major peaks and troughs with amazingly pinpoint precision.

One of the first, if not the first major prognosticator, to call for a super bull market in the 1980s, Gould sadly died a few years short of seeing his most extreme prediction materialize. Long forgotten in a world that mostly remembers recent headlines, Gould's writings are most significant in that they combine, as few have, the history of what has happened before, fundamental economics and basic crowd psychology. Most market timers tend to favor one of those three factors, or combine them badly. But Gould showed that calm observation of where we are in relation to what has happened before, and what the crowd is thinking, are the keys to market forecasting. His clarity, his sheer simplicity and his vision stand almost unique among market seers of modern history.

Investor's Press, 1966

JOHN MAGEE

OFF THE TOP OF THE CHARTS

The only relevant figure in the stock market is the stock price, a die-hard technical analyst would tell you. One such person is John Magee, who coauthored the first and what some call the definitive text on technical analysis in 1948, *Technical Analysis of Stock Trends*. Magee even dared to take a step further, saying it's possible, though not recommended, for a trader to trade in a stock knowing only its ticker symbol—and nothing else. The trader need not know the company, industry, what it produces or sells or how it's capitalized.

In keeping with this claim and philosophy, Magee went to great lengths to prevent any bit of fundamental knowledge from seeping into his life. He swore, "I will not be swayed or panicked by news flashes, rumors, tips or well-meant advice." He read only two-week-old *Wall Street Journals* (except for the daily quotes), boarded up his office window and operated from Springfield in his home state, Massachusetts, to avoid the business grapevine. Inside his quiet office, the air conditioner hummed and the harsh fluorescent light glared so that it was impossible to figure the time or weather. "When I come into this office, I leave the rest of the world outside and concentrate entirely on my charts. No chance to wander to the window and see a picket line forming. No chance to hear a radio blaring about an auto-production cutback in Detroit." He was fanatical about keeping his mind free of fundamental contamination, for a clear mind was key to operating the technician's most fundamental tools, charts.

Technical analysis, as defined by Magee, is "the science of recording, usually in graphic form, the actual history of trading (price changes, volume of transactions, etc.) in a certain stock or in 'the averages' and then deducing from that pictured history the probable future trend." The chart provides all the technician needs to know by illustrating all sorts of formations: head and shoulders, upside-down head and shoulders, right shoulders, necklines, drooping necklines. If he went much lower down the body, things could get really interesting, so he changed to flags at half mast and weak triangles. All of it is pattern and shape oriented. The jargon is baffling, especially to a layperson. The formations determine the main trend, or if and when it might change.

But to call technical analysis a science is deceiving. A science produces a definite number or answer and the ability to predict an outcome with a degree of predictable precision. But charting is open to interpretation, and there's no sure way to tell which interpretation is right. Indeed, when a technician misses calling a turn, he usually blames it on his own interpretation of his charts—not the charts or methods themselves—leaving technical analysis free of intellectual assault. The benefits of charts, Magee claimed, is that they're easy to maintain and require only a pencil, paper and the daily stock market quotes. That is an important aspect to the popularity of technical analysis—there is no financial barrier to participating in technical analysis, so anyone can do it.

Personally, Magee bordered on the eccentric. He resembled an absent-minded professor; thinning hair, a crinkled face marked with concentration lines, brown eyes, bushy brows and large ears. He looked like a nerd, was hard-working, regimented and attentive to detail, despite his preoccupied glare. He edited his town paper, *Our Home Town*, and directed the radio show, "The Voice of Springfield." Surprisingly, Magee painted abstract pictures for relaxation and even had one hanging in his office—"It keeps the room from being too bare, which in itself could be distracting." It is hard to conceive that he could have ever allowed himself to have an assistant who was good looking—might be a distraction, heaven forbid. Magee first married in 1928, fathered a son, then divorced five years later. He remarried in 1936 and fathered another son and two daughters.

He maintained daily charts on almost every stock on the New York and American stock exchanges—of course, there were fewer listed stocks then than there are now. It seems he charted everything. Once, while flipping through a binder filled with hundreds of charts of various companies, Magee stopped at one showing a slow-but-consistent downward line, interrupted at intervals by tiny upward spurts. He said to his visitor, author John Brooks, "I don't know how this one got in the book. It doesn't show any tactically significant formations, for the very good reason that it isn't a stock at all. It's a chart of my weight: I've been ordered by my doctor to reduce. As you can see, it's come down from around two hundred and twenty to a hundred and seventy-five. Those little upturns here and there—those are weekends." Good thing he couldn't take regular cholesterol readings or chart his dreams.

Before diving into charting as a career, Magee floundered in all types of fields. Born in 1901 in Malden, he graduated from MIT in 1923, then worked as a sales manager, cost estimator, advertising copy writer, Fuller Brush salesman and account executive. He was running his own mail-order business in cast phenolic plastics in 1942 when he met Bob Edwards, his coauthor and mentor in technical analysis. Edwards was also the brother-in-law of post-Dow theorist and former *Forbes* financial editor Richard W. Schabacker, who first applied the chart method to individual stocks, instead of sticking to the averages as Dow had done. Schabacker was an intellectual mentor to both Edwards and Magee.

Right away Magee had an "almost hypnotic fascination" with charting, "so I rushed right into the market, and promptly lost most of my savings." At 41, he became an investment counselor, a market researcher and trader. It is actually amazing that he could have started all this so late in life and made a big enough splash to be worthy of inclusion in this book. In 1953, he succeeded Edwards as senior analyst at the investment advisory firm, Stock Trend Services, for three years and then started up his own firm, John Magee, Inc.

"Next to my charts, operating in the market is what I like most. Frankly, I haven't done as well with my own investments, over the long haul, as I have with my recommendations to clients, but that's because of a shaky beginning." At first, before he succumbed to the power of the chart, he'd sell out his position if the stock started to drop.

Magee taught his specialty in the Springfield adult-ed program for about a decade. He died in 1987 at 86 of heart failure. Before his Big Chart ran out, he wrote, published and illustrated *The General Semantics of Wall Street* in 1958 and *Wall Street—Main Street—and You* in 1972. Magee was the dean of technical analysts and singularly gave birth to the process of predicting single stock price action based on charting. There are so many people today commonly engaged in charting stocks as part or all of their investment activity that it would be impossible not to include him in this book.

CHAPTER NINE

SUCCESSFUL SPECULATORS, WHEELER-DEALERS, AND OPERATORS

WILD ON WALL STREET—BUT QUIET AT NIGHT

Many of the folks in this section are often referred to as "robber barons." It's a label connoting greed and ruthlessness that was stuck on them during the Progressive Era just after the turn of the century. But it's not entirely accurate or suited to the unique and individual characteristics that each possessed. And in many instances it is actually unfair and inconsistent with the personalities involved, who, as we shall see, often cared little for luxury or extravagance. Greedy or not, who knows? Yet each of these Successful Speculators, Wheeler-Dealers and Operators helped the market evolve into what it is today, and that's not something to be overlooked, nor something to which most of the rest of us can lay claim.

In many ways, this group resembles latter day Dinosaurs. Like the Dinosaurs, when they didn't know how to do something or didn't like what they saw, they created new steps and imaginative ways to cross barriers they faced. Unlike the Dinosaurs, they went any which way the wind blew. Without an absolute process or methodology, and without the Dinosaurs' sheer power, their saving grace was their flexibility—having enough of it to survive when their environment about-faced.

This crew operated on gut instinct and courage. They climbed out on a limb to build empires, buy long and sell short and buck popular trends. In the end, their bravado paid off. Sounds admirable enough, but today, like the Dinosaurs, the successful Speculators, Wheeler-Dealers and Operators would be viewed as wild, too unruly and too unpredictable to be allowed the freedom to be themselves. They are the antithesis of today's "team player," but that's what made them successful.

Jay Gould, for instance, gave the market his all—literally. He had no meaningful family life, no real friends; instead, he dedicated his life to merging railroads and running them. Even in business, he operated alone, even when others thought they were his partners. He remained ever flexible and free to go in, out, long and short. He was hated for his independence throughout his career, but never more so than when he exited Wall Street with his large fortune intact and out of reach of other speculators and wheeler-dealers. Few folks anywhere are ready to pay the social and emotional price Gould paid to be a success.

Typically, the success stories are about those who focused almost solely on work, with few personal sidetracks. But occasionally, you'll find flamboyant and flashy types who made fortunes—and kept them—such as Diamond Jim Brady and Bet-A-Million Gates. Diamond Jim usually had a girl on his arm and diamonds on his fingers. But he was loved more for his genuine generosity than for his gargantuan looks. Women came and went in his life, no matter how many diamonds he furnished them—none stayed for good. He found solace in the stock market, where he gambled big and won big. He was probably more lucky than skilled, but sometimes luck is as important a factor as any. Brady at least had the courage to keep rolling the dice.

John Bet-A-Million Gates was brash, audacious, and full of life. Sporting diamond-studded suspenders, he lived up to his name, betting on bugs, horses and bull markets. He was a savvy salesman and either truly brazen or crazy, once giving Morgan a take-it-or-leave-it ultimatum in a railroad deal and winning. He ultimately blew it all in the 1907 Panic, but always willing to put himself on the line, he recouped his fortune in oil. Not as colorful, but quirky just the same, was James Keene. He was another infamous speculator who tipped the bottle and played the horses, but otherwise stayed true to the market.

In the rest of the Speculators' cases, it was their market activities that warranted attention, not their personal lives. Jay Gould, William Vanderbilt, Edward Harriman, Henry Rogers, John Raskob, Arthur Cutten, and Bernard Smith were not socially flamboyant The Fisher Brothers became socially prominent within the confines of their own community and then only after leaving the stock market; they did so in a private and quiet way, not with the spectacularly flamboyant and eccentric lifestyle, as we will see in a later chapter, common among unsuccessful speculators.

Generally, successful speculators keep their eyes on business, not the high life. To make it as big as these guys did, and keep it, it is almost axiomatic to be as driven and focused as these men were. Jim Brady's party life and ultimate market focus are rarely attainable within the same brain. It was as if these men's deals and risks acted as their only outlet for fun and adventure and provided them a full spectrum of vicarious thrills. Typically, the truly wildest of the speculators kept their private lives private, simple, and stable—pretty darn unwild. They knew when to separate family from fortune and work from play.

William H. Vanderbilt, for instance, was a tyrannical executive in the office, but a loving father at home. He built his own success, apart from his famous father's, driven purely by his love for business and profits. Vanderbilt used to say he worked for the stockholders, not the public, and the public hated him, but he didn't care. By working hard and staying close to home, he amassed a greater fortune and a closer family than his father ever came close to achieving.

Edward Harriman and James Hill both built railroads, fortunes, families and successors. Neither was too proud to compromise if it meant overcoming barriers, and both made successes of whatever projects they undertook. Harriman was a shy little man who raised hell in board rooms when others didn't agree with him, but still knew when to shut up. He specialized in taking over dilapidated railroads, pulling them out of debt and making them pay. Although he died with a robber-baron–size fortune, he lived life outside of the office like any regular guy with a wife and five kids. One son even followed in his footsteps, becoming a railroad magnate.

Henry Rogers, a great market manipulator, loved gambling. When the stock market was closed, he played poker! But his family life knew no scandal. Ditto for Arthur Cutten, the last of the big manipulators, who gambled high but lived quietly.

Sell-Em-Ben Smith thrived on the thrill of the market and, occasionally, a fast car. But for the most part, he was a Puritan who never smoked or drank, and a romantic when it came to his wife. In the market he operated fast and loose, and when the New Deal turned Wall Street upside down, Smith flexibly went with it and was still able to turn a buck.

John Raskob, the Fisher Brothers and Bernard Baruch were all operators who knew that quitting while they were ahead would preserve their success in the market. Raskob, speculator and General Motors executive, and Baruch, speculator who abandoned the market just weeks before the Crash, both left the Street for politics. The Fishers, prominent players in the 1920s bull market, didn't foresee the Crash like Baruch, but they had the sense to withdraw fast before their fortune was decimated. They returned to their homes, families and a lives of low-key social and private charitable events.

As we will soon see, unsuccessful speculators lacked the clarity of focus these men had. For some men, Wall Street and money is a means to an end. For others, the big successes, Wall Street is the end itself. The biggest and most enduring successes had an inner code that drove them, and they played the game for the game's sake. They weren't driven to earn the money so they could go spend it. They typically had no desire to immerse themselves in any form of hedonistic adventurism. A Brady or a Gates is the rare exception proving the rule. It is almost spiritually ironic that those who most want money for what it will buy, are those least likely to make and keep huge amounts of it. Success historically goes to those who pray at the game's altar rather than at the altar of luxury.

JAY GOULD

BLOOD DRAWN AND BLOOD
SPIT—GOULD OR GHOUL-ED?

If you were a 19th-century Gould family member, you were a social outcast. Market manipulator Jay Gould was America's most despised man, receiving weekly death threats, not because he wasn't a nice guy—he wasn't—but due to his uncanny skill at taking over other people's properties. He was one tough operator.

Nicknamed the "Mephistopheles of Wall Street," Gould built his fortune by manipulating railroads across America, buying unstable, smaller lines, then merging and renaming them. By fudging financial figures, he sold the "empires" for huge profits—and if they went bankrupt, he began all over again, buying the outfit cheaply. Absolutely ruthless.

Personally, I kind of like the guy, but maybe that's just the contrarian in me. Regardless, you have to respect him for his skill. Among the best of the robber barons, he bought stock cheaply, often driving prices down, then seized control of the firms, streamlining and unloading them for sizable profits. A man ahead of his time, today, he would compare with the best of our modern raiders, who buy firms cheaply and turn them into better entities. What one man began, Gould finished with finesse. A bull at heart, a bear when it suited him, he was a wolf always—a lone one—if it meant a big buck.

In 1857, Gould, age 21 and a partner in a tannery, prepared for Wall Street's dog-eat-dog competition by ousting his partner and tying himself to a big-city merchant with cash and connections. Moving onward, Gould speculated with company profits and borrowed money, trying to corner the hide market. But, when he failed and the creditors hounded the firm, his big-city partner shattered and committed suicide.

Gould seemed eerily emotionless. Pale, pasty, 5 foot 6, with dark, deep-set eyes beneath bristling black eyebrows and a rough-cut beard beneath a balding pate, Gould's expressionless face mirrored total coldness. He would have been good at poker. Or at manipulation. But you can't be completely devoid of emotion; if you can't show emotions, they find another outlet. Consequently, Gould endured chest pains, tuberculosis, and various ailments. He frequently spit blood. Lovely man.

Next, he dove into the market, speculating in railroads and inevitably clashing with the powerful industrialist, **Cornelius Vanderbilt.** Teamed with market veteran **Daniel Drew** and raider **James Fisk**—whose boodles he would later decimate—Gould conspired to seize control of the Erie Railroad in 1867, crushing Vanderbilt's chance to monopolize Manhattan rails. They succeeded by issuing a massive amount of illegal convertible bonds, diluting the millions Vanderbilt spent on Erie stock.

Vanderbilt reacted by sicking his pet judge on the three, outlawing their flagrant methods. Fleeing the law, the conspirators left Manhattan for Jersey City with $8 million in profits and Erie's books. A homesick Gould soon sought remedy, for as long as they were outlaws, they couldn't return to Wall Street. Sending carpetbaggers with $1,000 bills, he tried to buy off Vanderbilt's bribes of state legislators in a bidding war, which he finally won by spending over $1 million and even buying off Vanderbilt's own treacherous agents.

But the Erie episode endured. When Drew secretly met with Vanderbilt to settle the "whole damned business," Gould and Fisk, enraged, vowed revenge. With Drew off the board, they issued new Erie shares, flooding the market, driving the price from 68 to 35 and earning millions for themselves. Then, without telling Drew, who was selling short heavily, they bulled the price back to 62 using Treasury funds, again profiting and forcing Drew to cover his shorts at a huge loss—revenge. Grinning like a hyena, Gould ran Erie until 1872, continually selling Erie stock and his own to the market and personally raking in more than $20 million.

Gould raced through many deals, transforming manipulation into a science, leaving countless corpses behind. His most famous and grandiose scheme? Attempting to corner gold. While he is most noted for this effort, it was quite unusual for Gould, typically a stock market and railroad operator. It is also usually misunderstood. While he hoped to profit by his raid, his real goal was to achieve a higher price for gold. This ultimately meant a lower greenback dollar, which would entice foreigners to buy more grain, which would be railroaded on his baby, the Erie. Starting in 1869, Gould bought gold, blatantly bulling the price, and soon held over $50 million worth of gold contracts. Meanwhile, Gould, Fisk and well-connected market crony, Abel Corbin, focused on convincing Corbin's brother-in-law, President Ulysses Grant, to support high-priced gold.

Grant held the power to crush the corner by opening Treasury vaults to circulate $100 million in federal gold. And, despite Gould's and Fisk's wining and dining campaign, Grant did just that, freeing $5 million in gold on September 24, 1869—known as Black Friday—sending the market reeling. As gold plummeted, unsuspecting speculators splattered with it in one of history's most notorious failed corners. But Gould sidestepped disaster with what we now call insider information. Grant's wife informed her brother Corbin; and Corbin informed Gould, who neglected to inform Fisk. Fisk was selling short and was left holding the bag. Gould cleared $11 million as gold soared and then fell. Some conquered cohorts cursed Gould, others vowed revenge on both him and Fisk—unaware that Fisk was crushed too.

Gould had few Wall Street friends, but after Black Friday, he had none. In the next 20 years, he mellowed his modus operandi, but the deals continued. He bought and sold Union Pacific, Kansas Pacific, Central Pacific, Missouri Pacific, Texas & Pacific, Cleveland and Pittsburgh, Denver Pacific, and Manhattan Elevated Railway, running them all as well as he raided them.

Another Machiavellian Gould diversion was his 1870s purchase of the *New York World*. In it he mounted a magnificent publicity campaign against America's largest telegraph firm, Vanderbilt-run Western Union, labeling it the "most vicious" monopoly. The *World* extolled American & Pacific as an up-and-coming telegraph firm (coincidentally, owned by Gould). Promptly, Western Union lost millions in business, and so, to squelch Gould's attacks, it bought his American & Pacific for over $10 million. The *World* then heralded another Gould telegraph firm, causing Western Union to buy it, too. Next, he went into high gear. With his paper blatantly and fraudulently blasting Western Union and its condition, Gould used his profits to short the stock, driving it down. Finally he reversed his course to buy at low prices and gain control of Western Union. Poor Vanderbilt. Just like Drew and Fisk.

Gould's personal Black Friday came in 1884, when **James Keene** and a syndicate of bears slashed Gould with the very sword of his own style, running bear raids on multiple Gould holdings. They won, Gould lost, and by June, in declining health, he surrendered his yacht, his castle overlooking the Hudson, his Fifth Avenue home and many other holdings—to his enemies. Ever clever and willing to quit before total defeat, he escaped with what was valued at his death in 1892 as a $72 million estate.

Gould always gave the market his all, made his fortune and, in turn, was hated. Eventually, he required round-the-clock guards, as he received weekly death threats. An insomniac, he took to pacing the sidewalks while his guard stood watch. But you must admire his skill. A sad wheeler-dealer? Yes, but unlike so many others, instead of raiding and ruining companies, he raided and ran them—usually for the better. Also, he was unusually flexible and was able to bend when the trend ran against him, instead of fighting an unyielding market to the end. Unlike so many others who had it all—and lost it—Gould was able to keep it all. He was dedicated! Rough and ruthless in a ruthless time! At times illegal in an era when it was hard to go far enough to be illegal, Gould combined brilliance with flexibility and managerial skill. He saw the big picture and the little detail. With his blood-lined spittoon nearby, he fought the battles no one else could stomach, and won more than he lost, always brilliantly. He represents the best and the worst of a world we all look back on with dread and awe.

"DIAMOND" JIM BRADY

LADY LUCK WAS ON HIS SIDE—SOMETIMES

❝ Hell! Ya can't always win!" Diamond Jim used to holler, but win he did, at least during work hours. In his very first speculative venture he netted $1.5 million back in 1897! Here's how it went: On the heels of winning big, betting on President William McKinley's election, Diamond Jim chuckled, "Sure, I'll take a chance," and plunged into a railroad until it reached 26. When the stock hit 68, Diamond Jim simply unloaded his holdings, counted his profits and left the stock to take a sudden dip from his selling! When Jim Brady did something, he went all out. Extravagance was his trademark, calling card—and his salvation.

Whether it was speculating in the market, dazzling ladies with diamonds, adorning his house with lavish luxuries, or funding a stranger's sob story, Brady just flashed his fat wallet. "Did you ever stop to think that it's fun to be a sucker—if you can afford it?" Well-known for his generosity, James Buchanan Brady spent freely because he had no family to whom to bequeath his millions. Weighing 240 pounds, with heavy jowls, small close-set eyes, a homely face, and a stomach six times larger than the average person's, he moaned, "There ain't a woman on this earth who'd marry an ugly-lookin' guy like me." Since so many ugly people do marry successfully, one suspects Brady adopted this philosophy more out of choice than necessity based on experience. Regardless, Brady found solace in earning and spending, living a life of one-night stands with diamond-eyed girlfriends like the famous Jersey Lily and Lillian Russell.

Jim nurtured his brilliant sales career, selling railroad supplies and steel cars, writing million-dollar contracts and gathering a fortune in commissions. A New York City native, the poor, young Irishman began in railroads. At age 21, in 1877, he adorned himself in costly black suits and silk, stovepipe hats. After attending business school, he switched to sales and took to the road, where people naturally liked him. But that wasn't enough for Jim. A shrewd and discerning gambler, he played cards and dice in his free time—for diamonds instead of money. By gambling and driving hard bargains with pawnbrokers, Jim collected diamonds, using them in his sales pitch. He would pull out a pocketful of diamonds, which his customers often suspected were phony, to show how successful he was. But while they balked, he laughed last. To establish his credibility at that point, he needed only prove the diamonds were real, which he did by engraving his name permanently in their windows—sure-fire publicity with a flair.

As Jim became more and more successful, his diamonds grew in size and number. So, in his usual grandiose style, he gave a few of his prized possessions away to his best customers and friendly actresses. And he had plenty left over to adorn shirts, his cane, and even a bicycle for his sultry girlfriend of 40 years, Lillian Russell, thereby earning his nickname, Diamond Jim.

Once consuming 45 ears of corn in one sitting—on top of an already heavy meal—Brady was as infamous for his eating habits as his diamond fetish. And because he routinely downed 14-course meals, with four helpings of each rich main dish, Brady received few dinner invitations! When one daring hostess asked how he knew when he was satiated, Brady stoically stated, "Whenever I sit down to a meal, I always make it a point to leave just four inches between my stummick and the edge of the table. And then, when I can feel 'em rubbin' together pretty hard, I know I've had enough!" At 56, the man who faithfully kept a five-pound box of chocolate-covered nuts and coconut creams within reach was diagnosed as having unusually large gallstones—and at 61, he was dead, from diabetes and other illnesses. Small wonder!

In the market, Diamond Jim operated on a similarly grandiose scale in keeping with his reputation. With plenty of market-savvy friends to keep him well-informed, Brady had the bucks and brawn to follow through on hot, chancy tips. Yet, as successful as he was, it was his open wallet that put him in the spotlight. Always a salesman and never a producer, Brady rarely made things happen—he simply facilitated them and he excelled at making the most of what lay before him. One of the few times Diamond Jim masterminded his own coup resulted from his inspection of a small Georgia railroad, which he noticed was surrounded by a large maturing peach orchard. He envisioned that it would soon be transporting its produce over the line. Acting quickly, he returned to Wall Street and bought $70,000 of the line's bonds—and within five years sold out for over half a million! Ah, the luck of the Irish!

He really fell in love with Wall Street after participating in a pool formed in 1902 by **John "Bet-A-Million" Gates** as a syndicate against **J.P. Morgan**'s Louisville and Nashville Railroad. En route Brady netted $1.25 million with no effort and was hooked the way a gambler is hooked. Soon he found himself hanging out in the Waldorf-Astoria bar, buying drinks for Morgan confidante **James R. Keene.** When Keene drunkenly uttered, "Go long on July cotton," Diamond Jim listened, buying 100,000 bales the next morning. After two months, he heard another operator was short cotton, so Jim cornered the desperado the same afternoon, pinched him for information, and walked away with a cool million.

On rare instances, Brady lost in the market by acting on tips too soon—he'd be in and out of a stock before a pool even made its first move! But that was the exception, not the rule, maybe because Diamond Jim was lucky. And that may be the lesson of Diamond Jim's life. Some folks are just lucky. If you line up a few million folks and ask them all to flip coins, some lucky guy will flip a thousand heads in a row. It's just a matter of odds and luck. Some other folks might think that person was a good flipper. But luck, both good and bad, strikes where it does, and you can't really account for it.

It's important when considering the histories of successful investors to remember some of them may have looked smart but were merely lucky. As these bios show, most of the flamboyant types on Wall Street end up broke. Brady didn't. No one knows exactly how much he had when he died, but it was a plenty big boodle. And yet that is particularly rare for someone who never was much of a pioneer of theory or tactics and spent most of his time being extravagant. But in a book about minds that contributed to the market, it is wise to remember that luck makes the market, at times, as much as any idea.

Whatever it was that kept Diamond Jim in diamonds, it never carried over to his personal life. He was always the lone rogue with the one night stands—except once when he lived with a woman for 10 years and gave her over $1 million in jewels, but she too didn't work out. She took off with his best friend. So, as lucky as Diamond Jim Brady was in the monetary sense, he was never really lucky in love. But who can tell where luck will strike? Brady would have laughed about it, rolled the dice again, and said, "Hell, ya can't always win!"

WILLIAM H. VANDERBILT

HE PROVED HIS FATHER WRONG

William Henry Vanderbilt sighed with relief when his overbearing, multimillionaire father died in 1877—now he could really get to work. His first 43 years had been filled with disapproval from the hulking **Cornelius Vanderbilt**, who was sure his sickly, wimpy son would "go to the dogs." William was told, but never convinced, "You don't amount to a row of pins. You won't never be able to do anything but to bring disgrace upon yourself, your family, and everybody connected with you. I have made up my mind to have nothing more to do with you." Cornelius then banished the 21-year-old William, who was already married, to a Staten Island, New York farm to fend for himself and his fast-growing family of eight children. His father apparently thought he would never amount to more than a "dirt farmer." Just goes to show you that having a rich and powerful father doesn't guarantee an easy life!

After 20 years as a farmer—whether from pride, a strong will, or sheer hatred for a farmer's life—William gradually wove his way back into his father's life some 10 years before he died. He won his father's favor and respect and the majority of his $100 million estate. During the remainder of William's life, he did something that would have truly astonished his skeptical father—in just seven years, he doubled what Cornelius had earned in 30!

The young Vanderbilt first captured his father's favor by revitalizing a bankrupt Staten Island railroad, though he knew little of railroads at the time. By helping his father build a Manhattan railroad empire during the 1860s, William became a great manager, improving track and equipment, regulating rates, and reconciling with labor. For instance, during a widespread railroad strike, he rewarded Vanderbilt workers with a $100,000 bonus for their loyalty, thus preventing a strike. But despite his achievements, William became a full-fledged executive only when his father lay on his deathbed—the skeptical old man retained control until the bitter end!

When Cornelius finally died, William seized the reins of the Vanderbilt empire, greatly expanding its railroad system by adopting some of his father's dubious tactics, including stock manipulation and price-cutting. For example, when a competing line refused to sell out to him, he cut his line's rates, took his competitor's business, forced it into bankruptcy, then bought it cheaply and churned out millions in watered stock.

Another typical maneuver was organizing a dummy railroad construction firm while organizing a new railroad. This enabled Vanderbilt to have the construction firm charge the railroad three to four times the actual cost of the work. He issued millions in securities to pay for the exaggerated construction costs, keeping the excess. Building a Pennsylvania line, for example, cost only $6.5 million, but he issued $40 million in securities, taking over $30 million in pure profits! the *New York Times* heralded him as one of the greatest railroad men who ever lived, claiming what Vanderbilt didn't know about railroads simply wasn't worth knowing.

"I wouldn't walk across the street to make a million dollars," Vanderbilt once told the *Times*. He didn't have to. Income from his holdings was over $10 million per year! One of the reasons he was able to hang on to his money was that he learned not to operate on heavy debt the way many of his peers did. This was partially due to the 1883 panic, which caused him to sell stocks bought on margin and invest in bonds. "I shall buy no more than I have the actual cash to pay for out and out." After 1883, holdings consisted of government, state and municipal bonds, and some stocks and mortgages. By his death in 1885, Vanderbilt had some $70 million in government bonds. Yet, he still claimed faith in the American economy. "Everything will come out right. This country is very elastic ... like a rubber ball hit, it will spring up again."

In keeping with his father's reputation, Vanderbilt was despised by the public for his extensive wealth and bitter attitude, a trait he obviously inherited from his father. When a reporter asked him why he was eliminating an extra-fare express line, he bluntly blurted "Railroads are not run for the benefit of the dear public"—they're built for the stockholders' benefit "by men who invest their money and who expect to get a fair percentage on the same." He even admitted to not caring "a penny" for the public's safety or convenience, unless it meant profits. You can see why the public loved him. When it came to business, William was virtually indistinguishable from his father, crying, "The public be damned . . . I am rich and full of all manner of good. I will eat, drink, and be merry!"

At home, however, Vanderbilt was quite different. He was the loving father of eight, generous to charities and had simple personal habits and an overall temperate manner. He was known as fair, frank and a good judge of character—which his father wasn't. Toward the end of his life, Vanderbilt, aware of his failing health, resigned all railroad presidencies and ordered two sons to take his place. He wasn't about to repeat his father's mistake. He trusted his sons implicitly and died while discussing future railroad plans. He left $200 million equally distributed among his children.

Vanderbilt had to compete against an extremely insensitive father, but in the end, he won. He was known as a good father—and that was probably reward enough for him. Doubling his father's estate was mere icing on the cake, maybe. Compared with his dad, William was a nice guy, but because he got things done—and wasn't modest about his achievements—he was portrayed as just another insensitive Vanderbilt. It must have been easy for the press to do—Cornelius' ruthless reputation was only eight years old when William died.

William Vanderbilt is one of the rare examples of the sons of tremendously successful empire builders who have been able to go on to build still further. He teaches the lesson that his personal lifestyle—that of being modest, non-extravagant, family-oriented and dedicated to business—is common to those few who have been able to surmount their fathers' egos, empires, and control to create even more. He must have been emotionally stronger than anyone gave him credit for in his day.

JOHN W. GATES

WHAT CAN YOU SAY ABOUT A MAN
NICKNAMED "BET-A-MILLION"?

In 1900, the audacious John "Bet-A-Million" Gates was Wall Street's favorite speculator. In one instance, following a well publicized bet on a
horse named Royal Flush that earned him a half-million, Gates predicted
William McKinley's election would bring a bull market. Putting his money
where his mouth was, Gates bought $150,000 in options on 50,000 Union
Pacific Railroad shares costing an average of $58, announcing the stock would
soon cross par. "If McKinley is elected, I ought to make some money don't
you think?" he roared. Asked about his option costs, he said, "Well, it's a
bet on the election, and if I lose, I'll charge it up to Royal Flush!" McKinley
won—and within months, the bull market moved Union Pacific to $130 and
netted Gates another $2.5 million windfall!

Despite his Bet-A-Million nickname, Gates was savvy. Operating quickly
and on instinct, he once bet which fly would be the first to fly off a sugar cube.
In reality, Gates was an ingenious industrial and market wonder! Starting as
an unsatisfied-but-clever barbed-wire salesman, Gates climbed his way to the
top of the industry, revolutionizing it along the way. Then, still not satisfied,

he took on Wall Street, becoming a major speculative power. Yet, what makes his story so intriguing is that he held on to his bundle, in spite of his hype and whimsical ways, whereas most wheeler-dealer types invariably get their comeuppance.

Tall, with wide, blue eyes, black hair and a Cheshire grin, Gates' entire life attested to his saying, "When you want something, make up your mind you want it and how to get it—and then go after it with a vengeance." Whether it was a barbed-wire factory, a steel combine or smug revenge, Gates fearlessly went for what he wanted—and always got it. Born in 1855 of stern, frugal farmers from what's now West Chicago, the teenaged Gates made his first speculative venture with a threshing machine. With the profits, he married at 19 and started a small hardware store in his hometown. But feeling confined, Gates sold his store and entered the sapling wire business at 21, becoming a salesman for Col. Isaac Ellwood, who would later feel the sting of Gates' vengeance. A lot of these 19th century tycoon types seemed to have a penchant for starting early, and schooling rarely seems to have played a major role in their early years.

Characteristically, when Gates did something, he went all out. So, when he reached Texas to find no one buying barbed wire, he quickly adopted the outrageous methods of a smooth-talking medicine-show trickster, setting up a barbed-wire corral filled with 25 of the wildest steers he could find—smack in the middle of town! When the fencing held and the cattle settled down, Gates rounded up more orders than his boss, Ellwood, could keep up with. Feeling incredibly self-confident at having made his boss rich—and, en route, revolutionizing the Southwestern cattle industry—Gates demanded partnership. His boss flatly refused to part with any profits, so Gates immediately quit, and—knowing the money was in manufacturing—decided to set up shop in St. Louis (where he was almost sidetracked into a career as city mayor).

Despite harassing litigation by Ellwood, J.W. Gates & Co. was born. At age 25, in 1880, Gates formed the Southern Wire Co. and, two years later, formed the first modern-day consolidation. Absorbing rival companies and riding the crest of the now-booming wire business, Gates' wire interests grew into Consolidated Steel & Wire Co. and took the lead in wire, ousting Ellwood from his former position as industry leader. Everything Gates touched turned to gold!

Next, after courting his ex-boss to his side, Gates went on a plant-buying spree, offering owners irresistible millions and playing two-handed poker while awaiting their decisions. "I'll take it," was the usual response, "if I can get the cash tomorrow." After paying $7 million—in cash—for plants sight-unseen, the 40-year-old millionaire formed American Steel & Wire Co., capitalized at $24 million and underwritten by Wall Street. As quickly as American was organized and listed on the American Stock Exchange, Gates, a bull, formed a pool to manipulate its stock.

Inevitably, Gates clashed with J.P. Morgan, who denounced Gates as "a dangerous man" who could not be trusted. Yet, Morgan believed in Gates' consolidation concept, as he was in the process of forming the first billion-dollar corporation, U.S. Steel—and Gates' companies were key in completing its formation. So, Gates made Morgan pay through the nose for his firms—in exchange for Gates' $60 million in American Steel stock, Morgan gave him $110 million in U.S. Steel! But Morgan got his when he refused Gates a director's seat, saying "You have made your own reputation; we are not responsible for it." Stricken by this blow to his pride, Gates vowed revenge on Morgan—and, as usual, he got it. Out for blood, Gates campaigned to squash Morgan's railroad expansion in 1902 by buying control of the Louisville and Nashville line. Creating a Northern Pacific-like corner (see **James J. Hill**), Gates made Morgan squirm! Under pressure, Morgan sent a partner at 1:30 a.m. to see Gates, who negotiated in flowered PJs and a red robe! A keen negotiator, Gates made a take-it-or-leave-it offer of $150 per share (he had paid $100), plus a $10 million bonus! Morgan, of course had no choice.

Setting up shop in the Waldorf-Astoria hotel, Bet-A-Million played poker and bridge—and speculated in the 1901 Hill-Harriman battle for the Northern Pacific. Although he hated admitting a loss—he wasn't used to it—Gates admitted he got kicked around a bit and had to unload batches of securities to cover his shorts. But he recovered, forming Wall Street's largest brokerage house, Charles G. Gates & Co., commonly known as the "House of Twelve Partners." The firm, headed by his son Charles G. Gates—who, coincidentally, was as extravagant as his father—became known as the Street's largest speculative house by carrying as much as $125 million of stocks on margin.

The Panic of 1907 caught Gates' firm bogged down with Tennessee Coal and Iron, a company he had planned to pawn off on Morgan's U.S. Steel. But Gates didn't figure on a panic! Morgan, chuckling, didn't budge—forcing Gates to the wall, and triggering his firm's closure, while letting Gates' associates in the venture off the hook. This ended Gates' career on Wall Street for good. After a long vacation in Europe, he ventured in an oil exploration company called the Texas Oil Co. (Texaco) replenishing his fortune when the oil spurted! Meanwhile, he developed Port Arthur, Texas, dominating its real estate, industries and railroad, the Kansas City Southern, claiming, "I am not interested in the stock market. I am simply following the policy of the average business man; that is to attend to my own business."

Gates is one of the few wheeler-dealer types to end up on top. Yes, he had a boom/bust aspect to his life. He would almost have to with a name like Bet-A-Million. And yes, he was a flamboyant character right up until he took the ultimate plunge in 1911, always sporting three diamonds on each suspender buckle, but after his licking in the Panic of 1907, he husbanded his $50 million carefully and gambled only for fun.

EDWARD HARRIMAN

WALK SOFTLY AND CARRY A BIG STICK

E d Harriman never smiled. Not that he didn't have reason to—he died leaving a Morgan-sized, $100 million estate in 1909. He was just that type of guy. Small, skinny, stooped, and runny-nosed, Harriman was avidly antisocial and completely obscure, buried beneath Coke-bottle-lens glasses, baggy trousers, a walrus mustache, and soft hat pulled down to his eyes. Operating in the shadow of his beguiling guise, he stalked Wall Street over 40 years before creating what was at one point America's largest railroad empire. So, while splashy self-promoters speculated their fortunes away, Harriman skulked his way to the top ever so silently.

"All the opportunity I ask is to be one amongst fifteen men in a board room," Harriman once told Kuhn, Loeb financier Otto Kahn. Kahn knew if ever in such a situation, Harriman would be the lone soldier convincing the rest of the troops of his ideas. Harriman, particularly persuasive, thrived on challenge. Perhaps compensating for his lack of personality, he was also ferociously focused, determined, domineering and obstinate. Born in 1848 to a poor Episcopalian clergyman, Harriman began as a Wall Street office boy at 14, working his way up the ranks. One year after profiting in 1869's Black Friday panic, he bought a $3,000 Stock Exchange seat and set out independently, forming E.H. Harriman & Co. He was always the loner and always driven.

"My capital when I began was a pencil and this," Harriman used to say in his distinct low voice, tapping his noggin. He began speculating with accumulated commissions from clients like the Vanderbilts. (As he was just one in a crowd then, his trades were rarely recorded.) At age 28, Harriman married into a prominent N. Y. family that coincidentally dealt in railroads.

He then moved in on railroads, selling short during the collapse of the New Jersey Central and making $150,000. Within just a few years, he had mastered railroad management and manipulation, and developed his hallmark strategy.

While placing bonds for an Illinois Central acquisition, he bought Illinois stock for himself, became a director, won the confidence of its manager and began running the road from the inside, instead of from Wall Street. Completely revamping the line and nearly tripling its track mileage, Harriman knew that a line's physical property mattered first—and current profits, second. Whereas operators like **Jay Gould** and **Jim Fisk** would skin a line for profits, then dispose of it, Harriman quickly rebuilt and extended lines, dumping millions into them, then sat back to reap the profits. Never allowing equipment to deteriorate (he inspected track himself), he always provided ample funds for contingencies, avoided financial risk during slumps and when raising capital, exceeded his immediate needs, gaining outstanding credit for his lines.

He hit the jackpot in 1895 with his notorious reorganization of the near-fizzled Union Pacific. Not even Morgan would touch the debt-ridden line, which owed 30 years of interest plus principal—yet Harriman was eager to attach it to his Illinois line. So, he set out to intimidate his only competitor, investment banking firm, Kuhn, Loeb, wielding the Illinois' untarnished credit, which could guarantee hundreds of millions at under four percent! The two ultimately joined forces—remaining as such over 20 years—and bought the UP, paying over $45 million in cash, including interest, and issuing four-percent bonds and preferred stock. Within three years, he had dumped millions into the ramshackle road and extended UP track over 12,000 miles. The line was completely pulled out of debt and even showed profits! Harriman had accomplished what others thought impossible.

Harriman's only competitor was Morgan-affiliated **James Hill**, who dreamed as vividly as Harriman, but not as slyly! The two inevitably clashed over the Chicago, Burlington and Quincy system, as it brought both Harriman's UP and Hill's Northern Pacific closer to becoming transcontinentals. When Hill somehow obtained the line from right under Harriman's nose, and then refused Harriman's advances to monopolize, Harriman saw red. But he didn't get mad, he got even—if he couldn't have the Burlington, he was going to take Hill's Northern Pacific!

Ever so quietly, Harriman—via Kuhn, Loeb—began buying the $90 million of Northern Pacific stock needed to acquire control, but before he could finish, Hill woke up and started to do the same. Following a few days of frenzied buying, both parties claimed victory on the same day—but by then, the stock was cornered, prices propelled to $1,000 per share, and panic wafted through the air! It was either truce or panic, so the two conceded, forming a $400 million joint holding company called Northern Securities Co. Through the holding company, the unyielding Harriman had gained access to Hill's lines in the end.

Harriman also understood the era's power of consolidation and monopoly. In 1900, he bought nearly 50 percent of the Southern Pacific system by creating a $100 million mortgage on the UP and selling $40 million in 4 percent convertible bonds. Next, Morgan-like, he pooled his new acquisition with the UP, cutting costs in half and decreasing competition and staff. By 1907, Harriman controlled—either directly or indirectly—10 major railroads, five navigation firms, substantial interests in coal, real estate and oil and several street railway systems. Two years later, he died. Some say he worked himself to death.

The "little giant" of Wall Street was no slouch. He constantly sought new challenges, and just as often succeeded. Even in leisure, he loved jumping steep hurdles on horseback. Yet, he was a real family man, who loved spending the day with his wife and five kids and never compromised his family or moral position. The odd thing was that he never wielded more of a tycoon's image, though it was his modesty (or was that simply his camouflage?) that boosted his fortune—and kept it! Even today, modesty pays. If you look at the *Forbes* 400, you'll find quite a few people who have built a lot more than Donald Trump—Harriman's lesson is that they're more apt to keep it.

While Harriman's significance and power were hardly questioned by the bigwigs of his day, he didn't have the bigger-than-life image his success deserved—that is until his son, William Averell Harriman, followed in his father's footsteps. William became Union Pacific's powerful chairman and did his father justice. His son's success, rather than any fortune Harriman incurred during his lifetime, must be considered his greatest tribute.

Harriman's success stemmed from a strong-willed soul. He had a serious sense of purpose and was flexible enough to deal with any problem, even if it meant compromising. Like Jay Gould, who would bend with the market when the market bent against him, Harriman took what he received, thoroughly convinced he could do the best with it. Unlike many who feel it's either all or nothing, Harriman could improvise. And he was confident in his ability to handle hostile men. Absolutely nothing—or no one—could interfere with his success. All this and honor, too—that's quite a feat in the days when Gould's cut-throat tactics reigned on Wall Street.

The *Wall Street Journal* once explained, "When the Harriman mind is made up, that settles it. Panics may follow, boards of directors may be disrupted, officers may resign, financial powers at large may band against him, law may deny him, the money forces of the world may say him nay—but nothing matters. Isolated, regardless, persistent, defiant and courageous, he goes upon his way, caring neither for method, law nor man, so it may be that at the end he wins the prize at which he aims!"

JAMES J. HILL

WHEN OPPORTUNITY KNOCKS

You never know when opportunity might knock. One evening in 1856, for instance, a weary traveler stopping at the Hill farm in Ontario, Canada was delighted to see young James Hill, the son of Irish emigrants, willingly fetch a bucket of water for his thirsty horse. In return for his thoughtfulness, Hill was tossed an American newspaper and told, "Go there, young man. That country needs young citizens of your spirit!" Soon after, Hill left for the U.S. Northwest with itchy palms, always operating on the premise that "the man with the big opportunity today is the man in the ranks."

Assertive and astute, Hill found plenty of opportunity there—and when he didn't find it, he created it. During his life, he built railroad systems traversing the Northwest, developing traffic for his lines as the tracks were laid! Whether it was distributing bulls for farmers to breed or developing more cost-efficient ways to grow wheat, Hill—with an eye for detail—could always be found behind the scenes boosting development. In a 20-year period, he turned wilderness into farmland, developed towns and industries and tapped virgin markets, guaranteeing his lines' prosperity. From poor

Canadian emigrant to millionaire "Empire Builder," Hill worked with farmers, lumbermen, traders—even Wall Street's most powerful **J.P. Morgan**—to open up the Northwest for the first time.

An eager immigrant, Hill settled in St. Paul, Minnesota working in shipping. Ever the big thinker and operator, he married and started what would eventually become a family of 10. His first capitalist endeavor was to start a shipping company. Then he used that as a base to buy the St. Paul and Pacific railroad in 1873, which really got his career on track.

By 1879 his railroad venture was a profitable system integrating several smaller lines and capturing the Canadian railroad market. By 1889 he had become a big time operator by transforming his little St. Paul system into the Great Northern Railway Company. Sightless in his right eye, Hill worked feverishly, building and equipping a mile of track per working day at $15,000 a mile, insisting that operating costs be the lowest of all regional roads. In his early years, he was purely a railroad operator, not a stock market operator.

When **Jay Gould**, for instance, offered to capitalize Hill's system at double the cost, an indignant Hill replied, "We should build our railroad through and capitalize it for exactly what it costs; not a dollar more nor a dollar less ... I will not join with you in a real estate speculation, for a real estate speculation is not a railroad." Indeed, the furthest thought from Hill's mind was speculation—initially.

Some say the Hill lines were also noted for corruption—as Northwestern state legislatures and press basked in bribery money, expansion came easy. Gustavus Myers, in his 1907 book, *The History of Great American Fortunes*, notes that while it was probable that Hill was corrupt, nothing ever stuck—no one ever got the goods on him! So, Hill might have been a crook—but at least he was a discreet one! Discretion was key to anyone winning the support of the venerable Morgan.

But ultimately, to be real big in late 19th-century railroads you learned that all tracks lead to Wall Street. To build a truly big system you would have to acquire lines to access areas otherwise unattainable. For Hill, the "Prince of the Great Northern," the first bite was his former competitor, the Northern Pacific. He bought it cheaply after it failed in the 1893 panic. Moving closer to a transcontinental line, his next bite was to acquire 97 percent of the strategic Chicago, Burlington and Quincy line. This is where the picture gets more complicated because J.P. Morgan enters the picture by arranging a $215-million bond issue to finance the acquisition.

This enraged **Ed Harriman**. Not only had he, too, been coveting the Burlington for his own system, but seeing Hill suddenly backed by Morgan created a much more powerful foe than Hill had previously seemed on his own. Hill and Morgan together were the classic cross of Wall Street and Main Street—the ying and yang of capitalism. Harriman was ticked, and most likely afraid. So Harriman vowed revenge—and since his coveted Burlington was unavailable, he decided to go for the jugular—Hill's Northern Pacific!

Harriman, backed by Kuhn, Loeb Co., quietly bought up Northern Pacific stock until Hill noticed the sudden, sharp rise in price. Afraid his just-less-than-half interest in the line might not be enough for control in this instance, Hill hastened to buy needed shares to guarantee ownership, while Harriman did the same. Within the next few days, the stock was cornered and zoomed from under $100 to $1,000—one of the classic corners of all time! Panic ensued, culminating in Blue Thursday, May 9, 1901. As stocks tumbled, Hill—facing a ruined market—came to realize that compromise was in everyone's best interests. Harriman, who always saw himself as able to persuade any board to his view, agreed to let Hill have the presidency and control of a new holding company, which included the Northern Pacific, in exchange for granting Harriman a seat on the board, ending the battle in a win-win draw.

When he died in 1916 at age 77, Hill left a $53 million estate and a family of railroaders: One son took the Great Northern's presidency and another its vice-presidency. His third became overseer of Hill's iron-ore properties, but none ever achieved his father's fame. In the end, the rust streaks that he first bet on 30 years earlier were earning over $66 million per year and carried over 15 million tons annually!

The interesting role of Hill is as a legendary railroad operator who ultimately had to go to Wall Street to hold his own. You can be a small operator in business and ignore Wall Street, but the bigger your Main Street ambitions, the sooner and more certain will be your interaction with Wall Street. Hill's fame in Wall Street history and his main role in the evolution of the markets is his participation leading to the classic Great Northern corner. The notion of a corner is basic to human greed. Ironically, it was just this kind of monopolistic big corporate merger that created the impetus behind the antitrust laws that followed soon after the turn of the century. Corners are rare in the modern world, but not nonexistent. In an era of big pools of institutional money that can move with lightning speed, corners may become more likely now. After all, in a global financial market no local laws can possibly govern the entirety of the world market. Without folks like Hill who participated in corners, the evolution of securities laws and the Main Street businesses Wall Street represents would look very different than they do today.

JAMES R. KEENE

NOT GOOD ENOUGH FOR GOULD,
BUT TOO KEEN FOR ANYONE ELSE

He's been depicted as a wild and sleazy gambler, America's ablest pool operator and a great financier, but James Keene never saw his Wall Street career in black and white. The great market manipulator, who made possible some of the Street's greatest industrial coups, explained it this way: "Without speculation, call it gambling if you wish, initiative and enterprise would cease, business decay, values decline, and the country would go back twenty years in less than one." The way Keene saw it, he did the growing, turn-of-the-century American economy a favor by doing what he did best—simply buying and selling securities.

The way the "Silver Fox of Wall Street" operated, trading securities was anything but simple—it was an art form. Sure, the old adage advises—he bought cheap and sold dear—but it was never a matter of market timing—for he was the one who timed the market and indeed, made the market! He knew how to get action. For instance, Keene was able to do wonders with the Southern Pacific, a newly reorganized railroad that still had a droopy stock price, fed-up stockholders and no new investors. It was a classic case for the quick, sure, and bold manipulator. When no one else would touch the stock, he took it upon himself to drive up the stock price—and, of course, earn a pretty profit.

He started buying Southern Pacific stock in his characteristic sly and secretive way, making sure to sell some of the stock he'd just bought to keep the price down. Then—when he finished buying stock cheaply—he began buying recklessly, attaching his infamous name to the line. Keene's interest in the stock alone drove its price up some 20 points and prompted the weary investors to sell out, eager to accept a tiny, but certain profit. Meanwhile, Southern Pacific became a hot issue and other suckers gladly snatched up shares at any price! The new stock price secured and railroad management happy, Keene sold out quietly, taking a tidy bundle with him.

Born in England in 1838, the "Silver Fox" came to California at age 12 with his father. Sharp and perceptive, he made his living as a farmer, law student, cowboy, government mule-puncher, school teacher and San Francisco newspaper editor before making his first big bundle—$10,000—while mining silver in Nevada. Soon afterwards, he turned his modest kitty into $150,000 via the San Francisco Mining Exchange, at first acting as broker for other speculators, then forming his own deals. For a decade, Keene initiated bull and bear raids against stocks, made himself a name as a sagacious speculator, went bust a few times and always recouped his losses—gaining even more than he had in the first place.

The tall and slender Keene took his fortune to New York in 1876 with the intent of boating to Europe for a vacation. But the vacation never happened—Wall Street did. He arrived during a depressed market and was able to amass some $10 million speculating. He then teamed with the unscrupulous **Jay Gould** in a pool formed to bear Western Union stock. Once loaded up on the stock, however, Keene realized Gould had sold out his own position, taken his profits and left Keene holding the bag. This happened time and time again, until finally Keene was left with less than half his fortune—and then he vindictively roared, "I have ... $6,000,000. I guess I will stay right here and get that man's scalp!"

No matter how many times he tried, Keene never did get his foe's scalp. Gould continued to outmaneuver his "partner" during a few more deals, then ducked out of the market by the early 1890s, taking millions of Keene's former winnings. Gould, one of the best operators ever, was just too good for Keene. C'est la vie, Keene might have said, for he believed "all life is a gamble, whether in Wall Street or not." One of their most famous bouts was an attempt to corner the wheat market—and predictably, just as they were about to close in on the corner, Gould sold short, prices plummeted and Keene lost $7 million in a few days. Bust once again, Keene auctioned his valuables, including a painting that ironically wound up on Gould's wall—Gould re-named it, "Jim Keene's Scalp!"

Gould was to be Keene's one and only serious match—ever. No one ever got in his way again. Though he claimed he expected to be successful in only 51 percent of his endeavors, Keene cleaned up on practically every deal he made for himself and every job he was hired to do. He manipulated the stocks of sugar, railroad, tobacco and whiskey companies, to name a few. He also helped bring on the mini-panic of 1901, when **J.P. Morgan** hired him to buy 150,000 shares of Northern Pacific Railroad stock in one of the greatest railroad wars of all time. (See **E.H. Harriman** and **James Hill** for further details.)

By far Keene's most famous and most important job ever was creating a market for the first billion-dollar corporation, U.S. Steel. Again working for Morgan, he manipulated the stock so much that it became the center of a bull market. He repeatedly sold 1,000 shares, then bought back 100 to support the stock, driving its price up so as to attract speculators and small-time investors, alike. When asked why he took the job, which paid him about $1 million on top of his own already-secured fortune, Keene said, "Why does a dog chase his thousandth rabbit?"

With dignified eyes, a grave brow and nerves of steel, Keene died in 1913 leaving some $20 million. A widower, Keene was a loner, lived in the Waldorf Hotel and had no friends in which he could confide. His four favorite things in life were said to be his son Foxhall, who was a great daredevil auto racer and polo player; a great race horse, like the one he named his son after; a stock ticker; and the traditional mixture of black coffee and brandy that comprised his breakfast.

"Keene played 'em fast and furious, with the blue sky for a limit," Wall Streeter **Thomas Lawson** once said of Keene. "It was a greater pleasure to lose to him than to win from a bungler."

Used by everyone from Morgan to Gould, Keene was the classic 19th-century operator. Is there a lesson to Keene's life? Not really. Is his among the minds that made the market? Absolutely. On his own, he was as able as all but a few on Wall Street, and as a sidekick or operative, he was there in many of the big, hallmark battles of the market's formative years. Living old, dying rich, drinking more than he should without its getting to him, starting as a poor immigrant with a series of rough jobs, evolving out of the mining camps, this was a man who led a rough and tumble life in a rough and tumble time. He made himself as he participated in the making of the market. He was a man who correctly knew, as few do today, that the life of an investor, whether a speculator or a long-term holder, adds value to society and that by helping to make a market, he was helping the world. At a time when Wall Street is again increasingly coming under fire in the wake of the 1980's insider trading scandals, it would be wise for the world to see life from Keene's vantage point and recognize the value society receives from speculators and their speculation.

Henry Clews, Twenty-eight Years in Wall Street, 1887

HENRY H. ROGERS

WALL STREET'S BLUEBEARD: "HOIST
THE JOLLY ROGER!"

B ack at the turn of the century, Wall Street's version of Bluebeard was the dapper, dashing and debonair Henry Rogers, who found his buried treasure in the stock market. Profane and arrogant, the swashbuckler fit the part to a tee, swindling unsuspecting people and seizing properties for the unrelenting oil trust, Standard Oil. Rogers was shrewd, fiercely determined, bad-tempered, and utterly ruthless; he had the makings of a successful pirate. Former Standard crony **Thomas Lawson** once said of Rogers, "He is considerate, kindly, generous, helpful . . . but when he goes aboard his private brig and hoists Jolly Roger, God help you. He is a relentless, ravenous creature, as pitiless as a shark!"

They called him "Hell-Hound Rogers," and like every good pirate, he loved to gamble. "I am a gambler. Every now and then **John W. Gates** will come to me and say, 'Henry, don't you think it's time we had a little fun in the market?' We made lots of killings and had plenty of fun," the buccaneer roared. "I must have action. And on Saturday afternoons when the market is closed

I've got to have a poker game!" When Rogers wasn't tending to Standard Oil (he helped run the firm after its founder retired), he could usually be found with John Rockefeller's brother, William, scheming their next market coup (John Rockefeller despised stock gambling). Using their fat Standard Oil stock dividend checks and backing from **James Stillman**'s National City Bank, the two made the notorious "Standard Oil Crowd" a feared faction on Wall Street between 1897 and 1907.

Actually, the relationship between John Rockefeller and Rogers has interesting implications. While Rockefeller wasn't interested in tarnishing himself with Wall Street shenanigans, instead of turning his back on them, he used the pirate to get them done. Rogers was simply the black side of Rockefeller, and lived on after him. In today's world, we would see Rockefeller's hands as just as dirty for his agents' acts as if they were his own. But it made Rockefeller feel better that he wasn't the one Wall Streeting.

One of the Standard Oil Crowd's most famous maneuvers was creating Amalgamated Copper Company, a Standard Oil–like consolidation of midwestern copper mines. Rogers, who engineered the deal, arranged to buy several mines for $39 million. Then he and Rockefeller took title to the mines before forking over the $39-million National City Bank check, which they stipulated had to be deposited in National City. Meanwhile, Rogers organized the company, using Standard clerks as dummy directors, and transferred the mines to Amalgamated for $75 million in return for all of its capital stock! He then took the $75 million to National City, borrowed $39 million on it to cover his check, and sold the $75 million in stock to the public. With the proceeds, he paid off the bank loan and reaped $36 million in profits. Later, when the stock fell to 33, the group bought it back and resold it at 100! There hoists the Jolly Roger.

Rogers happened upon Standard Oil at the age of 34 while managing a Brooklyn, New York oil refinery taken over by John Rockefeller in his quest to form Standard Oil in 1874. Previously, Rogers had built a small refinery in Pennsylvania and worked in railroads.

The Fairhaven, Massachusetts native made his first killing at 14 as a newspaper boy. Early one morning when he first received his papers, quick-thinking Rogers noticed an article on the sinking of a vessel loaded with sperm oil bound for a local oil dealer. Instead of delivering his fifty cents' worth of papers to the community, he hurried to the oil dealer, showed him the article, then sold him the papers for $200! The dealer wasn't actually buying newspapers, Rogers reasoned, he was buying time that enabled him to corner the region's sperm oil before the news got out! In that transaction Rogers was evidencing Pirate traits. Fast on his feet, willing to double-cross and display disloyalty to his employer and his subscriber base, he was creative enough to see how to profit from others' misfortunes.

The great muckraking queen Ida Tarbell, who aimed her pen at Standard Oil, actually liked Rogers—or at least his no-nonsense, blunt attitude. He was a pirate, she said, but no hypocrite—he flew his black flag and made no bones about it! But on the flip side, Rogers was charitable. He helped out Helen Keller, Booker T. Washington, and even Mark Twain (when his finances hit rock bottom). Though Rogers didn't give Twain cash, he gave him his time and financial expertise to nurse Twain back to solvency.

Like his headquarters—a suite of interconnecting rooms allowing visitors to enter and exit without ever noticing one another—Rogers' investment portfolio was complex. He invested in gas companies, railroads and, believe it or not, tacks—and formed a $65 million smelting trust in 1899. He schemed and swashbuckled to the very end.

Just a few years before he died in 1909, Rogers was busy building and financing the Virginia Railroad for some $40 million—solely with his own resources and credit. Some say the stress of the project killed him, but this wasn't likely. If his zany stock market maneuvers and horrendous public scorn didn't kill him, it's doubtful a railroad could. Besides, by then he was already a semi-accomplished railroad man. He helped fund **Edward Harriman** in reorganizing the Union Pacific, served on other lines' boards of directors and was a Staten Island, transportation magnate, controlling its lines and ferries. Rogers was also a U.S. Steel director and founder of his hometown-based Atlas Tack Company, the world's largest tack company at a time when mass-produced tacks were a relatively new and hot product. He had his fingers in as many treasure chests as he could dig up!

Despite his sprawling fingers in personal investments, Rogers stuck to his roots at home, once he found them. Married at 52, he was widowed and remarried within two years. He had three daughters and one son, Henry H. Rogers II. A pirate in business, his personal life knew no scandal. And so, once more we see that success continues for those who place business before personal luxury. No ego-driven wild cavorter, Rogers was wild in business simply because he loved the game. Pirating came first. But when his second wife died, Rogers came unglued. The fact that his son found success in managing the tack firm and several railroads didn't seem to comfort him. "Everything is going away from me," he cried. "I am being left alone." The pirate in him was sadly gone.

A pirate can succeed on Wall Street. Perhaps today that is moderated by securities regulations, but Drexel Burnham's recent Junk Bond empire shows pirating is still possible. In recent years you could see pirating in the penny stock market in Denver or among the bond daddies in Arkansas—and venture capitalists are often pirates disguised as creators. All these folks owe their spiritual foundation to Rogers. And all Rogers would say to them, if he could see them from his grave is, "If it isn't profitable, it isn't fun and if there isn't anything in it for me, then to hell with you." Hoist the Jolly Roger!

Collier's, 1929

FISHER BROTHERS

MOTORTOWN MOGULS

To quit while you're ahead may not be fashionable—but it sure is profitable and smart. Take the Fisher Brothers of Detroit, for example. Well remembered in Detroit for their world-renowned innovations in car bodies, the hulking Fisher Building built in 1929, their part in local society and their many lavish gifts to Detroit charities, the Fisher Brothers had once been major Wall Street players. Their mere presence in New York bolstered confidence in the stock market so much that when they threw their support behind a stock, much of the public followed suit. But once the Fishers withdrew from the game immediately following the 1929 Crash—taking with them a hefty remainder of their generous fortune—Wall Street and the national media completely forgot about the Fishers, allowing them to live out their lives tucked away in palatial Detroit mansions. Ironically, if they had continued to fight on in the Crash and ensuing Great Depression and lost their fortune as so many others did, they almost certainly would have guaranteed their place in the media for the next decade. They also would have been broke.

The Fishers illustrate the lesson that it's smart to quit while ahead, yet at the same time, they dispute another equally important lesson: Stick to your knitting. **Jay Cooke**, for example, went from bonds to railroads, but in making the transition, he lost his shirt. The Fishers went from manufacturing automobile bodies—"Body by Fisher"—to dealing in the stock market, yet remarkably, they not only kept their shirts, they wound up with a big closet full of them.

The eldest brother, Fred, was responsible for the brothers' initial climb to success. Born in 1878 in Sandusky, Ohio, the grandson of a German wagon builder, Fred quit Catholic school at age 14 to master his father's black-smithing and carriage-building business. By 1902, he was ready for Detroit, the home of an infant auto industry, where his carriage-making skills were readily marketable. While rising through the ranks of a prominent carriage factory, which then doubled as the largest auto body manufacturer, Fred watched his brothers follow his footsteps and join him in Detroit as each came of age. In 1908, with an uncle and second eldest brother Charles, Fred ventured on his own to form Fisher Body Company, capitalized at $50,000.

Fisher Body designed sturdy, shock-resistant bodies specifically for autos, rather than modifying carriages to meet the new needs of an automobile. In 1910, they revolutionized the industry further by creating "closed" car bodies encased in glass. Drivers, who wore goggles to keep the dust from their eyes, thought anyone was crazy to ride in a glass-enclosed box, but the idea swept the nation. Fisher Closed Body was formed after Cadillac ordered a whopping 150 closed bodies—the first and largest order of its kind. By 1916, after having expanded into Canada, the Fishers merged their three firms into Fisher Body Corporation, a holding and operating firm capitalized at $6 million. The firm had a total annual capacity of 370,000 bodies and was the largest of its kind in America.

Tall and heavy-boned, the Fishers were literally giants in the auto indus-try, so naturally they attracted the attention of General Motor's overzealous **William Crapo Durant**. In 1919, GM acquired 60 percent of Fisher Body at a cost of some $27 million. The Fishers agreed to increase their 200,000 shares of common stock to 500,000 and sell the new issue to GM at $92 per share, and GM agreed to buy the majority of its bodies from Fisher Body at a price of cost-plus-17.6 percent. Seven years later, the Fishers sold their remaining 40 percent interest to GM in exchange for its stock, which then had a market value of $130 million.

Fisher Body quickly proved GM's most profitable acquisition. Following World War I, the firm constructed the world's largest auto body factory in Cleveland and until 1929, built and acquired some 20 factories nation wide. It made $23 million in 1923 on a volume of 417,000 bodies. By 1925, it was earning 18.9 percent on its assets. Some speculate GM wouldn't be what it is today without the Fisher acquisition—that in itself is quite an achievement in any book! But that's Main Street, not Wall Street.

Meanwhile, they had retained control of their firm and various GM sub-sidiaries. Fred was a GM vice president and general manager; William headed Fisher Body; and Lawrence headed Cadillac. Since selling out and amassing a fortune estimated at between $200 and $500 million, the Fishers had ached for something more. So, they set up Fisher and Company, their own personal investment firm, when Fred got a "hot tip" from a shrewd operator. The guy was looking for a mark to sell his stock to and after all, seven rough hewn and rich "mechanics" from Ohio must have been the best looking target in the world back then!

"Buy Baldwin Locomotive" was the tip, and being new to the stock market, the Fishers thought it looked as good as anything else. So they bought and, when it didn't go up as promised, they bought some more, and it still sagged! Eventually, the Fishers discovered they'd been buying Baldwin stock from the very source who tipped them—and the tipster, representing a pool and counting on the Fishers' ignorance, had unloaded all of their Baldwin stock on their victims and even shorted his position! The smug operator figured when the Fishers found out, they'd panic and unload their supply, which by then was so large that their selling would cause the stock to plummet, allowing the pool to cover its shorts for a song. But that's not what happened—the Fishers weren't just Motortown moguls.

The Fishers aggressively bought more Baldwin than ever, and gradually it started climbing. Wall Street was frantic over their bold move, but eventually others, like **Arthur Cutten**, also a newcomer on the Street, followed. The more they bought, the higher the stock zoomed—and it zoomed from $92 in 1926 to $233 in 1927. When it broke 15 points—because of Baldwin's president's claim that the stock wasn't worth $130—the Fishers kept their cool (they could afford to, really) and hired an engineer who "discovered" the stock was actually worth $350 per share! The Fishers kept buying and prompted the public's buying again, too, and the stock hit a new high of $265. Those who sold short lost millions.

After their wild introduction to Wall Street, the Fishers won coup after coup and became Wall Street's underdogs. They bought Texas Corp. at 50, and it went to 74; Richfield Oil at 25, and it went to 56. Everything they touched turned to gold, it seemed. They played for high stakes and paid what they had for a stock they wanted—and in this way, they helped bolster the climbing prices of the bull market. They flirted with Wall Street's biggest names, operated in pools with William Durant, and socialized with House of Morgan partners—they were taken in by Wall Street's finest as if they'd always been around.

But the Crash changed all that. In no time, the Fishers' paper profits were wiped out, but their original $100 million-plus fortune was still intact—more than enough on which to live like kings in Detroit. So they sold out, and, with their fortune, they quietly retreated to Detroit to become local legends. They lived charitable lives: They gave the Fisher branch to the YMCA, provided money to start the Sarah Fisher Infant's Home and built an annex for the care of foundling children. They lived cultured lives: Charles was a notorious arts patron; the youngest brother Howard became a yachtsman popular in the Great Lakes yachting circles; and Fred built a 236-foot yacht. They lived re-spectable lives: They built the Fisher Building, and Charles became a director of the National Bank of Detroit and a lay trustee of the University of Notre

Dame. And they lived simple lives—each of the seven brothers had his night to visit their elderly mother every night of the week.

The Fishers dropped from sight, except for sporadic news bits—like resignations from their GM posts and obituaries—beginning with Fred in 1941. And they probably liked it that way, since they were notoriously press-shy. But none of the articles written about them following their Wall Street departure makes any serious mention of their Detroit lives. Wall Street, ever self-centered, was as biased as ever and failed to recognize that the Fishers, while leaving the Street behind, had quit while they were ahead and that that was as much an achievement as doubling your wealth in the market—or going down with your ship.

The Fishers turned their backs on the flash and glamour of the Street, the ego, the adrenaline, and the roll of the dice. They had accomplished what they had set out to accomplish and more. When the game got tough, they recognized it and quit. There are an awful lot of others you can see in these pages, and for that matter through modern history, who would have done well to learn this lesson from the Fishers—especially in the modern era when so many money-hungry Wall Streeters are getting caught in their own traps. Just look at the Hunt Brothers, Ivan Boesky, Mike Milken and most recently, Donald Trump. . . . (Note: The Fisher brothers are no relation to the author).

JOHN J. RASKOB

PIONEER OF CONSUMER FINANCE

When John Raskob started buying stock in an infant General Motors, he did so with the simple intent of finding a safe outlet for his modest savings—but he got more than he bargained for. A savvy numbers man for E.I. duPont de Nemours and Company, Raskob, described in Henry Clews' *Twenty-eight Years in Wall Street*, became a GM vice president, director, and chairman of its finance committee. En route, "the man who has been called the financial genius of GM," according to the *New York Times*, helped build GM into one of America's greatest industrial concerns.

Raskob's 30-year GM career began suddenly in 1915 when he and his boss, Pierre duPont, were found to hold a block of shares that were vital to a battle for control between GM founder **William Durant** and GM's bank syndicate-financiers. Instead of simply voting, Raskob took control of the situation, proposing: "Why not allow each group to nominate seven directors for the stockholders they represent and duPont to name three, making a board of seventeen directors?" His proposal was accepted, and he became a GM director, and his boss, chairman of the board.

Straightforward, great with numbers, and Wall Street–smart, Raskob used his newfound power to expand GM, launching a major expansion program immediately after World War I. To finance the plan, he funneled some $50 million of duPont money into the firm and sold large blocks of GM stock to **J.P. Morgan**. While Durant wished GM to be entirely independent of bankers, Raskob knew a corporation was nothing without Wall Street connections.

In order to make an automobile revolution possible, Raskob revamped the car-payment system to accommodate the customer. In 1919, he popularized one of today's most common financing methods—the installment plan—for cars, forming the General Motors Acceptance Corporation, which allowed in-house credit for dealers and customers. The installment plan had previously been used for small-ticket items, but Raskob was the first to propose it for big-ticket items. At first, he met with opposition.

Raskob said his installment plan "was opposed by bankers, who saw in it only an incentive for extravagance. It was opposed by manufacturers because they thought people would buy automobiles instead of their products." Ultimately, the plan won everyone's favor. The popularization of installment sales as a mechanism for the purchase of expensive items singularly justifies Raskob's place in the history of American finance. The phenomenon would soon be applied to capital goods of all kinds—tractors, tools, appliances, and all of the big-ticket, almost infrastructure-like items that brought power to America's middle class in the 20th century. It is difficult to envision life today without consumer financing by big industrial producers. Raskob was the pioneer.

Optimistic and genial, Raskob also turned GM's finance department upside down as its finance chairman for eight years. He pushed for plump and prompt dividend payments, believing this would increase the value of the stock. Of course, he wasn't the first to see the importance of dividends. What made him different, however, was that he saw stockholders as potential customers, which they were. Any stockholder would be likely to believe in GM and buy its products.

He pushed just as hard to increase the number of stockholders. Of course, this had another effect. Companies had previously viewed public shareholders as a necessary evil, part of the after-burden of raising capital in a public stock sale. Many companies still do. But Raskob's other vision of them, as a constituency of value, pioneered their value for other firms. While few firms today value their shareholders for the potential to sell them products, many firms do value their shareholders and cater to their interests—a direct follow-through from Raskob's vision. During his term as chairman, he realized all his goals: multiplying the number of GM's stockholders by 14, its annual earnings by 18 and its sales ten-fold.

Raskob also got a little carried away with his overall finance-based consumerism. In a 1929 article he wrote for *Ladies Home Journal*, he suggested that people could have riveting results, similar to those he had achieved, by setting aside a mere $15 per month, then investing it in common stocks and reinvesting the dividends. This simple method, he professed, could make everyone rich, producing $80,000 within 20 years. When the Crash came, however, Raskob abandoned his plan, which had featured him as the peoples' financial advisor.

A small, compact man with a hard, sharp face, intense eyes, receding hairline, and an aquiline nose, he looked a little like Robert Duvall. Born in 1879, Raskob was the son and grandson of Alsatian cigar makers in Lockport, New York. While Raskob was a teenager, his father died, and he quit high school to support his mother and brother. Starting as a secretary, he began his 44-year career with duPont at 21. At age 27, in 1906, Raskob married. He and his wife had 13 children. That's a lot of children and an unlucky number: He and his wife later separated.

By the 1920s, Raskob had gained a giant reputation—so that any positive statement he made regarding GM caused the stock to jump which was great for duPont. Raskob had pushed duPont's investment to between 40 percent and 50 percent of GM's outstanding shares. When the Crash came, duPont and Raskob offset their modest losses by using the "wash sale" method, then favored by so many Wall Street bigwigs, like **Charles Mitchell**. Raskob sold $ 14 million of his securities to duPont, while at the same time buying $14 million of duPont's securities. Both were able to establish paper losses of about $3 million on their income tax returns and within two months both regained their securities via another two-way sale which reversed the initial transactions. Today this would be illegal.

A fierce speculator, Raskob—again, like most of his colleagues at the time—participated in stock pools to make quick profits. The most famous pool he participated in earned him about $300,000 in a week—with an initial investment of $ 1 million. The pool, managed by **Mike Meehan**, operated in one of the market's hottest issues, RCA, and bought and sold nearly 1.5 million shares with a total cash turnover of over $140 million! But in none of this part of his life was Raskob an innovator or important to the evolution of finance.

Raskob left GM as its chairman in 1928 to pursue politics with the Democratic Party. Why anyone would leave a successful business career that did much for the public in the commercial world in exchange for a life in politics is beyond comprehension. But he did. Public service, he said, allowed successful businessmen like him to pay his debt back to society. This author is baffled at the notion that successful businessmen have a debt to society. I thought criminals have debts to society, and politicians seem a lot more like criminals to me than business people. But in the topsy-turvy world of the 1920s, that may have been less clear to Raskob. Yet, perhaps, he learned the lesson. A decade later, he left politics and fell back on speculation and other investments and increasingly dropped from the public spotlight. He died of a heart attack at 71 in 1950. But his consumer financing lives on long after his death—the ultimate junction of Wall Street and Main Street— financing the purchases of items most folks couldn't afford to finance for themselves, so more items are in more hands. Raskob owed no debt to society. It was quite the other way around.

ARTHUR W. CUTTEN

BULLY THE PRICE, THEN CUT'N RUN

One of America's greatest speculators bullied markets with his buying, first in Chicago's grain market and later on Wall Street. This is a tactic that many have used before and since, but none have done it better. Today, operators have to disguise this tactic or go to jail. Arthur Cutten was the last of the big market manipulators.

Cutten frequently cornered his securities, borrowing heavily to play, then using his huge speculative profits to pay his debts. Whereas many operators borrow money, win a few rounds, then borrow more against their profits, Cutten always returned to a debt-free condition after a stock or commodity maneuver. This allowed him to fight off the 1929 Crash and Depression while smaller speculators were swatted like flies. Henry Clews', *Twenty-eight Years in Wall Street* asserts that, despite his incredible skill, his love for making money and his fortune estimated between $50 and $100 million when he died in 1936, the fragile, childless little man once remarked, "If I had a son I would keep him far away from the market. I would not let him touch it with a ten-foot pole, because there are so many wrecks down there!"

Another reason Canadian-born Cutten is of interest is that he is one of the few wild speculators of all time that never wound up a market wreck. Sure, he had a few losses early in his career, but he always about-faced—a rare trait—and profited later on. Arriving in Chicago at age 20 in 1890 with a bicycle and $60, Cutten worked on the Board of Trade. At 26, he traded corn for A.S. White & Co., scalping for himself on the side. When he had saved enough to trade on his own, Cutten delved into grain, faithfully following the fundamentals—weather, insects, transportation and statistics—elements he considered key to his market position. In just 10 years, the 37-year-old was married, a millionaire and internationally known in world grain markets.

Known for his tenacity and speculative acumen, Cutten turned a $4 million loss into a $15 million profit in his greatest grain coup. Buying wheat at $1 per bushel—while slowly and systematically concealing his purchases—he bulled wheat to over $2, accumulating millions of bushels. But while he was sunning in Miami—as wheat continued to rise—all hell broke loose! A bear raid, reputedly brought on by **Jesse Livermore**, who had been shadowing Cutten's moves, caused wheat to slide 16 cents in a few hours! Though Cutten was out some $4 million, he didn't abandon his position. Instead, he held on and increased his position, pushing it back up as the panic subsided, en route netting a $15 million profit! That year, he forked over $500,000 in income taxes, the most ever paid in Chicago at that time.

Operating from a small Chicago office, where his name was conspicuously omitted from his door, Cutten ventured to Wall Street in 1926 with $25 million in profits. (It was rumored government reporting requirements drove Cutten from grain.) Once hailed as "the leader of the largest and most influential group operating in the market today," Cutten sometimes worked in cahoots with **William Crapo Durant's** bull pools and formed syndicates of his own, but his personal speculations were far more interesting. Virtually unknown for a year, he used his time to become an insider and heavy holder of leading stocks.

He bought his favorites—International Harvester, RCA, Baldwin Locomotive and Standard Oil of Indiana—taking profits on 10–15 point swings, but more often Cutten held his stocks for long-term investment. When his 100,000 shares of Montgomery Ward, for instance, hit a whopping 624, Cutten held tight, even though he had paid between 80 and 100! He saw greater value there.

Later, when Cutten, a sharp dresser, sold his "Story of a Speculator" to *Everybody's* Magazine, he revealed his secrets:

1. Look for long-term investment.
2. Wait for undervalued situations.
3. Study the fundamentals.
4. Accumulate a position slowy.
5. Let the profits run!

But his seemingly easy steps to speculation would never work for the average investor. Most folks don't have the stomach or capital to keep throwing money into a market to push up what they've been buying. The other thing unique to Cutten was his ability, despite this basic strategy, to cut and run, cat-like. He was not only completely aware of his position but of his vulnerabilities—and cat-like, he had a knack for landing on his feet when he fell.

As Cutten's reputation grew, his moves became harder to camouflage, to his dismay—so he started using a dozen different brokers to avoid suspicion. And he didn't stop there. When buying stock, he ordered brokers to sell it back if its price rose too quickly. Buying 50,000 shares and then turning around and unloading most of them to keep the price down is pretty hard to conceal! Regardless of how inconspicuous he tried to be, Cutten stuck out like a sore thumb to the 1935 Senate committee that convicted him of violating the Grain Futures Act and suspended him from trading. Charged with reporting his holdings falsely and concealing his position in 1930 to 1931 to manipulate grain prices, Cutten blamed the inaccuracies on a new secretary. Through countless legal battles, Cutten fought all the way to the Supreme Court where he was finally cleared and restored to grain trading.

The 1929 Crash saw classic Cutten. When the market first turned against him, he lost $50 million and admitted being down to his last $17 million. But rather than digging in his heels, he characteristically turned to the bear side and sold short, winning back his losses. His basic posture of long-term fundamental thinking and big positions is rarely combined with the ability to turn around quickly when things go against the original course of action.

A bizarre story shows how determined Cutten was. Nine robbers once broke into his house, tied up his wife and him, and locked him in a wine vault to smother. "That," he said, "was an unnecessary, futile, and fiendish piece of cruelty." They stole cash, jewelry, and 25 cases of whiskey. Cutten vowed "I'd spend every dollar at my command, if necessary, to put them where they belong—behind the bars!" So, he spent eight years tracking them down and catching and prosecuting every last one of the nine. You didn't mess with big Arthur Cutten. He played to win, and he won. He was unique in his ability to be good at both long-term investing and short-term trading. Most folks can do one or the other. Cutten could do it all.

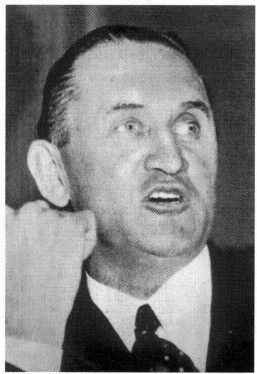

Saturday Evening Post, *1939*

BERNARD E. "SELL'EM BEN" SMITH

THE RICH CHAMELEON

If you were to envision one person to represent the old Wall Street—the wild and wooly, pre-regulation Wall Street—it would be Bernard "Sell' Em Ben" Smith, who died in 1961. While making his own indelible mark on Wall Street as "the market's greatest bear operator," Smith embodied the most outrageous qualities of Wall Street's most talked-about characters. He was as opportunistic as **John "Bet-A-Million" Gates**; as quick to make and lose fortunes as **Jesse Livermore**; and as flexible as **Joe Kennedy**. Ultimately, he died among the wealthier of them.

Smith's legend—and his catchy nickname—revolves around the 1929 Crash when he sold short as the market collapsed, raking in some $10 million, according to Henry Clews in *Twenty-eight Years in Wall Street* Previously, he had never been known as a bear raider; instead, he joined and even managed some of the largest speculative bull pools in the late 1920s. But when he heard news of the Crash while flying toward Canada, he quickly reversed his airplane—and trading methods—and called in orders to sell his securities. As soon as he reached Wall Street, he burst through his office doors shouting, "Sell 'em! They aren't worth anything!" Hence, a legend was made.

Before becoming a legend, Smith, like many other great Wall Streeters, lived through the rags-to-riches-to-rags-to-riches story—about as many times as Jesse Livermore. Born to Irish immigrants in 1888 in Manhattan, Sell 'Em Ben quit school at age 12, when his dad died, to be a delivery boy for a haberdashery. Back then, working at a ridiculously young age with scant schooling was typical. He next worked for a stockbroker, where he was regarded as a "diamond in the rough," marking quotations on the board and building his first fortune. By age 15, he'd turned $100 into a whopping $35,000 by acting on market tips and using good timing.

Within a year Smith was broke again, wiped out by the panic of 1903—but he bounced back, making another $15,000 before falling flat on his face yet again. Disgusted with Wall Street and an unpredictable bank roll, he stayed clear of the market for the next decade, first driving a Model T cross-country, then working as a copper-mine mucker, wartime ambulance driver and cartire distributor. For a short while, he was even a spectacular car salesman making deals with the wealthy, like **James Stillman** and **J.P. Morgan** (who actually died before taking delivery). But eventually Smith returned to Wall Street and made another fortune in time to cash in on the Crash.

As wild and racy as the times he lived in, Sell 'Em Ben flew anywhere at the blink of an eye. He raced automobiles, once racing back and forth nonstop to Montreal in 18 hours—about 1,000 miles at about 55 mph, which was pretty darn fast back then. He loved to shoot craps, play checkers and insult friends—yet, in his own little way, he was a Puritan, never touching tobacco, alcohol, coffee or tea. He was most famous for being a practical joker who played the part of a loud, obnoxious swaggering grouch. Yet friends would tell you it was just a farce—he was really a pussycat who loved to roar like a lion. One telltale sign: After proposing to his wife in 1918 on a Paris boulevard bench overlooking the Seine, he battled Paris officials to buy the bench and bring it home. He placed it in a prominent place in their backyard. Not just a puritan, but a romantic puritan.

Of modest height, with icy-blue eyes and broad shoulders, sporting a wrinkled overcoat and wilted collars, the image Smith conveyed on the Street was illustrated by what the press wrote about him. He was called "The Great Bear of the Street"—the most merciless of them all. The more he shorted stocks, leaving companies in shambles with worthless stock, the more he was viewed as a public villain—Wall Street's most ruthless operator. It's true that he shorted stocks without regard for the firm or the people involved with it—but so did lots of folks then. What really earned him the spotlight and raised eyebrows on the Street was his driving the stock of a threshing machine outfit from 500 to about 16, shorting it rigorously while the market bottomed out in 1932. It just so happened that the firm's principal investor and chairman of the board was Smith's own father-in-law, and Sell 'Em Ben's maneuvers ruined him!

Supposedly, Smith later gave his father-in-law about $1 million to make up for the damage.

When short selling became the potential scapegoat on which to blame the entire dismal economic condition, Smith was naturally the very first of the bears to be subpoenaed by the famous U.S. Senate Committee on Banking and Currency. Cocky and defiant, Smith strolled into the hearing room chuckling with reporters, telling them he was happy to give the committee "an earful." Smith did exactly that, relating in detail the way the big operators worked and how it was the bulls, not the bears, who precipitated the Crash. He told them about stock pools and that ethical conduct was seldom enforced on the stock exchange, but when it came to talking about himself. Smith was no stooge. When asked, "You are known as a big bear raider, aren't you?" Smith replied slyly, "Nobody ever called me that to my face!" Smith skulked out of the hearing room blame-free.

When Uncle Sam passed the Securities and Exchange Act of 1934, thereby creating the SEC, Smith laughed, "That law was long overdue—people could get away with murder in the market." Sell 'Em Ben was all for the law and realized an era was over. "I saw the handwriting on the wall. I had made money. I got out. The Exchange was way behind the times. It was supposed to regulate itself—it did, but never enough. A man could make millions literally, you know as well as I, without putting up a dollar of his own. It was too good to last. The market will never be the same again."

After bidding his goodbye, Sell 'Em Ben wasted no time in covering all his shorts and promising never to pound the market again. He abandoned his bear instincts for good on President Franklin D. Roosevelt's inauguration day in March, 1933,—it was no coincidence, since he was very much persona grata in Roosevelt's White House, a major Roosevelt financier. Unlike **Mike Meehan**, for example, who refused to acknowledge a new, reformed Wall Street—or **Jesse Livermore**, who wasn't able to kick up one more last fortune—Sell 'Em Ben stayed as flexible as ever. He knew when to strike and reversed his methods to play under the New Deal.

Now he plunged into gold, uttering, "Tell 'em I'm a bull now—a bull on gold!" and caught the 1934 rise when gold rose some 70 percent. His credo was that he was able to make a buck from any and all circumstances—and he did. In the following years, he invested in a Canadian cracker company and a Bendix washing machine (after his wife tested it and gave it her OK). Later, he became a respectable investment banker, joining Thomson and McKinnon and underwriting immensely successful Grumman Aircraft. A man for all seasons.

Sell 'Em Ben Smith was a dazzling operator who knew his limits and, most of all, knew when to strike. Although he personified the volatile days leading up to and surrounding the Crash, Smith was able to leave the old days behind and kick up his heels with the New Deal. In his later years, he lived in quiet respectability, retired and rich. More than any man I've encountered, the broad span of his life reflects the evolution of Wall Street during this era.

Is there a lesson to be learned from Smith's life? Surely, it is the lesson that flexibility pays. To make it and keep it, you can't be too rigidly adherent to any one investment religion. How will the world be different 40 years from today? Who knows? While it is impossible to envision the distant future, it is clear that, were Smith alive, he would change once more to reflect the present as it evolves into the next century.

BERNARD BARUCH

HE WON AND LOST, BUT KNEW
WHEN TO QUIT

How do you separate the man from the myth? You don't if it's Bernard Baruch. For a man whose Wall Street fortune flourished by ignoring trendy investment ideas and "hot tips," Baruch was surprisingly solicitous of his image, cultivating the press to build his reputation as a savvy man in the know.

Herbert Swope, the journalist who helped conjure Baruch's highly-publicized character, once openly speculated "whether his reputation is wholly deserved." But beneath the glitz and glory was a street-smart speculator who rightly boasted of amassing $100,000 for each of his thirty-two years. When speaking of his methods in his best-selling autobiography, *My Own Story*, the lover of Greek and Latin defined "speculator" by quoting the Latin word "speculari," meaning to spy out and observe. With keen observation and a shrewd ear, Baruch sought out and took advantage of opportunities, setting his stage for success.

Baruch came from humble origins in Camden, South Carolina, where his father, mother and three brothers lived in a two-story frame house. His father, a Confederate Army veteran, moved the family to New York in 1880, when Baruch was 10. With an early intent to study medicine, Baruch, at 14, entered the College of the City of New York. A political economy class, where he learned the law of supply and demand, sparked his interest in finance.

Baruch, a towering 6 foot 3 and sporting a pair of pince-nez glasses, pursued Wall Street in 1891. Due to his mom's efforts (and strategically-placed connections), "Bernie" became an office boy and runner for A. A. Housman & Company, earning $5 per week. He later learned to appreciate "connections" as a way of ensuring positive press to pander to his ego.

By the age of 27, a junior partner at Housman's firm, Baruch had begun speculating on his own, earning tidy sums and immediately blowing them. After carefully observing a sugar company's prospects, however, Baruch made his first major hit of $60,000. Now a well-to-do young gentleman, he married, launching a family of two daughters and one son, who probably never received the degree of attention from him reporters did.

As his success pyramided, he came to view tips as sucker-bait. Baruch, whose biggest career disappointment was never owning a railroad, went broke once again buying stock in America's largest liquor firm after following one of those "hot tips." Afterwards, he bitterly snarled, "The longer I operated in Wall Street, the more distrustful I became of tips and 'inside' information of every kind."

Suspicious of generally accepted wisdom, Baruch viewed tips circulating around the public as a measure of the public's misperceptions. He surmised if the shoeshine boy (most likely Wall Street's own **Patrick Bologna**) knew about a great deal, you could bet others were aware of it too, so it must be overpriced and couldn't work out. On that premise, Baruch—who struck out on his own in 1903, rarely managing others' money—ardently warned investors to "beware of barbers, beauticians, waiters—of anyone—bringing gifts of 'inside' information or 'tips.' "Instead, he credited his 1929 pre-Crash exit from stocks to seeing that too much of the public was bullish, so the market couldn't keep going up. According to Baruch, this crowd-watching bent came from the philosophical grounding he received from Charles Mackay's 1841 classic, *Extraordinary Popular Delusions and the Madness of Crowds.*

After the fact, and again to promote his public image, Baruch wanted everyone to know that he had foreseen the Crash—escaping financial disaster by literally weeks. He trumpeted, "I think that the depression of 1929 was due more to a world of madness and delusion than anything else." Baruch sold several times in 1928, "feeling that a break was imminent," but after returning from hunting in Scotland, he decided to sell everything he could. He was at least partly lucky in his timing. The market easily could have crashed while he was still tucked away in the Scottish woods.

Baruch's philosophies were formed from many mistakes, but the lessons he learned were taken to heart. Skeptical of definitive rules, his autobiography described 10 guidelines—the fruits of his experience:

1. Speculating is a full-time job.
2. Beware of anyone giving inside information.

3. Before buying a security, discover everything possible regarding the company's management, competitors, earnings and growth-possibilities.
4. Don't try to buy at the bottom and sell at the top. "This can't be done—except by liars."
5. Learn to cut losses quickly and cleanly—and don't expect to always be right.
6. Limit the number of securities bought, so that portfolios can be managed easily.
7. Periodically re-appraise all investments to check whether prospects have changed.
8. Study your tax position to know the best time to sell.
9. Never invest everything—always keep some cash in reserve.
10. Don't be a "jack of all investments": Stick to familiar fields.

After 25 years on Wall Street, Baruch left without regret for Washington to offer advice and solicit political power. A lot of this was based on his steady barrage of calls to reporters with advice and comments for public attribution. A reporter once remarked, "Either Baruch gives lousy advice or nobody takes it." Baruch responded, "I won't admit to the first part of that observation, but I cannot deny the latter." While he had the ear of many and was widely quoted, largely due to his continual public relations efforts, he held little or no formal power. Ultimately he portrayed himself to the media as an "Adviser to Presidents." And clearly he got the ear, if not the nod of FDR. And while Truman heard him out, at least partly perhaps because of the large cash contributions he gave, it is clear Truman viewed him as an "old goat."

Perhaps leaving Wall Street was the best thing Baruch could have done. His money was secure in the bank. Unlike some other opportunistic counterparts, like plungers **Jesse Livermore** and **William Crapo Durant**, who bet their fortunes one too many times when they were just a tad too old and slow to maintain a gunslinger's pace, Baruch's ego may have actually saved him from the financial disaster the others suffered. His ego, which drove him to be "Adviser to Presidents" might have saved him the humility of trying to remain forever "Mr. Big" on Wall Street. Sometimes it's better to quit while you're ahead.

Before his death in 1965, Baruch penned a second book, *The Public Years*, detailing his later years as the "Park Bench Statesman." Written in typical, Baruchian style—simply put, immodest—the man states, "America has always been considered the Land of Opportunity. I cannot say that I have discharged the debt I owe this country for what it has given me, but in good conscience I can say I have tried."

CHAPTER TEN

UNSUCCESSFUL SPECULATORS, WHEELER-DEALERS, AND OPERATORS

THEY GOT WHAT THEY WANTED MOST, AND FAILED

The Unsuccessful Speculators, Wheeler-Dealers and Operators lacked what their successful counterparts had—focus and flexibility. Focus is what drives the driven to win, and keep winning, and put everything in their lives second to the stock market. Flexibility enables the successful to turn their backs on a winning streak when they think it might end, and in fact, to turn their backs on their own egos, and withdraw from a bull market right before it crashes—and abandon old investment techniques when they don't fit the changing times. This becomes clear from the lives depicted in the previous chapter.

Not so for the group who couldn't hang on to their fortunes. Instead of being focused on the stock market, this group was unusually preoccupied with spending the money they were expecting to make or were too busy with wine, women and song. Instead of being flexible, the losers on Wall Street stick to their die-hard ways and, as a result, sink with their ships. Often they stuck to their ways because their egos wouldn't allow them to admit they were wrong, and bend when events trended against them.

James Fisk, F. Augustus Heinze, and Jesse Livermore lacked focus: All three were more concerned with making merry than making money. Fisk totally scandalized Wall Street by partying with actresses in his own opera house office and keeping a mistress who eventually blackmailed him. Ultimately, he died after his scheming mistress' boyfriend (and Fisk's ex-colleague) dealt Fisk a fatal shot to his fat stomach.

Heinze was a brash speculator who got off to a good start, but was later burned when he began burning the candle at both ends. His office doubled as a party cave. During the daytime he worked there, and all night long the bimbos and booze flowed through there. He simply womanized and drank too much and couldn't separate fun from his Wall Street role. He compulsively grew more interested in what his money could buy than in actually making it and as a result, lost everything. Finally, he died an alcoholic's death.

Jesse Livermore was willing to stay flexible, but was unable to focus on his operations. Here too, his excessive drinking and womanizing got in his way, and after booming and busting too many times, he chose another classic version of alcoholic death—he blew his brains out in 1940 in one of the more colorfully sad endings to a Wall Street legend, going down in history as a self-proclaimed failure and Wall Street's last great plunger.

Without focus and flexibility, a whole array of other negative qualities can come into play, including recklessness and fraud. Both the Van Swearingens and Durant were reckless and inflexible by virtue of their unstable operations. They operated via excessive leverage—borrowing compulsively—so when 1929's tough economic times hit, they toppled and couldn't rebuild themselves again. Charles W. Morse, too, was reckless via borrowing, and it led him to desperation and fraud. Yes, he was flexible, always turning to another business when one failed him, but it wasn't enough. Along with Heinze, Morse speculated in copper mining stocks while heading a chain of banks. When the stocks went belly up, so did his banks, and so did he.

Jacob Little was Wall Street's very first full-time operator and, by that factor alone, was a form of exception. His failure had more to do with inexperience than loss of focus or flexibility. He plunged through four fortunes, making lots of enemies who were always trying to squeeze him out of the market and his money. Ironically, he lost his final fortune because of bad timing; he was caught extended going into a bull market, so he had to cover his shorts at astronomical prices.

Successful Speculators, Wheeler-Dealers, and Operators were mostly homebodies and led fairly boring personal lives; wild on Wall Street but quiet at night. The Unsuccessful group tried to be wild whenever they felt like it, and they felt like it a lot. They were ego-driven and vain. They gambled, drank, and often would not compromise their positions. They lacked foresight in predicting the outcome of their own actions—whether it had to do with their wives, children, friends, or predicting troubled economic times. When they were out of their environment, like Livermore in a post-reform market, they were all but useless. And they didn't know when to quit, as William Durant had. Unlike those who kept their fortunes, they usually liked their luxuries a little too much. You have to ask yourself which is more important to you — success or the things money can buy? For the Unsuccessful Speculators, the answer was clear, and they paid the price to get what they wanted most.

Henry Clews, Twenty-eight Years in Wall Street, 1887

JACOB LITTLE

THE FIRST TO DO SO MUCH

I n his heyday, Jacob Little was heralded as a wild stock gambler—the first of his kind in the financial community. He was the first to operate on Wall Street full-time, the first to speculate aggressively and flamboyantly—and the first to initiate short selling. You might say he was Wall Street's very own Evel Knievel, doing what no other man thought possible—or reasonable. Back in the 1830s, wild speculating was frowned upon by the market's gatekeepers, which only encouraged Little—and he quickly made room for a new breed of operator. Though he had no mentors or prior scalawags to look up to, Little plunged his way through Wall Street and four fortunes. He ultimately died poor but left a tradition upheld over the years by spiritul descendants like **Daniel Drew** and **Jesse Livermore**.

Little started his career as a clerk for Jacob Barker, a well-to-do merchant who also brokered stocks on the side. In those days, at a time when the world was almost exclusively agricultural, there was a lot more interest in trading commodities than in trading stocks. Little learned by watching and doing for Barker and, in 1835, started his own brokerage operation—just in time for the peak of the stock market and the ensuing Panic of 1837. Little reasoned that investors should be able to profit regardless of whether prices were rising or falling, and with short selling, someone like him could make a tremendous killing in a bear market. It was here that he would make a fortune and an outrageous reputation as the American innovator of short selling. Since he was its innovator, he set its terms—ones favorable to him—which initially included an unusually long 60- or 90-day delivery period on stocks sold to other unsuspecting investors. That gave him time to drive the prices down before the required delivery, buy them back cheaply and pocket the spread.

The *New York Times* called Little a "gambler in stocks" who "always bet they were worthless." Having made the "bet," Little would make sure he won it by "breaking the public impression that the stocks had any value at all." To do this, he sold his targeted stock—stock he did not own—at steeply discounted prices, raising the public's suspicions and causing hordes of stockholders to panic and unload what they thought was worthless stock. Often, he'd quicken the process by planting false and damaging rumors about the company in major newspapers, a practice that grew in popularity even up until the introduction of federal securities regulations in the 1930s.

After the stock had fallen, Little bought back the shares to cover his short. If a good thing is good, two are twice as good, so Little not only bought back the shorted shares but took a long position as well at unusually cheap prices created by the panic-inducing activities of his shorting. With his shorts covered and a long position in place, he somehow drove the stock to unrealistically high prices by exactly the reverse tactic of what he had used to bang it down. Most of this fell on relatively unsuspecting market suckers who had never seen such tactics before on any broad scale. Yes, none of this would seem particularly radical in just a few decades, but for his time, it was innovation.

As a master speculator, Little was curt, cold, and distant. His life revolved around his speculative schemes—and nothing else. He was utterly obsessed with the market, and made a habit of personally delivering all the stocks he ever sold and keeping all his own books and records. Unlike others who dabbled in the market now and then, Little was far from being the social climber, so his colleagues at first laughed at him, then loathed him—and ultimately, feared him.

Regardless of what anyone thought of him, Little always displayed the ultimate cool. When he found himself in a bind, he remained astoundingly calm and looked for the loophole that would let him escape. Take the case of Erie Railroad, for example. Little was short the stock when a group of bulls aimed at giving him "the squeeze." They intended to drive the stock up until it was so high, his short position would be bought back in—sort of out from under him. It was during the railroad boom of the mid-19th century, when the Erie and other lines were not only traded in America, but in London as well, and here is what happened.

In 1840, Little had started a bear raid on Erie stock, unloading large blocks on "sellers options," with an amazingly long 6 to 12 months for delivery. Meanwhile, a group of bulls, including various Erie directors, set out to corner him by buying up outstanding shares, pushing up the price and thinking they then could force Little to cover his shorts on their terms, pushing the price up further and making their corner profitable. But Little outfoxed the bulls, with an escape hatch they hadn't envisioned. Years earlier Erie had issued convertible bonds in London. At the rising prices created by the group's cornering activities, the convertibles would be "in the money" and convertible into common shares on a one-for-one basis. Little went to the London market, bought the converts, and covered his shorts with them. And, he lived to play another day. He had squeezed out of their corner with forgotten convertibles overseas. It was a trick that future shorters including Drew, **Jay Gould** and **James Fisk** would attempt to replay with mixed success for decades.

In the spirit of a great plunger, the tall, slender, and slightly stooped Little went boom and bust four times before going down for the count in 1857. In this respect he was also a pioneer in a path that many others would follow: Most notably, Livermore—the last of the great plungers. Before Little's last and final blunder, he'd always picked up the pieces and started out anew, even making good his former debts.

But this time—the fifth and final time—was different. Ironically, his failure occurred at the onset of the 1857 panic—a time when bears usually reap their greatest profit. But Little was caught extended going into the last rally just before the crash. His timing was off, and he found himself in a rising market—instead of a falling one—and he couldn't cover his shorts "for cheap." Ultimately, he was caught short 100,000 shares of Erie as it rose, and he went from $2 million in the black to about $10 million in the red in December, 1856. Within a few months, Erie reversed course and finally bottomed out, falling from about 63 to 8. But all that happened after it was too late for Little. He had been wiped out before the stock hit its peak. Had he been able to hold on just a little longer, he would have ended up fine. But Little suffered the fate of short sellers in that it isn't sufficient to be right in the longterm as a shorter. You have to be right, right now.

After his failure, Little was a pathetic figure on the Street, trading a measly five shares at a time and being the butt of jokes. He couldn't quit the game, but he couldn't hack it either. He watched Daniel Drew step in and take his place as king manipulator. Drew ungraciously rubbed Little's nose in his failure, saying the only mistake Little ever made was being born 20 years too early. He had a wife but no children. And he was lonely, miserable, and sickly for the last few years of his life. He had little to do with Wall Street in the final five years of his life, but—perhaps delirious—before dying at age 68 in 1865, he murmured his last words, "I am going up. Who will go with me?" Was he talking about heaven, or stocks? Probably the latter.

JAMES FISK

IF YOU KNEW JOSIE LIKE HE KNEW JOSIE, YOU'D BE DEAD TOO!

He captured God-fearing men's tempers, wide-eyed ladies' love, and unsuspecting investors' money—all with exceptional ease. Diamond-studded stock-waterer Jim Fisk was an operator in business and pleasure. Short and rotund, Fisk was colorful, corrupt, crafty, and captivating—1860's America loved him and hated him, but always passionately. A gaudy, infamous robber baron, Fisk earned his lavish reputation during a mere seven-year Wall Street stint—plenty of time to shroud himself in scandal.

Ever opportunistic, Fisk began his career with luck, good timing, and ambition. At 31, the talkative Vermonter squirmed into a deal for the Street's king conniver **Daniel Drew**, The Great Bear, receiving a hefty commission and Drew's blessing when the deal was done. Fortunately for Fisk, Drew took to him, supplying him with an old friend's son as a partner, and setting them up in their own brokerage firm, Fisk & Belden. Soon, Fisk—a guy who'd slap men on the back and ladies on the butt—became known as Wall Street's jolliest operator, fueled by whiskey and cigars.

Soon, the stogy-smoking Fisk learned Drew's treacherous ways firsthand, profiting from his mentor's commissions and inside information. As Drew's broker, Fisk played in Drew's 1866 bear raid on Erie Railroad. They dumped Erie stock, sold Erie short, and sent its stock plummeting. After buying Erie back at bargain prices, they stuffed their pockets with profits and laughed as adversary **Cornelius Vanderbilt** kissed a million good-bye. Now Fisk, a peddler's son, was a millionaire—and flaunted it. He donned a large shirt-front diamond atop flashy fabric and bought a Boston mansion for his wife, while taking on the 22-year-old "actress" Josie Mansfield as his Manhattan mistress—and laughing steadily. He was a roly-poly ball of fun for everyone.

The next year, he joined Drew and the silent-but-deadly **Jay Gould** in a hair-raising fight against Vanderbilt for control of Drew's meal ticket, Erie. In the ruckus, they were temporarily banished to Jersey City by Vanderbilt's legal maneuvers. But, whereas the elderly Drew and the ever-somber Gould wanted to get back home to Manhattan, Jersey City was just another party for Fisk; he took an entire hotel floor and mistress Josie in one hand, pickled oysters and champagne in the other. Chubby Jimmy partied to his heart's content. It wasn't until Gould got the trio's legal rap fixed in Albany that the party ended.

Upon their return to Manhattan, Fisk shifted his alliance to Gould. The two teamed up seeking revenge against Drew, who, without his partners' approval or knowledge, reconciled with Vanderbilt. Too bad for Drew—he was about to get a taste of his own gut-wrenching medicine. Fisk and Gould, Erie directors, issued new Erie stock mercilessly, printing on Erie's own printing press. How Fisk cherished "freedom of the press"!

But he who takes a snake for a bedfellow must be prepared to be bitten. In Gould's most famous fiasco, an attempt to corner gold, he gave Fisk the fang. The scheme was basically to keep President Ulysses Grant from selling federal gold while they bought out all the market's supply, driving the price sky-high. Fisk's role, as the roly-poly ball of fun, was to wine and dine the President. Tough job. So with a twist of his finely-twined mustache, Fisk courted Grant with champagne and nights at the opera. But Grant was not so easily controlled.

As Gould moved in the market, Fisk, with unshakable faith, followed suit, buying gold right until the very end, when on Friday, September 13, 1869, the truly independent Grant freed $5 million in federal gold, sending the price plummeting. Shifty-eyed Gould, however, was forewarned of Grant's intentions, and while he appeared to be buying, he was secretly selling the majority of his $50 million in gold and finally turned successfully to the short side of the market as gold continued its tumble.

In the end, Gould earned $11 million, and Fisk was wiped out on paper. Sadly and dishonestly, Fisk reneged on his moral obligation to complete the trades he had executed. He refuted his purchases, leaving his partner William Belden holding the bag—and plumb broke. Believed to be Friday's co-mastermind, Fisk sought refuge in Erie's headquarters—a four-story, marble opera hall seating 2,600, and protected by corrupt Tammany Hall policemen.

From his mighty fortress, Fisk yelled at reporters, "A fellow can't have a little innocent fun without everybody raising a halloo and going wild!" But Fisk's fun was rarely innocent.

Fisk continued to go wild. He fought numerous lawsuits, juggled multiple enterprises—railways and steamboats—and made a fatal acquaintance with debonair socialite Edward Stokes. He and Stokes conspired to milk the Brooklyn Oil Refinery under the guise of granting it many of Erie's oil contracts. Meanwhile, in 1870, via Fisk, Stokes discovered Fisk's floozy, Josie—while Fisk discovered the excitement of show business, becoming sidetracked by running posh productions at his "Fisk's Opera Hall."

Now this was fun. But it wasn't really serious. Ever the flamboyant social outsider, Fisk's shows were shunned by high class New Yorkers. But Fisk was Fisk, and fun was fun, and the most fun were the scantily-clad showgirls prancing about his office. While Fisk was diverted by his bought beauties, Josie was largely back-burnered, and became bored and belligerent. As there is no wrath greater than a woman scorned, Fisk ignored the dangerous romantic liaison brewing between Josie and Stokes.

Josie, bored with her furnished, four-story brownstone, five servants, and free rides on the Erie and enthralled with Stokes' romantic fervor, teamed with Stokes in a blackmail scheme! Their efforts centered around threats to publish the many love letters Fisk had earlier sent Josie, in a 19th-century moral equivalent to today's palimony. Josie figured Fisk owed her and she wanted to collect some $20,000, though she upped the figure as the legal threat mounted.

As Fisk finally figured out the dime-store novel scenario he faced, New York papers were washing his dirty laundry in public. Outraged and spiteful, Fisk took Erie's oil contracts away from Stokes' Brooklyn Oil Refinery income source and destroyed his reputation. In the uproar, the real power in Fisk's life, Jay Gould, became embarrassed by the situation. Somber, ever unhedonistic and very unforgiving, Gould asked for Fisk's resignation from Erie when the publicity began adversely affecting Erie stock. Fisk was publicly destroyed.

But it was the love of Josie, or lack thereof, that physically destroyed Fisk. Ultimately, Josie's friend Stokes, embittered and enraged at how this scheme panned out, took his frustration out on Fisk, following him and eventually shooting him in his rotund, roly-poly belly. Fisk died the next day, January 7, 1872. Amazingly, despite the massive and flamboyant legend Fisk left behind, he was only 36 at his death.

Despite his faults, the scoundrel was genuinely missed for his promotional, fun-loving ways. Even Vanderbilt called upon Fisk's spirit, via the occult, for market tips. Endeared as much as he was despised, Fisk epitomized the zany, scandalous part of a society where freedom of action was valued above fairness or rules. The lesson of his life? Those who are interested in business for business' sake, as was Gould, are often lifetime commercial successes. But men like Fisk, who are mainly in business for ego gratification and hedonistic benefits money can buy—wine, women and song—rarely can keep their focus on the nuts and bolts of business on a continuous and never-ending basis, and themselves end up skewered by the "Goulds" of life.

WILLIAM CRAPO DURANT

HALF VISIONARY BUILDER, HALF WILD GAMBLER

When considering William Durant, it's key to recall "Prudence" was not his middle name—"Crapo" was. Likened to Halley's Comet, the overly-optimistic creator of General Motors (GM) blazed a trail through the auto industry in the early 1900s with exuberance and flair, only to fizzle back to earth. The notorious wheeler-dealer simply knew no moderation. He was venture-wise and prudence-poor. Durant began his tumultuous, rags-to-riches-to-rags life in New Bedford, Massachusetts in 1861. A high school dropout, Durant started his own insurance agency at age 21. At 40, he was beckoned toward the burgeoning auto industry after making a million as a dazzling buggy salesman in Flint, Michigan.

Forming GM was a series of whirlwind acquisitions, beginning with Buick Motor. The small spare cigar-smoker was handed control of the fledgling firm in 1904—when it could no longer operate without help—largely because he was a prominent citizen of Flint, Michigan (Buick's headquarters). Durant, sitting on Buick's board of directors, immediately increased capital stock from $75,000 to $300,000 and expanded production. Always the gambler and always the former insurance salesman at heart, Durant sold over 1,100 cars at a New York auto show before Buick had produced even 40! Soon, he was running the world's largest auto factory. With Buick now secure, Durant successfully created GM in September by the seat of his pants—without publicity or bankers. Durant slyly prepared for a colleague to incorporate GM as his holding company. Then, keeping his name secret, he arranged for a puppet GM board to acquire Buick for $3.75 million of stock and $1,500 in cash. All the while Durant controlled both firms. He financed it with "patents and applications against which the common stock could be issued." Only by year's end was it commonly known that Durant had spearheaded the GM consolidation.

Next, Durant moved on Olds Motor Works—buying Oldsmobile for just over $3 million. Though scorned for paying so much—after all, Buick, America's leading auto maker, was purchased for $3.75 million—Durant gambled on the magical "Oldsmobile" name. He figured the 1905 song, "In My Merry Oldsmobile," was still popular! In 1909, Durant cautiously courted the small, unstable Oakland Motor Car Company, acquiring today's Pontiac division just days before the owner's demise. Cadillac came next at the unheard-of price of $4.75 million, though Durant later boasted the entire sum was returned in only 14 months. But Durant laughed last in 1909 as GM earned a whopping $29 million profit.

Sadly, the splendor soon subsided. The cash outlay for Cadillac drained company capital, and while 1910 started strongly, Durant drained capital further by investing in Heany Lamp, an ill-fated electrical firm. GM lost over $12 million after Heany's tungsten-filament electric bulb patents were voided and deemed worthless. True to spirit, the wild gambler pushed on—declaring a stock dividend of 400 percent—but workers remained laid off for months, and GM stock fell from 100 to 25.

Durant sought capital feverishly. "I tried the large financial institutions. I tried the life insurance companies. I tried the men who were known to possess large fortunes—but while I was considered an excellent salesman and had a wonderful proposition to offer, my efforts in that direction were to no avail," he lamented. Life's tough!

So Billy sold his soul to the devil, bankers, to get the financing that saved GM—$15 million of six-percent notes. But the terms were severe. GM got just $12.75 million, with the bankers keeping the rest—plus a $6.1 million commission in GM stock—plus a blanket mortgage on GM's Michigan properties—plus control of GM via a voting trust for the loan's five-year term.

Durant remained active only briefly. "I had been given a title and a position, but the support, the cooperation, the spirit, the unselfishness that is needed in every successful undertaking, was not there," he remarked. So, he left GM to make a go at another one-man empire, and by early 1911, conjured up a new plan to regain control of his "baby." With retired Buick racer Louis Chevrolet's name, he set out to compete with the Model T. By 1914 he was marketing the "490" to rival the $490 Model T and the next year had sales of $11.7 million with net profits of $1.3 million.

In 1916, with the GM voting trust due to expire and the $15-million loan to pay off, Durant, like a lion awaiting its prey, bulled the market, buying GM stock heavily and asking friends to hang on to theirs. He scrambled to be ready for the September board meeting. Working from a three-room New York hotel suite, he used telephones in each room to purchase stock from all across America. GM stock rose from 82 in January to 558 by 1916's end. The visionary gambler was on the loose.

Having successfully overthrown the bankers by winning 54 percent of the stock, Durant felt great, especially with a board consisting of loyal friends and four neutral members—chairman Pierre duPont, duPont Company treasurer **John Raskob** and two of their associates. And again, Durant charged, forming United Motors Company and acquiring Frigidaire refrigerators.

But Durant didn't count on World War I, which sent GM stock plummeting. Most of his GM stock, bought on 10 percent margin, was wiped out, leaving him largely at the mercy of the duPonts. But Durant had a few more years of aggressive adventure with GM, finding support in duPont ally, Raskob. Between 1918 and 1919, GM expanded capacity and vehicle production, entered the tractor business, bought Fisher Body Corporation and built the $20-million "Durant" Building (later renamed the GM Building).

But 1920's recession delivered Durant his downfall, as car sales and GM stock declined sharply and his wild ways became criticized. The duPonts called upon America's most powerful investment banking house, J.P. Morgan & Company, to underwrite over $20 million in stock. As GM stock dropped to 21, Durant was actively participating in syndicates to support the price. By October, he was severely in the red, borrowing 1.3 million GM shares from duPont and margining them for further stock purchases. By November, GM plummeted to 13, leaving Billy $90 million in the red. December 1 ended his connection with GM—permanently.

But he couldn't quit the auto industry. At 59, he still thrilled for a challenge and, within six weeks, started Durant Motors. By writing to well-endowed friends and settling with GM for $3 million in stock, he capitalized Durant Motors with $7 million—some say purely "on personality." The stock quickly soared from 15 to over 80—and was even offered on layaway. But Durant's timing was off and he couldn't buck the coming depression. By 1933, his 150 acres of floor space across America had come and gone, and Durant Motors was liquidated.

Meanwhile, during the Roaring 20s, Durant became a Wall Street legend, gambling staggering amounts of money, even while touring Europe. Known as the "bull of bulls," he joined in then-legal "bull pools" with the Fisher brothers of auto-body fame, bidding a stock up, then selling for hefty profits. He handled over 11 million shares in 1928 and reportedly established a $50 million nest egg. But as usual, he won big and lost big. He foresaw the 1929 Crash and withdrew in time, but "Crapo" re-entered the market—on margin—in 1930, even borrowing from his wife's GM holdings. He had lost everything by 1932. In 1936, weary of repeated court actions from persistent creditors, he filed bankruptcy.

Durant tried entrepreneurship a few more times before dying virtually penniless at 86. Some say he dabbled in supermarkets, others say bowling alleys. In 1936, photos of Durant washing a dish in a New Jersey diner received widespread attention, yet the picture wasn't as tear-jerking as people believed—Durant was simply promoting the diner he owned and operated. Always selling.

Years later, Alfred Sloan, his successor at General Motors, claimed Durant's stock would have been worth more than $100 million by the time he died in 1947, had he held on to it. But that just wasn't Durant's style. He took big risks. Sometimes they paid off and sometimes they didn't. The lesson of Durant's life? Yes, be a visionary and take risks, but don't be a wild gambler, particularly on borrowed money, or you end up at the mercy of luck.

F. AUGUSTUS HEINZE

BURNED BY BURNING THE CANDLE
AT BOTH ENDS

F. Augustus Heinze, or "Fritz," loved a good time—his escapades were always the talk of the town. He was a lavish entertainer, loved beautiful women, and gambled as hard as he drank. Heinze also worked as hard as he played, burning the candle at both ends. During his career as a mine owner and Wall Street speculator, his extravagant nights seemingly never interfered with his success—that is until his extravagance trickled into his daytime activities. The effect wasn't immediate, but when it came, it was a swift and fatal blow. He died at 45 in 1914 from cirrhosis of the liver after being ruined on Wall Street, leaving a fortune a fraction of what it could have been.

A hulking, muscular figure standing 5 foot 10, weighing 200 pounds with an ivory-white face and big blue eyes, Heinze was born in Brooklyn in 1869, then educated in Europe's finest schools—a bit surprising from the sound of him. At 20 he returned home to pursue mine engineering in what was to become America's mining capital—Butte, Montana. Four years later, in 1893, he and two brothers formed a copper mining and smelting company just as copper mining became the region's top industry. Little did he know he was on a collision course with forces much bigger than he was.

Audacious, brash, bold and extremely sly, Heinze had what it took to make it in the cutthroat copper industry. In one case he convinced a mine owner to lease him a mine known for its high-grade copper, offering the owner a whopping 50 percent of the profits (as compared to the standard 20 percent lease). But there was one condition. Heinze would pay the 50 percent only if the mine continued to produce its high-grade ore; if the ore were low grade, Heinze would reap virtually all of the profits.

Mysteriously, from the day Heinze took over, the mine began producing only low-grade ore. He was secretly mixing waste rock with the high-grade ore, creating low-grade output and then reaping the profits! It was simple dishonesty, but it wasn't out of place in the era. During an unsuccessful law suit to claim lost profits, the duped mine owner—who once thought of himself as the craftiest around—yelled, "If I'd known that young fellow 10 years ago I'd have owned all of Butte (by now)!"

Next, in a move he repeated during Butte's later copper battle, and with his profits piling up, Heinze stormed—and manipulated—a remote town in the Kootenay region of British Columbia dominated by a single, powerful railroad, the Canadian Pacific. He bought the local newspaper, publicized himself as the region's savior from the unpopular line, and then lavished locals with grandiose promises of developing a mining industry, along with a railroad which would compete with the dominant Canadian Pacific.

The government, seeing Heinze as a sort of hometown hero, gave him valuable land grants on which to build his line. Heinze then borrowed money and appeared to begin construction of the new line, but in no time he turned around and simultaneously sold out to Canadian Pacific and announced to the public that he was overextended and would not go ahead with construction. He walked away with the valuable land grants and a cool million from the Canadian Pacific, which some speculated had been his goal all along.

Then, in Butte, Heinze battled with the huge Rockefeller conglomerate, Standard Oil, over the town's copper mines. (At this time, Standard Oil had begun forming a copper trust in the late 1890s: See **Henry Rogers.**) True to his craftiness, Heinze used his newly bought community newspaper to portray Standard Oil as an outsider trying to profit from local sweat—and himself as the local savior! He also bought a small interest in the oil company to bring numerous annoying minority stockholder suits against it. Above all, Heinze never let up! By 1906, Standard Oil was so fed up with him that it came through with a very tempting offer—$12 million. In a split second, Heinze about-faced on Butte, taking the company's money while agreeing to drop all his lawsuits and leave Butte, making him anything but a savior!

Money in hand, Heinze quickly forgot about Butte and boldly rushed to conquer Wall Street with Otto Heinze and Company, a brokerage firm he set up with his brothers in New York. "Otto" was his brother. Fritz set the firm up in his brother's name, partly because he hated his own—Frederick Augustus. Folks called him Fritz, which he also disliked. He referred to himself as "F."

You can see how a guy who lies, cheats, and steals and doesn't even like his own name might drink a lot and turn to more exotic escapes.

He stormed Manhattan, taking an elaborate double suite at the Waldorf Astoria, thinking if he could lick Rockefeller, he surely could lick Wall Street. He was confident, cocky—and wrong. What would happen in the next few years would be disastrous, both for his interests and the American economy.

In Manhattan, Heinze was in his element—at night, that is. His daytime office served as a nighttime party cave, where he surrounded himself with actresses and Manhattan's most active socialites. Somehow it never quite dawned on him that having a lot of actresses hanging around might cloud his Wall Street acumen. He threw gala parties. As his brother Otto recalled, "He entertained most lavishly—some forty or fifty men and women at a time. The favors were frequently of gold, the flowers profuse and beautiful, the food excellent and the champagne plentiful . . . These parties usually began late and did not end for many hours. F.A. would often play all night and work all day." His candle regularly burned at both ends.

If during the night, Heinze made all the right connections, he certainly made the wrong ones during the workday—in particular, with speculator and chain banker **Charles Morse.** Together, the two controlled 12 banks (one of which was owned by Heinze), and joined in speculative pools financed at their banks' expense. Their most famous venture was the United Copper pool operating between 1904 and 1907. The copper firm was overcapitalized and financed through one of the chain banks. Ironically, United Copper grew successful, and by 1906, closely rivaled Standard Oil's previously-untouchable copper trust, Amalgamated Copper, by underselling it in the metal market. Standard Oil vowed revenge, saying, "We are going to settle this but we are going to settle it in our own way."

Meanwhile, as the copper market showed signs of weakness, United Copper jumped from 37-1/2 to 60. The *New York Times* reported it was due to speculation, but what actually caused it was Heinze's and Morse's attempted corner on United Copper. The two didn't have their corner secured, and they were left holding large blocks of disintegrating United Copper stock. The Standard Oil group was rumored to have helped crush their corner and reportedly squashed any chance of financial aid Heinze could have gotten. In any case, the Panic of 1907 was in full force, and Heinze had helped create it. In return, during a three-week period, Heinze lost his financial standing in New York, his banks and prestige—and some $10 million!

At this point, Heinze's days were numbered. He just didn't know it. In 1909 he was acquitted of 16 charges of financial malfeasance as president of his bank. The next year he married an actress and had a son, but it was downhill from here, as his bad luck gained momentum every day. By 1912, his wife had flown the coop. Then, two years later, they reconciled for their son's sake—right before she died! Next, he lost a $1.2 million lawsuit for skipping out on the bank he had bought years earlier. His many years of hard drinking finally caught up to him, and he began deteriorating physically. Finally, in 1914, he died an alcoholic's death.

Heinze made all the classic mistakes—in life and on Wall Street. He partied and drank too much and entered a field he knew next to nothing about—banking. And he neglected Wall Street. The wild womanizing, parties, and drinking killed him, and his lack of humility and focus on Wall Street disgraced him. He is just one more nail in the coffin encasing the argument that anyone who is more interested in spending money than in the game of Wall Street itself is likely to fail in the financial markets.

CHARLES W. MORSE

SLICK AND COLD AS ICE,
EVERYTHING HE TOUCHED
...MELTED

Some people never learn. Charles Morse was a prime example. Everything he dipped his pudgy fingers into managed to go belly up. It wasn't just bad luck. Morse had a reckless, speculative streak (uncharacteristic of his New England upbringing) which triggered America's 1907 Panic. But nothing ever discouraged him from starting a new, more outrageous scheme. He was wild, out of control and totally reckless.

You wouldn't expect it of him. Morse was a small, stout, barrel-chested imp born in Bath, Maine in 1856. The word trouble was practically branded on his forehead. Even while working his way through Bowdoin College, he secured a job for himself at his father's office, then paid another to do it for less in his place! Morse, meanwhile, devoted himself to his studies and—more importantly— his thriving Manhattan ice business.

Morse made his initial fortune in ice, but by no modest means. He bribed city politicos, including the corrupt mayor, who backed Morse in forcing his competition to merge. Then he capitalized his company with more water than ice, watering the stock and greasing politicos' palms! His monopoly in place, the confident "Ice King" boldly pushed ice prices sky high, causing public uproar. Let the public roar all it wants, he figured—their mayor is invested in Morse stock! His next step was forming a holding company, manipulating its stock and taking some $25 million for himself, before corruption burst his bubble. The public had the last laugh. They booted the corrupt mayor from office, and the new one ended Morse's monopoly.

Hungry for another plunge, Morse dove into shipping shortly before his banking escapades. Using techniques similar to the ice scam, the "Admiral of the Atlantic Coast" created a watered-down near-monopoly in shipping along the eastern coast and milked it for all it was worth.

While his ice and shipping deals were pretty shady, nothing compared to his banking and speculative schemes. He started out borrowing hundreds of thousands from little people like his stenographer. Then, through a series of loans, he gained control of a series of banks. It was easy—Morse borrowed cash and with it, bought controlling shares in a bank. Then, he used the bank's assets against another loan, with which he'd buy another bank. The more banks he controlled, the more loans came in. Gradually, he and two partners formed a highly speculative dozen-bank chain—and it was then that United Copper stock caught their eyes.

United Copper was overcapitalized, and Morse liked that. But what he liked better was the chance to make a few bucks by manipulating its stock. So, he and his partners formed a pool to corner the stock, buying huge amounts of United Copper through various brokers. (The brokers were to "park" the stocks for the pool in their own names in order to keep the operation secret and prevent the stock's price from rising too high, too soon. Note that parking stock was the cause of Ivan Boesky's recent jailing. It's illegal now, but wasn't then.)

When a sudden outbreak of selling depressed the stock, Morse and his pool immediately suspected the brokers. So, when the price shot back up from 37 to 60 after hordes of short sellers covered themselves, Morse believed he and his cohorts had cornered United Copper, and that's when they made their move.

The pool called what they believed was their brokers' bluff. Thinking that the brokers were short and had insufficient shares to meet Morse's demands, the Morse pool requested delivery on all the United Copper stocks the brokers had been parking for the pool. If the brokers had indeed been treacherous and were short the stock, they would have to buy it all back, driving the price sky-high, and in the process, the pool would win millions. But if the brokers were not short and actually had the shares to deliver, the pool would be finished because, lo and behold, Morse didn't have enough cash to pay for all he'd purchased. He was playing big-time poker and calling a bluff by bluffing himself.

What happened was this: First, Morse hadn't really cornered United Copper. There were lots of small investors who still had pieces, and when the stock shot back up to 60, these small investors saw their chance to get out—and they did, selling to eager brokers. The brokers had been short—just as the pool believed, but now, as the small investors sold out, the brokers bought the stock and were able to meet delivery. And, yes, the pool didn't have the money to pay for the stocks! Morse and his cronies scrambled to raise enough cash to pay for the stock by unloading their United Copper stock on the market Naturally, United Copper plummeted because of their selling spree, first to 36, then to 10!

Damage might have been minimal had Morse been purely a speculator—and not a banker. But his involvement with banks—and his failure on Wall Street—now caused sheer panic on the Street. Depositors began a run on his bank, fearing for their accounts. And, because of their speculative nature, Morse's banks did not have much in the way of reserves. They lacked the cash and support of the Morgan-controlled Clearing House, a pre–Federal Reserve institution that oversaw the checks and credit among New York's larger banks and controlled smaller banks' access to credit. So when Morse requested Clearing House credit, the Clearing House demanded that he and his partners resign from all their banking interests, and only then did **J.P. Morgan** take action to rescue the economy from disaster. While it is clear that he didn't cause the Panic of 1907, which had been brewing in the normal fashion from a prior period of speculative fervor and excess, Morse was the trigger mechanism that starting the avalanche.

For his starring role in the panic, Morse was sentenced to 15 years in 1908. But because of appeals and a good lawyer, he served only two years, from 1910 to 1912. (Ironically, Morse skipped on paying his lawyer's bill.) Later, President Taft pardoned him after hearing he was dying. Actually, Morse had consumed a chemical soapsuds mixture calculated to produce fatal symptoms, but no real damage! It was enough to fool the president.

Hardly discouraged, the troublemaker returned to Wall Street with a vengeance, hellbent on a comeback. By 1915, his newly formed Hudson Navigation Co. was a growing power in shipping, later sued for unfair competition. The next year another Morse upstart in shipbuilding was contracted by Uncle Sam to build 136 vessels for World War I. As always, Morse borrowed to do this, and then completed only 22 ships—something's fishy!

Morse was charged with conspiracy to defraud the government during a postwar investigation revealing he had used much of the loan to build shipyards for his firm instead of ships! But before an indictment could be handed down, Morse sailed for Europe. En route, the attorney general cabled him to return, which he did—and Morse was again arrested, all the while protesting his innocence. Uncle Sam, meanwhile, was awarded some $11 million from Morse's company in 1925.

Morse died eight years later, a complete failure in all his business endeavors. He is as good an example as any of why you shouldn't operate on borrowed money. He borrowed and mis-speculated, he borrowed and defrauded, and en route he ended up poor and in jail. Most folks know borrowing can backfire if you don't know what you're doing. Morse proves borrowing also causes acts of desperation not otherwise undertaken. In the process you can lose integrity—and perhaps everything.

ORIS P. AND MANTIS
J. VAN SWEARINGEN

HE WHO LIVES BY LEVERAGE, DIES
BY LEVERAGE

Visionary opportunists Oris and Mantis Van Swearingen accomplished what most thought impossible. Riding on the coattails of the booming 1920s, they built a railroad empire via leveraged buyouts, strung together by holding companies—their hallmark. Though the hard-driving, dynamic twosome lost it all following the 1929 Crash—as quickly as they made it—their empire shows creative financing at its best and earliest stages. Of course, it also shows that he who lives by leverage, dies by leverage.

Looking like twins, the Van Swearingens, former office clerks, initially started small with real estate in 1900. Oris, 21, and Mantis, 19, contracted for an acre of land, selling it by offering tiny subdivisions and backing the buyers until the land could be resold for modest profits. The real estate market continued to look ripe to them, so they plunged. With their initial profits, plus money borrowed from friends, they bought 4,000 acres outside Cleveland, hoping to transform it into an upscale residential neighborhood,

Shaker Heights. This was early in the era of planned subdivisions, and most folks were skeptical of their plans.

Remaining bachelors, living together, even sleeping in twin beds, the brothers worked hard—never vacationing until 1930—and planned for Shaker Heights' lifeline, a railroad. Aiming to build a modest connection from their land to downtown Cleveland, the brothers instead stumbled upon a major line, the New York, Chicago & St. Louis Railroad, at the right price. Why settle for a simple suburban connection when you can build a kingdom? So, the brothers swept up the line for $8.5 million—paying $500,000 of their own, $2 million in bank loans and the rest in 10-year notes payable. It was that easy—just borrow! Then the brothers organized their first holding company. By floating the stock to the public, they effectively used the stock market to refinance their debt, and they were on their way—a trick they would repeat often in their career.

Railroad acquisitions became a breeze for the dynamic duo. The brothers snatched up lines, borrowed against past acquisitions and formed holding companies, pyramid-style—not unlike today's leveraged take-overs. They were among the first of the true pyramiders and, in that respect, were financial innovators. Just the opposite of **James Hill**, who was a railroad operator, first, and used Wall Street only when he had to, Oris and Mantis were financial operators, first, and stayed away from day-to-day operations. With savvy operators running their lines, the Van Swearingen empire flourished.

As with most pyramiders since, their initial successes built their reputation as innovative empire builders and increased financial support for the smalltown boys from Wall Street's heavy hitters, like the House of Morgan and influential N.Y. banker, **George F. Baker.** To receive Baker's support, the squeaky-clean brothers had to pass his homespun test: "Do you work, and do you sleep well?" When the brothers replied they slept like logs and never worried, Baker said, "All right, I am with you." But perhaps the Van Swearingens slept too soundly, for when 1929 rolled around the crash found them highly leveraged. A year later, with both earnings and securities depressed—and their money-hungry empire starving—the brothers fell to their knees, deeply indebted to Cleveland banks. I'll bet they slept poorly, if at all, that year.

Their pyramid was a group of operating companies owned by holding companies. But then the holding companies also owned partial shares of each other in a confusing spider web-like tangle that is more than vaguely reminiscent of a pea-and-shell game. Their pyramid, topped by the General Securities Corp. and the Vaness Co., which had interlocking ownership, stood at a standstill. So, naturally, their next step was exactly what you'd expect from money manipulators.

They made yet another deal, reaching far into Wall Street's deep pockets, the House of Morgan's in particular, to obtain a $48 million loan, using their properties as security. But that wasn't enough. Equity prices fell steadily in the early 1930s, so their collateral depreciated, and the pyramid needed more money. Pyramid building requires staying in tune with the financial scene to avoid the crunch of an imploding economy, but for the brothers it was too late. Without regular income, the Van Swearingens couldn't hack their leverage, and despite a relatively high degree of confidence and support from Wall Street, they defaulted in 1935, kissing their holdings good-bye as the Morgans auctioned them off! They had ridden all the way up in the 1920s and all the way down in five years. But sometimes down isn't out—particularly for wheeler-dealers.

There were two sealed bidders present at the bankruptcy auction—the House of Morgan and Midamerica Corp. Morgan, offering $3 million for the extensive system, expected to win and become the equity owner of the operating assets they had unsuccessfully loaned money to support. Midamerica, a surprise bidder, won with a $3.12 million bid—meaning an unrecoupable loss of some $45 million to the Morgans! But here is where treachery came in, as it often does in bankruptcy. Midamerica was controlled by a Van Swearingen friend, who bought the assets and tried to revert the system back to them. This is a tactic now common in bankruptcies, and is another place where the Van Swearingens made their mark on finance.

After all, who knows the assets better than the former owners? And by the time bankruptcy hits, there is no love lost between the owners and the creditors who were once allies. So the former owners turn on their creditors and find some other form of financing from a new set of allies, usually equity partners, who together compete in the bankruptcy process to win the assets cheaply. In this case, the Van Swearingens hoped to buy back their assets cheaply out of bankruptcy and get their railroads back, without the burden of all the debt they had originally assumed from Morgan and the Cleveland banks. En route they hoped to regain operating railroads that together had more total track footage than existed in all of England.

In this case, the new ally was George Ball—of "Ball Jar" fame. The deal between Ball and the brothers was to buy it back from him at previously-specified low prices over 10 years for a mere $8.250. But it never happened. Mantis, 54, died two months later. Oris followed his brother less than 12 months later, dying at 57—in debt over $80 million, more than half of which was owed to the House of Morgan!

Lessons? You can make a lot of money fast if you can borrow lots of money and buy lots of assets in a bull market. But there are three keys to making this work. First, you have to win and keep the confidence of your bankers throughout the bull market. Second, you have to be able to run the operations pretty well so you can withstand tough times, something at which few financial types are good. And third, you have to be able to see tough times coming at you—with enough lead time to be able to float enough stock to pay back your debts before falling security prices and a weak economy take you down. The problem usually ends up being that the market tends to fall before the economy does, so that your ability to float stock to a suckered crowd fades before you see the economy weakening on you.

Though the Van Swearingens wound up broke and in debt, their strategy would have worked had they just sold massive amounts of stock in 1929 and been able to enter the 1930s debt-free. But they didn't. Wheeler-dealers are usually playing a game where they roll the dice and assume the game won't end abruptly on them. Eventually, it almost always does. So, of course, this game is not for the faint of heart, and while it can't be proved, the death of both brothers so soon after the bankruptcy is a clear warning that heavy debt can be bad for your health—even fatal. He who lives by leverage, dies by leverage.

Investor's Press, 1966

JESSE L. LIVERMORE

THE BOY PLUNGER AND
FAILED MAN

Jesse Livermore was right when he said, "Speculation is not an easy business. It is not a game for the stupid, the mentally lazy, the man of inferior
emotional balance." He played anyway—and thrived, sometimes. But the excitable "J.L.," one of Wall Street's greatest speculators, spent his flamboyant
life on an emotional roller coaster, coasting between fame and ruin.

Far from stupid and nowhere near lazy, the blue-eyed "Boy Plunger" stayed
true to his trade, marrying three times while keeping an endless supply of
mistresses, drinking like a fish and yachting aboard his 202-foot Anita. "The
more I made, the more I spent," he whined. "I don't want to die disgustingly
rich!" A society page's dream, he reportedly courted **Diamond Jim Brady**'s
lover, Lillian Russell, and temporarily won her favor. But like everything else,
he could win, but he couldn't keep.

His career was boom or bust. He made himself a millionaire four different
times following bankruptcies, recouping his fortunes as spectacularly as he
lost them. Despite incredible resiliency, Livermore's comeback ability—and

his fortune—dwindled during the 1930s when new government regulations outlawed many of his tactics. The dapper dresser, in turn, marked the end of an era by blowing his brains out in 1940. Like the man said, speculation is not an easy business.

Making his name in the anything-goes, pre-SEC market, Livermore concealed positions, cornered stocks, bought heavily on margin, planted phony publicity and gathered inside information to make his killings. Operating on the sly and on his own (taking on pools and partners only when broke), he worked from a secret Manhattan penthouse staffed with statisticians. He swung with the market, foreseeing popular trends and avoiding them. He didn't really care which way the market moved, just as long as it moved and he could make a buck! In the 1929 Crash, for example, he started bullish, then switched sides, only to gain millions on the short side—and lose about as much in his long positions!

Livermore mastered market price fluctuations. Reading the ticker with uncanny accuracy, he first started trading in Boston bucket shops, which were considered an outrageous gamble to most. Bucket shops provided a chance to bet on the market without actually buying stocks. Like investors at a broker's office, "bucket shop investors" bet on which way a stock would move, paying commissions and a small margin, but, unlike a broker's office, actual orders to buy were discarded. As a general rule, and the one that kept the bucket shops in existence, people can't predict stock prices based on prior stock action, so trying to read the tape and bet on it is a game that, Las Vegas-like, pours money into the house and out of the customers' pockets. But Livermore was the exception that proves the rule—the very rare bird who could read the tape and tell where a stock was going.

Bucket shops were not particularly respectable, but for Livermore they were profitable. By 15, he won $1,000 speculating during lunch breaks of his first and only job as board boy for Paine-Webber! Then, encouraged by his first speculative venture "plunging" $10 in a railroad and winning $3 when he sold out—Livermore quit his job to buck bucket shops full time. In no time, he was beating every shop he entered, reaping profits and an unmerciful reputation!

Such success at bucket shops was unheard of, and, as a result, he received the highest degree of flattery—banishment from trading, not from one or two of them, but from all of them! Not willing to give up his meal ticket, Livermore resorted to aliases and disguises to continue speculating. The aliases worked at first, but the disguises became necessary when he developed the label of "the boy plunger!"

When it became hard to find a bucket shop in the Northeast where his reputation hadn't preceded him, he hopped a westbound box car for a tour of the country's bucket shops, trading all over the East Coast and Midwest. New York, Indianapolis, Chicago, St. Louis and Denver—Livermore won wherever he went, stashing away some $50,000. At that point, he headed for the big time—Wall Street, where they couldn't turn you down, but where you actually had to buy the stock in order to play.

Livermore came to Wall Street in 1906 confident and ready to conquer. Too cocky for his own good, he lost it all in his first bust. Never being one to diversify and spread his risks, the ego maniac also didn't understand how hard it is to build a big position. Buying stocks is different from reading the tape. If he saw a stock at 20 in the bucket shops and thought it would go to 24, he could "buy" at 20, and when it got to 24 he could "sell" for a 20 percent profit.

But on Wall Street he would take his $50,000 and plan to buy 2,500 shares of the stock. That was a hefty position in a market much smaller and less liquid than today's, and the spread between bids and offering prices was often huge. It wasn't abnormal to see a stock quoted at 20 bid, offered at 25—a 25 percent spread. Suppose he saw a stock that traded last at 20 but was quoted 19 bid, offered at 21. He started buying at 21, plus a commission. But then his own buying would drive the stock up. It might take him until 24 to get his entire position built. Then, if he thought it would fall and started to sell, it might be quoted at 23 bid, offered at 24. He'd then start selling but never get a better price than 23, less commission, and take a loss on his first sale. Then he would drive the stock down and take a loss on the liquidation of his remaining 2,500 shares. It's a lot harder to make money in reality than it is to do on paper—something which few people today, except for institutional money managers, seem to fully realize. For instance, investment newsletters "manage" portfolios the same way Livermore traded the bucket shops. But actually operating off the newsletters' advice is like Livermore's buying on Wall Street.

Livermore didn't get that at first. He just thought he couldn't read the tape fast enough on Wall Street. So, doing the only thing he knew to do, he headed back to replenishing his capital via the bucket shops. En route, the 29-year-old stumbled upon Union Pacific Railroad—on a lucky hunch. As Union Pacific rose, he sold short, anticipating a big swing. Then, just as he was about to be wiped out, his swing came in the form of the San Francisco earthquake, halting East–West money flow and sending the railroad plummeting! Livermore quickly covered his shorts, took a bundle, booming a second time.

World War I interfered with his boom and his profligate spending! This time coffee was the culprit. Expecting a rise in coffee, Livermore loaded up on it—and, sure enough, it rose. But, his coffee profits were dripped dry when government officials frowned on wartime fortunes, voiding his millions in coffee contracts. Tough luck—he was broke a third time. With broker-supplied capital (Livermore's commission-generating trading was often more valuable to them on a leveraged basis than on a small amount of capital), he resurrected himself again, masterminding bear raids and bull runs successfully throughout the 1920s. But the 1929 Crash left him bust for good.

To make the magic happen between busts, Livermore didn't wait for fate—instead, he used the media, mainly the *New York Times*, to move the market in his favor. For instance, while acquiring cotton in a rising market with few buyers, he assured his success via a 1908 article headlined, "July Cotton Cornered By Jesse Livermore." Never admitting to planting the article, Livermore reaped millions as new, excited buyers and panicked short-sellers scrambled to buy his holdings—at premium prices! The newly enthroned "Cotton King" followed three infallible steps during the next decade: (1) Gather a huge position whether long or short, (2) Publicize it, and (3) Unload on the suckers! Jesse, who detested shaking hands with men but loved touching women, believed the public was, on the whole, stupid. It somehow never seemed to dawn on him he was unscrupulous.

Recovering from a $3 million loss in grain in 1925, Livermore recouped by secretly heading a pool and pushing a stock from 19 to over 74 within a year. Even in the 1920s, when he lost, he resorted to bucket shops for quick cash. He also favored filing bankruptcy to clear his debts, which once exceeded $2 million, although he regularly paid back most of his debts even after his bankruptcy proceeding was completed. One time—once was enough—he tried to resort to his first wife's jewels, asking her to hock what he had previously bought for her! When she refused, he packed up and left, divorcing her a few years later to marry an 18-year-old. He was 41.

(**Arnold Bernhard**, the legendary founder of the *Value Line*, once told me about working for Livermore during the 1920s as a statistician. Bernhard was young, eager, and inexperienced but observant. The main thing he noticed about Livermore was that he wasn't observant. According to Bernhard, Livermore's vanity, even in his private office, got in the way of his ability to recognize reality.)

If the 1920s were Livermore's dream decade—lavish parties, estates, Rolls-Royces, two sons—the following decade was a quick lesson in reality. When the market bottomed after the Crash, he quickly followed suit. His sweet little 18-year-old second wife had since become an alcoholic and shot his favorite young son during a drinking binge. The son recovered, and Livermore quickly got rid of the wife and took a third. His career was equally dim. While he was never completely broke, the big time wheeler-dealer had to resort to trading in 100-share lots and returned once more to the bucket shops, just before their SEC-caused demise. In 1933, he cracked up, holed himself up in a hotel room, drank for 26 hours straight, then stumbled bleary-eyed into a police station, claiming amnesia. A real basket case. But it doesn't end here.

Haggard and worn out from too many icy-dry martinis, Livermore attempted to pawn his "secret" to success on the public, publishing *How To Trade Stocks* in 1940. Barely 100 pages, his flimsy and visually cheap book was available in two editions—a leather-bound volume or the "Anyman's" edition. But putting leather on the outside wasn't going to make this an esteemed item. It was a desperate last attempt at recovering his coveted reputation, and it showed. Despite his usual publicity efforts—big parties with free food and drink for the press—the book flopped, and Livermore finally fell over the emotional edge. Sipping two drinks in Manhattan's Sherry-Netherland Hotel, he penned an eight-page letter reiterating "My life has been a failure" to wife number three (who reputedly would have been out, had the book been a success). Next, he ducked into the empty hat-check room, slumped into a chair, held a pistol to his temple, and rid the world of his future. Since he had claimed he didn't want to die disgustingly rich, he may have considered himself a success.

Livermore's lessons? There are almost too many to list. He was among the most flamboyant and famous of all market operators, and, amazingly so, for someone who deserved it so little. It was his flash, extravagance, and publicity that caught attention. But when you think of him, it's important to remember that it's harder to buy stocks than it looks. Wild traders may make it on Wall Street, but they rarely keep it.

CHAPTER ELEVEN

MISCELLANEOUS, BUT
NOT EXTRANEOUS

LEGENDS AND MAVERICKS

Whenever you put 100 people into subgroupings, there will naturally be a few outcasts who don't quite fit into any one category. The four in this section refused to fit neatly in any of the other 10 chapters, but that fact doesn't in any way discount their significance. They're simply Miscellaneous, But Not Extraneous. And each Miscellaneous person—Hetty Green, Patrick Bologna, Cyrus Eaton, and Robert Young—is exceptional in his or her own way and had a distinct impact on the market.

First, there are the legends—Hetty Green and Patrick Bologna. To this day, there are blind references made to both of these rather obscure contributors. To wit, as I picked up the May 23, 1991, *San Francisco Chronicle*, I read Herb Caen's column as he talks about a local Hetty Green-like old woman and her personal money foibles.

The legacy of Hetty Green ballooned to legendary proportions primarily because of her phenomenal monetary success and her clearly weird ways. She was a conservative investor content with compounding moderate gains year after year. She was also a notorious social outcast, which suited her just fine. Unlike other successful operators who sought the limelight by wielding their wealth, Green sought to hide it, concealing her securities in her dirty and dated clothing and moving around a lot. She lived more cheaply than the poorest of the poor. And she was so cheap, and that's the word for her, she cost her son his leg to gangrene when she wouldn't pay for a doctor's visit. But as much as any person in this book, her penny-pinching profits were the stuff of legend.

Patrick Bologna had a truly obscure tie to Wall Street—he was its favorite shoeshine boy—yet, in that modest role, he affected the market in more ways than he ever could have imagined! Bologna symbolized the "hot" market tips that were notorious during the 1920s. He heard them from his important, higher-up customers, then spread them to the little guys for quarter tips. He was at the heart of the gossip machine that helped fuel the crowd's involvement in the stock market in the feverish years preceding the 1929 Crash. His eager involvement tipped off the lonely few who were able to translate his activities into an immediate danger signal and escape from the market before getting wiped out like all the rest.

Then, there are the mavericks, and mavericks typically are people who buck being categorized or labeled. Cyrus Eaton and Robert Young are little-known empire-builders who also bucked the Wall Street lasso when that just wasn't done. Eaton built an industrial empire and then an investment banking empire in Cleveland. Young boldly took over a previously Wall Street–affiliated railroad empire, and, en route, made the first case for competitive bidding between investment banking houses. Young escaped with his maverick reputation intact, but not his mind. He killed himself in 1958. Being a maverick has its cost.

Green and Bologna were accessible to the little guy as veritable street people. That is, you could get to them. Some wino might not know that the bag lady on the park bench next to him was worth $100 million. And I would have loved to have gotten my shoes shined by Bologna. Either of these characters, and the roles they played, would make movie models I'd pay to see. Not so with the mavericks. They were obscure, inaccessible and relatively bland compared to Green and Bologna, and yet, they made the market, too, in their own ways.

Miscellaneous, But Not Extraneous says it all. Green, Bologna, Eaton, and Young all contributed to today's financial landscape. And without them, there wouldn't be *100 Minds That Made The Market*—there would be just 96! While I couldn't fit these four neatly into any other grouping, there aren't another four who still had such lasting market impact.

HETTY GREEN

THE WITCH'S BREW, OR... IT'S NOT
EASY BEING GREEN

How would you picture Wall Street's first female finagler? It can't possibly compare with the miserly, eccentric Hetty Green who shrewdly turned a $6 million inheritance into $100 million. Not quite the business-schooled, gray-suit type, Green shrouded herself in foul-smelling black, outdated dresses in which she sewed untold securities. Donned daily in the same attire—complete with grimy black cotton gloves, bonnet, shabby umbrella, and cape—Hetty scurried between raunchy flats and her headquarters, the Chemical National Bank vault, fleeing the money-hungry spirits who "pursued" her. Eating graham crackers, oatmeal, and, on occasion, unwrapped ham sandwiches from the filthy folds of her pockets, Hetty sat cross-legged on the vault floor clipping coupons—stuffing them down her bosom. Within months of her Wall Street arrival, the middle-aged eccentric became known as "the Witch of Wall Street."

Yet, even a witch must possess an investment strategy—and hers was simple. In a pre-income tax world, she strove to make and keep 6 percent every year. To wit, Green operated under two rules. First, she never aimed for "big hits," preferring a great many good solid investments with relatively safe returns. Second, Green was stingy.

"There is no secret in fortune making. I believe in getting in at the bottom and out at the top. All you have to do is buy cheap and sell dear, act with thrift and shrewdness, and be persistent. When I see a good thing going cheap because nobody wants it, I buy a lot of it and tuck it away."

Inherent in Green's thinking was that most folks consume their investment harvests, but if you spend nothing, you keep it all, and it keeps compounding. If you compound $6 million at 6 percent for 51 years, without spending any of your 6 percents, you get $117 million. And that's exactly what Green did. She became the richest woman in America, but to accomplish her goal, as you will see, Green was also perhaps the most miserly.

Green bought stock heavily, but only in the depths of financial panics—and then, primarily railroad stocks. Otherwise, she bought real estate mortgages, government and municipal bonds, and other safe, income-oriented investments. Since she spent virtually nothing, she kept reinvesting at 6 percent. Stocks were the icing on her cake. She stepped into the breach of financial panics—her "harvest"—as she reveled at buying stocks from men gone broke. Never a late-bull market buyer, she simply bought in crashes, when no one else would. Considering her confidence and riveting results, one wonders whether she turned to women's intuition, or, perhaps, insider information. A well known example of her timely luck was her pullout from Knickerbocker Trust shortly before it failed in the 1907 Panic. Her clue? "The men in that bank are too good looking!" She bailed out, leaving her with abundant cash to loan sorry speculators.

Hetty was in the minority as the market's only woman—and she knew it. "I am willing to leave politics to the men, although I wish women had more rights in business and elsewhere than they now have. I could have succeeded much easier in my career had I been a man. I find men will take advantages of women in business that they would not attempt with men. I found this so in the courts, where I have been fighting men all my life."

She hit Manhattan after a ghastly childhood and unsatisfying marriage. Born Henrietta Howland Robinson in 1834, Hetty's father was a determined fortune hunter, who married her mother's old New England money. While momma had a fairy-tale life in mind for Hetty—princes and the like—Hetty was Daddy's Girl, and daddy, Edward "Black Hawk" Robinson, was money's slave. Growing up in the vulgar whaling city of New Bedford, Massachusetts, Hetty watched her father build a shipping empire by exploiting people, forfeiting luxuries, and scrimping on necessities. Following in her father's footsteps, Hetty, the richest girl in town, was clad in rags and learned "never to give anyone anything, not even a kindness."

The young ragamuffin scampered the wharves, absorbing dad's foul language, financial savvy, fierce temper, and frugal ways as her daintiness disintegrated. In 1865, with both mother, father and aunt dead, Hetty inherited nearly $6 million—and a deranged demeanor. Black Hawk's mission succeeded: Hetty was left as determined and callous as he, primed for Wall Street, with a chartreuse dollar sign for a heart.

Hetty was adept at getting her way. When nagging failed, she went for the tears! When tears failed, she initiated lawsuits. The only thing wrong with lawsuits was the lawyer's fee: She hated lawyers' fees more than the men themselves. Regardless, she employed a steady stream of them, refusing to pay each and every one! "I had rather that my daughter should be burned at the stake than to have her suffer what I have gone through with lawyers." Once, she even paid a $50 registration fee to carry a revolver "mostly to protect myself against lawyers."

Hetty picked up market tips from her free-spending millionaire husband, Ned Green, who made money in the Philippine tea and silk trade. It's a wonder she married at all, as she eyed each suitor with suspicion. But, at the start, Ned had the upper hand—dangling Street savvy above Hetty's head. They were wed in 1867. Some say she married not for love, but for free financial advice—and room and board! Regardless, they had two kids—a boy and a girl—while Hetty made money in American gold bonds, largely due to Green's speculative skill. When the Panic of 1873 hit, Hetty was caught on the long side, watching her stocks depreciate. En route she learned her lesson well, vowing to always "harvest" panics from then on, and she did.

Ned Green was soon appalled by his wife's penny-pinching ways, such as replacing their fine china with decrepit, cracked dishes, and haggling local merchants on every penny. But Hetty was as fed up with her husband as he was with her. When his speculative luck failed, Hetty bailed him out at least three times—after the fourth, she washed her hands of him. While they remained married, they never shared their lives again in any form.

Hetty's only real love was money. By 1900, she was reputedly worth $100 million, earning $20,000 per day. With money piling up faster than she could put it to work, she feverishly bought railroads, such as the Ohio and Mississippi in 1887, but not before being completely informed of her investment and rethinking it overnight. And, if it didn't yield 6 percent, forget about it! In 1892, she formed the Texas Midland road, combining the smaller lines Waco & Northwestern—for which she had her son outbid a bitter enemy. For Hetty, the roads were not only an income source, but a source of employment for her son, Ned.

Hetty groomed Ned as her successor, even paying his college tuition—only after securing his promise to stay single for 20 years after graduation. Ned was a momma's boy to the bone—as a kid, he resold his mother's newspaper each morning after she finished. Ned started as a clerk for her Connecticut River road, then graduated to overseeing her $5 million of Chicago real estate. As he raked in $40,000 per month for his mom, she paid him $3 per day—"training." Hetty, a proud mother, had aspirations for him—why, he could be another **Jay Gould**! But even with Ned, her love of money came first. When 14 years old, Ned injured his knee sledding downhill. Hetty fetched her shabbiest dress and waited unsuccessfully in line at a free medical clinic, after applying her useless treatment of hot sand and tobacco leaf poultices. When Ned's father learned of his son's unimproved condition, he sought a doctor without Hetty's consent, and paid $5,000 to have Ned's leg amputated—gangrene had set in.

Strive to get something for nothing—that was Hetty's motto. Following a stroke brought on by a fierce argument with a friend's cook, Green died in 1916 leaving behind a fortune—entirely in liquid assets—that she had acquired and protected ferociously. Attempting to keep her fortune within the confines of her immediate family—knowing that she couldn't take it with her—Green had constructed a restrictive will and prenuptial agreements to prevent in-laws from inheriting. Since her son and daughter had no children, her millions were eventually passed to more than 100 beneficiaries who never even knew Green.

Hetty teaches a lot of investment lessons. While her miserliness stands out as negative, her compounding success teaches us that frugality, when combined with reinvestment, is a powerful mechanism if even moderate rates of return can be achieved. Likewise, her insistence on safe 6 percent returns, while slightly low by modern standards, clearly points to the power of compound interest and the fact that most folks will do better getting a good safe return than gambling on a few risky and dramatic plays. If you happen to have $50,000 now in a tax-free retirement plan and could compound it at 15 percent per year for 50 years, as Hetty did her 6 percents, you would end up with more than $50 million. The power of compound interest—the witch's brew.

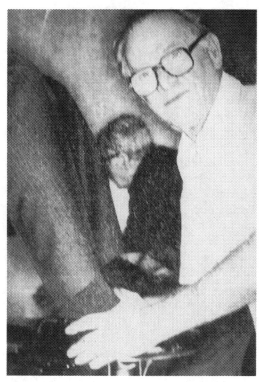

PATRICK BOLOGNA

THE EASY MONEY—ISN'T

W hen America was consumed with playing the stock market back in the late '20s, "hot" tips could be heard wafting through subway cars, hair salons, taxicabs, supermarkets, dance halls, and restaurants. As Wall Street figured out, after the fact, this wild fascination with the stock market was the hottest tip-off to the impending 1929 Crash—but few saw it in time.

Whether he knew it or not, Patrick Bologna symbolized the public's fervor to a handful of insightful Wall Street operators. The self-appointed "Bootblack to Wall Street" regularly gave his customers more than a 10-cent shine from his booth at 60 Wall Street. He put forth a stream of hot tips and relayed inside information from customer to customer while shining shoes. He had important regulars like **Charles Mitchell, "Sell 'Em Ben" Smith**, and **William Crapo Durant**, and, if they really ever gave him any worthwhile information, Bologna spoiled it all by passing it along to the next guy. But what he got out of passing the buck was exactly that, a buck or sometimes a quarter if the news was stale. The money added up—sometimes he could make more money in an hour playing investment advisor than he could shining shoes all day! Then, Bologna used his tips to play the stock market—the same hot tips he'd been passing around all along. "My money never leaves the Street. It's the best place in the world for it to be," he said before the Crash.

Legend has it one of those tips sparked **Joe Kennedy** into selling out his position months—some accounts say days—before the market crashed. One morning, while walking up Wall Street, Kennedy noticed Bologna was momentarily without customers and reading the *Wall Street Journal*. So, he climbed aboard the wooden chair and dug his heels into the footrests while Bologna put the paper down and picked up his brushes. The usual hellos had been exchanged when Bologna asked, "You wanna tip?" Kennedy said, "Sure" and listened to what his friend had to say.

Pat confided in Kennedy, "Buy oils and rails. They're gonna hit the sky. Had a guy here today with inside knowledge." Kennedy thanked his informer, pressed a quarter in his hand and chuckled to himself. If a shoeshine boy is predicting the market, he thought, this market must really be out of control. That night he told his wife he was getting out—and fast. Kennedy survived the Crash with his fortune intact, and, in fact, he magnified it by selling short as prices fell sharply lower. **Bernard Baruch** had a similar experience and supposedly decided to get out and then short. Baruch's comment on the subject is telling. "When beggars and shoeshine boys, barbers and beauticians can tell you how to get rich it is time to remind yourself that there is no more dangerous illusion than the belief that one can get something for nothing."

Meanwhile, Bologna had his entire savings wiped out—about $8,000 invested, or, as he said in a 1982 *Forbes* interview, $100,000 in today's purchasing power. "What did I do when I lost all that money? I was 21. What else would I do? I went out and got drunk!" Fully invested on margin, Bologna remembers Black Thursday well. At 10 A.M., he recalled, "People just stood there, stopped talking and looked towards the Stock Exchange. It was like the silence before the off at a big race." At 10:50 A.M., Bologna elbowed his way into a nearby brokerage house's customers' room that had previously welcomed his business. He sought advice about his margin and stocks, but help was nowhere to be found. Instead the room was jam-packed with nervous people like him trying to either sell out their positions or cover their margins.

Bologna retreated to his shoeshine stand with his holdings intact, remembering these words from his idol, Charles Mitchell: "A wise man never sells out at the first sign of trouble. That's for the pikers." Coincidentally, Bologna's holdings were in Mitchell's National City Bank.

By Monday, Bologna remembered most people on the subway ride into the city to be in a lighter mood than on Friday's depressing trip home. Most of the papers predicted a bankers' bail-out, and folks were joking and laughing at rich men suddenly gone broke. But when he reached Wall Street, Bologna found quite a different story. It was like a funeral parlor on the Street. On Tuesday "people who had battled through Thursday's Crash, who had been hit again by Monday's break, looked like they couldn't take it anymore. They were at the end of their resistance." That was the day Bologna finally surrendered, cashing in his thousands in National City stock for a mere $1,700.

Born Gennaro Pasquale Bologna in 1907 in Manhattan's Lower East side, the short and well-built Bologna was to remain a bootblack for the rest of his life. Business wasn't so bad during the Depression. "People realized they couldn't be buying new shoes all the time, so they took better care of all the old ones. You could support a family of four on $40 a week back in those days." And so he did, even putting his son through college and his daughter through secretarial school. And when the kids grew up and moved upstate to Suffern, Pat and his wife were able to follow, though he still commuted to his stand for a few hours each day.

Humbled by the Crash, Bologna didn't quit the market. In fact, he became something of an enigma to the next few generations of Wall Streeters, writing and distributing a tongue-in-cheek newsletter to his executive clientele from the 1940s to the 1980s. Even *Forbes* mentioned his stock market antics in 1982. Not exactly a literary genius, Bologna wrote rhythmic commentary that sometimes rhymed, and sometimes was seen as "startlingly shrewd." For example, in March 1966, before the Federal Reserve began manipulating our economy via the money supply, he wrote, "For if you want to stay ahead, keep one eye on the Fed."

Regarding his own investments, he said, "I'm too conservative. I only invest in good, dividend-paying blue chips. I'm still not even with 1929, counting in purchasing power, but that's all right. I'm not in a hurry."

Bologna was the personification of the hot tip. And the tip is the crowd, and the crowd is always wrong at the market's turning points and right in the middle of the move—and a loser overall. There has never been a tipster who made such an impact as Pat Bologna and, yet, who has been so unknown by name. All kinds of people know Kennedy and Baruch were contrarily influenced by a shoeshine boy. Almost no one knows it was Bologna. There is probably no better quote on the subject than that cited above from Baruch. But in a nutshell Bologna teaches us the easy money—isn't.

ROBERT R. YOUNG

AND IT'S NEVER BEEN THE
SAME SINCE

Robert Young took control of a $3 billion railroad empire with about $250,000 of his own cash—and a lot of guts. He flipped Wall Street on its back, grabbed power from the few dominant firms—and en route, revolutionized railroad financing. Although he thought of himself as a great reformer, he wasn't. Young's reforms came as a by-product of his colorful populist publicity stunts, but regardless, his reforms stuck and made history. Sadly, he killed himself in a 1958 money crunch.

The railroad empire that vaulted ambitious, aggressive Young to fame was built by the **Van Swearingen Brothers** during the 1920s. Their huge but jumbled corporate structure—strung together with elaborate holding companies, pyramid style—collapsed during the Crash when money, its most precious resource, became scarce.

In building their kingdom, the Van Swearingens leveraged buyouts, used past purchases as collateral—and faithfully returned to the House of Morgan, and sometimes Kuhn, Loeb for financing. Enter Robert Young. Small, prematurely gray, and otherwise looking like a dour Mickey Rooney, Young took control of the empire but incurred the wrath of the House of Morgan when he threatened to take the empire's financing business away from Morgan and offer it to whomever would complete bond financings at the lowest competitive bid. Morgan, of course, didn't like this. It just wasn't the way you did things in the Wall Street club where all roads led to Morgan—because the concept threatened the absolute dominance of Morgan in railroad finance. Young's move did, in fact, initiate Morgan's slide from dominance.

What frustrated Wall Street insiders was that the "daring young man from Texas" wasn't their kind. More like a 19th-century pioneering financier, he appeared out of practically nowhere. Born in 1897, the University of Virginia drop-out married at 19, then worked cutting rifle powder during World War I. Good timing and math skills landed him a job first at duPont, and then at General Motors' financial offices, where he learned enough to start his own investment firm with a million-dollar clientele, among them the legendary Alfred P. Sloan.

During the 1929 Crash, at 33, he made a killing selling short, then started picking up bargains among the ruins, including his diamond-in-the-rough— the debt-ridden Van Swearingen empire. Its $100 par stock had been selling for under $1 after the Crash! By 1937, Young had seized control of its top holding company, Alleghany Corporation, via two million shares from temporary owner George A. Ball for under $7 million—$4 million in cash, largely borrowed, and the rest in notes payable. He put up only $250,000 of his own. That's not so easy to do, so he must have been a heck of a salesman. Young, 40 at the time, took charge, knowing nothing about railroads!

But neither did most, so he appealed to the people, starting a proxy and publicity campaign. He started by calling the first of many press conferences—and allying himself with the New Deal, securities reform, and opposition to the classic Wall Street club's views. Some people maintain he had no problem adapting to securities regulation because, as a new entrant into the financial world, he wasn't entrenched in a career based on pre-regulatory ways.

At his first press conference, Young announced in his strong, confident voice he would "snap the old Van Swearingen chain" via fiscal independence and reinstate dividends for all the "Aunt Janes" of the investing public. But while he sounded confident, he must have been fearful inside, because later that year, in a fit of depression that would presage his eventual successful suicide, Young tried to kill himself in his summer estate—saved only by a neighbor who happened to drop by and pulled the revolver from his distraught hand. It took Young three months to regain his composure. Lesson 384: Never back someone financially who shows signs of mental problems. Some folks forget this simplest of lessons, otherwise Young's career would have been over almost immediately But people do silly things when it comes to money that they would never do with any other part of their lives.

What pressures could be so great as to make a man want to kill himself? Well, in those days, you just didn't take business away from the House of Morgan, and that's exactly what Young attempted to do. Meanwhile, the

House of Morgan engaged Young in a never-ending, exhausting power play that was to last his entire career. Young's most powerful weapon was publicity.

Fashioning himself the leader of a small-stockholders' army battling rich Wall Street bigwigs, he suggested that, instead of relying on Morgan, Alleghany and all of its underlings rely on competitive bidding to choose its backers! Young didn't devise competitive bidding, but he was the first to apply it to railroads. The true test came when Alleghany's only money-making line needed a bond issue and the predominantly Morgan-affiliated board of directors insisted on Morgan's underwriting—even though Young's choice of bankers offered a better deal! No problem. The persistent Young pranced around the board room, repeatedly chanting "Morgan will not get this business!" Then he threatened suit if the board didn't choose the better deal! They did.

Young remained under fire from Morgan and its affiliates until his death in 1958. Whereas takeover wars and bouts for control had once been fought in the market arena, Young brought the fight out in the open—and in the newspapers. While taking over the New York Central—not being able to buy the necessary amount of stock—he went after proxies! He courted stockholders, large and small, implementing the novel practice of sending doorbell ringers, brochures, and telemarketers to voice his cause and get their votes! And he won, taking control of the railroad. This major contribution to Wall Street methodology is today common practice, but it was only possible in a post–New Deal era that created the regulatory framework that outlawed pre-1929 stock-watering deals.

You might say Young bucked the system and survived, but he didn't. In another fit of depression, he succeeded where he had previously failed—by killing himself—in 1958. After sitting in a funk in the library of his Palm Beach, Florida mansion, he went downstairs to the billiard room in his basement and blew off his head with a shotgun. (I guess somebody told him you weren't supposed to make noise in a library.)

What brought on this depression? You can't really know what goes on in the mind of a suicide victim just before he ends it. There had been a recession that caused his New York Central Railroad to slide and angry stockholders to sue. In addition, his only child, a daughter, had died in a plane crash a few years before. Rumors had been spreading that doubted his financial stability. But these things happen to people. (I, myself, have had a daughter die and all kinds of problems, but I've never felt like ending the greatest game God gave to earth—life.) Most folks who have tough times recoil for a while and go on and recover without giving into depression. Young didn't. Wall Street is a place with tremendous inherent pressure. If you can't take the heat, get off the Street. Nobody's financial problems or image could be worth dying over.

Lessons from Young's life? Well, obviously, don't take yourself too seriously. But a simple and pragmatic tool is the power of the press, and the public, over any corporation. Young's use of this tool on Wall Street bucked the past clubby nature of Wall Street financing and corporate governance, and it's never been the same since.

CYRUS S. EATON

QUIET, FLEXIBLE, AND RICH

Most folks have never heard of Cyrus Eaton even though he left some $200 million upon his death in 1979 (the very least of his achievements, by the way). The reason for it is simple—he made his fortune without Wall Street's help. In fact, he ignored America's financial mecca, the supposed judge of who makes it and who doesn't. Although he dealt in the Street's roots—securities and investment banking—it had absolutely no say in Eaton's business. Morgan couldn't control him, Kuhn, Loeb lost business to him and New York banks were shunned by him. That angered plenty of people, but Eaton escaped their wrath unscathed, emerging as "perhaps as hardened a capitalist as the world contains."

Eaton never cared for Wall Street in the slightest. In fact, he had hoped to make his adopted hometown, Cleveland, a financial center that, along with Detroit, could rival New York. Though it never came to be, Eaton gave it his best shot, moving in on industries such as steel, railroads, investment banking, banking, iron ore and electric utilities ordinarily controlled by finance's biggest Wall Street–endorsed names. It was once said Eaton bought and sold entire industries—he certainly wielded the power and money to do so.

Born in Nova Scotia in 1883, Eaton had beginnings different from the typical Wall Street executive. At 17, he was intent on becoming a Baptist minister! So to Cleveland he went, where his uncle had his own congregation, which interestingly enough included John D. Rockefeller. While studying with his uncle, Rockefeller hired Eaton and later tried to dissuade him from the collar saying, "You've got what it takes to be successful in business." Eaton didn't listen at first, but later joined Rockefeller after graduating from college.

His very first start in business, spurred by Rockefeller, made Eaton a millionaire by 30. He was sent to Manitoba, Canada, to acquire franchises for a proposed series of power plants. When the deal was called off, Eaton, foreseeing tremendous opportunity, raised money from Canadian banks and built his own plants. Through consolidation, he set up Continental Gas and Electric Company extending throughout western Canada and the Midwest. In 1913, worth $2 million, Eaton returned to Cleveland and acquired a partnership in the established investment banking firm, Otis and Company.

With Otis and Company, Eaton pulled off spectacular coups against Wall Street. In 1925, he invaded the steel industry, and five years later had the third largest steel concern, rivaling Morgan's U.S. Steel and Schwab's Bethlehem Steel! Eaton found a debt-ridden Ohio steel firm, offered the exact amount of its indebtedness—$18 million—and took control. He took over several other firms, combining them into the $331 million Republic Steel Corporation in 1930.

In 1929, he began buying up public utility rival **Sam Insull**'s securities at the same time Morgan interests made it clear they wanted in on Sam Insull's empire. Whether it was to undermine Insull or, more probably, to tick off Wall Street, Eaton sold Insull his 160,000 shares for $56 million—about $6 million above market price—one of the first examples of what we would today call greenmail. This gave Eaton a tidy profit, assured Insull control of his pyramid-structured corporation (though not for long), and thus infuriated Morgan interests who had been intent on building their own public utilities empire by gaining control of Insull's.

Alongside glorious victory, however, came tremendous losses in 1929. The Crash took over $100 million from Eaton, and the *Nation* reported, "It was the final curtain in the grandiose empire-building of Cyrus S. Eaton." Left with almost no cash, he was forced to go into debt to ward off Bethlehem Steel's attempted takeover of Republic Steel. By 1931, he had won the challenge, but at the cost of most of his remaining personal fortune. Eaton spent most of the mid-1930s trying to put his leveraged empire on solid footing—with little progress—but no further setbacks. It was in 1938, after almost a decade of difficulty, that Eaton really made sparks fly. He aided a group aimed at fighting a Morgan and Kuhn, Loeb consortium for control of Alleghany Corporation and its trophy property-centerpiece, the Chesapeake and Ohio Railroad.

Morgan and Kuhn interests already sat on Allegheny's board, and the custom of the day routinely called for equity and bond issues to be handled by the firms of board members. So, when it came time for Alleghany to issue a $30 million bond issue, the houses of Morgan and Kuhn, Loeb presumed the offering would be theirs to handle. But Eaton led a group offering an outsiders' low-ball bid to do the offering cheaper (at a lower net interest rate to Alleghany) which would save the company $1.35 million. That was a huge discrepancy in pricing for the service of underwriting and provided a pricing wedge that simply demanded consideration.

The Morgan and Kuhn, Loeb interests tried to stampede the board into overlooking the Eaton offer on the grounds that he was unreliable. But the Eaton consortium threatened litigation against the whole board, charging that they weren't fulfilling their fiduciary obligation to their shareholders. Whether insecure in their ability to win the litigation, or simply not wanting the hassle, the board capitulated and accepted Eaton's offer—thus marking the birth of competitive bidding! By 1942, the SEC made competitive bidding mandatory, chalking up another victory for Eaton and another aggravating defeat for Wall Street! This phenomenon alone ensured Young and Eaton a prime spot in financial history.

Eaton kept going strong from this point on, creating a $2.6 billion empire by his death at 95. No more busts—strictly various and diverse booms that rebuilt his $200 million fortune. He was a director of some 40 firms, including Fisher Body, Detroit Steel and the Chesapeake and Ohio until he was 90! He had extensive public utility holdings worldwide, including ones in Tokyo, Berlin and Brazil, making him one of the first Americans to invest overseas, and particularly one of the first to invest overseas in lesser developed nations. He practically owned the rubber industry including Goodyear Tire and Rubber. He bought control of Sherwin-Williams paint firm and owned Cleveland Cliffs Iron Mining. Financial management of his concerns always centered in Cleveland.

Eaton's personal life was equally diverse. Married for almost 30 years, Eaton had seven kids, two of whom died young. He divorced in 1933 and remarried in 1957 at the age of 74. A staunch Republican until nearly 50, Eaton swung to the Democrats' side in 1930, feeling Herbert Hoover couldn't lift America out from under the Depression. At that point, he put his energies into supporting Franklin Roosevelt.

Later, he grew still more liberal in his politics, becoming an early advocate of American–Communist bloc relations. Nicknamed the "Kremlin's favorite capitalist," he was denounced as a traitor during the cold war and initiated the first Pugwash conference on nuclear weapons in 1957 at his home in Pugwash, Nova Scotia. Defending his patriotism, Eaton said he believed "a nation's social and economic system is its own affair. I wouldn't want Communism here, but if the Russians want it, that's up to them."

Eaton was one of those rare birds on the financial scene who worked un-obtrusively and disliked all sorts of hoopla. Yet in his hometown, Cleveland, he was a beloved personality supported by the people. In fact, a good part of Cleveland's population supported him by buying into Eaton enterprises. One writer once said, "If he should fall, so would most of Cleveland." Eaton had sort of a grass-roots effort behind him, and as we saw in **A.P. Giannini**'s case, that's the strongest form of support anyone can have, far stronger than Wall Street ties.

As a person, perhaps his most amazing quality was his ability to remain flexible into the later years of his life. Most folks get kind of rigid and set in their ways as they age, but whether it was getting wiped out and rebuilding his wealth, his political swings, his marital status which yo-yoed between ages 50 and 74, this was a man who could bend with the breeze and bounce off a fall. He brought life to old age.

CONCLUSION

THE NEXT 100

By now you've seen these *100 Minds* that made our market were exceptionally diverse. No rules could box these 100 in any singularly prescribed format. For every generality you can craft to describe them, you can find at least several exceptions to prove the rule. In many instances, these giants were simply above any rules. They and thousands of other lesser noted, or unnoted, leaders set the stage for today's markets through their innovations. But innovation never ends—even in a partially free market. And these leaders' efforts and the evolutions springing from them are not this story's end. History is a beginning—merely the stage being set for future history.

There are plenty of living legends who are, and always will be, more famous than many of these *100 Minds*. I'm talking about today's bigwig movers and shakers—or octogenarian legends from 20 years ago. Their stories will be written best when their lives are done and can be put in perspective. And their lives will tell still more about market innovation.

But many of the lessons we will learn from the next 50 have already been told by my 100. The next 50 will be no smarter, no more diverse, and no more creative; they still will have to grapple with many of the same issues faced by the 100.

These next 50 will show us more technical expertise, to be sure, as it pertains to rapidly evolving technology and a world where increased specialization in all fields seems insured. Yet, in finance, the key will be to deploy specialization without losing the overview and personal traits that made the original 100 so great. Specialization in finance without overview is useless. It's like a cog spinning wildly with no connections. And specialization without the right supporting character traits won't go any further than many of the geniuses we've examined who couldn't quite get past their own character flaws.

Time and again, we saw among the *100 Minds* separation based on character between those who endured as financial successes and those who gained-and-waned. The endurers cared more for the game they played than their egos or what their money could buy for them in earthly pleasures. The flash-in-the-pans were often just as smart, innovative and timely as the endurers, but often got diverted by some compulsive obsession, whether it was wine, women, ego, or all three. It will probably always be that way. And you may well take it to heart, and to the bank, in your own investment activities.

That there will be another 50 fabulous financial types, who could half-fill another book like this one, is certain. Between us, we could rattle off a third of them right here and now: Warren Buffett, Fred Carr, David Dreman, Phil Fisher, Rudolph Giuliani, Peter Lynch, Ned Johnson, Michael Milken, William O'Neil, T. Boone Pickens, Claude Rosenberg, Barr Rosenberg, William Sharpe, George Soros, John Templeton, Gerry Tsai, Robert Vesco. All are living, most are still contributing, and all are fabulous and fascinating. Think a tad harder and another third would pop into our minds without too much trouble. But coming up with those 50 names isn't really the issue.

What really counts is the 50 after that . . . the ones who haven't even started their financial legacies yet. Hopefully, we may some day see a book entitled, *The Second 100 Minds That Remade the Market*. If capitalism and Wall Street are to prosper, then behind them must be vivid minds twisting new ideas out of an ever-aging financial system to keep it renewed. Will those minds keep evolving to drive our financial system forward? Let us hope so. The future of capitalism depends on it. And to make it fun for us in the process, let us hope they are as fascinating as these *100 Minds That Made The Market*.

APPENDIX

BIBLIOGRAPHIES

CHAPTER 1: THE DINOSAURS

MAYER AMSCHEL ROTHSCHILD

Cowles, Virginia. *The Rothschilds: A Family of Fortune*. Alfred A. Knopf, 1973, pp. 1–139.

Glanz, Rudolf. "The Rothschild Legend in America." *Jewish Social Studies*. Vols. 18–19: Jan.–April, 1957, pp. 3–28.

Morton, Frederic. *The Rothschilds: A Family Portrait*. Atheneum, 1962, pp. 298.

"Nathan Rothschild." *The Banker*. Vol. 130: Jan., 1980, pp. 116–117.

NATHAN ROTHSCHILD

Cowles, Virginia. *The Rothschilds: A Family of Fortune*. Alfred A. Knopf, 1973, pp. 1–139

Glanz, Rudolf. "The Rothschild Legend in America." *Jewish Social Studies*. Vols. 18–19: Jan.–April, 1957, pp. 3–28.

Morton, Frederic. *The Rothschilds: A Family Portrait*. Atheneum, 1962, pp. 298.

"Nathan Rothschild." *The Banker*. Vol. 136: Jan., 1986, pp. 89.

STEPHEN GIRARD

Adams, Donald R., Jr. *Finance and Enterprise in Early America*. University of Pennsylvania Press, 1978, pp. 1–141.

Govan, Thomas Payne. *Nicholas Biddle*. The University of Chicago Press, 1959, pp. 45, 55–56.

Groner, Alex. *The History of American Business & Industry*. American Heritage Publishing Co., Inc., 1972, pp. 57, 67.

Minnigerode, Meade. *Certain Rich Men*. G.P. Putnam's Sons, 1927, pp. 3–30.

"Stephen Girard, Promoter of the Second Bank of the United States." *Journal of Economic History*. Vol. 2: Nov., 1942, pp. 125–148.

The National Cyclopedia of American Biography. James T. White & Co., Vol. 17: 1897, pp. 11–13.

JOHN JACOB ASTOR

Groner, Alex. *The History of American Business & History*. American Heritage Publishing Co., Inc., 1972, pp. 57, 67–68.

Holbrook, Stewart H. *The Age of Moguls*. Doubleday Co., 1953, pp. 9–10.

Minnigerode, Meade. *Certain Rich Men*. G.P. Putnam's Sons, 1927, pp. 31–50.

Myers, Gustavus. *The History of Great American Fortunes*. The Modern Library, 1907, pp. 93–175.

Porter, Wiggins. *John Jacob Astor: Business Man*. 2 vols. Harvard University Press, 1931, p. 1137.

Smith, Matthew Hale. *Sunshine and Shadow in New York*. J.B. Burr and Company, 1869, pp. 113–126.

CORNELIUS VANDERBILT

Clews, Henry. *Fifty Years in Wall Street: "Twenty-Eight Years in Wall Street." Revised and Enlarged by a Resume of the Past Twenty-Two Years Making a Record of Fifty Years in Wall Street*. Irving, 1908.

Fowler, William Worthington. *Twenty Years of Inside Life in Wall Street: or Revelations of the Personal Experience of a Speculator*. Reprint: Greenwood Press, 1968.

Groner, Alex. *The History of American Business and Industry*. American Heritage Publishing Co., Inc., 1972, pp. 88, 116, 119, 123–125, 136, 158–160, 165, 236.

Ingham, John N. *Biographical Dictionary of American Business Leaders*. 4 vols. Greenwood Press, 1983.

Minnegerode, Meade. *Certain Rich Men*. G.P. Putnam's Sons, 1927, pp. 101–134.

Myers, Gustavus. *The History of Great American Fortunes*. The Modern Library, 1907.

Sharp, Robert M. *The Lore & Legends of Wall Street*. Dow Jones-Irwin, 1989, pp. 98–99.

GEORGE PEABODY

Hidy, Muriel Emmie. *George Peabody: Merchant and Financier.* Arno Press, 1978.

Parker, Franklin. *George Peabody: A Biography.* Vanderbilt University Press, 1971.

Sobel, Robert. *The Big Board: A History of the New York Stock Exchange.* The Free Press, Macmilian Co., 1965, pp. 36–37.

JUNIUS SPENCER MORGAN

Carosso, Vincent P. *The Morgans: Private International Bankers.* Harvard University Press, 1987, pp. 18–145.

Parker, Franklin. *George Peabody.* Vanderbilt University Press, 1956, pp. 65–70, 140–145.

DANIEL DREW

Holbrook, Stewart. *The Age of Moguls.* Doubleday & Co., Inc., 1953, pp. 21–35.

Minnigerode, Meade. *Certain Rich Men.* G.P. Putnam's Sons, 1927, pp. 83–100.

White, Bouck. *The Book of Daniel Drew.* Original: Doubleday, 1910. Reprint: Citadel Press, 1910, pp. 100–200.

Sobel, Robert. *Panic on Wall Street: A History of America's Financial Disasters.* Macmillan Co., 1968, pp. 122–135.

JAY COOKE

Cooke, Jay. "A Decade of American Finance." *North American Review.* Nov. 1902. pp. 577–586.

Neill, Humphrey B. *The Inside Story of the Stock Exchange.* B.C. Forbes & Sons Publishing Co., Inc., 1950, pp. 74–76, 83, 97–98, 144.

Oberholtzer, Ellis Paxson. "Jay Cooke, and the Financing of the Civil War." *Century Magazine.* Nov. 1906, pp. 116–132; Jan., 1907, pp. 282+.

Sobel, Robert. *Panic on Wall Street: A History of America's Financial Disasters.* Macmillan Co., 1968, pp. 167–173, 189–194.

Sobel, Robert. *The Big Board: A History of the New York Stock Market.* The Free Press, Macmillan Co., 1965, pp. 69–71, 82.

CHAPTER 2: JOURNALISTS AND AUTHORS

CHARLES DOW

Nelson, S.A. *The ABC of Stock Speculation.* Original: S.A. Nelson, 1903. Reprint: Fraser, 1964.

Schultz, Harry D. and Coslow, Samuel, eds. *A Treasury of Wall Street Wisdom.* Investors' Press, Inc., 1966, pp. 3–24.

Sobel, Robert. *Inside Wall Street.* W. W. Norton & Company, 1977, pp. 117–121, 123, 127.

Stillman, Richard J. *Dow Jones Industrial Average.* Dow Jones-Irwin, 1986, pp. 9–26.

Wendt, Lloyd. *The Wall Street Journal.* Rand McNally & Company, 1982, pp. 15–84.

EDWARD JONES

Rosenberg, Jerry M. *Inside The Wall Street Journal.* Macmillan Publishing Co., Inc., 1982, pp. 1–19.

Sobel, Robert *Inside Wall Street.* W.W. Norton & Company, Inc., 1977, pp. 118, 127.

Wendt, Lloyd. *The Wall Street Journal.* Rand McNally & Co., 1982.

THOMAS W. LAWSON

Ingham, John N. *Biographical Dictionary of American Business Leaders.* 4 vols. Greenwood Press, 1983.

Lawson, Thomas. "Frenzied Finance." *Everybody's Magazine.* Vol. 12: pp. 173+.

Lawson, Thomas. "The Remedy." *Everybody's Magazine.* Vol. 27: Oct., 1912, pp. 472+.

Lawson, Thomas. *Frenzied Finance: Vol. 1. The Crime of Amalgamated.* Original: Ridgeway-Thayer, 1905. Reprint: Greenwood Press, 1968.

B.C. FORBES

"B.C. Forbes Dies." *Time.* Vol. 63: May 17, 1954, p. 105.

"B.C. Forbes Dies." *New York Times.* May 7, 1954, p. 24:3.

Forbes, B.C. *Keys to Success.* B.C. Forbes Publishing Company, 1917.

Forbes, B.C. *How to Get the Most Out of Business.* B.C. Forbes Publishing Company, 1927.

Forbes, Malcolm. *More Than I Dreamed.* Simon & Schuster, 1989.

"A Magazine of His Own." *Forbes.* Sept. 15, 1967, pp. 13+.

EDWIN LEFEVRE

"Chronicle and Comment." *The Bookman.* Vol. 43: Aug., 1916, pp. 582–585.
"Edwin Lefevre, 73, Financial Writer." *New York Times.* Feb. 24, 1943, p. 21:5.
Lefevre, Edwin. "New Bull Market, New Dangers." *Saturday Evening Post.* Vol. 208: May 2, 1936, pp. 14–15+; May 9, 1936, pp. 25+.
Lefevre, Edwin. *Reminiscences of a Stock Operator.* George H. Doran Co., 1923. Reprint American Research Council.
"Lefevre, Edwin." *The Bookman.* Vol. 69: August, 1929, p. 629.
Lefevre, Edwin. "Vanished Billions." *Saturday Evening Post.* Vol. 204: Feb. 13, 1932, pp. 3–5+.
Lefevre, Edwin. "When Is It Safe to Invest?" *Saturday Evening Post.* Vol. 205: Aug. 6, 1932, pp. 12–13+.

CLARENCE W. BARRON

Pound, Arthur and Moore, Samuel Taylor, eds. *They Told Barron: Conversations and Revelations of an American Pepys in Wall Street.* Harper & Brothers Publishers, 1930.
Rosenberg, Jerry M. *Inside Wall Street.* Macmillan Publishing Co., 1982, pp. 21–44, 120–123.
Wendt, Lloyd. *Wall Street Journal.* Rand McNally & Company, 1982, pp. 143–148.

BENJAMIN GRAHAM

Cray, Douglas W. "Benjamin Graham, Securities Expert." *New York Times.* Sept. 23, 1976, p. 44:1.
"Portrait of an Analyst: Benjamin Graham." *Financial Analysts Journal.* Vol. 24: Jan.–Feb., 1968, pp. 15–16.
Rea, James B. "Remembering Benjamin Graham—Teacher and Friend." *The Journal of Portfolio Management.* Summer, 1977, pp. 66–72.
"Remembering Uncle Ben." *Forbes.* Vol. 118: Oct. 15, 1976, p. 144.
Smith, Adam. *Supermoney.* Random House, 1972, pp. 173–199.
"The Father of Value Investing." *Fortune.* Vol. 116: Fall, 1988 Investor's Guide, p. 48.
Train, John. *The Money Master.* Harper & Row, Publishers, 1980, pp. 82–113.

ARNOLD BERNHARD

Brimelow, Peter. *The Wall Street Gurus.* Random House, 1986, pp. 4–5, 28–30, 85, 88, 156–167.

Kaplan, Gilbert Edmund and Welles, Chris, eds. *The Money Managers*. Random House, 1969, pp. 137–148.

Mayer, Martin. *Wall Street: Men and Money*. Harper & Brothers, Publishers, 1959, pp. 209–212.

Reynolds, Quentin and Rowe, Wilfrid S. *Operation Success*. Duell, Sloan and Pearce, 1957, pp. 54–68.

"Value Line's Arnold Bernhard: Making His Own Advice Pay Off." *Financial World*. Vol. 148: Jan. 15, 1979, p. 70.

"Value Line Figures It's Time To Go Public." *Business Week*. Jan. 24, 1983, p. 72.

Vartan, Vartanig G. "Arnold Bernhard is Dead at 86; Led Value Line Investor Service." *New York Times*. Dec. 23, 1987, p. D-18:1.

LOUIS ENGEL

Bird, David. "Louis Engel Jr., Ex-Merrill Lynch Partner, Dies." *New York Times*. Nov. 8, 1982, p. IV-15:1.

Engel, Louis. *How to Buy Stocks*. Bantam Books, Inc., 1967.

May, Hal. *Contemporary Authors*. Gale Research Co. Vol. 108: 1983.

Sobel, Robert. *Inside Wall Street*. W.W. Norton & Company, Inc. 1977, pp. 95, 103–106, 114–115, 130–132, 208–211.

"Use of Lingo of Middle-Income Class Advised To Get Group to Put Idle Funds in Securities." *New York Times*. Oct. 9, 1949, p. III-6:4.

CHAPTER 3: INVESTMENT BANKERS AND BROKERS

AUGUST BELMONT

Birmingham, Stephen. *Our Crowd*. Dell Publishing Co., Inc., 1967, pp. 25, 38–47, 76–82, 89–91, 101–102.

Black, David. *The King of Fifth Avenue*. The Dial Press, 1981.

Ingham, John N. *Biographical Dictionary of American Business Leaders*. 4 vols. Greenwood Press, 1983.

The National Cyclopedia of American Biography. James T. White & Co. Vol. 11: 1909, p. 500.

EMANUEL LEHMAN AND HIS SON PHILIP

Birmingham, Stephen. *"Our Crowd."* Dell Publishing Co., Inc., 1967, pp. 16, 20–21, 90–91, 100, 108–109, 156–158, 359–360, 392–394.

Ingham, John N. *Biographical Dictionary of American Business Leaders*. 4 vols. Greenwood Press, 1983.

Krefetz, Gerald. *Jews and Money: The Myths and the Reality.* Ticknor and Fields, 1982, pp. 45–83.
"Philip Lehman, 86, Noted Banker, Dies." *New York Times.* March 22, 1947, p. 13:1.
Smith, Arthur D. Howden. *Men Who Run America.* The Bobbs-Merrill Co., 1936, pp. 111–118, 199, 235, 251–252.
The National Cyclopedia of American Biography. James T. White & Co. Vol. 25: 1936, p. 98.

JOHN PIERPONT MORGAN

Baker, Ray Standard. "J. Pierpont Morgan." *McClure's Magazine.* October, 1901, pp. 506–518.
Birmingham, Stephen. *Our Crowd.* Dell Publishing Co., 1967, pp. 199–205.
Merwin, John. "J.P. Morgan: The Agglomerator." *Forbes.* July 13, 1987, pp. 275, 278.
Moody, John. *The Masters of Capital.* Yale University Press, 1919, pp. 1–34.
Sinclair, Andrew. *Corsair.* Little, Brown and Co., 1981, pp. 15–38, 159–191.
Sobel, Robert. "Junk Issues of the Past and Future." *Wall Street Journal.* Feb. 28, 1990, p. A14.

JACOB H. SCHIFF

Adler, Cyrus. *Jacob H. Schiff: His Life And Letters.* 2 vols. William Heinemann, Ltd., 1929.
Birmingham, Stephen. *Our Crowd.* Dell Publishing Co., Inc., 1967, pp. 184–236, 348–408.
Brooks, John. *Once in Golconda.* Harper Colophon Books, 1969, pp. 51–55.
Forbes, B.C. *Men Who Are Making America.* B.C. Forbes Publishing Company, Inc., 1916, pp. 328–335.
Ingham, John N. *Biographical Dictionary of American Business Leaders.* 4 vols. Greenwood Press, 1983.
Neill, Humphrey B. *The Inside Story of the Stock Exchange.* B.C. Forbes & Sons Publishing Company, Inc., 1950, pp. 135–140, 161, 165.

GEORGE W. PERKINS

Forbes, B.C. *Men Who Are Making America.* B.C. Forbes Publishing Company, Inc., 1916, pp. 278–287.
Garraty, John. *Right-Hand Man: The Life of George W. Perkins.* 1st ed. Harper, 1960, pp. 30–44, 130–146, 173–176, 233–234.

"George W. Perkins Dies In 58th Year." *New York Times*. June 19, 1920, p. 13–1.

Groner, Alex. *The History of American Business and Industry*. American Heritage Publishing Co., Inc., pp. 198–199, 220.

Ingham, John N. *Biographical Dictionary of American Business Leaders*. 4 vols. Greenwood Press, 1983.

Lewis, Corey. *The House of Morgan*. G. Howard Watt, 1930, pp. 257, 306–309, 378–386.

Malone, Dumas. *Dictionary of American Biography*. Charles Scribner's Sons. Vol. 14: 1934, pp. 471–2.

JOHN PIERPONT "JACK" MORGAN, JR.

Forbes, John D. *J.P. Morgan, Jr*. University of Virginia, 1982.

Ingham, John N. *Biographical Dictionary of American Business Leaders*. 4 vols. Greenwood Press, 1983.

"Mister Morgan." *Fortune*. Aug., 1930, pp. 57+.

Pecora, Ferdinand. *Wall Street Under Oath: The Story of Our Modern Money Changers*. Original: Simon & Schuster, 1939. Reprint: Augustus M. Kelley, 1968.

Sobel, Robert. *The Big Board: A History of America's Financial Disasters*. The Free Press, Macmillan Company, 1965, pp. 237–238, 295, 305.

United Press. "J.P. Morgan Dies, Victim of Stroke at Florida Resort." *New York Times*. March 13, 1943, p. 1.

THOMAS LAMONT

Brooks, John. *Once in Golconda*. Harper Colophon Books, 1969, pp. 46–48, 97, 102, 124–127, 282–286.

Carosso, Vincent P. *Investment Banking in America: A History*. Harvard University Press, 1970.

Carosso, Vincent P. *The Morgans: Private International Bankers*. Harvard University Press, 1987, p. 441.

Corey, Lewis. *The House of Morgan*. G. Howard Watt, 1930, pp. 430, 452.

Josephson, Matthew. *The Money Lords*. Weybright and Talley, 1972, pp. 91–92, 202–203, 345.

CLARENCE D. DILLON

"Dillon, Read Buys Dodge Motors For Over $175, 000,000." *New York Times*. April 1, 1925, p. 1:6+.

Ingham, John N. *Biographical Dictionary of American Business Leaders*. 4 vols. Greenwood Press, 1983.

Josephson, Matthew. *The Money Lords.* Weybright and Talley, Inc., 1972, pp. 18, 191.

Pecora, Ferdinand. *Wall Street Under Oath.* Simon & Schuster, Inc., 1939, pp. 48–50, 207–214.

The National Cyclopedia of American Biography. James T. White & Co. Vol. 62: 1984, pp. 243–244.

CHARLES E. MERRILL

"Charles Merrill, Broker, Dies; Founder of Merrill Lynch Firm." *New York Times.* Oct. 7, 1956, p. 1:1+.

Ingham, John N. *Dictionary of American Business Leaders.* 4 vols. Greenwood Press, 1983, pp. 930–933.

The National Cyclopedia of American Biography. James T. White & Co. Vol. 53: 1971, pp. 39–40.

"Wall Street: We The People." *Time.* Vol. 68: Oct. 15, 1956, p. 104.

GERALD M. LOEB

"Are There Men for All Seasons?" *Forbes.* Vol. 103: Jan. 15, 1969, p. 55.

Brady, Raymond. "Wall Street Beat: The Investment Individualist." *Dun's Review.* June, 1969, pp. 105–106.

Loeb, Gerald M. *The Battle for Investment Survival.* Simon & Schuster, 1965, 1971.

Martin, Ralph G. *The Wizard of Wall Street.* William Morrow & Co., 1965.

Shepherd, William G. "The Market According to Loeb." *Business Week.* May 20, 1972, p. 74.

"Customers' Brokers Seen Bettering Role." *New York Times.* Jan. 10, 1945, p. 35:6.

SIDNEY WEINBERG

"Director's Doctrine." *Newsweek.* Vol. 9: Jan. 14, 1957, p. 70.

"Everybody's Broker." *Time.* Vol. 72: Dec. 8, 1958, p. 96.

"Finance: Mr. Wall Street." *Newsweek.* Vol. 74: Aug. 4, 1969, pp. 76–77.

Kahn, E.J., Jr. "Directors' Director." *New Yorker.* Vol. 32: Sept. 8, 1956, pp. 39–40+.

"Lessons of Leadership: Part VII—Balancing Ability with Humility." *Nation's Business.* Vol. 53: Dec., 1965, pp. 44–46+.

"Wall Street: A Nice Guy from Brooklyn." *Time.* Vol. 94: Aug. 1, 1969, p.69a.

CHAPTER 4: THE INNOVATORS

ELIAS JACKSON "LUCKY" BALDWIN

Bancroft, H.H. "Dictation" prepared for *Chronicles of the Builders*. H.H. Bancroft Collection, University of California at Berkeley, ca. 1890–1891.

Dickinson, Samuel. *San Francisco is Your Home*. Stanford University Press, 1947, pp. 151–158.

Glasscock, C.B. *Lucky Baldwin: The Story of an Unconventional Success*. The Bobbs-Merrill Company, 1933.

Hunt, Rockwell. *California's Stately Hall of Fame*. College of the Pacific, 1950, pp. 287–292.

King, Joseph L. *History of the San Francisco Stock and Exchange Board*. Original: 1910. Reprint: Arno Press, 1975, pp. 256–259.

Parkhill, Forbes. *The Wildest of the West*. Henry Holt and Company, 1951, pp. 50–55.

Sear, Marian V. *Mining Stock Exchanges, 1860–1930*. University of Montana Press, 1973, pp. 39–45.

The National Cyclopedia of American Biography. James T. White & Company. Vol. 22: 1932, pp. 381–382.

CHARLES T. YERKES

"An American Invader of London." *Harper's Weekly*. Vol. 47: Jan. 17, 1903, p. 90.

Dreiser, Theodore. *The Financier*. Original: Boni and Liveright, 1925. Reprint: The World Publishing Co., 1940.

Dreiser, Theodore. *The Titan*. Boni and Liveright, 1914.

Gerber, Philip L. "The Financier Himself: Dreiser and C.T. Yerkes." *PMLA*. Vol. 88: Jan., 1973, pp. 112–121.

Roberts, Sidney I. "Portrait of a Robber Baron: Charles T. Yerkes." *Business History Review*. Vol. 35: Autumn, 1961, pp. 345–371.

THOMAS FORTUNE RYAN

Brooks, John. *Once in Golconda*. Harper Colophon Books, 1969, pp. 23–26, 40.

Everett, James F. "How a Great Merger is Handled in Wall Street." *Harper's Weekly*. Vol. 48: Nov. 26, 1904, pp. 1802–1804.

Ingham, John N. *Biographical Dictionary of American Business Leaders*. 4 vols. Greenwood Press, 1983.

"Like a Baby." *New Yorker*. Vol. 25: March 26, 1949, p. 18:1.
"Notes from the Capital: Thomas F. Ryan." *The Nation*. Vol. 105: Aug. 23, 1917, pp. 206–207.

RUSSELL SAGE

Groner, Alex. *The History of American Business & Industry*. American Heritage Publishing Company, Inc., 1972.
Ingham, John N. *Biographical Dictionary of American Business Leaders*. 4 vols. Greenwood Press, 1983.
Myers, Gustavus. *The History of Great American Fortunes*. The Modern Library, 1907, pp. 437, 447–477, 487–491.
Sarnoff, Paul. *Russell Sage: The Money King*. Ivan Obelinsky, Inc., 1965.
Sarnoff, Paul. *Puts and Calls: The Complete Guide*. Hawthorne Books, 1968.
Sharp, Robert M. *Lore and Legends of Wall Street*. Dow Jones-Irwin, 1989, pp. 155–158.

ROGER W. BABSON

Babson, Roger W. *A Continuous Working Plan for Your Money*. Babson's Statistical Organization, Inc., 1927.
Babson, Roger W. *Business Barometers and Investment*. Harper & Brothers Publishers, sixth edition, 1952.
Brimelow, Peter. *The Wall Street Gurus*. Random House, Inc., 1986, pp. 31–36.
"Sir Isaac Babson." *Newsweek*. Aug. 23, 1948, p. 47.
"Roger Babson, 92, Economist, Dead." *New York Times*. March 6, 1967, p. 33:4.

T. ROWE PRICE

Michaels, James W. "Thomas Rowe Price: 1898–1983." *Forbes*. Vol. 132: pp. 51–52.
Price, T. Rowe. "Stocks To Buy." *Forbes*. Vol. 121: May 29, 1978, pp. 126–127.
Scholl, Jaye. "Retracing the Route of an Investment Genius." *Barron's*. Vol. 63: Nov. 14, 1983, p. 62.
"The Money Men: An Old Curmudgeon's New Era." *Forbes*. Vol. 104: July 1, 1969, pp. 62–63.

"The Money Men: The Generation Gap." *Forbes*. Vol. 106: Nov. 15, 1970, pp. 46+.

Train, John. *The Money Masters*. Harper & Row, Publishers, 1980, pp. 139–157.

FLOYD B. ODLUM

Block, Maxine, ed. *Current Biography*. The H.W. Wilson Co., 1941, pp. 629–631.

Davis, Forrest. "Thinker of Wall Street." *Saturday Evening Post*. Vol. 210: July 10, 1937, pp. 14–15+.

"Floyd B. Odlum, Financier, 84, Dies." *New York Times*. June 18, 1976, p. IV-16:3.

"Floyd Odlum and the Work Ethic." *New York Times*. Jan. 28, 1973, p. III-1:7.

"Go-Getter for the Little Man." *Nation's Business*. Vol. 29: Nov., 1941, pp. 34+.

Hellman, Geoffrey T. "Collector of Trusts." *Review of Reviews and World's Work*. Vol. 88: Nov., 1933, pp. 48–49.

"The Chairman Negotiates a Business Deal." *Fortune*. Vol. 40: Sept., 1949, p. 91.

"The Phone Was Silent." *Newsweek*. Vol. 5: May 30, 1960, p. 69.

PAUL CABOT

"Faces Behind the Figures." *Forbes*. Vol. 104: June 15, 1970, p. 80.

"In Investing, It's the Prudent Bostonian." *Business Week*. June 6, 1959, pp. 56–74.

Metz, Robert. "Market Place." *New York Times*. Oct. 26, 1973, p. 64:3.

"The Money Men." *Forbes*. Vol. 103: Feb. 15, 1969, pp. 65+.

Train, John. *The Money Masters*. Harper & Row, Publishers, 1980, pp. 42–56.

GEORGES DORIOT

Dominguez, John R. *Venture Capital*. Lexington Books, 1974, pp. 13, 48–59.

Fuhrman, Peter. "A Teacher Who Made A Difference." *Forbes*. July 13, 1987, pp. 362+.

International Who's Who. Europa Publications Limited. Vol. 47: 1983.

"Pere Doriot." *Newsweek*. Vol. 67: May 16, 1966, p. 84.

"Profit-Minded Professor." *Time*. Vol. 81: March 8, 1963, pp. 88–89.
"Stock to be Sold by Textron Unit." *New York Times*. Oct. 16, 1959, p. 42:4.

ROYAL LITTLE

"As They See It." *Forbes*. Vol. 106: Dec. 15, 1970, pp. 38–41.
"Financial Scorekeeper." *Forbes*. Vol. 138: Nov. 17, 1986, p. 258.
Levy, Robert. "The Restless World of Royal Little." *Dun's Review*. Vol. 95: Feb., 1970, pp. 38–40.
Little, Royal. "How I'm Deconglomerating The Conglomerates." *Fortune*. Vol. 100: July 16, 1979, pp. 120+.
Little, Royal. *How To Lose $100,000,000 And Other Valuable Advice*. Little, Brown and Co., 1979.
"Royal Little Looks at Conglomerates." *Dun's Review*. Vol. 91: May, 1968, pp. 25–27.
Solow, Herbert. "Royal Little's Remarkable Retirement." *Fortune*. Vol. 66: Oct., 1962, pp. 124–126+.

CHAPTER 5: BANKERS AND CENTRAL BANKERS

JOHN LAW

Oudard, Georges. *The Amazing Life of John Law, The Man Behind the Mississippi Bubble*. Pawson & Clarke, Ltd., 1928.
Mackay, Charles. *Extraordinary Popular Delusions and the Madness of Crowds*. Original: Richard Bentley, 1841. Reprint: L.C. Page, 1932. Distributed by Fraser.
Wilding, Peter. *Adventures in the Eighteenth Century*. G. P. Putnam's Sons, 1937.

ALEXANDER HAMILTON

DiBacco, Thomas V. *Made in the U.S.A.* Harper & Row, 1987, pp. 63–74.
Hacker, Andrew. "Why We Are Hamilton's Heirs." *Fortune*. Oct. 18, 1982, pp. 231–234.
Hill, Frederick Trevor. *The Story of a Street*. Original: Harper & Brothers, 1908. Reprint: Fraser, 1969.
Ingham, John N. *Biographical Dictionary of American Business Leaders*. 4 vols. Greenwood Press, 1983.

McDonald, Forrest. "Understanding Alexander Hamilton." *National Review.* July 11, 1980, pp. 827–833.

Mitchell, Broadus. *Alexander Hamilton: A Concise Biography.* Oxford University Press, 1976, pp. 175–258.

Neill, Humphrey B. *The Inside Story of the Stock Exchange.* B.C. Forbes & Sons Publishing Company, Inc., 1950, pp. 9–21, 24, 56.

NICHOLAS BIDDLE

Catterall, Ralph C.H. *The Second Bank of the United States.* The University of Chicago Press, 1903.

Groner, Alex. *The History of American Business & Industry.* American Heritage Publishing Co., Inc., 1972.

Govan, Thomas Payne. *Nicholas Biddle: Nationalist and Public Banker.* The University of Chicago Press, 1959

Ingham, John N. *Biographical Dictionary of American Business Leaders.* 4 vols. Greenwood Press, 1983

Schlesinger, Arthur M. Jr. *The Age of Jackson.* Little, Brown & Co., 1945.

JAMES STILLMAN

Allen, Frederick Lewis. *The Lords of Creation.* Harper & Brothers Publishers, 1935, pp. 13, 52–53, 57, 81–99, 105–110, 122–125, 129–142.

Burr, Anna. *The Portrait of a Banker: James Stillman.* Duffield & Co., 1927.

Forbes, B.C. *Men Who Are Making America.* B.C. Forbes Publishing Company, Inc., 1916, pp. 368–374.

Holbrook, Stewart H. *The Age of Moguls.* Doubleday & Co., Inc., 1953, pp. 135–6, 169, 173.

Moody, John and Turner, George Kibbe. "Masters of Capital in America. The City Bank: The Federation the Great Merchants." *McClure's Magazine.* Vol. 37: May, 1911, pp. 73–87.

Winkler, John K. *The First Billion: The Stillmans and the National City Bank.* The Vanguard Press, 1934.

FRANK A. VANDERLIP

Forbes, B.C. *Men Who Are Making America.* B.C. Forbes Publishing Company, Inc., 1916, pp. 389–397.

"Frank Vanderlip, Banker, Dies At 72." *New York Times.* June 30, 1937, p. 23:1.

Ingham, John N. *Biographical Dictionary of American Business Leaders.* 4 vols. Greenwood Press, 1983.

The National Cyclopedia of Biography. James T. White & Company. Vol. 15: 1916, p. 29.

Vanderlip, Frank A. "From Farm Boy to Financier: My Start in Wall Street." *Saturday Evening Post.* Vol. 207: Dec. 22, 1934, pp. 14–26.

GEORGE F. BAKER

Forbes, B.C. *Men Who Are Making America.* B.C. Forbes Publishing Company, Inc., 1916, pp. 11–18.

Groner, Alex. *The History of American Business and Industry.* American Heritage Publishing Co., Inc., 1972, pp. 193, 211, 213–215, 282, 289.

Ingham, John N. *Biographical Dictionary of American Business Leaders.* 4 vols. Greenwood Press, 1983.

Sobel, Robert. *Panic on Wall Street: A History of America's Financial Disasters.* Macmillan Company, 1968, pp. 285, 312, 318, 323.

Thomas, Gordon and Morgan-Witts, Max. *The Day the Bubble Burst.* Doubleday & Company, Inc., 1979, pp. 94, 376.

AMADEO P. GIANNINI

"Branch-Bank King: A.P. Giannini Blankets California With Chain, Eyes Other States." *Literary Digest.* Vols. 123–124, May 29, 1937, pp. 38–39.

Dana, Julian. *A.P. Giannini: Giant in the West.* Prentice-Hall, 1947, pp. 3–40, 250–334.

Groner, Alex. *The History of American Business & Industry.* American Heritage Publishing Co., Inc., 1972, pp. 281–285, 319.

Ingham, John N. *Biographical Dictionary of American Business Leaders.* 4 vols. Greenwood Press, 1983.

"$30,000,000 for Giannini." *Time.* Vol. 35: May 13, 1940, pp. 86+.

Yeates, Fred. *The Little Giant.* Bank of America, 1954, 80 pp.

PAUL M. WARBURG

Brooks, John. "*Our Crowd.*" Dell Publishing Co., Inc., 1967, pp. 22, 189, 226–237, 415–451.

"Finance: Mr. Warburg Speaks Out." *Review of Reviews.* Vol. 81: June, 1930, p. 90

Forbes, B.C. *Men Who Are Making America.* B.C. Forbes Publishing Company, Inc., 1916, pp. 398–405.

"Paul M. Warburg." *The Nation.* Vol. 134: p. 132.

"Paul Warburg." *New York Times.* Jan. 25, 1932, p. 16:2.

Warburg, Paul M. "Political Pressure and the Future of the Federal Reserve System." *Annals of the American Academy of Political and Social Science.* Vols. 99–101: Jan., 1922, pp. 70–74.

Warburg, Paul M. *The Federal Reserve System: Its Origin and Growth.* 2 vols. The Macmillan Company, 1930.

BENJAMIN STRONG

Brooks, John. *Once in Golconda.* Harper Colophon Books, 1969, pp. 90–98.

Chandler, Lester V. *Benjamin Strong: Central Banker.* The Brookings Institute, 1958.

The National Cyclopedia of American Biography. James T. White & Co. Vol. 33: 1947, pp. 471–472.

Sobel, Robert. *The Great Bull Market.* W.W. Norton & Co., Inc., 1968, pp. 56–57, 114–116.

GEORGE L. HARRISON

Brooks, John. *Once in Golconda.* Harper Colophon Books, 1970, pp. 153–158, 170–177.

"George L. Harrison Dead at 71; Headed Federal Reserve Here." *New York Times.* March 6, 1958.

Josephson, Matthew. *The Money Lords.* Weybright and Talley, Inc., 1972, pp. 91–92, 100–102, 122–124, 135, 147–148, 155–156, 326–327.

"The Dollar: Harrison Is Not Stabilizing It, Thomas Finds." *Newsweek.* Vol. 4: July 21, 1934, pp. 27–28.

The National Cyclopedia of American Biography. James T. White & Co. Vol. 51: 1969, pp. 563–565.

NATALIE SCHENK LAIMBEER

"Business Women Answer Charges Laid Against Them." *New York Times.* July 26, 1925, p. VII-11:1

Ingham, John N. *Biographical Dictionary of American Business Leaders.* 4 vols. Greenwood Press, 1983.

"Mrs. Laimbeer Tells Girls How To Succeed." *New York Times.* May 27, 1927, p. 11:3.

"Mrs. N.S. Laimbeer, Noted Banker, Dies." *New York Times.* Oct. 26, 1929, p. 17:4.

"Sees More Women As Bank Officials." *New York Times.* Feb. 14, 1925, p. 16:1

Holbrook, Stewart H. *Age of the Moguls.* Doubleday & Co., Inc., 1953, pp. 340–342.

"Woman Banker Quits National City." *New York Times.* Oct. 14, 1926, p. 4:5.
"Woman Wins Place As Bank Executive." *New York Times.* Feb. 13, 1925, p. 1:2+.
"Women in the Public Eye." *Woman Citizen.* Vol. 9: March 7, 1925, p. 4.

CHARLES E. MITCHELL

Allen, Frederick Lewis. *The Lords of Creation.* Harper & Brothers Publishers, 1935, pp. 304–319, 323–326, 331, 346, 349, 358, 365.
Brooks, John. *Once in Golconda.* Harper Colophon Books, 1969, pp. 100–104, 112, 124, 155, 187.
"C.E. Mitchell Joins Blyth & Co., Inc." *New York Times.* June 18, 1935, p. 31:6.
Josephson, Matthew. *The Money Lords.* Weybright and Talley, Inc., 1972, pp. 35, 53, 85–88, 91–92, 116, 120, 122, 134, 136, 142.
"Mitchell Guilty, Tax Board Rules." *New York Times.* Aug. 8, 1935, pp. 1:7+.
Pecora, Ferdinand. *Wall Street Under Oath.* Augustus M. Kelley Publishers, 1968, pp. 71–130, 194–196.
Sobel, Robert. *Panic on Wall Street: A History of America's Financial Disasters.* Macmillan Company, 1968, pp. 353–354, 369–376, 379.
Thomas, Gordon and Morgan-Witts, Max. *The Day the Bubble Burst.* Doubleday & Company, Inc., 1979, pp. 79–84, 111, 120, 135–149, 206–208, 221, 229, 233, 238, 247–250, 420–422, 425.

ELISHA WALKER

"Elisha Walker, 71, Financier, Is Dead." *New York Times.* Nov. 10, 1950, p. 27:1.
James, Marquis and James, Bessie Rowland. *Biography of a Bank.* Harper & Brothers, 1954, pp. 297–346, 346, 353.
Josephson, Matthew. *The Money Lords.* Weybright and Talley, 1972, pp. 37–44, 77–79, 220.
Pecora, Ferdinand. *Wall Street Under Oath.* Augustus M. Kelley Publishers, 1968, pp. 175–180.

ALBERT H. WIGGIN

Allen, Frederic Lewis. *The Lords of Creation.* Harper & Brothers Publishers, 1935, pp. 259, 323–6, 332–335, 356–58, 396, 445.
Brooks, John. *Once in Golconda.* Harper Colophon Books, 1970, pp. 103–105, 120–124, 190–193.

Carosso, Vincent P. *Investment Banking in America.* Harvard University Press, 1970, pp. 278, 346–347, 368–385, 412–413.

Ingham, John N. *Biographical Dictionary of American Business Leaders.* 4 vols. Greenwood Press, 1983.

Josephson, Matthew. *The Money Lords.* Weybright and Talley, Inc., 1972, pp. 91–92, 120–127, 135–136.

Pecora, Ferdinand. *Wall Street Under Oath.* Original: Simon & Schuster, 1939. Reprint: Augustus M. Kelley Publishers, 1968, pp. 67–68, 131–201, 258–269.

CHAPTER 6: NEW DEAL REFORMERS

E.H.H. SIMMONS

"Capitalize Brains, Message To Youth." *New York Times.* May 23, 1926, p. 24:1.

Josephson, Matthew. *The Money Lords.* Weybright and Talley, Inc., 1972, pp. 91–91, 104.

"Simmons To Stay As Exchange Head." *New York Times.* March 26, 1929, p. 50:2.

"Simmons Advocates Tighter Blue-Sky Laws." *New York Times.* Dec. 7, 1927, p. 49:4.

"Simmons Asks Help In Bucket Shop War." *New York Times.* April 10, 1925, p. 30:5.

WINTHROP W. ALDRICH

Block, Maxine, ed. *Current Biography.* The H.W. Wilson Co., 1940, pp. 9–10.

Candee, Marjorie Dent, ed. *Current Biography.* The H.W. Wilson Co., 1953, pp. 2–5.

Johnson, Arthur M. *Winthrop W. Aldrich: Lawyer, Banker, Diplomat.* Harvard University, 1968, pp. 25–40, 49–53, 429–435.

Seligman, Joel. *The Transformation of Wall Street.* Houghton Mifflin Co., 1982.

JOSEPH P. KENNEDY

"Foreign Service: Chameleon & Career Man." National Affairs. *Time.* Vol. 30: Dec. 20, 1937, pp. 10–11.

Groner, Alex. *The History of American Business & Industry.* American Heritage Publishing Co., Inc., 1972, pp. 89–91, 97.

Ingham, John N. *Biographical Dictionary of American Business Leaders.* 4 vols. Greenwood Press, 1983.

Josephson, Matthew. *The Money Lords.* Weybright and Talley, 1972, pp. 85–88, 176–185.

Koskoff, David E. *Joseph P. Kennedy: A Life and Times.* Prentice-Hall, Inc., 1974.

"Wall Street's New Boss 'Knows the Game.' " *Literary Digest.* Vol. 18: July 21, 1934, p. 36.

JAMES M. LANDIS

Block, Maxine, ed. *Current Biography.* The H.W. Wilson Co., 1942, pp. 481–484.

"James M. Landis Found Dead In Swimming Pool at His Home." *New York Times.* July 31, 1964, pp. 1:4+.

Mayer, Martin. *Wall Street: Men and Money.* Harper & Brothers Publishers, 1959, pp. 129, 236.

"Nothing Much to Say." *Newsweek.* Vol. 62: Sept. 9, 1963, p. 31.

Ritchie, Donald A. *James M. Landis: Dean of the Regulators.* Harvard University Press, 1980, pp. 43–91.

Seligman, Joel. *The Transformation of Wall Street.* Houghton Mifflin Co., 1982, pp. 57–69, 79–89, 97–102.

"The Careless Crusader." *Time.* Vol. 82: August 9, 1963, pp. 15–16.

WILLIAM O. DOUGLAS

Block, Maxine, ed. *Current Biography.* The H.W. Wilson Co., 1941, pp. 233–235.

Brooks, John. *Once In Golconda.* Harper Colophon Books, 1969, pp. 241, 244, 251–252, 268.

Brooks, John. *The Go-Go Years.* Weybright and Talley, 1973, pp. 89–90, 275, 339.

Josephson, Matthew. *The Money Lords.* Weybright and Talley, Inc., 1972, pp. 258–259.

Sobel, Robert. *Inside Wall Street: Continuity and Change in the Financial District.* W.W. Norton & Company, 1977, pp. 168–172, 189–191.

Whitman, Alden. "William O. Douglas Is Dead at 81; Served 36 Years on Supreme Court." *New York Times.* Jan. 20, 1980, p. 1:1+.

CHAPTER 7: CROOKS, SCANDALS, AND SCALAWAGS

CHARLES PONZI

Josephson, Matthew. *The Money Lords.* Weybright and Talley, Inc., 1972, pp. 35–36.

Sobel, Robert. *The Great Bull Market*. W.W. Norton & Co., Inc., 1968, pp. 17–20, 98.

Kanfer, Stefan. "Pigs Always Get Slaughtered." *Time*. Feb. 26, 1990.

"Ponzi Is Deported, Hoping To Return." *New York Times*. Oct. 8, 1934, p. 3:1.

"Ponzi Dies In Rio In Charity Ward." *New York Times*. Jan. 19, 1949, p. 56:3.

SAMUEL INSULL

Allen, Frederick Lewis. *The Lords of Creation*. Quadrangle Paperback, 1935, pp. 247, 266–89, 348–358.

Forbes, B.C. *Men Who Are Making America*. B.C. Forbes Publishing Company, Inc., 1916, pp. 204–213.

Ingham, John N. *Biographical Dictionary of American Business Leaders*. 4 vols. Greenwood Press, 1983.

Josephson, Matthew. *The Money Lords*. Weybright and Talley, 1972, pp. 19, 34–43, 52–53, 68, 72, 81–86, 95–96, 131–132, 138, 142, 347–348.

McDonald, Forrest. *Insull*. The University of Chicago Press, 1962.

Michaels, James W. "History Lesson." *Forbes*. Dec. 24, 1990, p. 38–40.

IVAR KREUGER

"Europe's Newest Wizard of Finance." *Review of Reviews*. Vol. 79: April, 1929, pp. 24–25.

George, Manfred. *The Case of Ivar Kreuger: An Adventure in Finance*. Jonathan Cape, Ltd., 1933, pp. 256.

Parker, John Lloyd. *Unmasking Wall Street*. The Stratford Co., Publishers, 1932, pp. 154–187.

Shaplen, Robert. *Kreuger: Genius and Swindler*. Alfred A. Knopf, 1960.

"The Collapse of the Kreuger Legend." *Literary Digest*. Vol. 113: May 7, 1932, pp. 36–39.

"Why the House of Kreuger Fell." *Literary Digest*. Vol. 115: Feb. 4, 1933, p. 40.

RICHARD WHITNEY

Brooks, John. *Once in Golconda*. Harper Colophon Books, 1970, pp. 230–287.

Josephson, Matthew. *The Money Lords*. Weybright and Talley, Inc., 1972, pp. 90–107, 125–128, 173–184.

Neill, Humphrey B. *The Inside Story of the Stock Exchange.* B.C. Forbes & Sons Publishing Company, Inc., 1950, pp. 239, 252, 254, 260–263.
"Richard Whitney, 86, Dies; Headed Stock Exchange." *New York Times.* Dec. 6, 1974, p.42:1.

MICHAEL J. MEEHAN

"Broken Broker." *Time.* Vol. 28: Dec. 7, 1936, pp. 73–74.
Brooks, John. *Once in Golconda.* Harper Colophon Books, 1969, pp. 65–66, 78, 120, 278–279.
"Meehan: SEC's Show Has Broker As the Villain of the Piece." *Newsweek.* Vol. 6: Dec. 21, 1936, pp. 36–37.
"Present." *Time.* Vol. 26: Nov. 4, 1935, p. 74.
"Target For SEC: Meehan's Sky-Rocketing Operations in Stock Market Under Inquiry." *Literary Digest.* Vol. 122: Dec. 26, 1936, p. 37.
Weissman, Rudolph L. *The New Wall Street.* Harper and Brothers Publishers, 1939, pp. 130–134.

LOWELL M. BIRRELL

"Brazil: Hardly Diplomatic." *Newsweek.* Vol. 54: Aug. 31, 1959, p. 51.
"Brazil: The Improbable David." *Time.* Vol. 74: Aug. 31, 1959, p. 31.
Brean, Herbert. "A Master Rogue Unmasked." *Life.* Vol. 47: July 20, 1959, pp. 19–24.
Brooks, John. *The Go-Go Years.* Weybright and Talley, 1973, pp. 30–33, 75, 97.
Cormier, Frank. *Wall Street's Shady Side.* Public Affairs Press, 1962, pp. 26, 39, 146–162.
St. George, Andrew. "Fleeing Down To Rio ... America's Million-Dollar Fugitives." *Look.* Vol. 26: Feb. 27, 1962, pp. 124–130.
"The Birrell Break." *Newsweek.* Vol. 65: June 28, 1965, p. 72.
Wise, T.A. and Klaw, Spencer. "The Spoilers: The World of Lowell Birrell." *Fortune.* Vol. 60: November, 1959, pp. 170+.

WALTER F. TELLIER

Black, Hillel. *The Watchdogs of Wall Street.* William Morrow and Company, 1962, pp. 20–56, 79, 84–89.
Crane, Burton. "'Penny' Uranium Stock Expert Blasts S.E.C. and 'Fraud' Talk." *New York Times.* Nov. 4, 1955, p. 43:4.
"Tellier is Barred in New York State." *New York Times.* July 6, 1956, p. 31:5.
"Broker is Jailed in $900,000 Fraud." *New York Times.* April 13, 1957.

JERRY AND GERALD RE

Brooks, John. *The Go-Go Years.* Weybright and Talley, 1973, pp. 31–37.

Cormier, Frank. *Wall Street's Shady Side.* Public Affairs Press, 1962, pp. 15–43, 45, 50–51, 58, 64, 146–149.

"Stocks: Two Touts." *Newsweek.* Vol. 57: May 8, 1961, pp. 74+.

"Swindles: Father-and-Son Team." *Newsweek.* Vol. 57: May 15, 1961, pp. 83+.

"Trials: Re the Res." *Newsweek.* Vol. 62: July 22, 1963, p. 70.

CHAPTER 8: TECHNICIANS, ECONOMISTS, AND OTHER COSTLY EXPERTS

WILLIAM P. HAMILTON

Hamilton, William P. *The Stock Market Barometer.* Harper, 1922.

Neill, Humphrey B. *The Inside Story of the Stock Exchange.* B.C. Forbes & Sons Publishing Company, Inc., 1950, pp. 123, 144–147, 161–162.

Rhea, Robert. "The Dow Theory." *Barron's,* 1932, pp. 1–18.

Russell, Richard. *The Dow Theory Today.* Richard Russell Associates, 1960.

Stansbury, Charles B. "The Dow Theory Explained." *Barron's,* 1938.

Wendt, Lloyd. *The Wall Street Journal.* Rand McNally & Company, 1982, pp. 67–69, 78, 87, 109–111, 121, 146, 169, 196–203.

EVANGELINE ADAMS

Adams, Evangeline. *The Bowl of Heaven.* Reprint: Dodd, 1970.

"Evangeline Adams, Astrologer, Dead." *New York Times.* Nov. 11, 1932, p. 19:6.

The National Cyclopedia of American Biography. James T. White & Company. Vol. 25: 1936, p. 201.

Thomas, Gordon and Morgan-Witts, Max. *The Day the Bubble Burst.* Doubleday & Company, Inc., 1979, pp. 70–71, 205–206, 274–278, 369–370, 377, 403.

ROBERT RHEA

"Prophet in Bed." *Time.* Vol. 34: Nov. 20, 1939, pp. 77–78.

Rhea, Robert. *The Dow Theory: An Explanation of its Development and an Attempt to Define its Usefulness as an Aid in Speculation.* Robert Rhea, 1932.

"Robert Rhea." *New York Times.* Nov. 7, 1939, p. 25:4.

Schultz, Harry D. and Coslow, Samson, eds. *A Treasury of Wall Street Wisdom.* Investors' Press, Inc., 1966.

Stillman, Richard J. *The Dow Jones Industrial Average.* Dow Jones- Irwin, 1986, pp. 112–115.

"Tides, Waves, Ripples." *Time.* Vol. 31: June 20, 1938, p. 51.

IRVING FISHER

Allen, William R. "Irving Fisher, F.D.R., and the Great Depression." *History of Political Economy.* Vol. 9: Winter, 1977, pp. 560–587.

Fisher, Irving Norton. *My Father, Irving Fisher.* Comet Press Books, 1956.

Fisher, Irving. *The Stock Market Crash And After.* Macmillan Company, 1930.

Sobel, Robert. *The Great Bull Market: Wall Street in the 1920s.* W.W. Norton & Co., Inc., 1968, pp. 90, 97, 127, 157.

Zucker, Seymour. "Why Interest Rates Don't Follow Inflation Down." *Business Week.* June 21, 1982, p. 106.

WILLIAM D. GANN

Alphier, James E. and Williams, Thomas D. "W.D. Gann: The 'Mystic.'" *Commodities.* May 1982, pp. 62+.

Jones, Billy. "W.D. Gann: The Man." *Commodities.* May 1982, pp. 62–63.

Schultz, Harry D. and Coslow, Samson. *A Treasury of Wall Street Wisdom.* Investors' Press, Inc., pp. 133–139.

Stein, John. "Getting an Angle on Gann Techniques." *Futures.* Vol. 19: June, 1990, pp. 28–30.

WESLEY CLAIR MITCHELL

Burns, Arthur F. *Wesley Clair Mitchell: The Economic Scientist.* National Bureau of Economic Research, Inc., 1952, p. 387.

"Wesley Clair Mitchell." *New York Times.* Oct. 30, 1948, p. 14:3.

"Dr. Wesley Clair Mitchell, Economist, 74, Dies." *New York Times.* Oct. 30, 1948, p. 15:3.

Mitchell, Lucy Sprague. *Two Lives: The Story of Wesley Clair Mitchell and Myself.* Simon & Schuster, 1953, 575 pp.

Gann, William D. *Forty-Five Years in Wall Street: A Review of the 1937 Panic and 1942 Panic.* W.D. Gann, Publisher, 1949.

Collins, Edward H. "The Role of the National Bureau." *New York Times.* May 21, 1951, p.36:2.

"Obituary: Wesley C. Mitchell." *The Economic Journal.* Sept., 1949, pp. 448–469.
Van Dorem, Charles, Editor. *Webster's American Biographies.* G. and C. Merriam Co., 1974, p. 727.

JOHN MAYNARD KEYNES

"Baron Keynes of Tilton." *Fortune.* Vol. 29: May, 1944, pp. 146–147+.
Groner, Alex. *The History of American Business and Industry.* American Heritage Publishing Company, Inc., 1972, pp. 294–295, 302, 363.
Harris, Seymour E. *John Maynard Keynes: Economist and Policy Maker.* Charles Scribner's Sons, 1955.
Minard, Lawrence. "The Money Men: The Original Contrarian." *Forbes.* Sept. 26, 1983, pp. 42–44+.
Moggridge, D.E., ed. *Keynes: Aspects of the Man and His Work.* St. Martin's Press, 1974.

R.N. ELLIOTT

Beckman, R.C. *The Elliott Wave Principle As Applied To the London Stock Market.* Tara Books, 1976, pp. xi–39, 190–236.
Elliott, Margaret A. "The Champion Market Forecaster." *Fortune.* Jan. 5, 1987, p. 75.
Frost, Alfred John and Prechter, Robert. *The Elliott Wave Principle.* New Classics Library, 1978.
Prechter, Robert. "Hell Hath No Wrath Like An Elliott Wave Theorist Scorned." *Barron's.* Feb. 9, 1987, pp. 14+.
Reilly, Frank K. *Investment Analysis and Portfolio Management.* The Dryden Press, 1979, pp 121–132.
Warnecke, Steven J. "Hear This, Bob Prechter!: A Critic Attacks the Elliott Wave Theory." *Barron's.* Jan. 25, 1987, pp. 13+.

EDSON GOULD

"Edson Beers Gould Jr. Dies; Influential Stock Forecaster." *New York Times.* March 31, 1987.
Gould, Edson. "A Vital Anatomy." *Findings & Forecasts.* Anametrics, Inc.
Gould, Edson. "Edson Gould's 'The Sign of the Bull.'" *Findings & Forecasts.* Anametrics, Inc.
"The Selling of Edson Gould." *Dun's Review.* May, 1975, pp. 46+.
"The Successful 'Star Gazers.'" *Forbes.* Jan. 15, 1977, p. 98.
Smith, Paella. "Wall Street's Reigning Prophet Thinks the Bull Market Lives." *Money.* March, 1978, pp. 103+.

JOHN MAGEE

Brooks, John. *The Seven Fat Years: Chronicles of Wall Street*. Harper & Brothers, 1954, pp. 138–168.

Magee, John. *The General Semantics of Wall Street*. John Magee, 1953.

Magee, John and Edward, Robert D. *Technical Analysis of Stock Trends*. John Magee, Inc., Fifth Edition, 1966.

Magee, John. *Wall Street—Main Street—and You*. John Magee, Inc., 1972.

CHAPTER 9: SUCCESSFUL SPECULATORS, WHEELER-DEALERS, AND OPERATORS

JAY GOULD

Clews, Henry. *Fifty Years in Wall Street: "Twenty-Eight Years in Wall Street," Revised and Enlarged by a Resume of the Past Twenty-Two Years Making a Record of Fifty Years in Wall Street*. Irving, 1908.

Grodinsky, Julius. *Jay Gould*. University of Pennsylvania Press, 1957, pp. 627.

Holbrook, Stewart H. *The Age of the Moguls*. Doubleday & Co., 1953, pp. 30–43, 97–100.

Hoyt, Edwin P. *The Goulds*. Weybright and Talley, 1969, pp. 100–167.

Klein Maury. *The Life and Legend of Jay Gould*. John Hopkins University Press, 1986.

Minnigerode, Meade. *Certain Rich Men*. G.P. Putnam's Sons, 1927, pp. 135–188.

Sobel, Robert. *Panic on Wall Street: A History of America's Financial Disasters*. The Macmillan Co., 1968, pp. 127–156.

"DIAMOND" JIM BRADY

Ingham, John N. *Biographical Dictionary of American Business Leaders*. 4 vols. Greenwood Press, 1983, pp. 89–90.

Morell, Parker. *Diamond Jim*. Simon & Schuster, 1934.

O'Connor, Richard. *Duet in Diamonds: The Flamboyant Saga of Lillian Russell and Diamond Jim Brady in America's Gilded Age by John Burke*. Putnam, 1972.

WILLIAM H. VANDERBILT

Groner, Alex. *The History of American Business and Industry*. America Heritage Publishing Co., Inc., pp. 158–160, 176, 182.

Myers, Gustavus. *The History of Great American Fortunes*. The Modern Library, 1907, pp. 333–348.

"The Contentment of Croesus." *New York Times.* Oct. 10, 1882, p. 4:4.
"Mr. Vanderbilt on Stocks." *New York Times.* July 2, 1884, p. 1:7.
"Mr. Vanderbilt's Views." *New York Times.* Sept. 27, 1884, p. 1:3.

JOHN W. GATES

Groner, Alex. *The History of American Business and Industry.* American Heritage Publishing Co., Inc., 1972, pp. 170.
Warshow, Robert Irving. *Bet-A-Million Gates: The Story of a Plunger.* Greenberg, 1932.
Wendt, Lloyd and Kogan, Herman. *Bet A Million!* The Bobbs-Merrill Co.,
  1948.

EDWARD HARRIMAN

Birmingham, Stephen. *Our Crowd.* Dell Publishing Co., 1967,
  pp. 201–205, 354–365.
Eckenrode, H. J. and Edmunds, Pocahontas Wight Edmunds. *E.H. Harriman: The Little Giant of Wall Street.* Arno Press, 1981, pp. 3–81,
  204–238.
"Harriman and His Time." *The Nation.* Vol. 89: Sept. 16, 1909,
  pp. 248–249.
Ingham, John N. *Biographical Dictionary of American Business Leaders.*
  4 vols. Greenwood Press, 1983.
Myers, Gustavus. *The History of Great American Fortunes.* The Modern Library, 1907, pp. 491–503, 517–534.
Neill, Humphrey B. *The Inside Story of the Stock Exchange.* B.C. Forbes &
  Sons Publishing Company, Inc., 1950, pp. 135–140, 162–163.

JAMES J. HILL

Groner, Alex. *The History of American Business and Industry.* American Her-
  itage Publishing Co., Inc., 1972, pp. 165–166, 193, 200–203.
Myers, Gustavus. *The History of Great American Fortunes.* The Modern Li-
  brary, 1907, pp. 661–695.
Pound, Arthur and Moore, Samuel Taylor. *They Told Barron: Conversations
  and Revelations of an American Pepys in Wall Street.* Harper, 1930.
Pyle, Joseph Gilpin. *The Life of James J. Hill.* 2 vols. Peter Smith, 1936.
Redmond, George F. *Financial Giants of America.* The Stratford Co., 1922,
  pp. 131–145.
Sobel, Robert. *The Big Board: A History of the New York Stock Market.* The
  Free Press, Macmillan Co., 1965, pp. 133, 163–167.
Sobel, Robert. *Panic on Wall Street: History of America's Financial Disasters.*
  Macmillan Co., 1968, pp. 273–278, 291–295.

JAMES R. KEENE

"James R. Keene Left $15,000,000." *New York Times.* Jan. 5, 1913, p. 16:1.

"'Jim' Keene, The Avatar of Wall Street." *Current Literature.* Vol. 48: May, 1910, pp. 498–501.

Lefevre, Edwin. "James R. Keene, Manipulator." *World's Work.* Vol. 2: July, 1901, pp. 996–999.

"Personal Glimpses: James R. Keene." *Literary Digest.* Vol. 46: Jan. 18, 1913, p. 153.

Sharp, Robert M. *The Lore and Legends of Wall Street.* Dow Jones-Irwin, 1989, p. 127.

Sobel, Robert. *The Big Board: A History of the New York Stock Market.* The Free Press, Macmillan Co., 1965, pp. 115, 154–66.

Thomas, Dana L. *The Plungers and the Peacocks: 150 Years of Wall Street.* Putnam, 1967.

HENRY H. ROGERS

Abels, Jules. *The Rockefeller Billions.* Macmillan Co., 1965, pp. 154, 220–1, 256, 272.

Allen, Frederick Lewis. *The Lords of Creation.* Harper & Brothers Publishers, 1935, pp. 13, 21–22, 36, 72–74, 83–86, 94–99, 115–116.

Flynn, John T. *God's Gold.* Greenwood Press, Publishers, 1932, pp. 344–346, 437.

Ingham, John N. *Biographical Dictionary of American Business Leaders.* 4 vols. Greenwood Press, 1983.

Lawson, Thomas. *Frenzied Finance: Vol. 1. The Crime of Amalgamated.* Original: Ridgway-Thayer, 1905. Reprint: Greenwood Press, 1968.

McNelis, Sarah. *Copper King at War: The Biography of F. Augustus Heinze.* University of Montana Press, 1968.

Nevins, Allan. *John D. Rockefeller.* Charles Scribner's Sons. Vol. 2: 1940, pp. 431–432, 436–430.

FISHER BROTHERS

"Charles T. Fisher, 83, Is Dead; Founder of Auto Body Concern." *The New York Times.* Aug. 9, 1963, p. 23:2.

"H.A. Fisher Dead; of Auto Body Firm." *The New York Times.* April 1, 1942, p. 21:1.

Ingham, John N. *Biographical Dictionary of American Business Leaders.* 4 vols. Greenwood Press, 1983.

McManis, John. "Charles Fisher Rites in Cathedral Monday." *The Detroit News.* Aug. 9, 1963, p. 8:1.

Parker, John Lloyd. *Unmasking Wall Street.* The Stratford Co., Publishers, 1932, pp. 122–127.

Sparling, Earl. *Mystery Men of Wall Street.* Blue Ribbon Books, 1930, pp. 165–188.

Sobel, Robert. *Panic on Wall Street: A History of America's Financial Disasters.* Macmillan Co., 1968, pp. 363, 365, 374, 392.

JOHN J. RASKOB

Raskob, John J. "Everybody Ought to be Rich." *Review of Reviews.* Vol. 80: Sept., 1929, pp. 99+.

"Raskob's Bomb." *Literary Digest.* Vol. 108: March 21, 1931, pp. 8–9.

"Taxation: Old Linen." *Time.* Vol. 29: May 17, 1937, pp. 16–17.

Ingham, John N. *Biographical Dictionary of American Business Leaders.* 4 vols. Greenwood Press, 1983.

"John J. Raskob Dies Of A Heart Attack." *New York Times.* Oct. 16, 1950, p. 27:1.

"Raskob Radio Pool Realized $5,000,000." *New York Times.* May 20, 1932, pp. 1:4+.

"J.J. Raskob Quits His Du Pont Posts." *New York Times.* Feb. 19, 1946, p. 32+.

ARTHUR W. CUTTEN

Brooks, John. *Once In Golconda.* Harper Colophon Books, 1969, pp. 77–78.

Cutten, Arthur. "Story of a Speculator." *Everybody's Magazine.* Nov. 19, 1932, p. 26; Dec. 3, 1932, p. 10.

Ingham, John N. *Biographical Dictionary of American Business Leaders.* 4 vols. Greenwood Press, 1983.

Sharp, Robert M. *The Lore & Legends of Wall Street.* Dow Jones-Irwin, 1989, pp. 177–80.

Sobel, Robert. *The Great Bull Market: Wall Street in the 1920s.* W.W. Norton & Co., Inc., 1968, pp. 71–72, 132–137.

BERNARD E. "SELL 'EM BEN" SMITH

"Bernard E. Smith, Financier, Dead." *New York Times.* May 12, 1961, p. 29:1.

Brooks, John. *Once in Golconda.* Harper Colophon, 1969, pp. 79–80, 121–122, 143–144.

Davis, Forrest. "Sell 'Em Ben Smith: The Epic of a Rover Boy in Wall Street." The *Saturday Evening Post.* Vol. 211: Feb. 4, 1939, pp. 14–15+.

Josephson. Matthew. *The Money Lords.* Weybright and Talley, Inc., 1972, pp. 85–87, 94, 124–129. 175–187, 200, 213, 259.

Parker, John Lloyd. *Unmasking Wall Street.* The Stratford Co., Publishers, 1932.

"Sell-'em-Ben." *Newsweek.* Vol. 57: May 22, 1961, pp. 75–76.

BERNARD BARUCH

Akst, Daniel. "A Gallery of Moguls and Rogues." *Financial World.* Sept. 16, 1986, p. 34.

Baruch, Bernard. *My Own Story.* Henry Holt and Co., 1957, pp. 254–262.

Baruch, Bernard. *The Public Years.* Holt, Rinehart and Winston, 1960, pp. 217–225, 393–402.

Grant, James. *Bernard M. Baruch.* Simon & Schuster, 1983.

Grossman, Peter Z. "The Great Investors of the 20th Century." *Financial World.* June 15, 1982, pp. 22–23.

Schultz, Harry D. and Coslow, Samson, eds. *A Treasury of Wall Street Wisdom.* Investors' Press, 1966, pp. 161–172.

CHAPTER 10: UNSUCCESSFUL SPECULATORS, WHEELER-DEALERS, AND OPERATORS

JACOB LITTLE

Clews, Henry. *Twenty-Eight Years in Wall Street.* J.S. Ogilvie Publishing Co., 1887.

Sarnoff, Paul. *Russell Sage: The Money King.* Ivan Obolensky, Inc., 1965, pp. 84–86.

Sarnoff, Paul. *Puts and Calls: The Complete Guide.* Hawthorne Book, 1968.

Sharp, Robert M. *The Lore and Legends of Wall Street.* Dow Jones-Irwin, 1989, pp. 105–107.

Sobel, Robert. *The Big Board: A History of the New York Stock Market.* The Free Press, Macmillan Co., 1965, pp. 40–41, 60–62, 72.

"Stock Gambling." *New York Daily Times.* Dec. 12, 1856.

Warshow, Robert Irving. *The Story of Wall Street.* Greenberg, Publisher, Inc., 1929, pp. 663–679.

JAMES FISK

Dies, Edward B. *Behind the Wall Street Curtain.* Reprint: Books for Libraries, 1969.

Gordon, John Steele. "The Mating Game." *Forbes.* Oct. 22, 1990, pp. 62+.

Holbrook, Stewart H. *The Age of Moguls.* Doubleday & Co., Inc., 1953, pp. 30–48.

Hoyt. Edwin P. *The Goulds.* Weybright and Talley, 1969, pp. 69–85.

Minnigerode, Meade. *Certain Rich Men.* G.P. Putnam's Sons, 1927, pp. 189–210

Sobel, Robert. *Panic on Wall Street: A History of America's Financial Disasters.* Macmillan Co., 1968, pp. 127–156.

Swanberg, W.A. *Fisk: The Career of an Improbable Rascal.* Charles Scribner's Sons, 1959, pp. 100–135.

WILLIAM CRAPO DURANT

"Auto Biographies." *Motor Trend.* November, 1985, p. 102.

"Flashbacks." *Forbes.* March 30, 1981, p. 163.

Gustin, Lawrence R. *Billy Durant Creator of General Motors.* William B. Eerdmans Publishing Co., 1973.

McCall, Bruce. "Mr. DeLorean, Meet Mr. Durant." *Car and Driver.* July, 1982, p. 67.

Sobel, Robert. *Panic on Wall Street: A History of America's Greatest Financial Disasters.* Macmillan Co., 1968, pp. 363–365.

Sobel, Robert. *The Big Board: A History of the New York Stock Market.* The Free Press, Macmillan Co., 1965, pp. 200, 249–250.

Stovall, Robert H. "Durant's Legacy." *Financial World.* Sept. 16,1986, p. 180.

Winkleman, Barnie F. *Ten Years of Wall Street.* John C. Winston, 1932.

F. AUGUSTUS HEINZE

"F. Augustus Heinze, Mine Owner, Dead." *New York Times.* Nov. 5, 1914, p. 11:3.

Glasscock, C.B. *The War of the Copper Kings.* The Bobbs-Merril Co., 1935, pp. 141+.

Ingham, John N. *Biographical Dictionary of American Business Leaders.* 4 vols. Greenwood Press, 1983.

McNelis, Sarah. *Copper King at War: The Biography of F. Augustus Heinze.* University of Montana Press, 1968, pp. 28+.

Sobel, Robert. *The Big Board: A History of the New York Stock Market.* The Free Press, Macmillan Co., 1965, pp. 182–197.

CHARLES W. MORSE

Allen, Frederick Lewis. *The Lords of Creation.* Harper & Brothers Publishers, 1935, pp. 116–126.

Ingham, John N. *Biographical Dictionary of American Business Leaders.* 4 vols. Greenwood Press, 1983.

Malone, Michael P. *The Battle for Butte.* University of Washington Press, 1981, pp. 191–194.

Who Was Who In America. Marquis Who's Who, Inc. Vol. 4: 1968.

ORIS P. AND MANTIS J. VAN SWEARINGEN

Allen, Frederick Lewis. *The Lords of Creation.* Harper & Brothers Publishers, 1935, pp. 293–303, 319, 346–350, 365–370, 417.

Groner, Alex. *The History of American Business and Industry.* American Heritage Publishing Co., Inc., 1972, pp. 281–283, 291.

Kelly, Fred C. "Two Young Men Who are Real Estate Marvels." *American Magazine.* Vol. 83: March, 1917, pp. 50–51.

Ingham, John N. *Biographical Dictionary of American Business Leaders.* 4 vols. Greenwood Press, 1983.

Pound, Arthur and Moore, Samuel Taylor. *They Told Barron: Conversations and Revelations of an American Pepys in Wall Street.* Harper & Brothers, 1930, pp. 68, 290–291.

Sobel, Robert. *The Big Board: A History of the New York Stock Market.* The Free Press, Macmillan Co., 1965, pp. 244, 250, 296.

Sobel, Robert. *The Great Bull Market: Wall Street in the 1920s.* W.W. Norton & Co., Inc., 1968, pp. 81–88.

JESSE L. LIVERMORE

Brooks, John. *Once in Golconda.* Harper Colophon Books, 1969, pp. 74–78, 119–120,279.

Ingham, John N. *Biographical Dictionary of American Business Leaders.* 4 vols. Greenwood Press, 1983.

Josephson, Matthew. *The Money Lords.* Weybright and Talley, 1972, pp. 9–10, 20–21,86, 107–109.

Lefevre, Edwin. *Reminiscences of a Stock Operator.* Original: George H. Doran Co., 1923. Reprint: American Research Council.

Livermore, Jesse L. *How to Trade in Stocks: The Livermore Formula for Combining Time Element and Price.* Reprint: Investor's Press, Inc., 1966. Distributed by Simon & Schuster.

Sarnoff, Paul. *Jesse Livermore: Speculator-King.* Investors' Press, Inc., 1967.

CHAPTER 11: MISCELLANEOUS, BUT NOT EXTRANEOUS

HETTY GREEN

Grossman, Peter Z. "The Great Investors of the 20th Century." *Financial World.* June 15, 1982.

Holbrook, Stewart H. *Age of the Moguls.* Doubleday & Co., Inc., 1953, pp. 340–342.

Ingham, John N. *Biographical Dictionary of American Business Leaders.* 4 vols. Greenwood Press, 1983.

McGinty, Brian. "Hetty Green: The Witch of Wall Street." *American History Illustrated*. Sept. 1988, pp.30–31.

Sparkes, Boyden and Moore, Samuel Taylor. *Hetty Green: A Woman Who Loved Money*. Doubleday, Doran & Co., Inc., 1930.

PATRICK BOLOGNA

Baruch, Bernard. *Baruch: My Own Story*. Henry Holt and Company, 1957, p. 258.

Seneker, Harold. "Wall Street At Shoe Level." *Forbes*. Vol. 130: Nov. 22, 1982, pp. 45–46.

Thomas, Gordon and Morgan-Witts, Max. *The Day the Bubble Burst*. Doubleday & Company, Inc., 1979, pp. 143, 223, 250, 276, 283–284, 305, 312–314, 353–357, 384, 422–424.

ROBERT R. YOUNG

Borkin, Joseph. *Robert R. Young: The Populist of Wall Street*. Harper & Row, 1969.

Ingham, John N. *Biographical Dictionary of American Business Leaders*. 4 vols. Greenwood Press, 1983.

Josephson, Matthew. *The Money Lords*. Weybright and Talley, 1972, pp. 88, 188–246, 255.

CYRUS S. EATON

Crowther, Samuel. "Ohio Versus Wall Street." *World's Work*. Vol. 59: June, 1930, pp. 24+

"Eaton to the Wars." *Time*. Vol. 34: Dec. 11, 1939, p. 69.

Ingham, John N. *Biographical Dictionary of American Business Leaders*. 4 vols. Greenwood Press, 1983, pp. 333–337.

Noyes, Peter Helmoop. "The Last Days of Cyrus the Great." *The Nation* Vol. 136: June 21, 1933, pp. 700–701.

"Russia's Favorite U.S. Capitalist." *Newsweek*. Vol. 93: May 21,1979, p. 81.

INDEX

Printed in the United States
By Bookmasters